Uncertainty and Its Discont

MW00334422

This volume provides the first major study of worldviews in international relations. Worldviews are the unexamined, pretheoretical foundations of the approaches with which we understand and navigate the world. Advances in twentieth-century physics and cosmology and other intellectual developments questioning anthropocentrism have fostered the articulation of alternative worldviews that rival conventional Newtonian humanism and its assumption that the world is constituted by controllable risks. This matters for coming to terms with the uncertainties that are an indelible part of many spheres of life, including public health, the environment, finance, security, and politics – uncertainties that are concealed by the conventional presumption that the world is governed only by risk. The confluence of risk and uncertainty requires an awareness of alternative worldviews, alerts us to possible intersections between humanist Newtonianism and hyper-humanist Post-Newtonianism, and reminds us of the relevance of science, religion, and moral values in world politics.

Peter J. Katzenstein's work addresses issues of political economy, security, and culture in world politics. His recent books include *Protean Power: Exploring the Uncertain and Unexpected in World Politics* (co-edited with the late Lucia Seybert, Cambridge University Press, 2018) and *Downfall: The End of the American Order?* (co-edited with Jonathan Kirshner, Cornell University Press, 2022). He was elected to the American Academy of Arts and Science in 1987, the American Philosophical Society in 2009, and the British Academy in 2015. In 2020 he was named the twenty-sixth recipient of the Johan Skytte Prize.

Cambridge Studies in International Relations

Editors
Evelyn Goh
Christian Reus-Smit
Nicholas J. Wheeler

Editorial Board
Jacqueline Best, Karin Fierke, William Grimes, Yuen Foong
Khong, Andrew Kydd, Lily Ling, Andrew Linklater, Nicola
Phillips, Elizabeth Shakman Hurd, Jacquie True, Leslie
Vinjamuri, Alexander Wendt

Cambridge Studies in International Relations is a joint initiative of
Cambridge University Press and the British International
Studies Association (BISA). The series aims to publish the best
new scholarship in international studies, irrespective of subject
matter, methodological approach or theoretical perspective. The
series seeks to bring the latest theoretical work in International
Relations to bear on the most important problems and issues in
global politics.

Uncertainty and Its Discontents

Worldviews in World Politics

Edited by

Peter J. Katzenstein

Cornell University, New York

CAMBRIDGE
UNIVERSITY PRESS

CAMBRIDGE
UNIVERSITY PRESS

University Printing House, Cambridge CB2 8BS, United Kingdom

One Liberty Plaza, 20th Floor, New York, NY 10006, USA

477 Williamstown Road, Port Melbourne, VIC 3207, Australia

314–321, 3rd Floor, Plot 3, Splendor Forum, Jasola District Centre, New Delhi – 110025, India

103 Penang Road, #05–06/07, Visioncrest Commercial, Singapore 238467

Cambridge University Press is part of the University of Cambridge.

It furthers the University's mission by disseminating knowledge in the pursuit of education, learning, and research at the highest international levels of excellence.

www.cambridge.org
Information on this title: www.cambridge.org/9781316512661
DOI: 10.1017/9781009070997

First published 2022

A catalogue record for this publication is available from the British Library.

ISBN 978-1-316-51266-1 Hardback
ISBN 978-1-009-06897-0 Paperback

Contents

Figures

Contributors

BENTLEY B. ALLAN Associate Professor, Department of Political Science, Johns Hopkins University

MICHAEL BARNETT University Professor of International Affairs and Political Science, George Washington University

TIMOTHY A. BYRNES Third Century Chair of Philosophy, Politics, and Economics, Colgate University

PRASENJIT DUARA Oscar Tang Family Distinguished Chair Professor of East Asian Studies, Duke University

JAIRUS VICTOR GROVE Associate Professor, Department of Political Science, University of Hawai'i at Manoa

MARK L. HAAS Raymond J. Kelley Endowed Chair in International Relations in the Political Science Department, Duquesne University

PETER J. KATZENSTEIN Walter S. Carpenter, Jr. Professor of International Studies, Cornell University

MILJA KURKI EH Carr Professor in International Politics in the Department of International Politics, Aberystwyth University

HENRY R. NAU Professor Emeritus of Political Science and International Affairs in the Political Science Department and Elliott School of International Affairs, George Washington University

Preface

As I was cleaning out my office one quiet winter afternoon, I heard a colleague down the hall talk like a diligent gardener to a student about the "treatment effects" of various experiments on different political subjects. In sharp contrast, the daily news I have been reading, especially in recent years, reports scenes from the jungle. My political sensibilities tell me that gardening should not be the only occupation for students of world politics.

Why are we drawn so strongly to gardens rather than jungles when studying world politics, and why do we prefer the resolvable, risk-inflected world over the radical, uncertainty-marked one that we so often encounter?[1] The answer lies in a view of the world, for the most part held unconsciously, that prefers to highlight the features of politics which lend themselves more readily to systematic study and political control. Hence, students of world politics are habituated to focus their attention largely on the garden-like elements of world politics ruled by resolvable risks. They leave underattended the jungle-like elements marked by radical uncertainties. World politics encompasses both jungles and gardens, and uncertainty as well as risk. If we focus only on predictable risks, we are closing our eyes to a world filled with unpredictable potentialities waiting, for better or for worse, to be actualized by political action or inaction. They are always out there.

The 2020 pandemic illustrates the bone-shattering uncertainty of the world in which we live. People experience this uncertainty viscerally, as different forms of vulnerability: about their very lives, their economic livelihoods, their loved ones, and the communities in which they live. And the television is filled with incessant chatter by those in power who, often unavoidably, lack adequate knowledge about the virus and how it can be mitigated or contained. In the words of Nobel Prize–winning economist Paul Romer, "uncertainty is the overwhelming problem."[2] Dramatic environmental change in the wake of global warming,

---

[1] Kay and King 2020: 14.   [2] Romer, quoted in Seib 2020.

furthermore, may well make the pandemic a starter dish for a full menu that can pose "an unprecedented existential and temporal *uncertainty* concerning the future of ... Earth itself."[3] The pandemic illustrates a persistent problem. Many of the most momentous events in world politics are totally surprising to those professing special expertise in the analysis of world affairs.

During the last decade I have been trying to understand why. Together with Stephen Nelson – then a graduate student at Cornell and now a professor at Northwestern University – I wrote some papers to better understand the collective silence with which the discipline of political economy met the Great Recession of 2008, the greatest calamity that had hit the international economy since the Great Depression of the 1930s.[4] To my astonishment, I learned that economists, political economists, and Wall Street bankers had built their models on the assumption that we live in a world of knowable risk only. Once the crisis hit, those risk models proved to be both totally useless and totally wrong. Little has changed since. Uncertainty is still a marginal concept in finance.

The obliviousness to uncertainty, I sensed, had political roots and consequences worth probing further. Together with the late Lucia Seybert and a group of colleagues, I developed the concept of protean power to capture the unpredictable potentialities that exist all around us.[5] This was little more than a reminder that Machiavelli's writing about *fortuna* is as relevant to today's understanding of world politics as Hobbes's *Leviathan*. While we were developing this argument, the reaction of my colleagues was overwhelmingly skeptical. Did we need still another conceptualization of power, they asked, since the conventional one focusing on control seemed to have served us so well over the centuries? Brexit and the election of Donald Trump in 2016 changed that reaction, but only a little. Readers were willing to concede that they had been surprised by the outcomes of the referendum and the election, glossing over many other momentous, unexpected events they had conveniently chosen to forget. The seminars I attended and the lectures I delivered on the subject of protean power typically elicited an awkward silence followed by the question "This is very interesting. Let me try to translate what you are saying into my own language." That language inevitably was Newtonian and steeped in the notion of control power and manageable risk. I sensed that concepts, theories, and models were grounded in something more basic that made it very difficult – and often

---

[3] Hamilton 2019: 610.
[4] Katzenstein and Nelson 2013a, 2013b; Nelson and Katzenstein 2014.
[5] Katzenstein and Seybert 2018; Katzenstein 2020.

impossible – for members of these audiences to acknowledge the importance of uncertainty and the relevance of protean power effects for the
analysis of politics.

That more basic thing, the opening and closing chapters of this book
argue, lies in the conventional understanding of science, which most
students of world politics boil down to commonsense reasoning.
A Newtonian view of the world is baked deeply into our language and
sensory experience, and often holds sway over subconscious ways of
thinking. No stranger to fragility and uncertainty, journalist Thomas
Friedman advised the Biden presidential campaign in 2020 to adopt an
ad stating "I believe in the Enlightenment, Newtonian physics and the
Age of Reason. The other guy doesn't."[6] Really? Why would Newtonian
physics be the answer to a Post-Newtonian president trafficking in dis-
ruption and uncertainty?

The conventional theories, models, and hypotheses that inform our
study of world politics are grounded in a Newtonian worldview that has
no place for uncertainty. My chapters in this book attempt to uncover this
hidden foundation and to contrast it with a Post-Newtonian worldview
more attuned to the existence and importance of uncertainty. For more
than a century, theories and approaches grounded in this Post-
Newtonian worldview have generated remarkable progress in our understanding of the natural world. Is there something that students of world
politics, and the social sciences more generally, could learn from the
natural sciences that think of the world as filled with potentialities and
uncertainties? As Albert Hirschman observed about the social sciences,
including the study of world politics, a long time ago, they often "consider
it beneath their scientific dignity to deal with possibility until *after* it has
become actual and can then at least be redefined as a probability."[7] Today
it is a marker of the professional respectability of the best scholars of world
politics to be carefully trained in a broad array of statistical methods and
thus to acquire an intellectual disposition that overlooks ex ante possibilities by treating them as ex post probabilities.

The authors of the book's eight other chapters have a variety of interests
in their exploration of worldviews. Mark Haas and Henry Nau focus on
foreign policy ideologies and traditions interpreted from the perspective
of worldviews (Chapter 2); Milja Kurki on relational cosmology as
a central scientific contribution to the relational revolution in the natural
sciences and its implication for the analysis of world politics (Chapter 3);
Jairus Grove on relationalism as shown in American nuclear war prepar-
ations (Chapter 4); and Michael Barnett on Jewish nationalism and

---

[6] Friedman 2020a, 2020b.   [7] Hirschman 1980: xii.

cosmopolitanism in disparate Jewish communities (Chapter 5). Henry Nau (Chapter 6) and Prasenjit Duara (Chapter 7) reflect on these contributions through the lenses provided by their distinctive worldviews. Finally, Bentley Allan (Chapter 8) and Timothy Byrnes (Chapter 9) present challenging arguments about science and religion as today's two foundational worldviews. In short, this is a hybrid of an edited and single-authored book that analyzes both implicit and explicit worldviews.

I want to acknowledge here that my understanding of Newtonianism and Post-Newtonianism is that of a barely informed layperson. I bring no special expertise to any number of extremely complex subject matters and theoretical debates in physics and cosmology. Asked to read a few pages, a physicist friend of mine acknowledged that "physics is part of human culture, sure ... to try to lift someone's language about very arcane physics and paste it into some other situation should not be attempted."[8] None of what he had read, he argued, was of any relevance to the social sciences or humanities. I promised myself and him that, in the interest of full transparency, his unsparing judgment would be included in the book's Preface, possibly providing my colleagues in the social sciences some welcome cover for stopping their reading here.

Needless to say, I disagree. Physics is undeniably part of human culture, and the unwillingness of the social sciences to acknowledge uncertainty as a constitutive aspect of world politics and its tendency to equate uncontrollable uncertainty with manageable risk surely can be informed by a branch of science that takes uncertainty seriously.

Listening to David Mermin, a Cornell physicist, fed my curiosity at a ten-hour intellectual marathon I convened in the fall of 2016 in my living room for a discussion of Alex Wendt's *Quantum Mind*. Building on the argument that physics is part of human culture, Mermin, disagreeing with what he had read in Wendt's book, wrote in an email exchange with Wendt: "we're at opposite poles. I take human experience as given, and try to use it to make sense of quantum mechanics; you take quantum mechanics as given, and try to use it to make sense of human experience."[9] This opened the door for me to begin thinking and reading seriously about the effects of different scientific worldviews on the scholarly and the human enterprise.

Concerned with a few basic differences between two scientific worldviews, I am neither interested in nor qualified to adjudicate the intense and persisting arguments among physicists and cosmologists. My

[8] Eric Siggia, personal communication, August 30, 2020.
[9] Wendt 2015; David Mermin email correspondence with Alexander Wendt (September 2, 2016).

overriding concern is instead to show that students of world politics will be unable to integrate uncertainty into their theories and models as long as they remain committed, often unthinkingly, to a Newtonian world-view. As the natural sciences have moved in the last century to Post-Newtonian understandings of the world that integrate Newtonianism as a special case, why is that intellectual move so difficult for so many scholars of world politics, who insist that they are committed to the *scientific* study of world politics?

In this they are joined by public intellectuals and policymakers who often have no interest in science. Richard Haass's recent compendium on world politics offers a practical guide for readers seeking a better understanding of the global forces that shape their lives. As President of the Council on Foreign Relations and former director of Policy Planning in the US Department of State, Haass is well suited to this task. He dismisses academic debates and theories as "too abstract and too far removed from what is happening to be of value to most of us."[10] The literature on which Haass draws and to which his compendium contributes depends on a handful of foundational concepts, such as the balance of power, that have barely changed since the time of Hobbes and Newton. His book illustrates that the creation of knowledge in the field of global politics all too often is repetitive. In light of new circumstances, authors confront foundational issues with a handful of well-known concepts without adding new depth to our understanding of world politics – including our understanding of the unexpected.[11] This book is a prime target for Haass's criticism: it is about abstractions that are removed from daily events.

This, however, does not make it a purely academic exercise. Far from it. Newtonianism has a view of nature as inert and self-equilibrating that is at odds with the view of many natural scientists. The 2020 pandemic, firestorms, and floods are warning signs that should open our eyes to the prospect of much broader environmental challenges reflected in nature as active and utterly oblivious to any notion of an equilibrium. This will certainly change, and possibly transform, world politics in the coming decades. Being more self-aware of the various worldviews that shape our theories and models of world politics may turn out to be highly germane to those interested in policy.

I recall vividly a conversation with economic historian Charles Kindleberger in front of the Harvard Bookstore, a few years before his death. Charlie was an icon. When queried regarding what he was doing toward the end of his distinguished career, Charlie was, as always,

---

[10] Lawrence 2020; Haass 2020.   [11] Gabriel 1994.

unpretentiously laconic and wry. He replied cheerfully that he was tidying up his study: putting together in various books some of his myriad of articles and book chapters so that they would be more readily accessible for others after he was gone. This book has done the exact opposite for me. My study is not tidy. Far removed from my expertise, I have delved into fields of scholarship looking for insights that had escaped my attention, as they continue to escape the attention of most scholars of world politics. Working in fields I barely understand has made me appreciate once more the old adage "the more we know, the less we know."

This book was made possible and indelibly energized by two friends and intellectual companions. Alexander Wendt's monumental and audacious book *Quantum Mind* made him an astute and supportive critic at different stages of the project's evolution, and especially of my two chapters. Himself the editor of a book on worldviews, Henry Nau might well be tempted to update for this occasion Winston Churchill's World War II characterization of Charles De Gaulle: "the heaviest cross I have to bear is the Cross of Lorraine." This project was a serious test of his *Leidensfähigkeit* (ability to suffer), as it was at least for one of my German colleagues who introduced me to this delicious noun after reading excerpts from Chapters 1 and 10. I am immensely grateful to both Alex and Henry for their inspiration, perseverance, and, most importantly, their friendship.

I have received an enormous amount of help from many friends and colleagues, which I note at various places in Chapters 1 and 10. I am immeasurably grateful to Uriel Abulof, Begüm Adalet, David Bateman, Alexandra Blackman, Alexandra Cirone, Caryl Clarke, Matthew Evangelista, Roderick Floud, Jill Frank, Jeffrey Friedman, Peter Gourevitch, Ilene Grabel, Patrick Jackson, Sabrina Karim, Robert Keohane, Jonathan Kirshner, Stephen Krasner, Sarah Kreps, Douglas Kriner, Adam Levine, Patchen Markell, David Mermin, Henry Nau, Daniel Nexon, Leonardo Orlando, Richard Price, Yaqing Qin, Chris Reus-Smit, Bryn Rosenfeld, Rudra Sil, Divya Subramanian, Geoffrey Wallace, Christopher Way, and Alexander Wendt. Close to the end of this project, my colleagues at the Social Science Center Berlin (WZB) discussed excerpts of Chapters 1 and 10 in two seminars. I am very grateful for their generosity even though I was not able to follow all of their suggestions or answer all of their objections.

David Stuligross improved the writing in Chapters 1 and 10 immensely by editing the text from "within," as it were, nudging it toward communicating to readers just what I am trying to convey rather than from "without," improving only grammar and punctuation. I am immensely thankful for his work.

I also would like to thank Keenan Ashbrook, Colin Chia, Naomi Egel, Nina Obermeier, and Aditi Sahasrabuddhe for their expert research assistance; Cornell's Carpenter Chair for providing the funds necessary to carry out this project; and Cornell's Government Department for giving me, once again, the intellectual freedom and support to pursue an unconventional project.

This has been a deeply collaborative project. Without the help of a group of exceptional scholars and friends whom I invited to join me on this journey, I simply could not have ventured this far off the garden path. I would like to thank my coauthors, who agreed to draft discussion papers for a roundtable on the subject of worldviews at the 2019 meeting of the International Studies Association in Toronto. Their papers – and a memorable lunch after the public event – convinced me that this project might indeed be feasible. The coronavirus upended plans for a meeting at Cornell in April 2020. Full drafts were instead discussed in three Zoom meetings in June 2020. The revisions of our papers were aided enormously by the insightful and constructive critiques of four discussants. I thank John Owen, Richard Price, Robbie Shilliam, and Alexander Wendt for their written comments and active intellectual presence throughout our meetings.[12]

Every text has a subtext. Mine is a song without words. I dedicate this book and its song to Mary, the love of my life.

Bibliography

Friedman, Thomas L. 2020a. "This Should be Biden's Bumper Sticker," *The New York Times* (July 1): A 24.

Friedman, Thomas L. 2020b. "How We Broke the World," *The New York Times* (May 31): SR5.

Gabriel, Jürg Martin. 1994. *Worldviews and Theories of International Relations.* New York: St. Martin's.

Haass, Richard. 2020. *The World: An Introduction.* New York: Penguin.

Hamilton, Scott. 2019. "I Am Uncertain, but We Are Not: A New Subjectivity of the Anthropocene," *Review of International Studies* 45, 4: 607–26.

Hirschman, Albert O. 1980 [1945]. "Preface to the Expanded Paperback Edition," in *National Power and the Structure of Foreign Trade.* Berkeley: University of California Press, pp. v–xii.

Katzenstein, Peter J. 2020. "Protean Power: A Second Look," *International Theory* 12, 3: 481–99.

---

[12] I would also like to thank Stephen Kalberg for joining the meeting for the discussion of Bentley Allan's chapter.

Katzenstein, Peter J. and Stephen C. Nelson. 2013a. "Reading the Right Signals and Reading the Signals Right: IPE and the Financial Crisis of 2008," *Review of International Political Economy* 20, 5: 1101–31.

Katzenstein, Peter J. and Stephen Nelson. 2013b. "Worlds in Collision: Uncertainty and Risk in Hard Times," in Miles Kahler and David Lake, eds., *Politics in the New Hard Times: The Great Recession in Comparative Perspective.* Ithaca, NY: Cornell University Press, pp. 233–52.

Katzenstein, Peter J. and Lucia A. Seybert, eds. 2018. *Protean Power: Exploring the Uncertain and Unexpected in World Politics.* New York: Cambridge University Press.

Kay, John and Mervyn King. 2020. *Radical Uncertainty: Decision-Making Beyond Numbers.* New York: W.W. Norton.

Lawrence, Mark Atwood. 2020. "Intelligence Matters: Why Americans Should Educate Themselves about International Affairs," *The New York Times Book Review* (June 14): 14.

Nelson, Stephen C. and Peter J. Katzenstein. 2014. "Uncertainty, Risk, and the Financial Crisis of 2008," *International Organization* 68, 2: 361–92.

Seib, Gerald F. 2020. "In Coronavirus Fight, Uncertainty Emerges as the New Enemy," *The Wall Street Journal* (May 26): A4.

Wendt, Alexander. 2015. *Quantum Mind and Social Science: Unifying Physical and Social Ontology.* New York: Cambridge University Press.

1 Worldviews in World Politics

Peter J. Katzenstein

> The fact that financial markets went markedly into shock has to be attributed to a lack of confidence in policies and leadership. It's a failure of worldview.
>
> Adam Posen, March 2020[1]

> I found out to my intense surprise and disappointment that my father did not have, what I then thought was a basic necessity for any real person – a "Weltanschauung"! The subsequent history of my life and thought could probably be written in terms of the progressive discovery on my part how right my father had been.
>
> Albert O. Hirschman, March 1993[2]

Sometimes we get overwhelmed by the uncertainties of life and the open-endedness of the future. The pandemic gripping the world in 2020/21 is one such instance. As the virus spread, a sense of personal vulnerability and radical uncertainty spread as well, barely masked by incessant talk about changing risk calculations.[3] In such moments many of us do not turn to theories, models, or hypotheses. Instead, we turn to worldviews to give us some traction in a world suddenly turned upside down. President Trump's worldview valued national borders that could be closed to foreigners. Early on, he imposed a ban on travel from China. The World Health Organization and many others were aghast. Their world-view valued open borders and unobstructed travel. In January 2021, during his last day in office, President Trump lifted travel bans his administration had previously imposed, only to have the incoming Biden administration immediately reverse his decision. This is not to deny the obvious. After four years in office, President Trump's general

---

I thank Matthew Evangelista and Henry Nau for their careful read and invaluable comments on earlier drafts of this chapter; Robert Keohane and Chris Reus-Smit for their strategic advice how to position its argument; and Begüm Adalet, Peter Gourevitch, Patrick Jackson, Jonathan Kirshner, Stephen Krasner and Daniel Nexon for their general reactions.

[1] Phillips 2020: B4.   [2] Meldolesi 1995: v.   [3] Roberts 2020; Fisher 2020.

worldview had affected state and local officials of the Republican party, not to mention tens of millions of his supporters.[4]

The 2020/21 pandemic is merely the latest example of the kinds of uncertainties students of world politics confront on a daily basis.[5] On March 3–4, 2020, for example, it was unclear how the stock market would react to the biggest emergency rate cut of the Federal Reserve since the Great Recession of 2008. Most market analysts expected a bounce in stock prices; instead, the market tanked. A few weeks later – again to everyone's total surprise, as the real economy cratered and the number of unemployed topped 30 million – April 2020 turned out to be the best month Wall Street had recorded since 1987. Politics is similarly unpredictable. For example, the outcome of the Super Tuesday Democratic primary of March 2020 was entirely uncertain. Nobody had a clue how it would affect the relative standing of the main contenders. In the event, Joe Biden's string of victories stunned analysts and practitioners alike. Shomik Dutta, a veteran of Obama campaigns, lamented: "It's a bizarre feeling to realize that all the things I obsess over in politics ... did not seem to matter very much at all."[6] Eight months later, most pollsters agreed that Joe Biden would win the 2020 US Presidential election comfortably, and perhaps with a blow-out. Pollsters had tweaked their models, learning from their 2016 mistakes. All the hard work was to no avail. The cliffhanger election disproved a tsunami of surveys.[7]

With its unexpected turns and twists, time and again world politics has stumped participants and analysts with momentous events. The end of the Cold War, German unification, the peaceful disintegration of the Soviet Union, the 9/11 attacks on the World Trade Center and the Pentagon, the 2008 financial crisis and its aftermath, the Arab Spring, Brexit and the election of Donald Trump, the surge of protest across the United States after the murder of George Floyd, the coronavirus pandemic, and the wildfires engulfing the American West coast in 2020 were all big surprises. Insider knowledge and the political intuition of central protagonists are of little help. Chancellor Kohl's 1989 predictions about the process of German unification were wrong, as were those of Prime Minister Cameron in 2016 about the outcome of the Brexit referendum. And so too were the well-considered judgments of leading American international relations theorists. In the late 1970s and early 1980s, Kenneth Waltz bet that the Soviet Union would last another century, Robert Keohane that the era of American

---

[4] Lerer and Epstein 2021.   [5] Jervis 2017: 175–82.
[6] Quoted in Gamio and Goldmacher 2020.
[7] For a rare exception, see Enns and Lagodny 2021, who predicted a Biden victory with 54.5 percent of the popular vote and who accurately predicted 49 of 50 states, missing only Georgia. Their forecast incorporated operational uncertainty by running 70,000 simulations, analysis of which suggested that the probability of a Biden win was 60 percent.

hegemony had passed.[8] When the unexpected undermines or overturns our most respected theories, we often fall back on our worldviews for guidance.

For Theodore White, "It is the nature of politics that men must always act on the basis of uncertain facts ... Were it otherwise, then ... politics would be an exact science in which our purposes and destiny could be left to great impersonal computers."[9] Putting aside the concept of uncertainty, most students of world politics have followed economics in focusing their attention on calculable risk.[10] For example, in her authoritative and sophisticated analysis of risk and uncertainty in international politics, Rose McDermott writes that risk and uncertainty comingle.[11] She thus combines both as she identifies mechanisms of risk propensity that occur under conditions of "high" uncertainty. In the remainder of her book, however, she puts aside the problem of uncertainty and focuses exclusively on the domain of risk.

While it is not possible to scale the magnitude of uncertainty, it is possible to distinguish between two types: operational uncertainty and radical uncertainty. Known unknowns create operational uncertainty which, given more or better information, may transform into calculable risk. This, however, is not a panacea. Under conditions of operational uncertainty, better and more information and knowledge, as in the squeezing of a balloon, can simply push radical uncertainty into some other, unrecognized part of the political context.[12] On questions of security and political economy, this is standard practice in the analysis of world politics.[13] Uncertainty is conflated with the concept of risk and thus remains invisible.[14] McDermott acknowledges this fact. "It is impossible," she writes, "to predict the characteristics of many different variables simultaneously in advance, especially when they may have unknown interaction effects. Even the nature of many of the critical variables may be unknown beforehand."[15] Analysis proceeds based on the unrealistic assumption that, separated by different information, parties to a conflict in world politics share in the same understanding of how the world works. New information leads to revised risk calculations and thus offers a way forward.

Withdrawn from the precarious domain of uncertainty, the future is domesticated into the more agreeable form of risk, thus retaining a family

---

[8] Waltz 1979: 95; Keohane 1984: 244.   [9] White 1961: vii, quoted in Lepore 2020: 18.
[10] Classical realists are a notable exception. See Kirshner 2022 for a far-ranging, critical discussion of structural realism and bargaining models and their neglect of uncertainty and contingency in world politics. For longer discussions of uncertainty and risk, see Wenger, Jasper, and Cavelty 2020; Beckert and Bronk 2018; Katzenstein and Seybert 2018b: 41–50; Katzenstein and Nelson 2013a: 234–35, 238–42; Katzenstein and Nelson 2013b: 1103–109; Nelson and Katzenstein 2014: 361–69.
[11] McDermott 1998: 3–5, 30.   [12] Katzenstein and Seybert 2018c: 276–78.
[13] Katzenstein and Seybert 2018b: 42–50.   [14] Katzenstein and Seybert 2018b: 45–46.
[15] McDermott 1998: 5.

resemblance with the present and the past. Measurable confidence intervals strip the future of the deep anxiety that attends the unknown. We live life forward while understanding it backward. The malleability of the world is reflected in the multiple ways we have convinced ourselves of knowing the future. Prediction becomes a specific technology of "future making and world crafting," made possible by severing the link between a man-made future and religion.[16] This offers us an avenue for managing expectations and thus to exercise some control over time. But such efforts can run up against manifestations of uncertainty such as technological breakthroughs, authority crises, consensus breakdowns, revolutionary upheavals, generational conflicts, and other forces that restructure the political landscape.[17] Theories and models are thus defeated by the unpredictable as world politics moves beyond control.[18] And, as Ernst Haas observed long ago, theories and models can unwittingly exacerbate problems of turbulence by pretending to create predictability for parts of political reality while weakening our understanding of the whole.[19]

Worldviews differ in the salience they assign to risk and uncertainty. Approaches such as subjective probability theory explore ways of thinking about rationality and its relation to risk and uncertainty.[20] Rationality can take the form of different, situationally specific kinds of reasonableness. Since total chaos and existential uncertainty are terrifying, concepts such as ontological security probe different forms of reasonableness under conditions of risk and uncertainty.[21] And reasonableness differs in worldviews populated by different cosmologies, memories, imaginaries, emotions, and moral sensibilities: "It is not the information but the worldview that drives actors."[22]

The concept of a risk-inflected control of nature and society is so reassuring that we simply close our eyes to the self-evident: the ineluctability of the uncertainties of life. Why we do so is not self-evident. To be sure, the idea of risk is profound and has been immensely beneficial in human affairs. Indeed, a couple of centuries ago it was revolutionary to think that the future could serve the present, and that the chance of loss is an opportunity for gain.[23] But these important insights should not make us deny the obvious: uncertainty and an open future are important aspects of world politics. Uncertainty results in part from people holding different theories of how the world works. The financial meltdown of 2008 showed widely accepted risk models to have been utterly useless in

---

[16] Andersson 2018: 6, 75–97, 216.
[17] Rosenau 1990: 8; Rosenau and Durfee 1995: 33–44.   [18] Ridley 2015.
[19] Levine and Barder 2014, 873.   [20] Friedman 2019, further discussed in Chapter 10.
[21] Daston 2019: 45–53. Kinnvall and Mitzen 2020, further discussed in Chapter 10.
[22] Katzenstein and Seybert 2018b: 45.   [23] Bernstein 1996: 1, 337.

predicting the crisis. Very little has changed either in the specific field of finance or in the broader analysis of world politics. We have been so fully seduced by the Hobbesian notion of control that we overlook the surprises Machiavelli writes about. We have placed all of our bets on the all-controlling Leviathan, while forgetting about the jolts fortuna administers regularly.[24]

This is not to argue that uncertainty is the only factor shaping political life. Social science and common sense offer tools that equip us to cope with "knowable unknowns" and the risky aspects of life in a partly orderly world.[25] However, "unknowable unknowns" also exist, and these radical uncertainties shape a reality not amenable to risk analysis. Compared to the Great Recession of 2008, the 2020 pandemic raised broader uncertainties, thereby linking challenges in public health to escalating individual and social fears, and to collapsing economies. And this global pandemic is mild compared to the dramatic environmental changes that may well be unfolding under conditions of global warming. That crisis, Scott Hamilton writes, may pose "an unprecedented existential and temporal *uncertainty* concerning the future of human subjectivity, and of the Earth itself."[26]

The first typical reaction to our encounters with uncertainty is bafflement at the unexpected, and subsequently a labored process of normalizing the abnormal, followed by amnesia. Metaphors help. Echoing George Kennan's insistence that we are gardeners, not mechanics, former Secretary of State George Shultz once remarked that "diplomacy is like gardening. The layout of the garden is set. It just has to be tended."[27] But times have changed. For many students of politics, today's world looks and feels like a jungle. Robert Kagan, a prominent neoconservative public intellectual, captures this mood in the title of his book, *The Jungle Grows Back*.[28] He explains that liberalism "took root, spread and evolved" in an order that "was always artificial and tenuous, challenged from within and without" by the natural forces of an anarchic geopolitics. "Like a garden, it can last only so long as it is tended and protected. Today, the US seems bent on relinquishing its duties in pushing back the jungle."[29] Susan Rice, who served as National Security Advisor under President Obama, concurs

---

[24] Katzenstein and Seybert 2018a, 2018b, 2018c; Seybert and Katzenstein 2018.

[25] Putting aside the question of unknowable unknowns, the most creative and important work on operational uncertainty and risk focuses on combining specific forecasting question clusters about the short term with broad scenarios about the long term, thus giving decision-makers an evolving sense of plausible futures that leaves unanalyzed inescapable, radical uncertainty. Scoblic and Tetlock 2020: 16–18. See also Tetlock and Gardner 2015.

[26] Hamilton 2019: 610 (emphasis in the original).

[27] Kennan 1966/1954: 93; Shiraishi 2020: 3.   [28] Kagan 2018a.   [29] Kagan 2018b.

when she speaks of "Trump's Hobbesian jungle."[30] And an unflappable, rational former physicist, Germany's Chancellor Merkel, watches as the liberal multilateral world she helped sustain is "shoved aside by the law of the jungle."[31] Like Germany, Canada too must learn how to navigate a "jungle-like world."[32] Today, the jungle has become a common metaphor for the many disruptions and weirdnesses of the unpredictable.[33] Jungle and garden metaphors are stand-ins for worldviews that often remain unspoken while helping us navigate the turbulent currents of world affairs.

We should be wary, though, of loading the dice only on the side of looming threats. Jungles and forests are not only places of dread but also sites of hope. Uncertainty can reveal vulnerabilities that lead to creative responses and empowerment of the disempowered. Such bigger issues could be environmental or social. Viewed in a broader context, Jared Diamond argues, a "successful resolution of the pandemic crisis may motivate us to deal with ... bigger issues that we have until now balked at confronting."[34] Aided by the shocking vulnerabilities of African Americans revealed once again by the pandemic, the explosion of the Black Lives Matter movement in America in the summer of 2020 created a powerful multiracial coalition that vented its fury at police violence as one among many instances of systemic racism. This was the latest installment of a rights revolution that has spread globally during the last half-century, in fits and starts to be sure, and often in unpredictable directions.

Although they provide important anchors at many moments of uncertainty, the lack of attention to worldviews in the analysis of world politics is striking. Measured by Google Books Ngram Viewer, in sharp contrast to the concepts of "theory" and "model," Figure 1.1 shows that the concept of "worldview" is barely used.[35] Two decades ago, Peter Haas popularized the concept of epistemic communities, writing in the most cited article of *International Organization*, the highest-ranked journal of world politics in the United States, that epistemic communities refer to networks of knowledge-based individuals "who share the same worldview."[36] While many scholars have followed his lead in developing the concept of

---

[30] Rice 2020.   [31] Barber and Chazan 2020.   [32] The Economist 2019.
[33] Liik 2019; Erlanger 2018; Le Vine 2018; Wainer 2016.   [34] Diamond 2020.
[35] The *Ngram Viewer* is a research tool for "quick-and-dirty heuristic analysis" (Chumtong and Kaldewey 2017: 8). It is worth remembering that this tool does not measure what people are talking about but what they are publishing about, only in English, and only in texts that Google has digitalized.
[36] Haas 1992: 27.

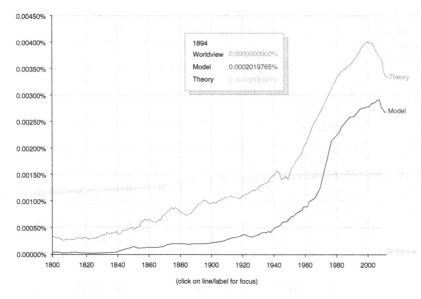

Figure 1.1 Ngrams: worldview, theory, model

epistemic community, none, to my knowledge, has followed up to inquire into the concept of worldview. While we might be vaguely aware of uncertainty's role in global politics, we seem to prefer not to look this challenge in the face by examining our worldviews.

In conceiving and contributing to this book, I have ventured for a third time off the conventional garden path of international relations scholarship. As was true of all other scholars of world politics, the end of the Cold War caught me by surprise. I wanted to understand why and turned to cultural sociology for new insights. *The Culture of National Security*,[37] mainstream realists and liberals thought in the mid-1990s, was no more than a futile exercise in postmodern flim-flam that had nothing to do with respectable social science. It turned out, however, that cultural sociology was central to the constructivist theories of international relations that quickly secured for themselves seats at the high table of theory. Seeking to understand the Great Recession of 2008–09 two decades later, I tracked the broader political implications of uncertainty and developed a conceptualization of power that was less materialist and less focused

---

[37] Katzenstein 1996.

on Hobbesian notions of control. Film and cultural studies provided me with valuable insights into the dynamics of unpredictable possibilities and potentialities of what Lucia Seybert and I called *Protean Power*.[38] The evident difficulty that book's argument created for many of my colleagues, as it forced them to come to terms with uncertainty and potentiality, has led me in this book to turn to the natural sciences, which for more than a century have been no strangers to these two concepts. *Uncertainty and Its Discontents* seeks to show the deep Newtonian roots of the firm convictions of what a scientific study of world politics entails, and our never-ending amazement when the unexpected derails those scientific endeavors. I will argue that "the relational revolution" in twentieth-century physics, and many of the natural sciences more generally, can enrich sociological relationalism in the social sciences.[39] It embeds risk-based, Newtonian thinking about a "world of being" in an uncertainty-inflected, Post-Newtonian thinking about a "relational world of becoming." Thus, it explicitly acknowledges uncertainty and the open-ended potentialities of world politics.

This chapter seeks to better understand the scientific worldviews that make us overlook uncertainty as a central aspect of world politics. It examines the concept of worldview (Section 1.1); considers for the field of world politics the substantive and analytical formulations of world-views in the form of political and analytical paradigms, as well as substantialist and relational ontologies and epistemologies that are embedded in them (Section 1.2); differentiates between Newtonianism and Post-Newtonianism (quantum mechanics) and humanism and hyper-humanism (scientific cosmology) as two dimensions structuring different worldviews (Sections 1.3 and 1.4); exemplifies the resulting four world-views as presented in greater detail in Chapters 2–5 (Section 1.5); and concludes briefly with two illustrations (Section 1.6).

This chapter's presentation of four strikingly different worldviews is balanced in Chapter 10 by a discussion of some workarounds and commonalities that provide a shared intellectual space for Newtonianism and Post-Newtonianism. Newtonianism prefers sharp distinctions. Philosophically, Post-Newtonianism does not. Chapter 10 thus adheres to Samuel Beckett's admiration of "greyness."[40] Moving from clearly demarcated "either–or" conceptual spaces in Chapter 1 to entangled "both–and" spaces in Chapter 10 suggests a radical reconceptualization

---

[38] Katzenstein and Seybert 2018a.　　[39] The term is coined by Smolin 2013: xxviii.

[40] "Whether all grow black, or all grow bright, or all remain grey, it is grey we need, to begin with, because of what it is, and of what it can do, made of bright and black, able to shed the former, or the latter, and be the latter or the former alone. But perhaps I am the prey, on the subject of grey, in the grey, to delusions." Beckett 1958: 17.

of conventional understandings of science operating at both macro- and microlevels. Specific approaches in the field of scientific cosmology and quantum mechanics put the individual human experience rather than objective laws of nature at the center of the universe. This eliminates the traditional insistence on the difference between the natural and social sciences and holds forth the promise for the analysis of uncertainty *and* risk, rather than the insistence that world politics is marked simply by risk.

1.1 Worldviews

Worldviews offer global overviews evident in relatively constant, repetitive habits of beliefs and emotions that mediate the relations between an individual or group and the world.[41] They are animated by a sense of being in the world and of viewing how the world works or should work. Worldviews are neither purely descriptive nor purely explanatory. They contain both prescriptive and practical elements. Far from immutable, they are susceptible to fluctuations brought about by personal experience and change in the world. They comprise a flexible conceptual apparatus rooted in values. Relationally mediated by discourses and institutions, worldviews create narratives about what is possible, what is worth doing, and what needs to be done, as well as what is impossible, what is shameful, and what needs to be avoided. They thus have effects on the purposes and interests that shape policies and practices. Many techniques and rules, on their own terms, might be considered inadequate or too weak to justify policy and practice, yet they acquire a deeper legitimacy when embedded in a broader worldview. What Daston writes about natural orders is also apposite for worldviews: they are "long-lived, polyvalent, and evocative of powerful emotions."[42] Operating at different levels of abstraction, several authors in this book point to a close relationship between worldviews and other, commonly used concepts. For example, in Chapter 5, Michael Barnett disaggregates holistic worldviews and points to the internal contradictions of their different components; and in Chapter 8 Bentley Allan considers worldviews built from more encompassing cosmologies.

Worldviews are concerned with viewing the world and understanding one's place in it. They are suffused with epistemologies and ontologies. But in the discipline of international relations, in the words of John Ruggie, "epistemology is often confused with method, and the term

---

[41] Gollwitzer 1980: 176–77; Geuss 2020: xiii. This section has benefitted enormously from discussions among this book's authors in a series of Zoom meetings in June 2020.
[42] Daston 2019: 33.

'ontology' typically draws either blank stares or bemused smiles."[43] Today, almost without fail, social theories "posit an ontological beginning point ... that one takes to be the foundations of the (world-) view being explored or posited."[44] As epistemologies, worldviews concern the scientific or religious basis for knowing the world. Worldviews can be analytic or substantive. Paradigms, theories, models, and the explanatory constructs they deploy are analytic. Liberalism, Realism, and Marxism are substantive. Worldviews provide elastic interpretive guides to help navigate the world. They differ from both universal, trans-historical cosmologies and more specific, time-bound ideologies. The concept of worldview is contested and, for some, considered inherently contestable.[45] The chapters in this book provide ample material for both contestation and inherent contestability.

Because they are foundational, worldviews are important for understanding and evaluating human choice. Embodied in both views and practice, they both passively "re-flect" and actively "re-present" the world, offering views both *of* and *for* the world.[46] Because "we believe what we do largely because of the way our beliefs fit into our worldview,"[47] our diagnoses and solutions are not cheap talk. Worldviews consist of big yet simple ideas that operate at both individual and collective levels. They reflect and shape individual ideas, experiences, memories, and imaginations that always remain open to modifications and reinterpretations.[48] They are also collective systems of thought that offer some measure of coherence and consistency in an often unfathomable world.[49] Worldviews can incorporate contradictory and tension-inducing elements. Loosely coupled, they compete, coexist, and coevolve with one another.

The growing schisms dividing "metro" from "retro" have prompted a few observers to apply the concept of worldview to contemporary American politics.[50] Reflecting on the partisanship of the 1990s and early 2000s, cognitive scientist George Lakoff writes that "contemporary American politics is about worldview."[51] Conservatives and Liberals have a very difficult time understanding each other because they rely on different commonsense notions as they interpret what they experience. Conservatives hold to a "Strict Father," Liberals to a "Nurturing Parent" trope. In a similar vein, and adapting Max Weber to twentieth-century America, Eric Oliver and Thomas Wood try to capture the different intuitions and modes of reasoning that distinguish American's disenchanted and enchanted worldviews.[52] Marc Hetherington and

[43] Ruggie 1993: 170.   [44] Arfi 2012: 191.   [45] Geuss 2020: 22.
[46] Phillips and Brown 1991: 29; Griffiths 2007: 1–2; Haukkala 2011: 30–38.
[47] Dewitt 2004: 11.   [48] Rösch 2015: 11–16.   [49] Betz 1980.
[50] Meyer 2001: 1–2, 22–23.   [51] Lakoff 2002: 3.   [52] Oliver and Wood 2018: 4–5.

Jonathan Weiler, finally, develop a related argument that focuses on two worldviews epitomized by pick-up truck and Prius, John Wayne and Jane Fonda, meatloaf and vegetable biryani, and a preference for a fixed or fluid politics.[53] During the last half-century, operational political ideologies have increasingly lined up with such underlying worldviews and are now creating a polarized politics that is threatening the very fabric of American democracy. The notion of a unique and singular American worldview captured by the trope of American exceptionalism is mistaken. American worldviews express political inclinations and moral sensibilities that differentiate liberals from conservatives along a number of dimensions. On closer inspection, though, all of these dualities are oversimplified and fail to capture the fractal patterns of political change in America.[54] Despite such qualifications, it is difficult to deny that worldviews play a substantial role in American politics.

Individually experienced yet irreducibly social, worldviews circulate through society.[55] They have emotional and rational components that are seamlessly fused.[56] As modern neuroscience tells us, one does not exist without the other.[57] "Emotions are not irrational pushes and pulls," Martha Nussbaum writes. "They are ways of viewing the world. They reside at the core of one's being, the part of it with which one makes sense of the world."[58] For Nussbaum, emotions are "appraisals or value judgements which ascribe to things and persons outside the person's own control great importance for the person's own flourishing."[59] The Latin root of the word emotion means to "move out" from the individual toward others and the world. Although emotions are individual, they also have an inherently social character.[60] Their collective reality is closely linked to individual identity.[61] Emotions are an important aspect of how we view the world. This is not to deny that a worldview is also grounded in rational beliefs with little or no emotional content. Newtonian and Post-Newtonian scientific worldviews, for example, differ in their rejection or acceptance of uncertainty as a constitutive aspect of both the natural world and the political world.

Emotional and rational worldviews, Miriam Steiner has argued, can appear in a modified form that acknowledges the fuzzy boundary between

---

[53] Hetherington and Weiler 2018: ix–xiii, 17–18, 215–24; Hetherington and Weiler 2009.
[54] Putnam 2020.
[55] Intergroup emotions theory has informed a number of clinical experiments (Sasley 2011: 458–65). See also Wolf 2012a, 2012b.
[56] Bially-Mattern 2014: 590–91.
[57] This line of thought is not pursued further here. For one example, see Damasio 1994.
[58] Nussbaum 1995: 375.   [59] Nussbaum 2001: 4.
[60] Fierke 2013: 79, 92–93; Hutchinson 2016: 18–20.   [61] Koschut 2018: 321–29.

optimization and intuition.[62] A modified rationalist worldview incorporates the notion of bounded rationality operating under constraints that encourages satisficing rather than optimizing behavior.[63] A modified nonrationalist worldview highlights the importance of intuition and subjective awareness. Some rationalist elements are always present in predominantly nonrationalist views, and vice versa. A comprehensive worldview integrates elements of both, featuring complex configurations of rationality and non-rationality.[64] Feelings of being in the world and being anchored in a particular worldview thus can challenge or reinforce our core beliefs. Such complementarities or contradictions can reinforce worldviews, alter them, or make them crumble.

The concept of worldview operates at a higher level than several related concepts that scholars of world politics have deployed in their analyses of world politics.[65] Foreign policy ideologies, belief systems, strategic cultures, operational codes, causal beliefs, cognitive maps, narratives, and policy and political paradigms are all related to, though distinct from, overarching worldviews. For example, worldviews are less coherent than Mark Haas's foreign policy ideologies.[66] They are conceptually less clear than Ole Holsti's belief systems, Alastair Iain Johnson's strategic cultures, and Nathan Leites's operational codes.[67] They are broader than the causal beliefs that interest Jeffrey Legro and the cognitive maps Robert Axelrod has deployed, and less determinative than the narratives that concern Ron Krebs.[68] They are less cognitive, less influenced by academic and bureaucratic experts, and socially and culturally more deeply embedded than are policy paradigms.[69] And they are overtly less political than political paradigms.[70]

Worldviews can act as both stabilizing anchors and emergent processes. They can be both explicit and implicit. The very idea of a choice of worldview is itself the product of a specific worldview. In fact, some strands of neuroscience suggest the possibility that reason and consciousness set in only after – rather than before – the act of choosing has

---

[62] Steiner 1983: 376–79, 382–83. Steiner's distinction resonates with the Japanese one between *tatemae* (formally established rational principles) and *honne* (authentic feelings and desires that cannot be openly expressed).

[63] Simon 1956: 129, 136.   [64] Steiner 1983: 392–400, 409–12.

[65] Terhalle 2015: 77–80. The concept of worldviews is mentioned briefly in a number of texts; See Bain 2020: 16–17; Chuang, Manley, and Petersen 2020; Maas 2018; Suleman 2017; Narlikar and Narlikar 2014: 6; Narang and Staniland 2012: 76–77; Kagan 2008; Pouliot 2008: 260; Hurrell 2007: 17; Tan 2007; Vennesson 2007: 8–9; Kagan 2003: 3; Nisbett 2003: xx; James 2002: 69; Keohane 2002: 45; Norwine and Smith 2000; Tilford 1995; Sanders 1989: 13; Sharma 1989: 324–25; Sabel: 1984: 14; Range 1961.

[66] Haas 2012.   [67] Holsti 2006; Johnson 1995; Leites 1951.

[68] Legro 2005; Axelrod 2015; Krebs 2015.   [69] Hall 1993; Wilder and Howlett 2014.

[70] Gilpin 1975: 215–62.

occurred.[71] Worldviews shape the views of both scholars and of the various actors they study. Worldviews connect the interpretation of the self in the analysis of the other and the world. In this chapter, for example, I am particularly interested in the scientific worldviews of scholars and the effect they have on the neglect or recognition of the constitutive importance of uncertainty in world politics. By contrast, in Chapter 2 Mark Haas and Henry Nau examine the worldviews of political leaders and the effects these worldviews have on political norms and practices. In Chapter 7, Prasenjit Duara covers the worldviews of both scholars and leaders.

These general characteristics of worldviews find more specific expression in the difference between the Newtonian and Post-Newtonian scientific worldviews that concern me here.[72] In the analysis of world politics and the social sciences, Newtonianism has been hegemonic. In contrast, quantum mechanics, with its insistence on the centrality of uncertainty at the subatomic level, has occupied a marginal position in the social sciences – including the study of world politics.[73] Furthermore, the relational revolution in scientific cosmology and several other branches of the natural sciences puts the concept of uncertainty into a much broader context. Both quantum mechanics and scientific cosmology are instances of a Post-Newtonian scientific worldview with far-reaching ramifications for our understanding of society and history. Yet, students of world politics have shown little interest in exploring and learning from Post-Newtonianism.

Newtonian uncertainty is cast in agentic terms and is believed to be manageable through the exercise of control power and risk management. In Post-Newtonianism it is considered systemic and can include protean power effects that thrive in the domain of the unexpected.[74] In the analysis of world politics, scholars with a Newtonian worldview typically downplay or overlook the distributed agency that is highlighted by Post-Newtonianism. Newtonianism offers a commitment to intervening in the world by accountable agents who seek to achieve some purpose or value. Post-Newtonianism is less focused on individual accountability. It points instead to the inherent contradiction within a Newtonian worldview, with its firm belief in laws or causal mechanisms that deny or limit freedom and

---

[71] Jairus Grove made this point several times in our discussions. See also Damasio 1994.

[72] The distinction between Newtonianism and Post-Newtonianism focuses on the difference between the ontology and epistemology of classical and quantum physics, but also goes beyond it to incorporate other natural sciences, such as scientific cosmology, which have taken a relational turn in the twentieth century. Even though it went well beyond Newton, nineteenth-century energy physics was classical. I am concerned here with scientific worldviews rather than the science of worldviews Dilthey tried to develop, as I discuss in Section 1.4.

[73] Wendt (2015) is the notable exception.   [74] Katzenstein and Seybert 2018a.

agency while at the same time insisting on the primacy of agency and accountability. Although Newtonianism reigns supreme in the analysis of world politics and some of the other social sciences, it has been sidelined in physics and the natural sciences. Debates in quantum mechanics, for example, do not seek to attack or defend Newtonianism in general; they focus instead on which elements of a closed Newtonian system can be usefully incorporated in a broader view of a universe that is open.

The determinism and certainty of Newton's macro world, softened by the laws of probability, has been replaced by the indeterminism and uncertainty of the micro world of quantum physics. According to Feynman, Mermin, and Baeyer, Newtonian and quantum physics are examples of scientific worldviews.[75] Taken together, these two scientific worldviews illuminate a politics marked by risk and uncertainty. In the Newtonian worldview, "the future after a fashion repeats the past."[76] Novelty in Newtonianism is conceived of as recombinatorial, in contrast to the possibility of radical creativity and innovation in Post-Newtonianism. In the conventional understanding of world politics, the world is viewed as closed and inhabited by actors who feel threatened by uncontrollable uncertainty. Envisaging a world that is open and actors who are enabled by new possibilities seems implausible and uncomfortable.

Only a handful of scholars of world politics have explicitly introduced the concept of worldview into their analysis. For Patrick James, building on Rosenau, worldviews provide complex, holistic foundations for scientific research. They are not analytically consistent.[77] They subsume paradigms, theories, models, and hypotheses that seek to understand and explain patterned or specific events. Worldviews are inescapably normative and shape the understanding and explanation of reality. They are often self-confirming and sometimes self-invalidating. Divergent worldviews do not get resolved by appeals to logic and evidence but through individual experiences and social processes.[78] In contrast to James, worldviews for Jürg Gabriel are extremely simple and highlight a few

---

[75] Mermin 1990: 175, 195; Baeyer 2016: 185, 192, 195. I justify my radical simplifications of an exceedingly complex analytical terrain because doing so highlights the central distinction I wish to make between two scientific worldviews (Baeyer 2016: 140). This discussion abstracts therefore from different interpretations of quantum mechanics, such as pilot-wave, spontaneous reduction, many-worlds, modal, consistent history, and spontaneous collapse (Bächtold 2008: 843–44; Baeyer 2016: 235–39). For a general overview, see Lewis 2016.

[76] Wiener 1948: 42.

[77] James 2002: 68–72; Rosenau 1997: 26–31. See also Rösch 2015: 11–16; Krell 2000; Nau 2012.

[78] James 2002: 72.

concepts that for centuries have remained largely unchanged.[79] He identifies optimists among scholars who believe in a general accumulation of
knowledge, and pessimists who are frustrated by the fact that, beyond
a handful of small islands, accumulation is smothered by a proliferation of
often incommensurable approaches. In contrast to the cumulative process of knowledge creation in the natural sciences, knowledge creation in
international relations is repetitive. Time and again, students of world
politics deal with foundational issues and concepts in light of new circumstances and information.

The stabilization of an uncertain world through worldviews is
a political act.[80] Worldviews offer basic ideas that shape the questions
we ask or fail to ask, provide us with explanatory and interpretive concepts, and suggest hunches or plausible answers.[81] They are a handle that
organizes many of the world's unknown or poorly understood facts. For
Max Weber, a world image (*Weltbild*) or worldview consists of concepts
and judgments that can provide the groundwork for a thoughtful ordering
of the world and a narrative shaping of "salient areas of daily, human
practice."[82] But, contra Weber, worldviews operate in all societies and in
all historical times.[83] They are imaginaries that are built around basic and
often unarticulated assumptions such as "time, space, language and
embodiment."[84] Worldviews contain arguments about the ontological
building blocks of the world, the epistemic requirements of acceptable
knowledge claims, and the origin and destiny of humanity. They find
expression in institutional and symbolic orders. They are legitimated by
being part of the natural order of things, privilege some actors, such as
priests or scientists, and embody shared values that are considered "natural." Within a given worldview there can always exist a variety of different and often competing ways of understanding. Christianity's religious
wars are one example. Scientific schisms between Aristotelian and modern science and within modern science, between classical physics and
quantum mechanics, are another. Lacking tight internal integration,
worldviews infuse meaning into world politics. Inchoate as they often
are, worldviews are central to our readiness to accept uncertainty as
a constitutive aspect of world politics.

---

[79] Gabriel 1994: 1–2.   [80] Allan, Chapter 8, this volume.
[81] The concept of *Weltanschauung* is normally translated as "worldview" even though the
German *anschauen* describes a conscious activity, while viewing can also be unconscious
(Rösch 2015: 11).
[82] Weber 1956: 253, 260, 414–17, 430; Naugle 2002: xvi, 291–92, 297–303.
[83] Trownsell et al. 2020; Waters 1999.   [84] Phillips, Brown, and Stonestreet 1991: 24.

1.2   Paradigms, Substantialism, and Relationalism

In their discussions of worldviews, students of world politics have tended to collapse this concept's multifarious analytical and political components into the more mundane "paradigm." [85] Specifically, since the 1970s they have debated both Thomas Kuhn's work on analytical paradigms and substantive political paradigms such as liberalism, realism, and Marxism. Commitments to Newtonian substantialism and Post-Newtonian relationalism, and the attendant (in)ability to conceptualize uncertainty as a constitutive part of world politics, are embedded in discussions about both types of paradigm.

Paradigms. Historian of science Thomas Kuhn used the concept of paradigm to characterize and distinguish the foundational assumptions of different scientific approaches.[86] Scientific progress was not a story of continuous and cumulative progress. It consisted instead of periods of normal science interrupted by brief periods of revolutionary science. Normal science is marked by the ascendance of a single paradigm that determines the central research questions, theoretical vocabulary, and acceptable methods and criteria for assessing how well a given question has been answered. When fully institutionalized, weak links of dominant paradigms are no longer recognized, foundational assumptions are no longer questioned, and anomalies are consistently overlooked or considered as lying outside of acceptable research programs. Revolutionary science occurs in brief spurts when scientists are frustrated by increasing numbers of anomalies, interested in new research questions, and committed to developing new approaches that might resolve troubling anomalies. Once the insurgents have acquired sufficient clout, conditions are ripe for the emergence of a new paradigm. Controversially, for Kuhn, paradigms are incommensurable with one another, so it is impossible to integrate or compare theories developed within different paradigms.

Kuhn's argument about "paradigm shift" and "paradigm incommensurability" is analytical.[87] It tells us nothing about the world itself. His argument is about the perception of reality and not about the real world. In a *Gestalt*-flip paradigm shift, we do not necessarily lose the ability to see the rabbit or the duck, but we may not be able to see them at the same time. The argument about incommensurability that captured the imagination of the humanities and some of the social sciences resonates with shifts in the "soft" parts of paradigms. It fails, however, to capture their "hard" parts that deal with predictive accuracy, explanatory depth, and

---

[85] I thank Rudra Sil for commenting helpfully on this section.
[86] Kuhn 1962. Sil and Katzenstein 2010a: 4–5, 26–34. Sil and Katzenstein 2010b.
[87] Sil and Katzenstein 2010a: 13–16.

power. The incommensurability account mischaracterizes the process of inquiry in the modern natural sciences, specifically in the maturing of paradigms and their theoretical developments over time.[88] Difficulties of understanding across paradigms are not the same as the impossibility of understanding. The question of "what is," after all, is not the same as "what is known" or "what can be made meaningful."[89] Such difficulties do not imply that all statements about truth are contingent.[90] As a matter of fact, Kuhn's later writings reflect a modified view on incommensurability, toward a more circumscribed claim about meaning variance across paradigms and the limits of our ability to translate adequately from one paradigm to another.[91] In any case, as Gunnell observes, "philosophy is no more the basis of science than social science is the basis of society."[92] For those who believe that there is a reality outside of and apart from the observer, it makes little sense to ask a natural or social scientist whether they have nature or society right.

Kuhn sometimes likened revolutionary, paradigm-shifting scientific progress to the process of Darwinian evolution: nondirectional improvement with no specific purpose. By contrast, change during normal times, within a well-understood paradigm, is directional.[93] There are multiple truths in all scientific endeavors and, on the record of the last several centuries, natural scientists have ruled out many things previously thought to be true. There is thus justified hope of movement in the direction of greater truth.[94] That hope is weaker in the social sciences – which Kuhn saw as lingering in a preparadigmatic state[95] – including the analysis of global politics, especially as long as it is captured by a worldview that fails to recognize the constitutive effects of uncertainty.

Since the middle of the twentieth century, students of world politics have debated their worldviews, first by employing the terminology of images and subsequently of substantive political paradigms. Carried by the unspoken assumption that we live in a world of probabilistic laws and risk, uncertainty has not been a subject in any of those debates. In the 1950s, the debate focused on the "image" of international relations.[96] For Wright, a synthesis of different mental images defined each scholar's perspective on international relations.[97] The world thus generates a uniform picture that lines up with the worldview accepted by individuals or groups. McClosky, Boulding, and Waltz all assumed that a stable, external world is reflected in multiple, shifting, subjective representations that scholars imagine to be images of unified, coherent

[88] Weinberg 1998.   [89] Wight 1996: 301.   [90] Morris 2011 part 3: 10; part 4: 1.
[91] Jackson and Nexon 2009: 910–11. Jackson 2015: 19–21.   [92] Gunnell 2011: 1467–68.
[93] Weinberg 1998: 14.   [94] Weinberg 2015: 6–7.   [95] Wight 1996: 292, fn 7.
[96] Hamilton 2017: 148–55. See also Kristensen 2016.   [97] Wright 1955: 484, 492–95.

wholes.[98] The image of world politics thus was embedded deeply in a Newtonian worldview. As Robert Dahl wrote in a foundational article on power in 1957, power and risk may be complicated, but "they don't defy the laws of nature as we understand them."[99] The role of uncertainty in the world was not a matter of concern within a Newtonian worldview or paradigm.

In the late 1960s, Graham Allison shifted away from anchoring international relations scholarship in images.[100] He developed three conceptual lenses or paradigms to capture how individuals, organizations, and governments behave. Allison was not interested in developing a comprehensive view of the world as much as picking up different pieces of the world that warrant explanation. As was true of the 1950s, his perspective betrayed a Newtonian worldview. His conceptual lenses perceived a real, known, and knowable world that remained an external and stable reference point.

This was true also for the prolonged discussion of realist, liberal, and Marxist paradigms by scholars of international relations in the 1980s and 1990s, which paralleled the discussion of rationalism, institutionalism, structuralism, and culturalism in the field of comparative and American politics.[101] Paradigmatic "isms" became the foundational worldviews or approaches for understanding world politics. Disagreements among analytical or substantive paradigms occurred on the firm ground of a single, real, stable world that was subject to law-like generalizations or mechanism-based analyses. The uncertainties of that world did not figure in the discussions. Furthermore, substantive political paradigms offered communities of purpose and value and focused on the problem of alternative consequences of action. With no single paradigm prevailing, each one asserted its own particular view as sacrosanct.[102] Indeed, each paradigm sought to "convey a world view more basic than theory"[103] and, following Kuhn (indeed, often directly inspired by him), viewed itself as incommensurable with all other paradigms. Hence, engagement with proponents of competing paradigms was viewed as a futile exercise. These paradigmatic worldviews were not dynamically competing but frozen in Newtonian time and space; and so too were the risk-based, theoretical worlds they generated.[104]

---

[98] McClosky 1956: 283; Boulding 1959: 120; Waltz 1959: 6, 10, 12.
[99] Dahl 1957: 214.   [100] Allison 1970: 249, 279.
[101] Gilpin 1975: 215–62; Rosenau and Durfee 1995: 9–69; Lichbach and Zuckerman 2009.
[102] Little 1984: 7.   [103] Banks 1984: 15.
[104] Hamilton 2017: 153; James 2002: 215–21. In contrast to explicitly political paradigms, analytical perspectives such as rationalism and constructivism offer different discourse communities and a shared concern with the problem of alternative causes of action.

Substantialism and Relationalism. Analytical and political paradigms[105] deal with epistemological problems of the relation between the observing mind and the observed world. They can also embody substantive onto-logical claims about the world and objects in it.[106] Their more or less explicit epistemological and ontological claims take the form of substan-tialism or relationalism.

In Newtonianism, substantial entities such as individual objects or persons exist with their internal characteristics prior to interacting with other entities. Social entities are aggregates of individuals.[107] In short, substantialism takes pregiven entities as the starting point and imbues them with properties and agency. Strong versions assume that individual choices are driven by objective or intersubjective features of the world.[108] Substantialism thus includes actor-centered approaches that rely on the logic of appropriateness.[109] Norms, culture, and identity are structural features that shape individual and state action. Both rational choice and norm-based approaches view individual human action as the elementary unit of social life. For rational choice approaches, preexisting actors typically "generate self-action" that is consistent with preexisting interests and attributes. Similarly, many norm-based approaches view individuals as "self-propelling ... entities" that follow internalized norms that are fixed for the timespan under investigation.[110] Substantialism expresses the Newtonian worldview in which classical conceptions of atoms as the smallest entities constitute the physical world, just as independent social entities are the building blocks of the social and political world.

Two key concepts in relationalism are processes and yoking.[111] Rescher defines processes as "coordinated group[s] of changes in the complexion of reality, an organized family of occurrences that are system-atically linked to one another either causally or functionally."[112] He emphasizes processes as prior (and irreducible) to substances, arguing

---

[105] There exists a vast literature in different fields of scholarship that discusses different formulations of these two concepts (Emirbayer 1997: 290–91). I provide here no more than stylized sketches to advance my argument. I thank Nina Obermeier for her excel-lent work in helping me draft this section, and Patrick Jackson for reading and com-menting on an earlier draft. See also Nordin and Smith 2019.

[106] Gunnell 2011: 1452–53, 1455, 1462, 1465–66; Jackson and Nexon 2013: 551. Wight 1996: 291–95.

[107] Abbott, 1995: 860–64.   [108] Jackson and Nexon 2013: 555.

[109] Jackson 2010; Jackson and Nexon 2013; McCourt, 2016; March and Olsen 1998.

[110] Structural arguments focus on social aggregates and do not take individual human action as their starting point. But they, too, adhere to the view of "durable, coherent entities" as the starting point of analysis and therefore are further examples of substan-tialism (Emirbayer 1997: 284–85).

[111] Nexon 2010; Jackson and Nexon 1999: 301; Rescher 1996; Abbott 1995.

[112] Rescher 1996: 38.

that this allows for an approach that prioritizes change. Unowned processes, such as nuclear proliferation and the growth of economic interdependence, cannot be viewed as the product of any particular agent's actions.[113] Rescher ties a process-oriented view of the world to quantum physics, which suggests that "at the microlevel, what was usually deemed a physical *thing*, a stably perduring object, is itself no more than a statistical pattern – a stability wave in a surging sea of process."[114] He regards the shift away from the atom to particle physics in the understanding of the physical world as analogous to the shift from substantialism to relationalism.

Focusing on boundaries rather than entities, Abbott shares Rescher's interest in relations.[115] According to his analysis, social entities come into existence when actors tie social boundaries together in specific ways. He defines boundaries as "difference[s] of character," which are gradually sorted into two sides to form stable properties through social interactions.[116] The idea of *yoking* refers to the connection of such boundaries by social actors in a way that defines entities inhabiting one or the other side of the social boundary. Abbott offers the example of the concept of social work, which did not exist prior to the late nineteenth century. It was created by the yoking together of different boundaries related to gender, training, and prior professional attachments. Abbott's description of relationalism thus stresses intersubjectivity and social context in a way that Rescher's process-oriented philosophy does not.

Extending this perspective, Laura Zanotti follows Karen Barad's lead by taking "quantum ontologies" as the starting point for her analysis of a strong version of relationalism.[117] The fundamental ontological indeterminacy in the natural world "can only be contingently resolved in the intra-action between the observer, and the observed, the human, and the non-human." In giving relations rather than substances primary ontological status, this is similar to the approaches discussed earlier. But it goes beyond them in positing a specific relationship between human and nonhuman aspects of the world. Zanotti relies on the concept of "apparatus" – ways of engaging with the world – to refer to the means by which boundaries and properties of objects are determined and ontological closure is achieved. Agency should not be considered a property that individuals possess. It operates, rather, through the apparatuses we use "to bring about differentiated forms of materialization of matter and the social."[118] Agency is not a free-floating means for humans to enact their will on the world. It is instead caught up in

---

[113] Rescher 1996: 42; Jackson and Nexon 1999: 303.
[114] Rescher 1996: 98 (emphasis in the original).   [115] Abbott 1995.
[116] Abbott 1995: 862.   [117] Barad 2007; Zanotti 2018: 4, 57–58.
[118] Zanotti 2018: 67.

complex entanglements of the human and nonhuman.[119] This version of relationalism incorporates uncertainty even more fully into its analysis than versions that focus on processes or boundaries.

In the field of political economy, the Open Economy Politics (OEP) approach exemplifies some of the advantages and disadvantages of substantialism and relationalism. OEP is readily intelligible and generates useful baselines for what to expect in the world. But it lacks "sensitivity to the social fabric of international politics."[120] That shortcoming was readily apparent after the financial meltdown of 2008–9. After the dust had settled, OEP had precious little to offer by way of analysis or interpretation to help in our understanding of the greatest uncertainty-induced calamity in the international political economy since the 1930s.[121] Similarly, international relations scholars often characterize international interdependence in substantialist terms. They describe international interdependence with a focus on the strategic interaction among purposive actors. According to Milner, under conditions of interdependence, states' "actions and attainments of their goals are conditioned by others' behavior and their expectations and perceptions of this."[122] This conceptualization emphasizes preexisting entities with interactions that affect their ability to achieve various objectives. An alternative, relational account of interdependence might "focus on the ways in which trade and other networks are constitutive of boundary conditions of the state and other projects," as Jackson and Nexon argue.[123] These examples highlight the differences between a substantialist approach that takes entities as the starting point for analysis and a relational approach that looks at how one set of relations gives rise to others. Indebted to Newtonianism, substantialist approaches tend to focus on the concept of risk and neglect uncertainty's central place in world politics.

In short, substantialism expresses a Newtonian worldview. A wide range of outcomes in closed systems can be explained with reference to a few abstract, universal principles.[124] Autonomy refers to the notion that "actors are analytically distinguishable from the practices and relations that constitute them."[125] Rational choice approaches seek to abstract from specific contexts. Models are generally transposable. This produces "timeless, context-free, and abstract knowledge,"[126] as opposed to a relational, practice-oriented Post-Newtonian worldview. It emphasizes an indeterminacy that can be resolved in contextually specific processes of materialization. Mayntz and Scharpf's actor-centered relationalism

---

[119] Kaufman 2008: 23–46.   [120] McCourt 2016: 482.
[121] Nelson and Katzenstein 2014.   [122] Milner 1991: 83.
[123] Jackson and Nexon 1999: 304.   [124] Zanotti 2018: 29.
[125] Jackson and Nexon 2013: 553, 555.   [126] McCourt 2016: 476.

combines actor autonomy with contextual factors.[127] It does not give explanatory primacy "to specific features of the immediate spatial-temporal environment in which actors operate."[128] Instead, it assumes that social relations embed actors and constrain their autonomy. The relations in which actors are embedded generate key actor attributes, capacities, and characteristics. Contextualism can be either "thin" or "thick." Thin contextualism allows for some level of generalization about actor relations and positions; actors and context are analytically separable. In contrast, "thick contextualism" focuses on immediate life-worlds and the local experiences of actors; actors do not have a clear analytical status independent of their contexts and analysis is more resistant to generalization.[129]

Yaqing Qin's eclectic view of world politics draws on both substantialist and relationalist elements.[130] It is partly substantialist and Newtonian, as it highlights the importance of cultural background knowledge of civilizational communities. Culture for him is an indelible birthmark, a crystallized background knowledge of worldviews and all theoretical systems. Qin argues that practice theorists such as Adler and Pouliot limit their notion of communities of practice with shared background knowledge too severely to those that form around specific groups (such as activists, diplomats, and epistemic communities) operating in bounded issue areas (such as national security, the environment, or the economy).[131] He defines culture as "the way of life of a people who share a lot in terms of behaviors, values, beliefs, and perspectives without consciously knowing them ... [A] cultural community is a group of people bound by background knowledge."[132] According to Qin, the differences between, for instance, Western and Chinese cultures mean that scholars based in these cultures develop different social theories of how the world works.[133] Like Huntington, this formulation flirts with a reification of culture as a unified object neglecting contestation and conflict within and encounters and engagements between cultures and civilizational complexes.[134]

Qin is also a Newtonian humanist. While Mustafa Emirbayer, like Jackson and Nexon, views relations as a "general term ... [that] may involve human and non-human factors," Qin's approach specifically concerns relations between humans in a Newtonian manner;[135] the Confucian and Daoist philosophies Qin draws on understand relations

---

[127] Mayntz and Scharpf 1995; Scharpf 1997.   [128] Jackson and Nexon 2013: 553.
[129] Jackson and Nexon 2013: 554–55.
[130] I thank Yaqing Qin for checking the accuracy of my rendition of his book.
[131] Qin 2018: 36–37.   [132] Qin 2018: 41.   [133] Qin 2018: 204.
[134] Huntington 1996; Katzenstein 2010, 2012a, 2012b.   [135] Qin 2018: 112.

between humans to be the foundation of social theory and ethics. Importantly, "state actors" are treated as humans and, apparently, as unitary actors. And so are civilizational complexes, as illustrated by Qin's discussion of the relations between China and the Soviet Union.[136]

The focus on human relations entails a focus on human agency. Qin critiques the concept of yoking as a "temporo-spatial chance with few human elements involved. In other words, nothing would happen if the necessary processes were not related, perhaps by chance."[137] By contrast, his focus on human relations puts human agency at the center of relationalism. This is reflected in his discussion of Jackson and Nexon's view of "relations before states," by which they mean that relations are ontologically prior to states.[138] Qin does not believe that relations should be seen as prior to actors. Instead, relations and actors are constitutive of one another: actors are defined by their relations, and relations are always between actors. In this way, actors and relations are coconstitutive "processual simultaneities."[139] The agency implicit in these relations between human actors is in turn important for harmony and balance, key concepts in Qin's approach. He argues that "human agency provides the sufficient condition for harmony ... When both the self and the other have learned through education and self-cultivation how to behave appropriately, their behavior is neither too aggressive nor too humble. ... As a result, the relationship between the self and the other is harmonious and society is harmonious, too."[140] Culture, harmony, balance, and human agency are indelibly linked in the production of social orders.

In his treatment of dialectics, in contrast, Qin leans toward processualism and articulates a relational Post-Newtonian worldview. He argues that Western notions of dialectics, typically relied on by both substantialist and relational approaches, are fundamentally different from the idea of "*zhongyong* dialectics" in Confucian and Daoist thought.[141] While Western notions of dialectics – drawn mainly from Hegel – emphasize difference, conflict, and irreconcilability, *zhongyong* dialectics are based on harmony and "immanent" relationships between polarities.[142] In Qin's understanding of a dialectical relationship, each pole is inclusive of its opposite; they are both "always engaged with each other in the

---

[136] Qin 2018: 118.   [137] Qin 2018: 112.   [138] Qin 2018: 117.   [139] Qin 2018: 117.
[140] Qin 2018: 193.
[141] Qin, 2018: 169–92. This is not an instance of Confucian or Daoist exceptionalism. For example, in his discussion of the Haitian revolution Shilliam (2017: 279) speaks of "Vodou's investment in the cosmological conceit of seminal relationality rather than fidelity towards the principle of categorical segregation embraced by colonial science."
[142] Qin 2018: 174.

process of becoming the other."[143] In contrast to Abbott, entities are not yoked – that is, socially constructed through the tying together of proto-boundaries – as much as each side of a boundary already includes the other.[144] The social world is thus marked by harmony or balance between different poles. Qin's eclecticism works along the substantialist–relationalist continuum. His reliance on both Newtonian and Post-Newtonian world-views remains implicit, and the potential for incorporating both risk and uncertainty into his analysis remains unexplored. In Qin's approach, world-views inform analytical perspectives more or less directly. Conversely, and less strongly, analytical perspectives can occasionally have a small impact on worldviews. Both are coevolving, competing, or complementary ways of understanding or engaging with the world. Since Newtonian concepts are baked into our conventional language, Qin's anthropocentrism takes for granted absolute dimensions of time and space as a background into which political actors are placed and analysis is conducted at a distance. In contrast, Post-Newtonianism acknowledges no background, and time and space are active processes of becoming that shape politics and political analysis.

Students of world politics have relied on paradigms as the core con-struct to debate both analytical and substantive views of the world. With rare exceptions, the substantialism and relationalism that inform their approaches never question a deeply ingrained Newtonian worldview.[145] Typically, that worldview encompasses a substantialist ontology, a probabilistic epistemology, and a commitment to replicable techniques that can help in error reduction. As John Ruggie observed almost thirty years ago, "As for the dominant positivist posture in our field, it is reposed in deep Newtonian slumber wherein method rules."[146] It is this Newtonian slumber that conceals the constitutive part of uncertainty in world politics.

1.3   Newtonianism vs. Post-Newtonianism (Quantum Mechanics)

To grasp more fully the implicit worldview that makes it so difficult for students of world politics to accept uncertainty as a constitutive factor of world politics, this and the next section discuss some salient differences between Newtonianism and Post-Newtonianism (quantum mechanics) on the one hand, and humanism and hyper-humanism (scientific cosmol-ogy) on the other. My discussion of quantum mechanics and scientific

---

[143] Qin 2018: 175.   [144] Abbott 1995.
[145] Wendt 2015 and Zanotti 2018 are notable exceptions.   [146] Ruggie 1993: 170.

cosmology is selective. Many of the issues I touch on are considered either peripheral (by most experimental physicists) or contestable (by scientific cosmologists). That is not to say that there are no widespread agreements on the meaning of the stunning and rapidly accumulating experimental and observational findings in both fields, as is true, for example, of the broad support for the Copenhagen interpretation of quantum mechanics. I have tried to capture how both fields are thinking about the natural world, in sharp contrast to Newtonianism and the conventional view shared by most students of world politics, which leaves no space for uncertainty.

Although scientific discoveries often defy common sense, worldviews integrate them into social and political life.[147] In the analysis of world politics, the best Newtonian scientific knowledge searches for law-like correlational statements and causal mechanisms.[148] The external world is real. Representational knowledge is located in absolute dimensions of time and space. And knowledge has a status that is independent of the observer. The simple billiard ball model of international relations, conventionally taught to first-year college students, is a good example of a mechanistic application of cause-and-effect reasoning. Following the example of economics, many scholars of world politics look to Newtonian physics as their main source of scientific inspiration.[149] But after he had listened to a Nobel Prize economics lecture, physicist David Mermin observed pithily that with its integrals and derivatives, economics was just "like physics, except physics works."[150]

Newtonianism. Newton's laws of motion articulate a universal set of principles to account for planetary movements: "The prototype for the order of universal natural law is universal gravitation, set forth in all its magisterial generality by Isaac Newton in his *Mathematical Principles of Natural Philosophy.*"[151] Newton assumed that movement occurs in relation to absolute space and time. Imagined as a large empty container or background, each bit of space is exchangeable. God invented matter and created the moving objects that fill this space. Nature is governed by objective principles. Thus, Newton arrived at the view of a clock-like universe: a consistently working machine that reflects a hidden order, captured by the universal laws of motion and accessible to human reason and observation.[152]

---

[147] Kurki 2015: 788.   [148] Jackson and Nexon 2013: 549; Wæver 1997.
[149] Mirowski 1989: 4–5, 357, 366, 374–95. For the cosmological configuration that enabled this affinity, see Grove, Chapter 4, this volume.
[150] Mermin 2016: 132.   [151] Daston 2019: 23.
[152] Maudlin 2012; Smolin 1997: 141–42.

A scientific Newtonian worldview began to replace a metaphysical religious one in sixteenth-century Europe. Knowable laws of a predictable Nature replaced the unknowable arbitrariness of an all-knowing God. Science encouraged self-organization and undermined existing hierarchies. In the hands of Kepler, Galileo, Descartes, Newton, Spinoza, and Leibniz, mathematics as the most knowable of the sciences was always also philosophical or even religious. The Newtonian worldview does not deny God as the creator of the world. But it does make God a mathematician and His logical plan becomes available for scientific interrogation. Human perception of the world is skewed; mathematics is not. It can fully understand and predict the linear interactions between the discrete objects of this world. Matter is dead; the human mind is not. And it can control and bend Nature to humanity's will. Relying on an inherent universalism, linearity, and reductionism, and superseding Aristotle's syllogistic logic and Descartes' deductive tendencies, Newton's inductive scientific methodology led him to the higher scientific truths articulated in his three laws:[153] "Newton, more than any other man, had banished mystery from the world by discovering a "universal law of nature," thus demonstrating what others had only asserted: that the universe was rational and intelligible through and through, and capable, therefore, of being subdued to the uses of men."[154]

Newtonianism has a powerful grip on the social sciences, including important strands in political science and, specifically, international relations.[155] In the Newtonian worldview, "the world was considered to be deterministic. Blended with the atomized and axiomatic approaches to the study of science, reason had in many senses become rationalism. Society was there to be solved."[156] It made "the world feel less anarchic and more predictable," and "strengthened the commonsense belief in a world designed by a higher intelligence and a superior force" – for some God, for others the Laws of Nature.[157] The assumed order of the world held forth the promise of control. The sciences do not eliminate from our lives the irrational, mystical, and religious. Far from it. But, as illustrated by conventional scientific practices, the notion of control continues to have a powerful grip on students of world politics and the social sciences more generally, at times as a metaphor "with a quasi-poetic function."[158] Since the eighteenth century, atomistic natural philosophy and, specifically, Newton's image of the universe, has left an indelible mark on political thought.[159]

---

[153] Louth 2011: 66–67.   [154] Louth 2011: 68.   [155] Kurki 2020: 42–46.
[156] Louth 2011: 73.   [157] Hage and Kowal 2011: 7.   [158] Hage and Kowal 2011: 9.
[159] Camilleri 2011: 51; Allan 2018: 207–62.

As the reigning scientific worldview, Newtonianism thus informs the conventional understandings of world politics. For example, the mechanical foundations of Newtonianism have had a strong effect on the progressive imagination of the American Founding Fathers and modern theorists of a recurrent balance of power.[160] Liberalism and realism share the Newtonian view of the political universe as self-sustaining and self-regulating objects or actors. In both, the flux of events is viewed as subject to fixed laws or statistical regularities. Entities are knowable and can be governed by humans. And humans are set apart in nature by the power of their reason.[161]

In search of intellectual simplicity, the analysis of world politics typically homogenizes reality by conflating a large number of diverse political phenomena and entities under a small number of concepts. It also adopts strong assumptions about how world politics works, using statistical analysis or experiments to support its search for simple causal relations. This approach to understanding the world hews closely to Newton's own words: scientific truth is to be found, "in the simplicity, and not in the multiplicity and confusion of things."[162] When we explain world politics by making simple distinctions – East and West, land and water, then and now – we follow Newton's advice.

As a matter of fact, Newton encountered multiplicity and confusion in human affairs, and painfully so. In the spring of 1720 he sold his shares of the South Sea Company, pocketing a 100 percent profit of £7,000. The price of the shares continued to rise. Not wishing to lose out on this speculative frenzy, Newton bought shares back at three times the price of his original investment. The bubble burst a few months later and decimated Newton's savings as he reportedly lost the equivalent of $3 million in today's money. He subsequently lamented that "I can calculate the motion of heavenly bodies but not the madness of people."[163] This "multiplicity and confusion of things" is central to a Post-Newtonian worldview.

Although students of world politics share Newton's befuddlement about the unexpected, they hold fast to his orderly worldview. The typical response to the often shocking predictive and explanatory failures of their preferred constructs has been to reexamine their theories and models with the hope that, eventually, the Newtonian strategy of simplification will lead to the discovery of valid laws and causal mechanisms that generate compelling explanations and

[160] Foley 1990; Allan 2018: 22, 117–35.
[161] Kurki 2020: 131–32; Grove and Chandler 2017: 79.
[162] Snobelen 2005: 273: fn 154.
[163] Lehrer 2007: 27; Christianson 1984: 571; Westfall: 1980: 861.

accurate predictions.[164] This, however, is not how it turned out in physics. Most physicists agree that quantum mechanics has super-seded Newtonian physics and simply get on with their work.[165] Modern physics and cosmology have discarded Newton's notion of absolute space and time. Although the classical model remains a convenient computational tool for many practical problems, it con-veys a misleading view of nature as orderly and accessible to neutral observation, when the reality is rather disorderly and often barely accessible. Furthermore, despite its practical usefulness, the classical model is inadequate for understanding the subatomic world and thus fails to account for the many practical applications of particle physics. It does not offer a general explanatory framework.[166] To be sure, some physicists held tight to their belief in a Newtonian world. Slowly but surely, however, most acknowledged the failings in their worldview and moved on. This process became less difficult after a plausible alternative presented itself.

Post-Newtonianism. In the late nineteenth century, experimental phys-ics began to probe the subatomic structure of matter. Electrons, quarks, photons, gluons, neutrinos, and a few "Higgs bosons" are the elementary particles studied by quantum mechanics.[167] It describes these particles and their movement. They are not real, like little pebbles; "They are the elementary excitations of a moving substratum … miniscule moving wavelets."[168] Einstein's special relativity theory of time and space, and relativistic quantum field theory more generally, opened up an invisible world of energy governed by randomness. Nineteenth-century philosoph-ical relationalism inspired the first, philosophically informed generation of quantum physicists to think relationally about many of the new phe-nomena they discovered with ingenious experiments. Only subsequently did a materialist and quantized version of relationalism claim to be foundational because it was "real." Although the weirdness of the

---

[164] Searle (1984: 75) argues that we must abandon the idea that the social sciences are like physics before Newton and that we are waiting for the arrival of a set of Newtonian laws of mind and society. Many students of world politics disagree. They subscribe to a scientific approach based on a Newtonian worldview, hoping that they are in the process of articulating scientific laws.

[165] Barad 2007: 134, 440 fn6; Unger and Smolin 2015: 373–84, 391–92.

[166] Barad 2007: 24, 134, 440 fn6; Unger and Smolin 2015: 373–84, 391–92; Smolin 1997: 125. Kauffman 2008 extends that criticism to include all of physics, Newtonian and quantum.

[167] Physicists who work on different portions within this broad perspective describe the new field of theory as quantum theory, quantum mechanics, quantum physics or particle physics. All four of these terms will be used (more or less) interchangeably in this chapter.

[168] Rovelli 2016: 32.

quantum world has defied all attempts at explanation, the new theory became a marvel of predictive accuracy. It has generated technological innovations and applications that continue to revolutionize the social and political world despite the scant attention paid by students of world politics.[169]

Early on, though, some prominent political scientists recognized the importance of new developments in physics. William Bennett Munro, President of the American Political Science Association, delivered his address on the topic of "physics and politics" in 1927, regretting that the study of government was "still in bondage to the eighteenth-century deification of the abstract, individual man."[170] In *Scientific Man vs. Power Politics*, which he described toward the end of his career as his favorite among his voluminous writings, Hans Morgenthau explicitly recognized the significance of changes in physics for the analysis of world politics.[171] This work was published in 1946, a few decades after the quantum revolution, and Newtonian physics for Morgenthau already was "a ghost from which life has long since departed."[172] Since the classical model had been disproven and rejected by physicists, it no longer could serve as an adequate guide for the social sciences and students of world politics. It needed to be replaced by the complex worldview of quantum mechanics. Morgenthau argued that the scientific studies of world politics would have to settle for a disquieting mixture of the knowable and the unknowable.[173] Quantum physics had introduced indeterminacy and thus radically transformed the calculable, determinist universe of the classical model.[174] Complete knowledge of either past or future had become a chimera, as scholars came to acknowledge that their current approach to understanding world affairs would never yield reliable predictions of individual events: "The next quantum jump of an atom is as uncertain as your life and mine."[175] Out-of-equilibrium nature does not know its own future, and neither do we. And while probabilistic predictions and scientific laws can provide insights into the modal tendencies of statistical aggregates, they are like quantum physics in that they cannot provide any insight into individual units of observation. Morgenthau thus called for a thorough revision of simplified social science modeling.[176] He

---

[169] For a few notable exceptions, see Uphoff 1992; Barad 2007; Wendt 2015, 2022a, 2022b; Zanotti 2018; Der Derian and Wendt 2020. James Der Derian's Project Q, housed at the University of Sidney, has tried to act as a catalyst.

[170] Munro 1928: 3.   [171] Frei 2001: 206.   [172] Morgenthau 1946: 132.

[173] Uncertainty was central to the work of economist Frank Knight, Morgenthau's colleague at Chicago, whom he singles out for special thanks in the preface to his 1946 book.

[174] Morgenthau 1946: 132.   [175] Morgenthau 1946: 136.

[176] Morgenthau 1946: 144–45.

pleaded that the unification of the natural and the social sciences should be triggered by their shared ignorance when confronting the unknowable and the insuperable. We can thank Morgenthau for positing that, when we take quantum mechanics rather than the classical model as our guide, "the structure of the natural world finds its exact counterpart in the social world."[177] Seventy-five years later, students of world politics are still trying to catch up.

Many baffling aspects occur in the subatomic world. Quantum physics cannot be visualized. It is not determinist. Quantum effects depend on the size of an object multiplied by its typical momentum; for electrons moving in an atom, quantum uncertainties predominate.[178] The world is not a causal machine but a creative generator of realized and unfolding propensities and potentialities.[179] The inventors of quantum theory also discovered the observer-created reality that flies in the face of notions of objectivity.[180] Quantum mechanics directs our attention to apparatuses of measurement and argumentation, and the performances and practices they entail.[181] They bring to light relational aspects of difference; the boundary-producing effects of measurement and argumentation; and the entanglements between objects and subjects, matter and meaning, and the natural and social worlds.[182]

Life does not evolve in space and time conceived, respectively, as a collection of preexisting points in an empty container that matter inhabits and as a succession of evenly spaced intervals available as a referent for all bodies. Instead, following Einstein, life is an iterative evolution of four-dimensional spacetime.[183] Space is not empty. Far from being vacant, a vacuum teems with possibilities.[184] The fields that make up the world are subject to tiny fluctuations. Basic particles have ephemeral existences that are continually created and destroyed:[185] "The world is a continuous, restless swarming of things, a continuous coming to light and disappearance of ephemeral entities ... A world of happenings, not of things."[186] Indeterminacy provides the condition for an open future. Possibilities are not static. They are always reconfigured and reconfiguring.[187] New possibilities open up as others close down. Although the world's presentation of an infinitude of relational possibilities cannot be controlled, it can be captured by conventional experiments and the imposition of isolated, efficient cause-and-effect chains. In this view, uncontrollable surprises are normal in a world of changing possibilities. Subatomic particles are

---

[177] Morgenthau 1946: 136.   [178] Pagels 1982: 90.   [179] Popper 1995: 17–20.
[180] Pagels 1982: 64–66, 72.   [181] Barad 2007: 29–30.
[182] Barad 2007: 26, 72, 75–88, 93.   [183] Rovelli 2017: 69–91.
[184] Barad 2007: 92, 141.   [185] Rovelli 2016: 33.
[186] Rovelli 2016: 33; Rovelli 2017: 79–84.   [187] Barad 2007: 234–35.

wrapped up in infinities of possibilities that have changed our image of the atom and our practices of imagining.[188] Quantum mechanics puts uncertainty, indeterminacy, potentiality, and possibility, rather than constraint and necessity, at its center. It offers an alternative to Newtonianism that students of international relations are largely unaware of as they think about the nature of world politics and its many uncertainties.

A century of astoundingly successful experimental work has yielded no agreement about the meaning of quantum theory.[189] However, it has generated powerful experimental results establishing, for example, particle entanglement without any observable mechanisms, creating what Einstein called "spooky action at a distance." Different approaches and interpretations illustrate that crucial aspects of the meaning of quantum physics remain unresolved.[190] But most physicists would agree with Rovelli that the key insight of quantum physics is "the *relational* aspect of things."[191] Smolin goes so far as calling "the 20th-century revolution in physics the relational revolution . . . in full swing in the rest of science."[192] Although it is not free of internal contradictions, what has come to be known as Niels Bohr's Copenhagen interpretation remains the most widely accepted. This is not to deny the existence of important critics of Copenhagen, including Albert Einstein, David Bohm, Hugh Everett, and John Bell.[193] Disagreement centers on the nature of measurement.[194]

"Quantum Realists" believe that the history of the world is a history of endless splits, which occur every time a macroscopic body is tied to a choice of quantum states. This view stipulates the existence of an inconceivably large number of uncorrelated multiverses. For David Mermin, this is "the *reduction ad absurdum* of reifying the quantum state."[195] Its plausibility, furthermore, is impaired by the requirement that conditions in our universe have to be just right.[196] Realists are waiting for a post-quantum revolution that, perhaps, would make quantum mechanics a special case of a more general theory, such as "objective collapse models" or some other theory not yet invented. Such a revolution could thus repeat a new cycle in which quantum physics would be subsumed, just as it subsumed Newtonian physics in the early twentieth century. Physics Nobel Prize winner Steven Weinberg characterized that quest as interesting but also "to some extent whistling in

---

[188] Barad 2007: 354.   [189] Weinberg 2017: 3.
[190] The online *Stanford Encyclopedia of Philosophy* is an excellent source for tracking some of these discussions: https://plato.stanford.edu/.
[191] Rovelli 2017: 119 (emphasis in the original).
[192] Smolin 2013: xxviii. See also Smolin 2000: 49–65; Smolin 1997: 276–84.
[193] Barad 2007: 249–52, 414–15 fn48; Cushing 1994; Healey 2017; Freire 2015; Becker 2018: 49–50, 84, 271; Ney and Albert 2013.
[194] Weinberg 2017: 5–8.   [195] Mermin 2019: 6, fn15.   [196] Kauffman 2008: 27–30.

the dark."[197] And while physicists work, scholars of international relations wait and remain beholden to Newtonianism and the denial of uncertainty as a constitutive part of world politics.

"Quantum Instrumentalists" believe that measurements of the world taken by humans themselves affect that world at a most fundamental level. The world is therefore not governed by impersonal physical laws that control human behavior together with everything else. Discussed further in Chapter 10, Quantum Bayesianism (or QBism), for example, offers a radically subjective interpretation of quantum mechanics that provides a coherent, unconventional answer to the mysterious meaning of the subatomic world.[198] The probability that one or another quantum state will emerge is not regulated by firm Newtonian laws that are irrevocable and universal. Instead, individual human actors assign these probabilities on the basis of their private beliefs. Based on past experience, updating that experience with new information, and adhering to the rules of Bayesian statistics, individuals calculate what might happen next. This process does not involve any physical laws or mechanisms operating on the wave function conceived of as a mathematical abstraction, rather than as an objective entity existing out there in the real world. It involves only individual experience, belief, and updating. Individual experience is intrinsically private and cannot be accessed by others. This does not mean that the world exists only in an individual's head. QBism is not solipsistic. Instead, each individual holds to the subjective belief, with the highest degree of confidence ($p=1.0$), that others experience the world as oneself does, and all rely on verbal or nonverbal communication to create the intersubjectivity and entanglement which, in turn, create a social world out of individual experience and belief. We are not free to make up our own individual world. QBism provides instead for a world that exists external to each actor without reifying that world as an extant, external entity.

QBism differs diametrically from Wendt's pathbreaking book on quantum consciousness.[199] Wendt's research program is foundational. He seeks to create a consistent, coherent, and complete system of knowledge, grounding human consciousness in the materiality of the world. His work is in line with the view of 2020 Nobel Prize–winning physicist Roger Penrose. QBism is pragmatic. It takes experience (or Wendt's consciousness) as given before making its argumentative move. QBism works in the tradition of Dewey's pragmatism.[200] Knowledge is not a set of securely anchored systematic propositions. "The claims to knowledge we can

---

[197] Henderson 2020: 39.   [198] Mermin 2019.   [199] Wendt 2015.
[200] Sil and Katzenstein 2010: 43–48.

defend by our impressive scientific successes," writes Nancy Cartwright, "do not argue for a unified world of universal order, but rather for a dappled world of mottled objects."[201] Knowledge is a set of successive attempts to cope with problematic situations that are more or less successful in historically variable, polymorphic contexts.[202] Like all of physics, QBism is a product of human thought and culture. For QBism there is no "reality" out there; it is all in our heads and the world is created through individual experience, beliefs, information updating, apparatuses of measurement and argumentation, and the creation of intersubjectivity through communication. For QBism, human experience (or Wendt's consciousness) is foundational and creates the quantum world; for Wendt, quantum physics is the foundation on which he grounds his far-ranging search for consciousness (or QBism's experience). For QBism, the move is from individual experience (or consciousness) to the world; for Wendt, the move is from the world to individual consciousness (or experience). For QBism, worldviews are epistemologically grounded; for Wendt, individuals are ontologically walking wave functions. These research programs and argumentative moves are opposite but not necessarily antithetical. Chewing on different ends of the same stick, it is not a far-fetched hope that somewhere, sometime, someone will succeed in making them meet.

1.4   Humanism (Dilthey and Weber) vs. Hyper-Humanism (Scientific Cosmology)

The concept of worldview is tied indelibly to the names of two iconic humanists: Wilhelm Dilthey and Max Weber. Both were committed to empirical investigations of intellectual and social history, including the analysis of worldviews. Both tried to find regularities in human affairs, eschewing metaphysical certainties. Dilthey's basis of historical processes is a feeling for and an attitude toward life as expressed in religious, artistic, and philosophical worldviews.[203] Max Weber focuses on the tensions introduced by modern capitalism into the civilizational legacies of the past, specifically the relationship between ideas and the structure of social action. Different in their intellectual focus and temperament as well as methods, both grappled with the issue of historical relativism: Dilthey retrospectively, by highlighting human self-analyses in history as acts of creativity; Weber prospectively, by inquiring into social necessities in history that increasingly came to circumscribe human existence.[204] For

---

[201] Cartwright 1999: 10.   [202] Geuss 2020: xii, 17–22, 28–30.
[203] Dilthey 1931: 3–42.   [204] Bergstraesser 1947: 92–95, 108–10.

both, the analysis of worldviews is a part of their encompassing historical inquiries.

Hyper-humanism offers a different vision of the world. Hyper-humanism refers here to a worldview that goes "beyond" humanism.[205] It describes "the 'more-than-human' character of human existence."[206] Conceptualizing the cosmos as an evolving set of processes and relations is quite common in, for example, biology, chemistry, and geology.[207] At the macro level, hyper-humanism can be found in scientific cosmology. It suggests our scientific theories and models are not representations of the universe but integral parts of its evolution.

Humanism. For Dilthey, worldviews touch on foundational questions about the meaning of life in the face of death.[208] He thus shifts the problem of history and philosophy from the universalism of concepts such as the world-in-itself (*Welt an sich*) to inherently partial and plural notions of worldviews (*Welt-ansicht*).[209] Emerging from the totality of life, worldviews serve as the foundation of religion, art, and philosophy.[210] Each of these three domains makes different demands on mental faculties. Religions mobilize will, art feeling, and philosophy thought. In the history of humankind, religion preceded the other two. Like prophets, poets and philosophers seek answers to the basic riddles of existence: its purpose and meaning, its transitory nature, and its beginning and end. Reality and its artifacts are texts that invite interpretation. For Dilthey, human existence is lived interpretation of these texts. He might well have agreed with Lucretius, for whom "our appetite for life is voracious, our thirst for life insatiable."[211] For Dilthey, life is the basic root of all worldviews.

In a nutshell, Dilthey distinguishes between three phases of history that are expressed in the worldviews of the monotheistic Abrahamic religions, all of which envision salvation through communion with a living God. These contrast with the philosophies of Greece and Rome, which articulated universally valid patterns of thought and developed rules, laws, and obligations for the imperium and its people. This was turned on its head

---

[205] Morton 2013: 2; Cudworth and Hobden invoke "posthumanism" (2018: 5, 7; 2013: 651–54). Ferrando's 2013 discussion of the many overlapping and contradictory strands and meanings of posthumanism, transhumanism, antihumanism, metahumanism, and new materialisms have made me choose hyper-humanism for the purpose of this discussion. It shares with much of Ferrando's discussion the insistence on dismantling strict dualisms including between matter and language, as in Barad's 2007 version of new materialism, and between humans, animals, and technology, as in Haraway's 1991 cyborgs. See also Banerji and Paranjape 2016.

[206] Kurki 2020: 115–16, 124–26, 134–35.   [207] Kauffman 2008.

[208] Koltko-Rivera 2004: 6.   [209] Ermarth 1978: 323; Kurki 2020: 13–14.

[210] Dilthey 1931: 26–42; Mul 2004: 269–83.

[211] Lucretius, Book III, line 1084, quoted in Rovelli 2016: 79.

in the modern era of science, starting with the European Renaissance. For Dilthey, the modern European worldview contains elements of all three.[212] Dilthey also distinguishes between three philosophical world-views: pluralistic naturalism (Democritus, Hobbes, Hume, and positivism), dualistic idealism of freedom (Plato, Descartes and Kant, with antecedents in Christian and Muslim doctrines), and monistic holism or, in Dilthey's terminology, objective idealism (Spinoza, Leibniz, Hegel, and Chinese and Indian antecedents).[213]

Worldviews are not purely rational constructions that explain the world scientifically. They try instead to understand the world synthetically, thus giving life a broader meaning.[214] Incorporating ideals and purposes, they offer insights into what is and postulates of what ought to be. Yet Dilthey develops a science of worldviews that operates at a higher level of abstraction than do worldviews themselves. It analyzes patterns of prescientific meaning that are reflected in major systems of thought. The science of worldviews is not seeking to specify causal laws, but offers instead descriptions of relationships.[215] In specifying types of worldviews, it generates conceptual knowledge and circumscribed generalizations. The science of worldviews seeks to overcome atomistic empiricism and monocausal explanations. It sidesteps both causal inference and transcendental values. For Dilthey, the science of worldviews is always heuristic and provisional: worldviews have an inner dialectic and are open to immanent critiques and thus remain always subject to change. Dilthey's science of worldviews does not rest on a stable and timeless point of observation outside of history. Instead, worldviews allow for shifting perspectives and evaluations that affect them from both inside and outside. The limits and changeability of all worldviews take some sharp edges off the unavoidable conflicts between them.[216]

For Dilthey, life and human experience in all of its richness is part of the ongoing reconfiguration of a world that is always becoming and always full of unexplored potentialities. Dilthey accords to the individual a central role in the world and in the (cultural) sciences. Individuals are both the starting point and the final goal of his investigations. Since he did not present an explicit theory concerning the nature of the individual's formation, Amnon Marom has provided a synthetic interpretation based on a close reading of Dilthey's voluminous writings. Marom's synthesis consists of three ideas about universality, particularity, and potentiality that Dilthey developed at great length. First, human beings can

---

[212] Masur 1952: 98–100.   [213] Makkreel 2020: 325.   [214] Mul 2004: 272.
[215] Dilthey 1924: 378–404.
[216] Ermarth 1978: 326–27, 334, 336; Orth 1985: 16–17; Plantinga 1980: 82, 139; Bulhof 1980: 89.

understand only what already exists in their own personal experience. This content is not affected by historical or cultural differences. It is a faculty, or inner universal content, that, with the requisite effort, makes it possible for every human being to understand all humans and human creations from all cultures and eras. Second, all humans share a cross-cultural and ahistorical immanent human nature. Third, this commonality resides in nature and is built on human potentialities. Each of these ideas is of course debatable, but their synthesis, Marom argues, offers a "theory of subjectivity as a unique realization of universal possibilities ... This actual fulfillment of different possibilities is what gives each individual their uniqueness."[217] Dilthey was interested in discovering ways to transcend human limits and enable limitless human understanding. He tracked and theorized "limitless shared understanding" in the domains of religion, the arts and philosophy. QBism does the same for quantum physics and the sciences.

Dilthey's core insight – an understanding of the world grounded in the interpretation of meaning – had a profound influence on Max Weber's general approach to sociology as an interpretive science, and, specifically, on his cross-cultural and cross-civilization sociology of religion.[218] Since they are scattered throughout his writings, Weber's ideas on the subject of worldviews are difficult to track. The comprehensive and highly regarded Max Weber dictionary, for example, does not contain a single entry under this subject heading.[219] My brief account relies on Stephen Kalberg's authoritative summary guide and interpretation.[220] Generally for Weber, worldviews of an ethical universe are somewhat autonomous from other social and political realms of belief and practice. Specifically, they differ greatly from random and strategic, means–ends calculated action: "Orientation to this ethical universe involves an uprooting of action from its common random, pragmatic, and utilitarian flux and flow, and its guidance by a constellation of values."[221]

For Weber, worldviews offer answers to some of the most profound human questions about the meaning, purpose, and conduct of life. The main carriers of worldviews are charismatic, ethical, or exemplary prophets.[222] They make available to their followers "a unified view of the world derived from a consciously integrated meaningful attitude toward life."[223] Prophets give social and cosmic events a systematic and coherent meaning that should govern man's conduct if he aspires to salvation. Their work is a matter of practical evaluation, not logical

---

[217] Marom 2014: 3, 11.   [218] Rickman 1979: 173–74; Byrnes, Chapter 9, this volume.
[219] Swedberg 2005.   [220] Kalberg 2012: 73–91.   [221] Kalberg 2012: 76.
[222] Weber 1978, I: 439–51; Joas 2012: 17–20, 27 fn34.   [223] Weber 1978, I: 450.

consistency. It is a conscious effort to bring order into life's variegated manifestations and to help organize man's practices in ordinary life. The discrepancy between this coherent, religiously infused view of the world and empirical reality is the source of the strongest tensions between inner life and external relationships. Prophecy, priestly guidance, and secular philosophy are all concerned with alleviating such tensions.[224]

Linking religion and secularism was Weber's central contribution. In his seminal *Protestant Ethic and the Spirit of Capitalism*, Weber develops a distinctive monocausal approach.[225] The economic ethic or spirit of capitalism was for Weber of central importance and required a cultural analysis, specifically of sixteenth and seventeenth century ascetic Protestant sects and churches, mainly Calvinist. The Protestant ethic furthered rationalization, especially in economic life but also in all other spheres, and set a standard that all other religions, including Catholicism, failed to meet. The economic practices of Protestant believers were ultimately shaped by answers they gave to the question of salvation rather than by utilitarian considerations. The faithful, Weber argues, came to believe that their capacity for methodical and profitable work and their success in accumulating wealth in this world served as evidence of their salvation. Faith convinced them, therefore, that the conditions of salvation were shaped by their personal conduct. Work acquired religious meaning. Methodical work became sanctified as a religious calling. Looking for signs of redemption sent by God, Protestants saw one such sign in economic success. Weber shows how believers arrived at their conclusions as they created a religious world and subjectively meaningful lives. Asceticism in this world gave the capitalist economy and the West a vital push to greater dynamism and efficiency. Eventually, the religious ethic of small groups of believers transformed into its secular successor: the spirit of capitalism.[226] The religious and magical basis of legitimacy of different religious traditions thus gave way, eventually, to different kinds of rationalisms. Although Weber's analysis of Hinduism, Confucianism, and the three Abrahamic religions acknowledges that each experienced its own distinctive rationalization process, he does not extend that argument to civilizations that believe in magic rather than mastering worldly affairs through calculation. In Weber's analysis, Western civilization remains unique and superior to many others.[227] Yet, the eventual disenchantment of life could not be stopped as science and technology eroded deeply held religious convictions and values, first in the West and eventually

---

[224] Weber 1978, I: 450–51.
[225] Weber 2009. In his subsequent comparative sociology of religion, Weber moves to a multi-causal analysis.
[226] Kalberg 2016.   [227] Shilliam 2009: 152–56; Weber 1946: 267–301.

everywhere. As religious beliefs were increasingly replaced by beliefs in science and technology, durable worldviews were replaced by the thin veneer of custom and interest as the main motivation for individual and group interests and practices.

It is worth noting that Weber does not consider the implications of different scientific worldviews in the era of disenchantment he bore witness to.[228] This is ironic since Weber was writing at the dawn of the revolution in quantum physics. He could not know that the twentieth century would give physics a "Chinese face," generating wonderfully precise predictions and practical applications without providing any convergent understanding of the meaning of quantum mechanics. In the social sciences and in international relations, Newtonian physics retains a strong grip on scholars whose research relies on the everyday technological products of the quantum revolution. Failing to consider the very possibility that modern physics offers a different worldview than the Newtonian one they take for granted is no small matter. It discourages the pursuit of non-Newtonian knowledge of and insights into the social and global world, including on matters of uncertainty.

Dilthey and Weber agree: worldviews express values. But they deployed that construct differently. In contrast to positivists who believe that social inquiry can be value-free, for Dilthey and Weber all inquiry is individually generated, historically shaped, and inescapably relative. On the issue of what constitutes truth, these two positions appear to be irreconcilable. When truth becomes a shared convention, "agreement makes truth, rather than truth inviting agreement."[229] Since time scales matter, this contradiction is not inevitable: "Just as truth ultimately serves to create consensus, so in the short run does acceptability."[230] Max Weber opted for an eclectic combination of both positions. He emphasizes how values shaped the selection of all objects of inquiry. He also argues for the possibility, though not necessity, of a value-free social science, emphasizing that worldviews are important for empirical theories, models, and hypotheses for three reasons: they shape the questions science pose by articulating the presuppositions that legitimize, define, and make such questions salient; they offer key concepts that become the building blocks for varieties of theoretical constructs and practices; and they provide the context in which information acquires political significance.

Hyper-humanism. Hyper-humanism includes the natural world in its animate and inanimate life forms. The human is a messy medley and the nonhuman is more than background.[231] This concept does not reject humanism altogether. Far from it.[232] But it rejects those elements of

---

[228] Allan 2018: 36, fn28.   [229] Bunge 1996: 97.   [230] Galbraith 1998: 7.
[231] Kurki 2020: 135.   [232] Kauffman 2008.

humanism that regard the human species as somehow exceptional or unique and distinct from the rest of nature.[233] Haraway, for example, argues that the universe consists of collectively produced systems rather than self-regulating ones.[234] Such systems lack self-defined spatial and temporal boundaries and rely on information and control provided by distributed components linked symbiotically in multiple, complex forms of relationships. Humans, as we are being taught once again in 2020, are not self-contained but are an inseparable part of others existing within (bacteria and viruses) and around (plants, animals and other humans) them.

All humans exist inside of this world, not outside of it, looking in. Kohn, among others, advocates an anthropology that stretches "beyond the human" and explores representational forms that go beyond conventional linguistic or symbolic forms.[235] Humans share with other living organisms semiotic modalities that pervade what he calls "the open whole."[236] Similarly, a German forester and global bestselling author, Peter Wohlleben, describes forests as systems of complex interdependence among trees that share a resilient, communal life.[237] For him the forest is a site for the comfort offered by slow evolutionary change. No apocalyptic news disturbs Wohlleben's forest. Below, soft-floor fungal bodies feed trees and extend themselves in skeins that bind roots, nurture organisms, and offer a collaborative, meshed net.[238] Feeling and thinking forests live relationally. In short, humans are not existing in special social settings apart from the natural world. They are porous and relationally connected, rather than self-contained and singular.

Broadly speaking, scientific cosmology shares this worldview.[239] It studies unfolding processes and relations in the cosmos, including the ideas, beliefs, and theories about the cosmos.[240] Contrary to the Newtonian worldview of the world as a closed system, scientific cosmology views the world as an open system and continuously interrogates many of its basic assumptions. Cosmology is "a human intellectual creation, not merely a collection of facts ... [that] can be done differently by different peoples in different places at different times."[241] It can change

---

[233] Cudworth and Hobden 2018: 8; Smith 1991.
[234] Haraway 2016: 33; Kurki 2020: 120–22.   [235] Kohn 2013: 8–10, 224–25.
[236] Kohn 2013: 27–68; Smith 1991.
[237] Wohlleben 2017; Weidermann 2018. Suzanne Simard's (2021) scientific work supports the same perspective with experimental work that raises the question of whether plants possess some kind of sentience or agency that might be interpreted as either collaborative or a form of reciprocal exploitation. See Jabr 2020.
[238] Tsing 2015: viii, 4
[239] This section on scientific cosmology is greatly indebted to Kurki 2020.
[240] Kurki 2020: 2–3, 14–16, 41–42.   [241] Hetherington 1993: 6.

rapidly as it seeks to incorporate new data and speculations as they become available. To the question "how do we think without Newtonianism?" In Chapter 3 Kurki gives the laconic and understated answer "with some difficulty." In scientific cosmology, the cosmos pushes back against the always imperfect and incomplete ideas and beliefs humans hold about it.

In the temporally understood postmodernity that Nau invokes in Chapter 6, the natural sciences are profoundly empirical and experimental. Yet modern natural sciences often do not line up with this characterization by students of politics. What postpositivists always suspected is now embraced as a cornerstone of "a new, emerging scientific worldview" built around the concept of emergence.[242] However, all too often, even now, laws or mechanisms express a mechanical view of the natural and political universe. International relations scholarship has not yet wrested itself from the Newtonian worldview. What is truly remarkable is how out-of-step with much of current scientific beliefs and practices this view is. This shift "makes the mechanical, 'scientific' construction of the social world in international relations appear like a superstitious oddity handed down from ancient times."[243]

Building on data that astronomers had collected through the ages, in the 1920s scientific cosmology started exploring various experimental and mathematical ways of solving Einstein's field equations. This endeavor evolved subsequently into probing matter, energy, and the cosmos at large.[244] Mathematical, experimental, empirical, and non-testable inquiries have continued to define the history of scientific cosmology and its contemporary debates.[245] Vortex theory and cosmophysics then, string theory and multiverse models now are some of the examples of historical dead-ends and contemporary disagreements. New knowledge has rapidly accumulated as new technologies have permitted the generation of new data that support, for example, the theory of the existence of many flat galaxies in an expanding universe rather than the now-discarded belief in the existence of a one-layered galaxy existing in a steady-state universe. Cosmic Background Radiation points to the beginning of the universe as an explosion yielding many observable features, such as matter and energy linked in spacetime, dark matter, and dark energy. Scientific cosmology is forever open to new information and data that pushes back on existing theories and models. It is constituted by a set of processes and relationships that encompass all thinking observers. Scientific cosmology does not view science (in the singular) as an abstract enterprise gazing at its subject matter

---

[242] Kauffman 2008: ix, 5, 43, 231.   [243] Katzenstein and Seybert 2018c: 294.
[244] Kragh 2011: 87–116; 2012; 2013.   [245] Kurki 2020: 25–31.

from a distance. In its practice, scientific cosmology embraces instead the sciences (in the plural) as an engaged human enterprise deeply entangled with their various subject matters.

The evolution of scientific cosmology over the last 400 years has yielded the Standard Model, often referred to as the Big Bang Model.[246] It incorporates both particle physics and cosmology, and is today accepted as the standard story informing theories in all of the natural sciences. It accepts the notion of the big bang, a moment of infinitely dense matter and energy about 13.6 billion years ago, followed by an expanding universe marked by smoothness and homogeneity in the distribution of matter and energy, with life emerging about 10 billion years later. Stars and galaxies evolved from the universe's physical and chemical elements rather than from God's will, as Newton believed. Elementary particles of matter waves with sixteen discernible properties make up atoms and electrons, and create the atomic level and everything beyond it that exists in the universe. Alternative theories – among them multiverse models, string theory, evolutionary and cyclic models, and variable law models – seek to address puzzles that the standard model cannot explain in its original form.

The greatest of these is how to theoretically and mathematically integrate relativity theories of gravity with the quantum world.[247] At the beginning of the universe, its moment of singularity, the very big and the very small, cosmology and quantum, were one. At the macro level of relativity theory, spacetime is viewed as curved and smooth; at the micro level of quantized spacetime, that smoothness disappears as discrete quanta jump over a flat spacetime governed by global symmetries:

> The two towering achievements of 20th century physics are the general theory of relativity for the large-scale structure of gravity in the universe that replaced Newtonianism and quantum mechanics for the microscopic subatomic world. Both theories remain partial and contradict one another. In one world space is curved and everything is continuous. In the other, space is flat and made discontinuous by leaping quanta.[248]

The hope is that, eventually, general relativity and quantum mechanics can be brought together and thus provide "the basis for cosmology, the study of the entire universe."[249] That overarching theory runs under the label of "quantum gravity." There, "time and space have disappeared altogether, and the world is dissolved into a swarming cloud of probability that the equations can, however, still describe."[250] Like Escher's famous picture *Ascending and Descending*, it is right now "an impossible

---

[246] Kurki 2020: 46–49.   [247] Smolin 2000: 3–5.   [248] Rovelli 2016: 40–41.
[249] Pagels 1982: 54–55.   [250] Rovelli 2016: 48.

construction which looks sensible in its local details but does not fit together into a coherent whole when using presently existing building materials."[251] In the absence of such a unifying theory, acceptance of our imperfect knowledge and partial pattern recognition remain the most viable strategies for our understanding of the natural world.[252]

Lee Smolin's relational cosmology and loop quantum gravity theories attempt to meet at least some of these intellectual challenges.[253] It does not purport to offer scientific truth but a philosophically and conceptually productive perspective that supports a rethinking of science, knowledge, meaning, and humanity's position in the evolving universe.[254] Relational cosmology is a wholistic critique of a Newtonianism that seeks to break all systems apart so as to fit its experimental methodology. The Newtonian approach is fundamentally ill-suited to approach questions of cosmology. Contra Newton, space is not a flat background condition with coordinates filled by thing-like objects, such as particles or planets, that move according to the logic of universal laws of motion and that are subject to human codification or control. Even though relativity and quantum theories have shown background-independent theorizing to be wrong, Smolin suspects that many scientists still hope to gain access to eternally valid laws of the universe; they have lost confidence in Newton's laws but not in the idea of laws. Mathematics is a powerful tool in the endeavor to find the universal and the eternal. But the problem with mathematics is that it looks at things in the universe from the outside, as if things were moving against a neutral background. Relational cosmology and loop quantum gravity break with this implicit Newtonianism.[255] To be sure, while astronomers have developed many theories in recent decades, the cosmos itself existed for billions of years before the discipline of astronomy was "invented" or "evoked."[256] Smolin argue that a single, open, and causally highly complex cosmos comprises the universe, but that nothing exists beyond it.[257] The universe is what it has evolved into being – specifically, networks of relationships in time. The relationships that have evolved in the universe cannot be explained by scientific laws any more than they can be explained by religious entities.[258] We are all in and of the universe – and not in or of anything else.

---

[251] Weinstein and Rickles 2018: 2.   [252] Pagels 1982: 127–34, 154.

[253] Smolin 1997; 2000; Unger and Smolin 2015.   [254] Kragh 2011: 316–20.

[255] Smolin 2000: 106–24.

[256] Unger and Smolin 2015: 422–23. Morris 2011, Part 5: 15, fn89.

[257] Smolin 2000: 17; Unger and Smolin 2015: 355, 371; Kurki 2020: 58–86.

[258] This explains Smolin's (1997: 207–08) critique of the weak version of the anthropic principle, which in his view reflects the nostalgia for a world in which there is a divine or scientific stance outside of the world. See also Kragh 2011: 224–25.

"That said, the Newtonian assumption about 'background' is deeply implanted into our conceptual vocabulary and continues to exercise a profound effect on social practices and social sciences."[259] Scientific cosmology insists on the "simple fact that all possible observers are inside the system they study."[260] And, in real time, that system is teeming with mini matters that are forever opening up and closing down new possibilities and thus constitute the universe as a history of its relationships.[261] Newton was brilliantly successful for many practical purposes. In contrast to quantum mechanics and relational cosmology, he told a coherent story about the world we experience with the five senses Newton was aware of. Newton's lesson is that, for all intents and purposes, the universe is background and the world is a machine that is governed by simple laws – except, of course, when the uncertainties that inhere in that world trip up the predictions that are based on theories and models grounded in a Newtonian worldview.[262]

By theorizing space and time without smuggling in Newtonian assumptions, loop quantum gravity complements the insights of relational cosmology at the micro level. Space is an integral part of the universe's evolving relationships, rather than neutral background, and it is bumpy rather than smooth. Points in space have no existence in themselves but only as particular features of networks of relationships.[263] Made of mathematically described or imagined quanta, space consists of looped spin-networks. These networks are not things and do not exist in space. They are relationships that give rise to space. Time, in this view, is a measure of change in the evolution of the universe's relationships. Everything changes in this relational universe, including change – that is, time. It is not only phenomena that change but also the observed regularities, the supposed laws and constants of nature.[264] In short, at both the micro and the macro levels and in both space and time, the evolution of the universe is relational. And since all we have of the universe is incomplete descriptions by various observers of various states of the universe, what we are left with is not a multiplicity of different worlds but multiple interpretations of the singular universe with nothing existing outside of it.[265] And that singular universe is constituted in part by an uncertainty that Newtonianism has great difficulty accepting as a central aspect of world politics.

---

[259] Smolin 1997: 13–14; Wertheim 2011.   [260] Smolin 2000: 3.
[261] Unger and Smolin 2015: 385–89; Smolin 2000: 25.
[262] Clarke and Primo 2012: 93–97 argue that prediction is usually the wrong standard by which to evaluate models.
[263] Smolin 2000: 22; Rovelli 2016: 39–49; Unger and Smolin 2015: ix.
[264] Unger and Smolin 2015: 8, 356.   [265] Kurki 2020: 60–67.

1.5   Four Worldviews

Different configurations of Newtonian and Post-Newtonian as well as humanist and hyper-humanist worldviews implicate denial or acceptance of uncertainty as a constitutive factor of world politics. The two dimensions that map the analytical space for four worldviews in Figure 1.2 express different epistemological and ontological commitments that can be independent from one another – but might not be. All too often, people use various interpretations of common sense to distinguish between the physicality of the real world and the social constitution of the human world, separating clearly the two dimensions of Newtonianism and Post-Newtonianism and humanism and hyper-humanism. Most such interpretations presuppose an actor-independent reality in which the observer can be placed at a distance from the world. In short, common sense reflects an implicit Newtonian worldview. But, as Rovelli argues, most modern sciences acknowledge that the physical world is not what it appears to be.[266] If physics is a product of human thought and culture, as QBism and scientific cosmology hold, then this commonsensical view

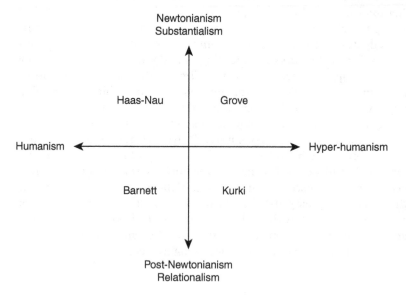

Figure 1.2 Worldviews and analytical perspectives

[266] Rovelli 2017.

is mistaken, and the two dimensions in Figure 1.2 are not orthogonal. Instead, they capture the epistemological commitments of four different world*views*. The ontological aspect of worldviews is concerned with "being" rather than "viewing," for example, with experiencing the overlapping, meaning-making domains of science and religion discussed at the end of Chapter 10.

Presented here as a heuristic device, Figure 1.2 summarizes schematically the four worldviews that typically inform the analysis of world politics: a "humanist substantialism" that focuses on discrete individuals, groups, states, and objects, and a "hyper-humanist relationalism" that emphasizes entangling processes. Humanist substantialism foregrounds individuals or things operating in a world of risk, hyper-humanist relationalism entangling processes unfolding under conditions of uncertainty. Figure 1.2 also yields two other worldviews: humanist relationalism and hyper-humanist substantialism. Each of the next four chapters exemplifies one of these four worldviews. The denial of uncertainty as a constitutive feature of the world is strongest in the most widely shared worldview: humanist substantialism.

Some worldviews put at their center substantial "entities": individuals, groups, states, or "things."[267] For example, the conventional idea of individual decision-making is based on the assumption that conscious, intentional desires and beliefs will lead to action in a world marked by risk.[268] Its substantialism is humanist and adheres to a Newtonian worldview that accommodates the assumptions of both "universal rationality" and "contextual reasonableness." A strong form of substantialism can focus on "actor identity," as in the analysis of ideology and foreign policy traditions that Mark Haas and Henry Nau offer in Chapter 2. An attenuated form might highlight "embedded agency," as in Jairus Grove's analysis of presidential war-making powers in Chapter 4. Other worldviews put "processes" at the center of their relationalism.[269] For example, indebted to scientific cosmology, Kurki's hyper-humanism in Chapter 3 engages the world through "practices of knowing and doing" that sidestep issues of individual agency and the responsibilities that go with engaging the world.[270] This worldview contradicts the belief in the existence of objective, natural laws or causal mechanisms that are unaffected by scientific measurement apparatuses and practices. In this uncertainty-laden view, analysis focuses on causal forces "coming together in specific (and contingent) ways."[271] Relationalism also takes different forms – "thicker" in its

---

[267] Jackson and Nexon 1999.   [268] Fearon and Wendt 2002: 59; Pouliot 2008: 257.
[269] Rescher 1996: 83–103; Adler 2019: 45–76; Massumi 2002: 6–9; Emirbayer 1997.
[270] Zanotti 2018: 60.   [271] Zanotti 2018: 61.

philosophical and quantum form and "thinner" in its sociological variant. Grove and Barnett illustrate that difference in Chapters 4 and 5.

Although Figure 1.2 presents dichotomies, it would be a mistake to conclude prematurely that the four types exist each one in a specific place in each quadrant and all in separate silos. Chapters 2–5 illustrate that worldviews are often fluid and can blend into one another. The complementarities between "either–or" and "both–and" logics are explored further in Chapters 6–9. Chapter 10 deepens that analysis. It relies on the metaphors of garden and forest to explore important differences between the practices of experiments and experimentation, and it deploys the metaphor of the park to inquire into the overlays of Newtonianism and Post-Newtonianism.

Humanist Substantialism: Haas and Nau (Chapter 2). Using ideologies and foreign policy traditions as their empirical material in an analysis of political worldviews, Mark Haas and Henry Nau build an argument for the centrality of "substantive and individualist ideas," "human agency," and individual responsibility and accountability: "Actors are free to imagine new or escape old group relationships. Above all, individuals are always responsible for the effect their ideologies have on the freedom of choice of other human beings." Haas and Nau grant in passing that individuals and groups are never completely independent;[272] however, they strongly oppose a deep relationalism that reifies the whole, where the entanglement of a holistic world eliminates separate individual identities.

Their chapter examines two types of political worldviews: political ideologies coded along liberal and authoritarian party lines, and four universal foreign policy traditions arrayed along the substantialist–relationalist dimension: nationalism is close to the substantialist end and social constructivism to the relationalist end, with realism and institutionalism holding the two intermediary positions. The empirical discussion of domestic ideologies and foreign policy traditions focuses on the degree of overlap or divergence. Overlap points to peace or cooperation, divergence to conflict or war. Haas and Nau conclude that

> our Weberian agency-oriented approach has important advantages that are eviscerated in more relationalist and holistic approaches . . . In holistic worlds, there is no contestation of political or religious perspectives. There is no good and evil. Nothing can be questioned because boundaries are uncertain and everything is in the process of becoming. There are no certainties, no firm truths. Seen critically, the holistic vision is an appeal to disarm intellectually, to abandon the pivot of individual inquiry and insight, to blur any distinction between points of view, and to lose choice which is the very essence of freedom.[273]

---

[272] Nau addresses this issue more fully in Chapter 6.   [273] Chapter 2, this volume.

Some of these arguments derive from the rhetorical strategy the chapter adopts. Haas and Nau are "splitters" while the relationalists they criticize are "lumpers." The variable-based analysis of Haas and Nau is grounded firmly in the substantialist camp, which leaves no room for processes that are "all bundled together" with mutually constituted variables.[274] Thinking perhaps about Haas and Nau's concession that complete independence of actors is a chimera, Grove asserts that "we are all relationalists, just some better and more explicit than others."[275] In contrast to Kurki, who insists on the existence of many relationalisms, Haas and Nau write about relationalism in the singular.[276] They argue that Weber's agency-oriented approach is "eviscerated" by relationalism, downplaying the relational elements of one of the founders of modern sociology. They also insist that relationalism denies the existence of an objective world, is relativist, and prevents the statement of firm truths.[277] This creates a strong disagreement with Kurki in particular, who draws on different kinds of relationalism and shows an interest in their varied cultural and scientific manifestations. Her discussion focuses prominently on Smolin's holistic, objective, relational cosmology, which shares many aspects with Kauffman's "new scientific worldview."[278] For what it is worth, in my reading, Smolin's and Kauffman's twenty-first-century versions of relationalism are no less scientific than the seventeenth-century Newtonianism that informs Haas and Nau.

Haas and Nau do not shy away from stating the implications of their argument. The natural sciences study things lacking consciousness as it is conventionally understood; the social sciences study human beings and their groups or institutions. Like Dilthey, Haas and Nau thus make a sharp distinction between the human and the natural sciences.[279] Human science cannot eliminate that distinction – that is, not without the loss of personal freedom.[280] Kauffman's "new scientific worldview" erases that difference. Nature is not predictable, law- or mechanism-governed lifeless matter but teeming processes of ever-changing possibilities which we meet with courage and faith moving forward as if we knew an unfathomable future.[281] Even though uncertainty appears to be perfectly compatible with their version of Weberianism, implicit in the

---

[274] Chapter 2 .   [275] Chapter 4, this volume.
[276] Kurki 2020. In Chapter 6 Nau elaborates on the different worldviews discussed in this volume. Unlike Kurki, he refers to relationalism in the singular.
[277] Chapter 2 .   [278] Kauffman 2008.
[279] Based on a subjective view of quantum physics and scientific cosmology, Chapter 10 suggests an argument that differs from their conventional adoption of Dilthey's position.
[280] Chapter 2 .   [281] Kauffman 2008.

Newtonianism of Haas and Nau is the neglect of uncertainty as a constitutive feature of world politics.

Hyper-Humanist Relationalism: Kurki (Chapter 3). In the form of quantum mechanics and scientific cosmology, hyper-humanism jettisons the distinction between humans and things. Insisting on the unity of all sciences implies that the cosmos extends to all aspects of nature and all forms of life. This can be viewed as undermining a belief in human agency and individual responsibility. But it can also be heard as a call for a radical "ethics of alterity," an ethics that contests humanism, its privileging of sameness, and its exclusion of difference.[282]

In her chapter, Milja Kurki draws on the insights of scientific cosmology to articulate a relational worldview that is radically at odds with Haas and Nau. She directly challenges core ontological, epistemological, and empiricist conceptions of humanist substantialism, most notably the separation of nature from society, and the urge to control people and things. For Kurki, the relational turn opens up "questions around religion, secularism, and indeed reason and affect in how we engage the world." Kurki's chapter does not offer definitive answers to pressing questions. Instead, it is a productive provocation for deliberation and dialogue.

For Kurki, relationalism appears as a singular only when compared to substantialism. Itself, it is cut by various dynamic tensions. "Explanation" becomes "explication": the characterizing of processes rather than the specification of variables. And it shifts away from "how we do politics." Kurki positions her argument against the humanist Newtonian worldview shared by most realist, liberal, constructivist, and critical theories. In that view, "humans" are separate from and stand above the "environment," and the world is made up of distinct "things" operating against a background. Contra Haas and Nau's Newtonian-grounded analysis, Kurki insists on giving up on a "God's eye view." Instead, she defines humanity as situated knowers in a relational universe.[283] The environment is not a background for Kurki, the climate crisis is not a human coordination problem, and global warming is not external to human communities and experiences and thus an issue to be managed. She points to the existence of polyphonic families of worldviews "with quite different orientations to substances and relations, human and nonhuman, nature and society." Confronted with enormous ecological challenges, she argues, the conventional analysis of international relations has come to its limits and is failing; the study of world politics must be pushed to consider a radical shift.

---

[282] Zalloua 2009: 3.   [283] Haas and Nau, Chapter 2; Kurki 2015.

In the relational universe there are no things, space is not empty background, history is a set of processes, and the categories and dichotomies with which we conventionally work do not operate. Worldviews are not so much views as fleeting moments of being in a world of becoming, filled with uncertainties. The conceptualization of practices in a thickly relational view of the world deviates from approaches commonly accepted in the analysis of world politics. To Lenin's question "what is to be done?" Kurki offers no actionable answer. In her broader conception of the world, institutional frameworks, global governance structures, patterns of practice, and intersubjective narratives and discourses fail to capture the richness of life in a relational universe. Practice lies beyond policy and politics as conventionally understood. Instead, "the aim is to 'loosen' actors (at the boundaries) to understand co-being, entanglement and co-negotiation across 'beings', actors, species" in a universe built around immanent relationships between polarities in what Qin has called *zhongyong* dialectics that are antithetical to Western liberal and realist understandings of the world.[284] Kurki is agnostic as to whether this politics will save us, but she insists that it offers alternatives to the simplified political practices that have so miserably failed too many humans and nonhumans alike.[285] Kurki's hyper-human relationalism has no difficulty accepting uncertainty as a constitutive aspect of world politics.

Hyper-humanist Substantialism: Grove (Chapter 4). Grove's relationalism is empiricist and focuses on how people and things actually work, rather than making claims about how they should or would work. His approach is "characterized by inhuman encounters and deep relational processes across geographical scales."[286] The human is not the sole focus of thinking and acting. And yet "we can de-center the human without letting go of the very specifically human and often national assemblages."[287] In this formulation, human agency is neither autonomous, as in Haas and Nau, nor fully submerged in relational processes, as in Kurki; instead agency is embedded in thick processes. Problems of accessing the world (representation) and meaning-making (hermeneutics) coexist with other relations. Observation and interpretation are part of the relations that make the world, rather than standing apart from or above the world. Investigating emergent processes tells stories about complex and highly distributed formations and agencies rather than

---

[284] Qin 2018: 175.

[285] Allan 2017 conceptualizes how the climate became a distinct object through processes that over time came to constitute it. From this perspective the climate is not a pregiven natural system as typically treated in analytical perspectives building on a Newtonian worldview.

[286] Grove 2019: 10.   [287] Grove 2019: 10.

about agents and variables which, for Grove, are the effects of processes. Distinctions between dependent and independent variables or agents and structures are arbitrary. The causal relations between them are not bearing any essences but are an effect of the investigation, specifically of the scale at which a question is posed and an answer is sought. Methodological individualism is not a natural unit of analysis. It is instead the result of the feeling we have about the unity of the "I." But relationalism goes all the way down in social as in natural processes. "We are not constituted *by* relations," Grove writes, "we *are* relations." In stressing the relationality of different elements within the individual, Grove's reading of Weber thus differs sharply from Nau's methodological and substantive Weberian individualism.[288]

Grove applies his relational approach to the case of nuclear warfare. That case shows the world as marked by highly distributed agencies and thick relations. For Grove, violence as a relational process illustrates that no specific ethics is associated with relationalism:

the geopolitical project of planet Earth is a violent pursuit of a form of life at the cost of others – full stop. ... [T]he violence of geopolitics is an ecological principle of world making that renders some forms of life principle and other forms of life useful or inconsequential ... Geopolitics, enacted through global war, is itself a form of life.[289]

In his rendering of nuclear violence, sovereignty is an assemblage which incorporates the office and person of the President who does not call the plays. He is "more like a mascot than a quarterback."[290] Instead, various assemblages and networks are the sites where the play involves many distributed agents.

In his far-ranging account, Grove acknowledges that the reduction to unitary actors or instrumental logics is not necessarily useless. As is true of Newtonian physics, reductions and simplifications can yield insights even when they are inaccurate. For example, the President's nuclear sovereignty appears in full sight only when methodological individualism primes the observer to look for an already constituted single decider. But a sovereign nuclear decision is not self-constituted or self-causal. It requires a field of relations and resonances. Yet, Grove does not seek simply to replace sovereignty with assemblages and networks. He insists, rather, that there are many scales of complexity and causality that such simplification conceals. His case study points to the limits that the conventional legal-moral and strategic anthropocentrism and anthropomorphism imposes on our

---

[288] Chapter 4, this volume. See also Damasio 1994.   [289] Grove 2019: 3.
[290] Grove, Chapter 4 .

view of nuclear politics and on possibilities of intervention in that domain of policy.

Grove's stance is motivated by strong normative claims. Camping on the hill of liberal internationalism or "in the dark woods of political realism," the field of international relations is in a weird state of denial of the horrors of the world and potentially apocalyptic change.[291] For Grove this is more than irrationalism or ignorance. It bears the stamp of a deep and corrosive nihilism stemming from a denial of experience in and of the world.[292] The moral engagement that Haas and Nau ask for in their critique of Kurki, Grove delivers in spades on conventional international relations scholarship, informed by his hyper-humanist substantialist worldview. Specifically, he calls out "these old white men [who] still strut around the halls of America's 'best' institutions as if they saved us from the Cold War, even as the planet crumbles under the weight of their failed imperial dreams."[293]

Humanist Relationalism: Barnett (Chapter 5). Within a humanist world-view, Barnett focuses on relational and internal value tensions that can further both the integration and the destabilization of worldviews stretching from the supernatural to the earthly world. Worldviews themselves are constituted by bounded communities and thus are ontologically related to them. As concepts of analysis and practice, nationalism and cosmopolitanism qualify as worldviews for Barnett. Agency is relationally embedded. Politics can lead to change in as well as restabilization of worldviews, specifically how different Jewish communities imagine the relationship between nationalism and cosmopolitanism. In line with his sociological relationalism, the duality of nationalism and cosmopolitanism are intertwined and mutually constituted. Zero-sum and positive-sum views of their relationship are two analytical extremes. Pulls in both directions often occur simultaneously, involving unavoidable political contestations that are shaped by developments in the dominant Christian community; "As the Christians go, so go the Jews."[294]

Among the concentric circles of compassion that define the obligation of a political community to others, tribal nationalism's is small, prophetic cosmopolitanism's large. Tribal nationalism asks "is it good or bad for the Jews?" Prophetic cosmopolitanism insists that identity and duty extend to all of humanity.[295] Because Jewish people are diasporic and transnational, the reconciling of different identities and interests with different calls of obligations issued in different institutional contexts is an unending

---

[291] Grove 2019: 21.   [292] Grove 2019: 22.
[293] Grove 2019: 21, quoted in Kurki 2020: 17.   [294] Barnett, Chapter 5, this volume.
[295] Barnett 2016: 9–10.

and unstable political process. Identification with the Jewish people and Israel pulls toward particularism and an inward-looking nationalism, while values associated with American identity pull Jewish communities there toward universalism and an outward-looking cosmopolitanism.[296] Survival, boundaries, the weight of external forces, and conditions of possibility are thus important and incessantly debated topics; "As the punchline to several Jewish jokes goes: two Jews, three synagogues."[297]

In sum, substantialist and relational analytical perspectives are grounded in four competing worldviews. The greatest difference exists between Haas/Nau and Kurki. Haas and Nau commit to a humanist Newtonianism of being and the individual accountability of taking a stance. Kurki's hyper-humanist relationalism highlights the existence of distributed agencies with no apparent link to individual morality and resonates with the concept of becoming. Grove and Barnett operate in distinct, intermediary analytical spaces. The depth of commitments to these four different perspectives is not readily explicable without excavating the links to the worldviews that ground the analysis. The participants in this project learned this important lesson from each other during their intense discussions and interactions. And it is those worldviews which obliterate more or less compellingly, or acknowledge more or less explicitly, the constitutive role of uncertainty in world politics.

1.6   Conclusion

Why should we deny what is so striking in our everyday life and in all domains of world politics: the constitutive role of uncertainty? Why should we indulge ourselves with an exclusive preoccupation with probabilities in a world that is shaped also by uncertainty? Why should the scientific study of world politics, modelled after the natural sciences, remain stuck exclusively in Newtonian thinking when quantum mechanics and scientific cosmology, among others, began to move on more than a century ago? What, more specifically, might be gained by broadening our scientific worldview beyond conventional Newtonianism? I give here two illustrative answers to these questions: one focusing on the planetary politics of the environment, the other on complementary concepts of control and protean power.

Some Earth scientists argue that we are at the beginning of a new era: the Anthropocene. Humans have become geological agents. Their

---

[296] Barnett, Chapter 5, also discusses diasporic nationalism and prophetic Zionism that global and local political developments sidelined in Israel and the United States.
[297] Barnett, Chapter 5.

activities have become a great force that enmeshes natural and social processes.[298] Human activities are adding new biophysical factors that shape some of the Earth's major systems. Old-style determinism and the concept of control no longer work as before. Everything now is simultaneously human and natural. Nonhuman "actans" (viruses, microbes, materials, and devices) can fundamentally alter human and natural possibilities;[299] "Humankind is no longer the anomaly, the freak of nature. We become *the key* to nature-as-a-whole."[300] And in this process, the subjectivity of the individual Cartesian "I" will quite possibly be transformed into the collective planetary "We." If this is a plausible conjecture, the consequences for world politics will be immense and contradictory. The tension between globalism and nationalism will acquire a new intensity and salience, and may come to encompass not only global and planetary politics, but local and national processes as well.

In the Anthropocene, Gaia is not inert matter that is moved by predictable, physical laws. Past experience of the Earth's system no longer offers a reliable guide for predicting future developments. No place on Earth can now be considered "natural." Man-made instead, nature is becoming "artificial." Entangled with human practices, the universe is undergoing a process of destructive and creative becoming. Nature is not a pristine, unmoved, and balanced landscape that exists apart from man. Human practice is instead endowing nature with its own agency. It often acts with unpredictable effects upon humankind and other living organisms and the cosmos at large, possibly with catastrophic or even existential consequences for humanity.[301] For the most part, existing international relations scholarship is unaware of hyper-humanism, ignores new unpredictabilities, and fails to engage seriously with the possibility of civilizational collapse in the face of disasters of unimaginable scope and scale. And when a pandemic strikes, as it did in 2020 with the Covid-19 virus, it is once again speechless in its surprise.[302] Broadening our scientific worldview by moving the environment beyond the status of a discrete policy issue and an inert object of human control might help us think more capaciously and deeply about incorporating more aspects of the profound ecological challenges we confront under conditions of radical uncertainty.

Control over nature is only one manifestation of the tenacious grip that a Newtonian-inflected, Hobbesian notion of control power has over students of politics in general and world politics in particular. In the

---

[298] Harrington 2016: 479, 490–91; Underdal 2017: 3; Hamilton 2019.
[299] Latour 2014: 11–13; Harrington 2016: 490–91.   [300] Hamilton 2019: 609.
[301] The Economist 2020; Pelopidas 2020; Mitchell 2019.   [302] Roberts 2020.

conventional understanding, power equals control: over nature, territory, people, risk, or political outcomes. Although this understanding is helpful in elucidating important aspects of the world, it is far from complete. The coronavirus crisis of 2020 is a vivid reminder that there also exists a second kind of power. The incalculable offers a context and experience for what Lucia Seybert and I have called protean power: "the effect of actors' improvised and innovative responses to an incalculable environment or their experience of the world as filled with uncertainties."[303] It cannot be harnessed consciously. Instead, not unlike the collapse of the wave function's creation of one reality out of an infinity of possibilities, protean power effects emerge in specific moments as they circulate across different political domains. They are always an inextricable part of the admixture of uncertainty and risk that characterizes world politics, bypassing all attempts at control. For Emmanuel Adler, all control power is an illusion, an ephemeral phase of a constantly emerging and reconfiguring reality. In this view all forms of power are special, transient, and unstable instances of protean power effects. The indeterminate condition of the natural and social world rather than lack of perfect knowledge shapes politics.[304] Even without going this far, it is understandable that political analysts and actors are frustrated by the existence of protean power effects. But rather than live in denial, why not acknowledge the existence of such effects and thereby enrich political analysis? After all, Machiavelli theorized *fortuna*'s whims long before Hobbes reconceived power as *Leviathan*'s control and laid the foundation for a convention that has blinded us to the obvious: the role of uncertainty in world politics.

The four chapters in Part I of this book map the contours of four worldviews that resist or accept the importance of uncertainty in world politics. The most resistant one – humanist substantialism – is articulated by Mark Haas and Henry Nau in Chapter 2. Their style of analysis is familiar to most students of world politics, whatever their methodological proclivities may be. Three other worldviews round out Part I. In Chapter 3 Milja Kurki's relational hyper-humanism offers a radical alternative to Haas and Nau. In Chapter 4 Jairus Grove analyzes the nuclear capacities of the United States. His analysis shares in Kurki's thick relationalism, while leaving some space for the substantialism of Haas and Nau. Finally, Michael Barnett's analysis of nationalism and cosmopolitanism of Jewish communities in Chapter 5 is both humanist and relational.

The two chapters in Part II offer disparate reflections on the chapters in Part I. In Chapter 6 Henry Nau mounts a strong attack on relational conceptualizations of world politics that are not rooted firmly in humanist

---

[303] Katzenstein and Seybert 2018b: 10–11; Katzenstein 2020.   [304] Adler 2020.

substantialism. In sharp contrast, in Chapter 7 Prasenjit Duara develops a relational argument that incorporates a broad notion of individual and distributed agency by humans and nonhumans and looks toward the future through the prism of oceanic counterfinalities and environmental catastrophe.

The two chapters in Part III look at scientific and religious worldviews as different and possibly complementary ways of meaning-making in an uncertain world. Bentley Allan argues in Chapter 8 that scientific worldviews are always temporary and contested efforts at the political stabilization of cosmological elements. With a specific focus on Weber's theory of science, Allan highlights how processes of disenchantment and rationalization have shaped materialism and object orientations as the foundation of understanding contemporary world politics. In Chapter 9, Timothy Byrnes argues that religion and politics are not separate variables but coconstitutive and relational ways of seeing and being in the world. More attuned to uncertainty than science, dogmatic and nondogmatic religions alike require a life-defining, faith-supported leap into the unknown.

The concluding Chapter 10 builds on the conjunctive "both–and" logic presented in Chapters 7–9 by tracking different worldviews through the use of garden, forest, and park metaphors. It critically examines the adoption of controlled experiments in the social sciences and the analysis of world politics as the latest manifestation of Newtonian gardens and their insistence on an orderly and predictable world. It contrasts this to forest-like practices of experimentations that point to a world marked by novelty and uncertainty. It explores complementarities and workarounds, relying on the metaphor of parks as zones of contact between garden and jungle, Newtonianism and Post-Newtonianism, and humanism and hyper-humanism. The chapter ends with a discussion of science and religion as meaning-making practices, of experiencing a world marked by both uncertainty and risk.

Bibliography

Abbott, Andrew. 1995. "Things of Boundaries," *Social Research* 62, 4: 857–82.

Adler, Emanuel. 2019. *World Ordering: A Social Theory of Cognitive Evolution.* Cambridge: Cambridge University Press.

Adler, Emanuel. 2020. "Control Power as a Special Case of Protean Power: Thoughts on Peter Katzenstein and Lucia Seybert's *Protean Power: Exploring the Uncertain and Unexpected in World Politics*," *International Theory* 12, 3: 422–34.

Allan, Bentley B. 2017. "Producing the Climate: States, Scientists, and the Constitution of Global Governance Objects," *International Organization* 71, 1: 131–62.

Allan, Bentley B. 2018. *Scientific Cosmology and International Orders*. New York: Cambridge University Press.

Allison, Graham T. 1970. *The Essence of Decision: Explaining the Cuban Missile Crisis*. Boston, MA: Little, Brown & Company.

Andersson, Jenny. 2018. *The Future of the World: Futurology, Futurists, and the Struggle for the Post-Cold War Imagination*. New York: Oxford University Press.

Arfi, Badredine. 2012. *"Khôra* as the Condition of Possibility of the Ontological *Without Ontology," Review of International Studies* 38, 1: 191–207.

Axelrod, Robert, ed. 2015. *Structure of Decision: The Cognitive Maps of Political Elites*. Princeton, NJ: Princeton University Press.

Bächtold, Manuel. 2008. "Interpreting Quantum Mechanics according to a Pragmatist Approach," *Foundations of Physics* 38, 9: 843–68.

Baeyer, Hans Christian von. 2016. *QBism: The Future of Quantum Physics*. Cambridge, MA: Harvard University Press.

Bain, William. 2020. *Political Theology of International Order*. New York: Oxford University Press.

Banerji, Debashish and Makarand R. Paranjape, eds. 2016. *Critical Posthumanism and Planetary Futures*. New York: Springer.

Banks, Michael. 1984. "The Evolution of International Relations Theory," in Michael Banks, ed., *Conflict in World Society: A New Perspective on International Relations*. Brighton: Wheatsheaf Books, pp. 3–21.

Barad, Karen. 2007. *Meeting the Universe Halfway: Quantum Physics and the Entanglement of Matter and Meaning*. Durham, NC: Duke University Press.

Barber, Lionel and Guy Chazan. 2020. "Angela Merkel warns EU: 'Brexit is a Wake-Up Call'," *Financial Times* (January 16). www.ft.com/content/a67850 28-35f1-11ea-a6d3-9a26f8c3cba4. Accessed 01/16/20.

Barnett, Michael N. 2016. *The Star and the Stripes: A History of the Foreign Policies of American Jews*. Princeton, NJ: Princeton University Press.

Becker, Adam. 2018. *What Is Real? The Unfinished Quest for the Meaning of Quantum Physics*. New York: Basic Books.

Beckert, Jens and Richard Bronk, eds. 2018. *Uncertain Futures: Imaginaries, Narratives and Calculation in the Economy*. New York: Oxford University Press.

Beckett, Samuel. 1958. *The Unnamable*. New York: Grove Press.

Bergstraesser, Arnold. 1947. "Wilhelm Dilthey and Max Weber: An Empirical Approach to Historical Synthesis," *Ethics* 57, 2: 92–110.

Bernstein, Peter. 1996. *Against the Gods: The Remarkable Story of Risk*. New York: John Wiley.

Betz, Werner. 1980. "Zur Geschichte des Wortes 'Weltanschauung'," in *Kursbuch der Weltanschauungen*. Frankfurt/M.: Ullstein, pp. 18–28.

Bially-Mattern, Janice. 2014. "On Being Convinced: An Emotional Epistemology of International Relations," *International Theory* 6, 3: 589–94.

Boulding, Kenneth E. 1959. "National Images and International Systems," *The Journal of Conflict Resolution* 3, 2: 120–31.

Bulhof, Ilse N. 1980. *Wilhelm Dilthey: A Hermeneutic Approach to the Study of History and Culture*. The Hague: Martinus Nijhoff.

Bunge, Mario. 1996. *Finding Philosophy in Social Science*. New Haven, CT: Yale University Press.

Camilleri, Kristian. 2011. "Atom and Individual: The Trajectory of a Metaphor," in Ghassan Hege and Emma Kowal, eds., *Force, Movement, Intensity: The Newtonian Imagination in the Humanities and Social Sciences.* Melbourne: Melbourne University Press, pp. 51–55.

Cartwright, Nancy. 1999. *The Dappled World: A Study of the Boundaries of Science.* New York: Cambridge University Press.

Christianson, Gale E. 1984. *In the Presence of the Creator: Isaac Newton and His Times.* New York: The Free Press.

Chuang, Frank, Ed Manley, and Arthur Petersen. 2020. "The Role of Worldviews in the Governance of Sustainable Mobility," *PNAS* 117, 8: 4034–42.

Chumtong, Jason and David Kaldewey. 2017. "Beyond the Google Ngram Viewer: Bibliographic Databases and Journal Archives as Tools for the Quantitative Analysis of Scientific and Meta-Scientific Concepts." University of Bonn, Forum Internationale Wissenschaft, FIW Working Paper 08.

Clarke, Kevin A. and David M. Primo. 2012. *A Model Discipline: Political Science and the Logic of Representation.* New York: Oxford University Press.

Cudworth, Erika and Stephen Hobden. 2018. *The Emancipatory Project of Posthumanism.* London: Routledge.

Cushing, James T. 1994. *Quantum Mechanics: Historical Contingency and the Copenhagen Hegemony.* Chicago, IL: The University of Chicago Press.

Dahl, Robert A. 1957. "The Concept of Power," *Behavioral Science* 2, 3: 201–15.

Damasio, Antonio R. 1994. *Descartes' Error: Emotion, Reason, and the Human Brain.* New York: G.P. Putnam Sons.

Daston, Lorraine. 2019. *Against Nature.* Cambridge, MA: The MIT Press.

Der Derian, James and Alexander Wendt. 2020. "'Quantizing International Relations': The Case for Quantum Approaches to International Theory and Security Practice," *Security Dialogue* 51, 5: 399–413.

Dewitt, Richard. 2004. *Worldviews: An Introduction to the History and Philosophy of Science.* Malden, MA: Blackwell.

Diamond, Jared. 2020. "Lessons from a Pandemic," *Financial Times* (May 28). www.ft.com/content/71ed9f88-9f5b-11ea-b65d-489c67b0d85d. Accessed 07/13/2021.

Dilthey, Wilhelm. 1924. *Gesammelte Schriften.* Vol. 5. *Einleitung in die Philosophie des Lebens. Erste Hälfte: Abhandlungen zur Grundlegung der Geisteswissenschaften.* [Introduction to the Philosophy of Life. First Half. Treatise on the Foundations of the Humanities]. Leipzig: Teubner.

Dilthey, Wilhelm. 1931. *Gesammelte Schriften.* Vol. 8. *Weltanschauungslehre: Abhandlungen zur Philosophie der Philosophie.* [Worldview Analysis: Treatise on the Philosophy of Philosophy]. Leipzig: Teubner.

The Economist. 2015. "The Science of Swing" (August 29). www.economist.com/obituary/2015/08/27/the-science-of-swing. Accessed 2/2/2021.

The Economist. 2019. "Canada in the Global Jungle" (February 9). www.economist.com/the-americas/2019/02/09/canada-in-the-global-jungle. Accessed 2/2/2021.

The Economist. 2020. "What's the Worst that Could Happen? The World Should Think Better about Catastrophic and Existential Risks" (June 25). www.econo

mist.com/briefing/2020/06/25/the-world-should-think-better-about-catastrophic-and-existential-risks. Accessed 2/2/2021.

Emirbayer, Mustafa. 1997. "Manifesto for a Relational Sociology," *American Journal of Sociology* 103, 2: 281–317.

Enns, Peter K., and Julius Lagodny. (2021). "Forecasting the 2020 Electoral College Winner: The State Presidential Approval/State Economy Model," *PS: Political Science & Politics* 54, 1: 81–85. https://doi.org/10.1017/S1049096520 001407. Accessed 2/2/2021.

Erlanger, Steven. 2018. "Is the World Becoming a Jungle Again? Should Americans Care?" *The New York Times* (September 22). www.nytimes.com/2018/09/22/wor ld/europe/trump-american-foreign-policy-europe.html. Accessed 01/28/20.

Ermarth, Michael. 1978. *Wilhelm Dilthey: The Critique of Historical Reason.* Chicago: The University of Chicago Press.

Fearon, James, and Alexander Wendt. 2002. "Rationalism v. Constructivism: A Skeptical View," in Walter Carlsnaes, Thomas Risse, and Beth A. Simmons, eds., *Handbook of International Relations*. London: Sage Publications, pp. 52–72.

Ferrando, Francesca. 2013. "Posthumanism, Transhumanism, Antihumanism, Metahumanism, and New Materialisms: Differences and Relations," *Existenz* 8, 2: 26–32.

Fierke, Karin M. 2013. *Political Self-Sacrifice: Agency, Body and Emotion in International Relations*. New York: Cambridge University Press.

Fisher, Max. 2020. "Coronavirus 'Hits All the Hot Buttons' for How We Misjudge Risk," *The New York Times* (February 13). www.nytimes.com/2020 /02/13/world/asia/coronavirus-risk-interpreter.html. Accessed 2/2/2021.

Foley, Michael. 1990. *Laws, Men and Machines: Modern American Government and the Appeal of Newtonian Mechanics*. London/New York: Routledge.

Frei, Christopher. 2001. *Hans J. Morgenthau: An Intellectual Biography*. Baton Rouge: Lousiana State University Press.

Freire Jr., Olival. 2015. *The Quantum Dissidents: Rebuilding the Foundations of Quantum Mechanics (1950–1990)*. New York: Springer.

Friedman, Jeffrey A. 2019. *War and Chance: Assessing Uncertainty in Politics*. New York: Oxford University Press.

Gabriel, Jürg Martin. 1994. *Worldviews and Theories of International Relations*. New York: St. Martin's.

Galbraith, John Kenneth. *The Affluent Society*. Boston, MA: Houghton Mifflin, 1998.

Gamio, Lazaro and Shane Goldmacher. 2020. "Five Takeaways from a Super Tuesday that Changed the Democratic Race," *The New York Times* (March 4). www.nytimes.com/interactive/2020/03/04/us/politics/super-tuesday-2020-res ults.html. Accessed 03/26/20.

Geuss, Raymond. 2020. *Who Needs a World View?* Cambridge, MA: Harvard University Press.

Gilpin, Robert. 1975. *US Power and the Multinational Corporation: The Political Economy of Foreign Direct Investment*. New York: Basic Books.

Gollwitzer, Helmut. 1980. "Weltanschauung als Massenproblem (am Beispiel der Bundesrpublik heute) [Worldview as a people problem (exemplified by today's Federal Republic)]," in *Kursbuch der Weltanschungen*. Frankfurt/M.: Ullstein, pp. 171–200.

Griffiths, Martin, ed. 2007. *International Relations Theory for the Twenty-First Century: An Introduction*. New York: Routledge.

Grove, Jairus Victor. 2019. *Savage Ecology: Geopolitics at the End of the World*. Durham, NC: Duke University Press.

Grove, Kevin and David Chandler. 2017. "Introduction: Resilience and the Anthropocene: The Stakes of 'Renaturalising' Politics," *Resilience* 5, 2: 79–91.

Gunnell, John G. 2011. "Social Scientific Inquiry and Meta-Theoretical Fantasy: The Case of International Relations," *Review of International Studies* 37: 1447–69.

Haas, Mark L. 2012. *The Clash of Ideologies: Middle Eastern Politics and American Security*. New York: Oxford University Press.

Haas, Peter M. 1992. "Introduction: Epistemic Communities and International Policy Coordination," *International Organization* 46, 1: 1–35.

Hage, Ghassan and Emma Kowal. 2011. "The Newtonian Fantasy and Its 'Social' Other," in Ghassan Hage and Emma Kowal, eds., *Force, Movement, Intensity: The Newtonian Imagination in the Humanities and Social Sciences*. Melbourne: Melbourne University Press, pp. 1–7.

Hall, Peter. 1993. "Policy Paradigms, Social Learning, and the State: The Case of Economic Policymaking in Britain," *Comparative Politics* 25, 3 (April): 275–96.

Hamilton, Scott. 2017. "A Genealogy of Metatheory in IR: How 'Ontology' Emerged from the Inter-Paradigm Debate," *International Theory* 9, 1: 136–70.

Hamilton, Scott. 2019. "I am Uncertain, but We are Not: A New Subjectivity of the Anthropocene," *Review of International Studies* 45, 4: 607–26.

Haraway, Donna J. 1991. *Simians, Cyborgs, and Women: The Reinvention of Nature*. New York: Routledge.

Haraway, Donna J. 2016. *Staying with Trouble: Making Kin in the Chthulucene*. London: Duke University Press.

Harrington, Cameron. 2016. "The Ends of the World: International Relations and the Anthropocene," *Millennium* 44, 3: 478–98.

Haukkala, Hiski. 2011. *The EU–Russia Strategic Partnership: The Limits of Post-Sovereignty in International Relations*. New York: Routledge.

Healey, Richard. 2017. *The Quantum Revolution in Philosophy*. New York: Oxford University Press.

Henderson, Bob. 2020. "The Quantum Mechanic," *The New York Times Magazine* (June 28): 36–39, 54–55.

Hetherington, Marc and Jonathan Weiler. 2009. *Authoritarianism and Polarization in American Politics*. New York: Cambridge University Press.

Hetherington, Marc and Jonathan Weiler. 2018. *Prius or Pickup? How the Answers to Four Simple Questions Explain America's Great Divide*. Boston, MA: Houghton Mifflin Harcourt.

Hetherington, Norriss S. 1993. ed. *Cosmology: Historical, Literary, Philosophical, Religious and Scientific Perspectives*. New York: Garland.

Holsti, Ole R. 2006. *Making American Foreign Policy*. New York: Routledge.

Huntington, Samuel. 1996. *The Clash of Civilizations and the Remaking of World Order*. New York: Simon & Schuster.

Hurrell, Andrew. 2007. *On Global Order: Power, Values, and the Constitution of International Society*. New York: Oxford University Press.

Hutchison, Emma. 2016. *Affective Communities in World Politics: Collective Emotions after Trauma*. New York: Cambridge University Press.

Jabr, Ferris. 2020. "The Social Life of Forests," *The New York Times Magazine* (December 6): 32–41.

Jackson, Patrick T. 2010. *The Conduct of Inquiry in International Relations: Philosophy of Science and Its Implications for the Study of World Politics*. New York: Routledge.

Jackson, Patrick T. 2015. "Fear of Relativism," *International Studies Perspectives* 16: 13–22.

Jackson, Patrick T. and Daniel H. Nexon. 1999. "Relations Before States: Substance, Process, and the Study of World Politics," *European Journal of International Relations* 5, 3: 291–332.

Jackson, Patrick T. and Daniel H. Nexon. 2009. "Paradigmatic Faults in International Relations Theory," *International Studies Quarterly* 53: 907–30.

Jackson, Patrick T. and Daniel H. Nexon. 2013. "International Theory in a Post-Paradigmatic Era: From Substantive Wagers to Scientific Ontologies," *European Journal of International Relations* 19, 3: 543–65.

James, Patrick. 2002. *International Relations and Scientific Progress: Structural Realism Reconsidered*. Columbus: The Ohio State University Press.

Jervis, Robert. 2017. "One World or Many?" *Critical Review* 29, 2: 170–88.

Joas, Hans. 2012. "The Axial Age Debate as Religious Discourse," in Robert N. Bellah and Hans Joas, eds., *The Axial Age and Its Consequences*. Cambridge, MA: The Belknap Press of Harvard University Press, pp. 9–29.

Johnson, Alastair Iain. 1995. "Thinking about Strategic Culture," *International Security* 19, 4 (Spring): 32–64.

Kagan, Robert. 2003. *Of Paradise and Power: America and Europe in the New World Order*. New York: Random House.

Kagan, Robert. 2008. "New Europe, Old Russia," *The Washington Post* (6 February): https://carnegieendowment.org/2008/02/06/new-europe-old-russia-pub-19898. Accessed 07/ 13/2021.

Kagan, Robert. 2018a. *The Jungle Grows Back: America and Our Imperiled World*. New York: Knopf.

Kagan. Robert. 2018b. "The Cost of American Retreat," *The Wall Street Journal* (September 7). www.wsj.com/articles/thecost-of-american-retreat-15363304 49. Accessed 01/27/20.

Kalberg, Stephen. 2012. *Max Weber's Comparative-Historical Sociology Today: Major Themes, Mode of Causal Analysis, and Applications*. Burlington, VT: Ashgate.

Kalberg, Stephen. 2016. "Protestant Ethic," in George Ritzer, ed., *The Blackwell Encyclopedia of Sociology*. New York: Wiley. https://doi.org/10.1002/97814051 65518.wbeos0826.

Katzenstein, Peter J., ed. 1996. *The Culture of National Security: Norms and Identity in World Politics*. New York: Columbia University Press.

Katzenstein, Peter J. ed. 2010. *Civilizations in World Politics: Plural and Pluralist Perspectives*. New York: Routledge.

Katzenstein, Peter J. ed. 2012a. *Sinicization and the Rise of China: Civilizational Processes beyond East and West.* New York: Routledge.

Katzenstein, Peter J. ed. 2012b. *Anglo-America and Its Discontents: Civilizational Identities beyond West and East.* New York: Routledge.

Katzenstein, Peter J. 2020. "Protean Power: A Second Look," *International Theory* 12, 3: 481–99.

Katzenstein, Peter J. and Stephen Nelson. 2013a. "Worlds in Collision: Uncertainty and Risk in Hard Times," in Miles Kahler and David Lake, eds., *Politics in the New Hard Times: The Great Recession in Comparative Perspective.* Ithaca, NY: Cornell University Press, pp. 233–52.

Katzenstein, Peter J. and Stephen C. Nelson. 2013b. "Reading the Right Signals and Reading the Signals Right: IPE and the Financial Crisis of 2008," *Review of International Political Economy* 20, 5: 1101–31.

Katzenstein, Peter J. and Lucia A. Seybert, eds. 2018a. *Protean Power: Exploring the Uncertain and Unexpected in World Politics.* New York: Cambridge University Press.

Katzenstein, Peter J. and Lucia A. Seybert. 2018b. "Uncertainty, Risk, Power and the Limits of International Relations Theory," in Peter J. Katzenstein and Lucia A. Seybert, eds., *Protean Power: Exploring the Uncertain and Unexpected in World Politics.* New York: Cambridge University Press, pp. 27–56.

Katzenstein, Peter J. and Lucia A. Seybert. 2018c. "Power Complexities and Political Theory," in Peter J. Katzenstein and Lucia A. Seybert, eds., *Protean Power: Exploring the Uncertain and Unexpected in World Politics.* New York: Cambridge University Press, pp. 267–301.

Kauffman, Sturt A. 2008. *Reinventing the Sacred: A New View of Science, Reason, and Religion.* New York: Basic Books.

Kennan, George F. 1966[1954]. *Realities of American Foreign Policy.* New York: Norton.

Keohane, Robert O. 1984. *After Hegemony: Cooperation and Discord in the World Political Economy.* Princeton, NJ: Princeton University Press.

Keohane, Robert O. 2002. *Power and Governance in a Partially Globalized World.* New York: Routledge.

Kinnvall, Catarina and Jennifer Mitzen. 2020. "Anxiety, Fear and Ontological Security in World Politics: Thinking With and Beyond Giddens," *International Theory* 12, 2: 240–56.

Kirshner, Jonathan. 2022. *An Unwritten Future: Realism and Uncertainty in World Politics.* Princeton, NJ: Princeton University Press.

Kohn, Eduardo. 2013. *How Forests Think: Toward an Anthropology Beyond the Human.* Berkeley: University of California Press.

Koltko-Rivera, Mark E. 2004. "The Psychology of Worldviews," *Review of General Psychology* 8, 1 : 3–58.

Koschut, Simon. 2018. "No Sympathy for the Devil: Emotions and the Social Construction of the Democratic Peace," *Cooperation and Conflict* 53, 3: 320–38.

Kragh, Helge. 2011. *Higher Speculations: Grand Theories and Failed Revolutions in Physics and Cosmology.* Oxford: Oxford University Press.

Kragh, Helge. 2012. "Criteria of Science, Cosmology, and Lessons of History," *History and Philosophy of Physics*, https://arxiv.org/abs/1208.5215. Accessed 2/2/2021.

Kragh, Helge. 2013. *Conceptions of Cosmos: From Myths to the Accelerating Universe: A History of Cosmology*. Oxford: Oxford University Press.

Krebs, Ronald R. 2015. *Narrative and the Making of US National Security*. Cambridge: Cambridge University Press.

Krell, Gert. 2000. *Weltbilder und Weltordnung: Einführung in die Theorie der Internationalen Beziehungen. [World images and world order: Introduction to the theory of international relations]*. Baden-Baden: Nomos.

Kristensen, Peter Marcus. 2016. "Discipline Admonished: On International Relations Fragmentation and the Disciplinary Politics of Stocktaking," *European Journal of International Relations* 22, 2: 243–46.

Kuhn, Thomas S. 1962. *The Structure of Scientific Revolutions*. Chicago, IL: The University of Chicago Press.

Kurki, Milja. 2015. "Stretching Situated Knowledge: From Standpoint Epistemology to Cosmology and Back Again," *Millennium: Journal of International Studies* 43, 3: 779–97.

Kurki, Milja. 2020. *International Relations in a Relational Universe*. Oxford/New York: Oxford University Press.

Lakoff, George. 2002. *Moral Politics: How Liberals and Conservatives Think*. 2nd ed. Chicago, IL: The University of Chicago Press.

Latour, Bruno. 2014. "Agency at the Time of the Anthropocene," *New Literary History* 45: 1–18.

Le Vine, Steve. 2018. "Rising European Fear: Strongman-Dominated Global 'Jungle'," *Axios* (September 12). www.axios.com/kagan-anti-establishment-movements-democracy-114b7f22-079e-4b70-875f-bef9d179bee5.html. Accessed 01/28/20.

Legro, Jeffrey W. 2005. *Rethinking the World: Great Power Strategies and International Order*. Ithaca, NY: Cornell University Press.

Lehrer, Jonah. 2007. *Proust Was a Neuroscientist*. Boston, MA: Houghton Mifflin.

Leites, Nathan. 1951. *The Operational Code of the Politburo*. New York: McGraw-Hill.

Lepore, Jill. 2020. "All the King's Data," *The New Yorker* (August 3 & 10): 18–24.

Lerer, Lisa and Reid J. Epstein. 2020. "Abandon Trump? Deep in the GOP Ranks, the MAGA Mind-Set Prevails," *The New York Times* (January 14). www.nytimes.com/2021/01/14/us/politics/trump-republicans.html. Accessed 02/02/21.

Levine, Daniel J. and Alexander D. Barder. 2014. "The Closing of the American Mind: 'American School' International Relations and the State of Grand Theory," *European Journal of International Relations* 20, 4: 863–88.

Lewis, Peter J. 2016. *Quantum Ontology: A Guide to the Metaphysics of Quantum Mechanics*. New York: Oxford University Press.

Lichbach, Mark Irving and Alan S. Zuckerman, eds. 2009. *Rationality, Culture and Structure*. 2nd ed. New York: Cambridge University Press.

Liik, Kadri. 2019. "Into the Jungle," *Berlin Policy Journal* (January/February). https://berlinpolicyjournal.com/into-the-jungle/. Accessed 01/28/20.

Lijphart, Arend. 1974. "The Structure of Theoretical Revolution in International Relations," *International Studies Quarterly* 18, 1: 41–74.

Little, Richard. 1984. "Teaching International Relations: Working with Paradigms," *Interstate: A Journal of International Relations* 1: 3–10.

Louth, Jonathan. 2011. "From Newton to Newtonianism: Reductionism and the Development of the Social Sciences," *Emergence: Complexity and Organization* 13, 4: 63–83.

Maas, Matthias, ed. 2018. *The World Views of the Obama Era*. New York: Palgrave.

Makkreel, Rudolf A. 2020. "Metaphysics and the Hermeneutical Relevance of Worldviews," *The Review of Metaphysics* 74: 321–44.

March, James G. and Johan P. Olsen. 1998. "The Institutional Dynamics of International Political Orders." *International Organization* 52, 4: 943–69.

Marom, Amnon. 2014. "Universality, Particularity, and Potentiality: The Sources of Human Divergence as Arise from Wilhelm Dilthey's Writings," *Human Studies* 37, 1: 1–13.

Massumi, Brian. 2002. *Parables for the Virtual: Movement, Affect, Sensation.* Durham, NC: Duke University Press.

Masur, Gerhard. 1952. "Wilhelm Dilthey and the History of Ideas," *Journal of the History of Ideas* 13, 1: 94–107.

Maudlin, Tim. 2012. *Philosophy of Physics: Space and Time.* Princeton, NJ: Princeton University Press.

Mayntz, Renate and Fritz W. Scharpf. 1995. "Der Ansatz des akteurzentrierten Institutionalismus, [The actor-centered institutional approach]" in Renate Mayntz and Fritz Scharpf, eds., *Steuerung und Selbstorganisation in staatsnahen Sektoren [Steering and Self-organization in Sectors Close to the State]*, pp. 39–72. Frankfurt am Main: Campus.

McClosky, Herbert. 1956. "Concerning Strategies for a Science of International Politics," *World Politics* 8, 2: 281–95.

McCourt, David M. 2016. "Practice Theory and Relationalism as the New Constructivism," *International Studies Quarterly* 60, 3: 475–85.

McDermott, Rose. 1998. *Risk-Taking in International Politics: Prospect Theory in American Foreign Policy.* Ann Arbor, MI: University of Michigan Press.

Meldolesi, Luca. 1995. *Discovering the Possible: The Surprising World of Albert O. Hirschman.* Notre Dame, IN: University of Notre Dame Press.

Mermin, N. David. 1990. *Boojums All the Way Through: Communicating Science in a Prosaic Age.* New York: Cambridge University Press.

Mermin, N. David. 2016. *Why Quark Rhymes with Pork: And Other Scientific Diversions.* New York: Cambridge University Press.

Mermin, N. David. 2019. "Making Better Sense of Quantum Mechanics," *Reports of Progress in Physics* 82: 1–16.

Meyer, John M. 2001. *Political Nature: Environmentalism and the Interpretation of Western Thought.* Cambridge, MA: The MIT Press.

Milner, Helen. 1991. "The Assumption of Anarchy in International Relations Theory: A Critique," *Review of International Studies* 17, 1: 67–85.

Mirowski, Philip. 1989. *More Heat than Light: Economics as Social Physics – Physics as Nature's Economics.* New York: Cambridge University Press.

Mitchell, Audra. 2019. "Can International Relations Confront the Cosmos?" in Jenny Edkins, ed., *Routledge Handbook of Critical International Relations.* Routledge: New York, pp. 51–64.

Morgenthau, Hans J. 1946. *Scientific Man vs. Power Politics*. Chicago, IL: The University of Chicago Press.

Morris, Errol. 2011. "The Ashtray," *The New York Times Opinionator* (March): 6–10.

Morton, Timothy. 2013. *Hyperobjects: Philosophy and Ecology after the End of the World*. London: University of Minnesota Press.

Mul, Jos de. 2004. *The Tragedy of Finitude: Dilthey's Hermeneutics of Life*. New Haven, CT: Yale University Press.

Munro, William Bennett. 1928. "Physics and Politics – An Old Analogy Revised," *The American Political Science Review* 22, 1: 1–11.

Narang, Vipin and Paul Staniland. 2012. "Institutions and Worldviews in Indian Foreign Security Policy," *India Review* 11, 2: 76–94.

Narlikar, Amrita and Aruna Narlikar. 2014. *Bargaining with a Rising India: Lessons from the Mahabharata*. New York: Oxford University Press.

Nau, Henry R. 2012. "Introduction: Domestic Voices of Aspiring Powers," in Henry R. Nau and Deepa M. Ollapally, eds., *Worldviews of Aspiring Powers: Domestic Foreign Policy Debates in China, India, Iran, Japan, and Russia*. New York: Oxford University Press, pp. 3–35.

Naugle, David K. 2002. *Worldview: The History of a Concept*. Grand Rapids, MI: Eerdmans.

Nelson, Stephen C. and Peter J. Katzenstein. 2014. "Uncertainty, Risk, and the Financial Crisis of 2008," *International Organization* 68: 361–92.

Nexon, Daniel H. 2010. "Relationalism and New Systems Theory," in Mathias Albert, Lars-Erik Cederman, and Alexander Wendt, eds., *New Systems Theories of World Politics*. New York: Palgrave, pp. 99–126.

Ney, Alyssa and David Z. Albert. 2013. *The Wave Function: Essays on the Metaphysics of Quantum Mechanics*. New York: Oxford University Press.

Nisbett, Richard E. 2003. *The Geography of Thought: How Asians and Westerners Think Differently . . . And Why*. New York: Free Press.

Nordin, Astrid H. M. and Graham M. Smith, guest eds. 2019. "Towards Global Relational Theorizing," Special Issue, *The Cambridge Review of International Affairs* 32, 5.

Norwine, Jim and Jonathan M. Smith, eds. 2000. *Worldview Flux: Perplexed Values among Postmodern Peoples*. Lanham, MD: Lexington Books.

Nussbaum, Martha. 1995. "Emotions and Women's Capabilities," in Jonathon Glover and Martha Nussbaum, eds., *Women, Culture, and Development*. New York: Oxford University Press, pp. 360–95.

Nussbaum, Martha. 2001. *Upheavals of Thought: The Intelligence of Emotions*. New York: Cambridge University Press.

Oliver, J. Eric and Thomas J. Wood. 2018. *Enchanted America: How Intuition and Reason Divide our Politics*. Chicago, IL: The University of Chicago Press.

Orth, Ernst Wolfgang. 1985. "Einleitung: Dilthey und die Gegenwart der Philosophie [Introduction: Dilthey and contemporary philosophy]," in Ernst Wolfgang Roth, ed., *Dilthey und die Gegenwart der Philosophie*. Freiburg: Karl Alber, pp. 7–27.

Pagels, Heinz R. 1982. *The Cosmic Code: Quantum Physics as the Language of Nature*. New York: Simon and Schuster.

Pelopidas, Benoît. 2020. "Power, Luck, and Scholarly Responsibility at the End of the World," *International Theory* 12, 3: 459–70.

Phillips, Matt. 2020. "Trillions in Value Erased, and Then a Surge of Hope," *The New York Times* (March 14): B1, B4.

Phillips, W. Gary, William E. Brown, and John Stonestreet. 1991. *Making Sense of Your World*. Chicago, IL: Moody Press.

Plantinga, Theodore. 1980. *Historical Understanding in the Thought of Wilhelm Dilthey*. Toronto: University of Toronto Press.

Popper, Karl. 1995. *A World of Propensities*. Bristol: Thoemmes Press.

Pouliot, Vincent. 2008. "The Logic of Practicality: A Theory of Practice of Security Communities," *International Organization* 62, 2: 257–88.

Putnam, Lara. 2020. "Rust Belt in Transition," *Democracy Journal* 57 (Summer). https://democracyjournal.org/magazine/57/rust-belt-in-transition/. Accessed 2/2/2021.

Qin, Yaqing. 2018. *A Relational Theory of World Politics*. New York: Cambridge University Press.

Range, Willard. 1961. *Jawaharlal Nehru's World View: A Theory of International Relations*. Athens, GA: University of Georgia Press.

Rescher, Nicholas. 1996. *Process Metaphysics: An Introduction to Process Philosophy*. Albany: State University of New York Press.

Rice, Susan. 2020. "Trump's Hobbesian Jungle," *The New York Times* (April 8): A25.

Rickman, H.P. 1979. *Wilhelm Dilthey: Pioneer of the Human Studies*. Berkeley: University of California Press.

Ridley, Matt. 2015. *The Evolution of Everything: How New Ideas Emerge*. New York: Harper Collins.

Roberts, Siobhan. 2020. "Embracing the Uncertainties of the Pandemic," *The New York Times* (April 8): A4.

Rosenau, James N. 1990. Turbulence in World Politics: A Theory of Change and Continuity. Princeton, NJ: Princeton University Press.

Rosenau, James N. 1997. *Along the Domestic Foreign Frontier: Exploring Governance in a Turbulent World*. New York: Cambridge University Press.

Rosenau, James N. and Mary Durfee. 1995. *Thinking Theory Thoroughly: Coherent Approaches to an Incoherent World*. Boulder, CO: Westview Press.

Rösch, Felix. 2015. *Power, Knowledge, and Dissent in Morgenthau's Worldview*. New York: Palgrave.

Rovelli, Carlo. 2016. *Seven Brief Lessons on Physics*. New York: Riverhead Books.

Rovelli, Carlo. 2017. *Reality is Not What It Seems: The Journey to Quantum Gravity*. New York: Riverhead Books.

Ruggie, John Gerard. 1993. "Territoriality and Beyond: Problematizing Modernity in International Relations," *International Organization* 47, 1: 139–74.

Sabel, Charles F. 1984. *Work and Politics: The Division of Labor in Industry*. New York: Cambridge University Press.

Sanders, David 1989. *Losing an Empire, Finding a Role: An Introduction to British Foreign Policy since 1945*. New York: St Martin's.

Sasley, Brent E. 2011. "Theorizing States' Emotions," *International Studies Review* 13: 452–76.

Scharpf, Fritz W. 1997. *Games Real Actors Play: Actor-Centered Institutionalism in Policy Research*. Boulder, CO: Westview.

Scoblic, J. Peter and Philip E. Tetlock. 2020. "A Better Crystal Ball: The Right Way to Think about the Future," *Foreign Affairs* (November–December): 10–18.

Searle, John. 1984. *Minds, Brains and Science*. Cambridge, MA: Harvard University Press.

Seybert, Lucia A. and Peter J. Katzenstein. 2018. "Protean Power and Control Power: Conceptual Analysis," in Peter J. Katzenstein and Lucia A. Seybert, eds., *Protean Power: Exploring the Uncertain and Unexpected in World Politics*. New York: Cambridge University Press, pp. 3–26.

Sharma, Ritu. 1989. "Nehru's World-View: An Alternative to the Superpowers' Model of International Relations," *India Quarterly* 45, 4: 324–32.

Shilliam, Robbie. 2009. *German Thought and International Relations: The Rise and Fall of a Liberal Project*. New York: Palgrave.

Shilliam, Robbie. 2017. "Race and Revolution at Bwa Kayiman," *Millennium* 45, 3: 269–92.

Shiraishi, Takashi. 2020. "Between the 'China Dream' and the 'Pacific Alliance': Japanese Strategy in an Age of US–China Rivalry," *Discuss Japan – Japan Foreign Policy Forum* 58 (June 8). www.japanpolicyforum.jp/diplomacy/pt20200608180915.html. Accessed 2/2/2021.

Sil, Rudra and Peter J. Katzenstein. 2010a. *Beyond Paradigms: Analytic Eclecticism in the Study of World Politics*. New York: Routledge.

Sil, Rudra and Peter J. Katzenstein. 2010b. "Analytic Eclecticism in the Study of World Politics: Reconfiguring Problems and Mechanisms across Research Traditions," *Perspectives on Politics* 8, 2: 411–31.

Simard, Susan. 2021. *Finding the Mother Tree: Discovering how the Forest is Wired for Intelligence and Healing*. New York: Knopf.

Simon, Herbert A. 1956. "Rational Choice and the Structure of the Environment," *Psychological Review* 63, 2: 129–38. https://doi.org/10.1037/h0042769. Accessed 2/2/2021.

Smith, Michael F 1991. "Letting in the Jungle," *Journal of Applied Philosophy* 8, 2: 145–54.

Smolin, Lee. 1997. *The Life of the Cosmos*. New York: Oxford University Press.

Smolin, Lee. 2000. *Three Roads to Quantum Gravity*. London: Phoenix.

Smolin, Lee. 2013. *Time Reborn: From the Crisis in Physics to the Future of the Universe*. Boston, MA: Houghton Mifflin Harcourt.

Snobelen, Stephen David. 2005. "Isaac Newton, Socinianism and the 'One Supreme God'," in Martin Mulsow and Jan Rohls, eds., *Socinianism and Arminianism: Antitrinitarians, Calvinists and Cultural Exchange*. Leiden: Brill, pp. 241–98.

Steiner, Miriam. 1983. "The Search for Order in a Disorderly World: Worldviews and Prescriptive Decision Paradigms," *International Organization* 37, 3: 373–413.

Suleman, Arsalan. 2017. "Return of the Clash: Operationalizing a Tainted Worldview," *The Washington Quarterly* 40, 4: 49–70.

Swedberg, Richard, with Ola Agevall. 2005. *The Max Weber Dictionary: Key Words and Central Concepts*. Stanford, CA: Stanford University Press.

Tan, Paige Johnson. 2007. "Navigating and Turbulent Ocean: Indonesia's Worldview and Foreign Policy," *Asian Perspective* 31, 3: 147–81.

Terhalle, Maximilian. 2015. *The Transition of Global Order: Legitimacy and Contestation*. New York: Palgrave.

Tetlock, Philip and Dan Gardner. 2015. *Superforecasting: The Art and Science of Prediction*. New York: Random House.

Tilford, Earl H. 1995. "World View: The 1995 Assessment from the Strategic Studies Institute." Carlisle Barracks PA: US Army War College, Strategic Studies Institute (February 10).

Trownsell, Tamara A. , Arlene B. Tickner, Amaya Querejazu, et al. 2020. "Differing about Difference: Relational IR from around the World," *International Studies Perspectives* 22, 1: 25–64.

Tsing, Anna Lowenhaupt. 2015. *The Mushroom at the End of the World: On the Possibility of Life in Capitalist Ruins*. Princeton, NJ: Princeton University Press.

Underdal, Arild. 2017. "Climate Change and International Relations (After Kyoto)," *Annual Review of Political Science* 20: 169–88.

Unger, Roberto Mangabeira and Lee Smolin. 2015. *The Singular Universe and the Reality of Time*. Cambridge: Cambridge University Press.

Uphoff, Norman. 1992. *Learning for Gal Oya: Possibilities for Participatory Development and Post-Newtonian Social Science*. Ithaca, NY: Cornell University Press.

Vennesson, Pascal. 2007. "European Worldviews: Ideas and the European Union in World Politics," *EUI Working Papers* RSCAS 2007/07. Florence: European University Institute.

Wæver, Ole. 1997. "Figures of International Thought: Introducing Persons instead of Paradigms," in Iver B. Neumann and Ole Wæver, eds., *The Future of International Relations: Masters in the Making*. New York: Routledge, pp. 1–37.

Wainer, Andrew. 2016. "Global Politics is Basically Anarchic – We're Ruled by the Law of the Jungle," *The Guardian* (July 2). www.theguardian.com/global-development-professionals-network/2016/jul/02/global-politics-is-basically-anarchic-were-ruled-by-the-law-of-the-jungle. Accessed 01/28/20.

Waldner, David. 2017. "Schroedinger's Cat and the Dog that Didn't Bark: Why Quantum Mechanics is (Probably) Irrelevant to the Social Sciences," *Critical Review* 29, 2: 190–233.

Waltz, Kenneth N. 1959. *Man, State and War: A Theoretical Analysis*. New York: Columbia University Press.

Waltz, Kenneth N. 1979. *Theory of International Politics*. Boston, MA: McGraw-Hill.

Waters, Malcolm, ed. 1999. *Modernity: Critical Concepts. 2 Volumes*. New York: Routledge.

Weber, Max. 1946. "The Social Psychology of World Religions," in H.H. Gerth and C. Wright Mills, eds., *From Max Weber: Essays in Sociology*. New York: Oxford University Press, pp. 267–301.

Weber, Max. 1956. *Soziologie, Weltgeschichtliche Analyse, Politik*, ed. Johannes Winckelmann. Stuttgart: Alfred Kröner.

Weber, Max. 1978. *Economy and Society, Vol. 1,* ed. Guenther Roth and Claus Wittich. New York: Bedminster Press.

Weber, Max. 2009. *The Protestant Ethic and the Spirit of Capitalism with Other Writings on the Rise of the West,* translated and introduced by S. Kalberg. New York: Oxford University Press.

Weidermann, Volker. 2018. "Wald als Widerstand," *Der Spiegel* 14 (March 31).

Weinberg, Steven. 1998. "The Revolution That Didn't Happen," *The New York Review of Books* (October 8). www.nybooks.com/articles/1998/the-revolution-that-didnt-happen. Accessed 9/10/2019.

Weinberg, Steven. 2015. "Eye on the Present – The Whig History of Science," *The New York Review of Books* (December 17). www.hrstud.unizg.hr/_news/3 4443/Pages%20from%20New%20York%20Review%20of%20Books%20-%2017%20December%202015-2.pdf. Accessed 03/20/20.

Weinberg, Steven. 2017. "The Trouble with Quantum Mechanics," *The New York Review of Books* (January 19). www.nybooks.com/articles/2017/01/1 9/trouble-with-quantum-mechanics/. Accessed 03/20/20.

Weinstein, Steven and Dean Rickles. 2018. "Quantum Gravity," *The Stanford Encyclopedia of Philosophy* (Summer 2018 Edition), Edward N. Zalta (ed.). https://plato.stanford.edu/archives/sum2018/entries/quan tum-gravity/. Accessed 2/2/2021.

Wendt, Alexander. 2015. *Quantum Mind and Social Science: Unifying Physical and Social Ontology.* New York: Cambridge University Press.

Wendt, Alexander. 2022a. "Why IR Scholars Should Care about Quantum Theory: Part I. Burdens of Proof and Uncomfortable Facts," *International Theory* 14:1: 119–129.

Wendt, Alexander. 2022b. "Why IR Scholars Should Care about Quantum Theory: Part II. Critics in the PITs," *International Theory* 14:1: 193–209.

Wenger, Andreas, Ursula Jasper, and Myriam Dunn Cavelty, eds. 2020. *The Politics and Science of Prevision.* New York: Routledge.

Wertheim, Margaret. 2011. *Physics on the Fringe: Smoke Rings, Circlons and Alternative Theories of Everything.* New York: Walker and Company.

Westfall, Richard S. 1980. *Never at Rest: A Biography of Isaac Newton.* New York: Cambridge University Press.

White, Theodore W. 1961. *The Making of the President 1960.* New York: Atheneum.

Wiener, Norbert. 1948. *Cybernetics: Or Control and Communication in the Animal and the Machine.* New York: John Wiley.

Wight, Colin. 1996. "Incommensurability and Cross-Paradigm Communication in International Relations Theory: 'What's the Frequency Kenneth?'," *Millennium* 25, 2: 291–319.

Wilder, Matt and Michael Howlett. 2014. "The Politics of Policy Anomalies: Bricolage and the Hermeneutics of Paradigms," *Critical Policy Studies* 8, 2: 183–202.

Wohlleben, Peter. 2017. *The Hidden Life of Trees: What They Feel, How They Communicate – Discoveries from a Secret World.* Vancouver: Greystone.

Wolf, Reinhard. 2012a. "Der 'emotional turn' in den IB: Plädoyer für eine theore-tische Überwindung methodischer Engführung [The 'emotional turn' in international relations: appeal for a theoretical overcoming of methodological narrowing]," *Zeitschrift für Außen-und Sicherheitspolitik* 5: 605–24.

Wolf, Reinhard. 2012b. "Prickly States? Recognition and Disrespect Between Persons and People," in Thomas Lindemann and Erik Ringmar, eds., *International Politics of Recognition*. London: Paradigm Publishers, pp. 39–56.

Wright, Quincy. 1955. *The Study of International Relations*. New York: Appleton-Century-Crofts.

Zalloua, Zahi. 2009. "Introduction to Focus: Posthumanism," *American Book Review* 30, 2: 3–4.

Zanotti, Laura. 2018. *Ontological Entanglements, Agency and Ethics in International Relations*. London: Routledge.

Part I

Substantialism and Relationalism

2 Political Worldviews in International Relations
The Importance of Ideologies and Foreign Policy Traditions

Mark L. Haas and Henry R. Nau

In this chapter we apply a Weberian analysis to selective foreign policy decisions made by US and European elites in the twentieth century concerning war and peace. We look at the behavior of individual actors and the groups they form because, following Max Weber, individuals "give meaning" to the world around them. They interpret the historical setting in which they find themselves and act to shape the world they seek in the future. Individual and group worldviews overlap and compete. They overlap to become the basis of relationships and structures that shape a particular historical period, and they compete to establish a range of options from which leaders may choose. They operate against an objective reality of power, institutions, and ideas. We can test their effectiveness and hold the individuals or groups that espouse them accountable. At times, as we will show, ideas trump power in determining an actor's behavior; at other times, power trumps ideas. Causation is discrete and sequential.

Relationalist worldviews say this type of analysis is a mirage. Individuals and the groups they form are not free to interpret and choose the circumstances around them, let alone play a significant role in shaping their future. The past and future are baked in the cake. A quantum rather than Weberian worldview prevails in which individuals and groups do not exist except as they emerge upon investigation. They materialize from a quantum world of wave functions in which every possible action is already prescribed by multiple probabilities. What exists after investigation is not a substance such as an individual but an entangled relationship of the observer, observed, and environment. This entangled "subject" is ephemeral and cannot be tested against an objective world because there is no objective world beyond what is observed. From a relationalist perspective, the free individuals we emphasize in this chapter are not free at all. They are deeply embedded in historical processes and contemporary relationships. They don't choose their political party, class status, national citizenship, interpretation of history, or alliance preferences. They *are* those relationships. Actors have little room in the present to reinterpret the cosmological and historical context they inherit. Causation is mutual and holistic.

This is a worthwhile debate.[1] We see worldviews as substantive and individualist ideas by which individuals define their identities and decide which groups or communities they wish to join or remain a part of. These ideas in turn prescribe their objectives and their use of power and diplomacy in international affairs. We recognize that individuals and the separate groups they form are never completely autonomous. There is always overlap ("smearing," as relationalists say). Bundles of relationships, fuzzy boundaries, and even structures of relationships exist that may be hard to change. The Cold War, for example, was thought to be permanent. But the whole point of Weberian rationalist thinking, which we affirm, is that individuals can be educated liberally to become self-critical and eventually form and change their worldviews on rational and accountable grounds. Because worldviews are substantive, their differences and relative significance can be measured. What Haas calls "ideological distance" tells us whether worldviews are close or far apart and, over time, converging or diverging. It shows us where boundaries between worldviews lie and how far individuals or groups must move to cross over from one worldview to another. Now, we can compare ideological worldviews relatively against the influence of other variables, such as the distribution of power and the role of institutions (relationships). The "distribution of ideologies," for example, may involve similar ideologies across states (all democracies), while the "distribution of power" is skewed – the democratic peace under American hegemony. An objective world remains against which worldviews can be tested.[2] Ultimately, individuals make choices; they are not simply prisoners of deep-seated cosmological and historical processes or ciphers for atoms and wave functions in a purely materialist world.

Our focus in this chapter is on distinct, individualist worldviews associated with political rather than religious or cosmological ideas.[3] Having made clear our worldview as scholars, we now apply the worldview concept to specific political leaders acting in the foreign policy arena. We examine in particular two types of political worldviews: domestic political ideologies (e.g., liberalism, fascism, communism, and

---

[1] See Nau, Chapter 6 in this volume, for more on this debate.

[2] By posing an objective world, this analysis follows contemporary social science approaches to international relations, such as realism (power), liberalism (interdependence and institutions), and constructivism (both type and shared ideas/identity), all of which we analyze in Section 2.2.

[3] We stick with the term "worldviews" even though political ideologies and foreign policy orientations operate at a lower level of analysis than cosmological or religious worldviews developed in other chapters of this volume.

Islamism) and foreign policy orientations (nationalism, realism, institutionalism, and constructivism). We ask in each case how these worldviews interact and affect policy outcomes, especially at the international level. In both cases, distinctive ideas and how they converge and diverge and interact causally with one another in the international system play a central role in creating threats and opportunities for the advancement of actors' international interests, and thus are critical to the likelihood of war and peace, confrontation and cooperation. In short, ideational orientations espoused by specific individuals or groups of individuals define the map of international contestation, much in the way that power disparities define conflict in materialist ontologies, or institutional rules and roles define conflict in liberal ontologies.

This chapter is divided into two main sections. Section 2.1 examines the role of distinctive political ideologies as causes of world affairs. It details the pathways that connect political ideologies to perceptions of threat and consequent foreign policy behavior. Section 2.2 explores the role of distinctive foreign policy worldviews and demonstrates how these worldviews compete with one another to shape foreign policy outcomes. It demonstrates how distinctive individualist worldviews (what we call type as opposed to role identity) sometimes override realist, institutionalist (relationalist), and social constructivist worldviews.

2.1   Ideological Worldviews

Ideological worldviews operate at all levels of analysis: individual leaders, political parties, national identities, foreign policy orientations, transnational groups, and international institutions. We are particularly interested in ideologies at the individual and domestic levels of analysis: the goals and self-image actors articulate that motivate, guide, and give meaning to their international pursuit of power and participation in international institutions.[4] What core institutional, political, economic, and social goals do leaders advocate and try to realize in their group or country? This domestic worldview in turn conditions their view for ordering international society.[5] Do individual politicians or political parties, for example, advocate for their country and for the world the creation or continuation of representative or authoritarian political institutions? Capitalist or socialist economies? Theocratic or secular values? Ethnic or civic citizenship? Prominent ideologies that meet this definition include communism,

---

[4] Haas 2005: 5 and Nau 2002: 28.
[5] For other studies that define ideology in similar ways, see Owen 2010; Walt 1996; Haas 2012a; Nau 2015a; Easton, Gunnell, and Stein 1995: 8–9.

fascism, liberalism, monarchism, and Islamism. These ideologies do not map neatly on the more holistic worldviews examined in other chapters of this volume. Nevertheless, liberal ideologies tend to emphasize rational faculties (explicit knowledge, reason) and lower levels of analysis along Weberian worldview lines. Authoritarian ideologies tend to emphasize nonrational faculties (tacit knowledge, traditions) and higher holistic levels of analysis along quantum worldview lines.

Political ideologies motivate actors to champion particular institutions and values against rival ones. To the extent they overlap, they form political in-groups. To the extent they diverge, they define political out-groups. Ideologies, in other words, encapsulate the shared or conflicting ideas around which domestic and transnational political parties and movements coalesce or collide. Group leaders draw on these ideas as they mobilize supporters and advance their ideology against rival ideological groups. Politics is about ideas and morality (right and wrong), not just about power, processes, and accommodation. Worldviews, as we understand them, are always contested – sometimes peacefully, sometimes not. They do not suffuse individuals in relationalist processes that limit individual choice. They involve individual and human agency. Actors are free to imagine new or escape old group relationships.[6] Above all, individuals are always responsible for the effect their ideologies have on the freedom of choice of other human beings.

Actors' ideological beliefs have profound effects on foreign policy behavior. Most importantly, the degree of similarity and difference among ideological beliefs – "ideological distance," as noted earlier – has major effects on threat perceptions, which in turn critically shape foreign policies. As Haas argues, "There exists a strong relationship between the ideological distance dividing states' leaders and their understandings of the level of [international] threat ... The greater the ideological differences dividing decision-makers across states, the higher the perceived level of threat; the greater the ideological similarities uniting leaders, the lower the perceived threat." Nau addresses the same issue through the concept of national identity – that is, a country's self-image which motivates the use of force: "If [national] identities ... diverge, hostile nations create a dangerous balance of power. On the other hand, if identities converge, communities of nations may

---

[6] In the 1980s, for example, Soviet leader Mikhail Gorbachev rejected orthodox Marxism–Leninism in favor of the much more liberal ideology of "New Thinking," having a significant effect on world affairs. See later discussion in this chapter.

moderate the balance of power." Alastair Iain Johnston also deploys the variable of "identity":

The greater the perceived identity difference, the more the environment is viewed as conflictual, the more the out-group is viewed as threatening . . . Conversely, the smaller the perceived identity difference, the more the external environment is seen as cooperative, the less the out-group is perceived as fundamentally threatening . . . Most critically, variation in identity difference should be independent of anarchy.[7]

Johnson's last point is very important, and it is one that we develop later in Section 2.2 on foreign policy orientations. The effects of ideological distributions are independent of the effects of other variables such as power disparities emphasized by realist arguments, institutional constraints emphasized by liberal arguments, and holistic ideas emphasized by social constructivist perspectives. Ideologies shape the real world of power, institutions, and social identities. They are separate, sequential causes of events not simply rationalizations of power (realism), mutually constituted variables (constructivism), or bundled entanglements (relationalism).

Ideological distances shape actors' threat perceptions and consequent international security policies by three main pathways – conflict expectations, demonstration effects, and miscommunications.[8]

2.1.1 Conflict Expectations

First, domestic ideological differences play a key role in affecting how actors assess one another's international intentions. As Michael Barnett observes, "states apparently attempt to predict a state's external behavior based on its internal arrangements."[9] The greater the ideological differences dividing states' decision-makers, the more likely they are to assume the worst about one another's objectives. As Secretary of State James Byrnes told President Harry Truman in late 1945, "there is too much difference in the ideologies of the US and Russia to work out a long term program of cooperation."[10] Byrnes understood that the greater the ideological distance between actors, the more likely they believe that serious conflict between them is inevitable in the long run. This expectation, measured concretely at one point in time, drives perceptions at later times. Even if ideological counterparts exhibit no hostility toward one another in the present – or even cooperate with each other currently – leaders will often assume that such amicability is temporary

---

[7] For quotations in this paragraph, see Haas 2005: 4; Nau 2002: 21; Johnston 2008: 199.
[8] Much of the following analysis of the causal links between ideologies and threat is taken from Haas 2005: 5–14. See also Haas 2012b: 420–21.
[9] Barnett 1996: 367. [10] Quoted in Marc Trachtenberg 1999: 16.

and is bound to be replaced with overt animosity.[11] Soviet leader Vladimir Lenin, for example, noted that Germany's cooperation with the Soviet Union in the early 1920s did nothing to eliminate the two states' underlying enmity due to ideological differences: "Germany wants revenge [against France and Britain], and we want revolution. For the moment our aims are the same, but when our ways part, they will be our most ferocious and greatest enemies."[12] To Lenin, "international imperialism [i.e., capitalist states] ... could not, under any circumstances, under any conditions, live side by side with the Soviet Republic ... In this sphere a conflict is inevitable."[13] These views led Soviet leaders to try to export communist revolution to Germany in the early 1920s, despite major material incentives to maintain cooperative relations with that state.[14] Former Soviet Foreign Minister Maxim Litvinov similarly stated in an interview in 1946 that the "root cause" of the incipient Soviet–American confrontation, despite years of alliance during World War II, was "the ideological conception prevailing [in the Soviet Union] that conflict between the Communist and capitalist worlds is inevitable."[15] Interestingly, when Gorbachev gave up that conception in the late 1980s, the Cold War moved toward its end (see Section 2.2.3).

Assuming enmity, politicians dedicated to opposing ideological beliefs frequently take actions that ensure such a hostile relationship. Adolf Hitler, for example, repeatedly told the Wehrmacht leaders that the origins, objectives, and means of fighting the unavoidable war with the Soviet Union were rooted in the ideological differences between the two powers. Three months before Germany's attack on the Soviet Union, he told his generals that the "struggle [with the USSR] is one of ideologies and racial differences and will have to be conducted with unprecedented, unmerciful, and unrelenting harshness .... The commissars are the bearers of ideologies directly opposed to National Socialism. Therefore the commissars will be liquidated." In fact, the "main theme" of Hitler's reasoning for attacking the Soviet Union, according to the Chief of the

---

[11] The relationship between high expectations of conflict and conflictual policies is not tautological, though it may be self-fulfilling. The less intense expectations are at the outset and the greater the interval between hostile expectations and eventual outcomes, the more likely the expectations will be independent of outcomes. In this interval, leaders may or may not take actions that make the expectations self fulfilling. Much depends on intervening circumstances such as ideological polarity (or the number of prominent ideological groupings in a system) in which a third country comes into play that is even more ideologically hostile to the first country. On the tendency for ideational variables to create self-fulfilling dynamics, see Wendt 1999: 184–89. On the international effects of ideological polarity, see Haas 2014: 715–53.

[12] Quoted in Walt 1996: 187.   [13] Quoted in Walt 1996: 130.   [14] Walt 1996: 187–89.

[15] Quoted in Roberts 1953: 366.

Armed Forces High Command, Wilhelm Keitel, was to engage "the decisive battle between two ideologies."[16]

When leaders have similar ideological beliefs, they are less likely to make worst-case assumptions than leaders whose beliefs are dissimilar. Policymakers who share core ideological principles are likely to trust one another more and to assume that they share major interests – including containing ideological enemies – that will result in cooperative relations. These relationships help explain the significant cooperation that often exists among co-ideologues, including monarchists (Concert of Europe), fascists (Germany, Italy, and Japan in World War II), religious funda-mentalists (Taliban Afghanistan and al Qaeda), communists (Soviet Union and China in 1950s), and especially liberals ("the liberal peace"). They also demonstrate why ideological convergence, or increas-ing ideological similarities among states, is often an important source of resolving international conflict.[17]

Because ideological relationships determine the threat posed by power variables, fears of power shifts and intense security dilemmas will exist more frequently among states that are dedicated to disparate ideological beliefs. Ideologically similar regimes, in contrast, will often form a "security community." Members of a security community rule out the use of force as a means of settling disputes and instead possess stable expectations of peaceful change.[18] Among these states, power distribu-tions are not an important source of war and peace. As Nau explains:

In a world where national orientations significantly converge, for example today in the EU or North Atlantic region, traditional balance of power forces recede in importance from interstate relations ... In a world of sharply diverging sociocul-tural and political orientations, on the other hand, the balance of power assumes preeminence to mediate security and wider disparities (for example, in Arab-Israeli relations). Military and economic balances do not themselves guarantee stability; but states are unlikely to feel safe or comfortable in a world of widely differing state identities unless they have an independent capability to defend themselves. The security dilemma, in short, is primarily a function of diverging identities not decentralized power.[19]

---

[16] Quotations from Shirer 1960: 830 and 846. The second quotation is a summary of a "comprehensive political speech" by Hitler to his generals in June 1941.

[17] For case study analyses demonstrating that that ideological convergence is a key source of international conflict resolution, see Owen 2010: 54–55, 68–70, 77, 115–19, 154–57, 196–99, 267–69; Haas 2005: 61–65; 70–72, 90–92, 192–94, 197–10; Haas 2007: 145–79; Miller 1995: 39–42, 53–55, 241. For quantitative analyses showing the importance of ideological similarities to states' alliance policies, see Werner and Lemke 1997: 529–546; Peceny, Beer, and Sanchez-Terry 2002: 15–26.

[18] On security communities in international relations, see Adler and Barnett 1998, espe-cially chapters 1 and 2.

[19] Nau 2011: 462–63. See also Haas 2005: 215–17.

Indeed, decentralized power exists, it might be argued, precisely because countries have diverging identities. When those identities converge – as, for example, among liberal democracies – decentralized power or anarchy raises fewer if any serious security concerns. Liberal nations exist separately without threatening one another militarily.

2.1.2   *Demonstration Effects*

A second prominent way in which ideological differences are likely to shape leaders' threat perceptions is by endangering their most important domestic interests, namely the preservation of their political power and the ideological system (political institutions and values) they support. Leaders often worry that the success of ideological enemies abroad will be contagious, ultimately boosting the political fortunes of like-minded individuals at home, even to the point of revolution. This concern will be greater the more vulnerable the regime is to domestic opposition.[20] In short, leaders fear the demonstration effects of other ideologies succeeding abroad and weakening their control at home. The greater the ideological differences dividing decision-makers in different states and the greater their internal vulnerability, the greater their fears of domestic subversion are likely to be, by which we mean the likely undermining at home of one set of ideological principles and the spread of a rival one.

In the 2000s, for example, Russia's illiberal leaders worried that the "color" liberal revolutions in Georgia, Ukraine, and Kyrgyzstan would spread to Russia. Vladislav Surkov, the Deputy Director of the Presidential Administration and a top advisor to President Vladimir Putin, claimed that these revolutions had "made a very strong impression on many [Russian] politicians," and he worried that the spread of these political changes to Russia was a "very real threat."[21] Putin expressed similar fears in justifying Russia's annexation of Crimea after the revolution in Ukraine in 2014 that ousted President Viktor Yanukovych, a Putin ally.[22] Chinese leaders have articulated the same concerns. As Aaron Friedberg summarizes (writing in 2012):

China's rulers . . . remain deeply fearful of encirclement and ideological subversion. And despite Washington's attempts to reassure them of its benign intentions, Chinese leaders are convinced that the United States aims to block China's rise and, ultimately, undermine its one-party system of government . . . Although limited cooperation on specific issues might be possible, the ideological gap

---

[20] On how high levels of regime vulnerability (susceptibility to major ideological changes at home) tend to make leaders' ideological identities highly salient to their perceptions and policies, see Haas 2021; Haas 2022.
[21] Quoted in Ambrosio 2007: 241.   [22] Myers and Barry 2014.

between the two nations is simply too great, and the level of trust between them too low, to permit a stable modus vivendi.[23]

The US–China trade war initiated by the Donald Trump administration offers further evidence of an ideological explanation of worsening relations. In January 2019, Li Ruogu, a former chairman of the Export-Import Bank of China and former deputy governor of China's central bank, asserted that the trade war was primarily a product of ideological not economic fears. According to Li, "the conflict wasn't about the United States being threatened by China's growth … but by its vision of state-led capitalism. 'This is the conflict of systems. It won't end easily.'"[24]

Whereas ideological enemies tend to view one another as subversive dangers to their core domestic objectives, the opposite threat relationship often holds for leaders who are dedicated to similar ideological beliefs. Elites will frequently view the success of ideologically similar regimes with approval since others' victories are likely to benefit the former's domestic interests. By demonstrating the advantages or staying power of particular ideological beliefs, a party's success in one state is likely to aid the political fortunes of like-minded groups throughout the system, thereby increasing the incentives for cooperative relations. Russian leaders, for example, provided generous aid to Belarus for much of the 2000s largely due to a belief that the continuation of the two countries' illiberal political systems was interconnected. As Belarus's authoritarian leader Alyaksandar Lukashenka observed in 2005: "A revolution in Belarus is a revolution in Russia," meaning that a revolution in Belarus threatened revolution in Russia. Key Russian politicians clearly sympathized with this position.[25] This perceived interconnectedness of domestic interests created powerful incentives for Russia's illiberal leaders to aid Lukashenka's regime lest its demise undermine Russia's system of governance. The same thinking led Saudi Arabia to tighten its alliance with Bahrain (both countries are monarchies) in response to the spread of popular protests throughout much of the Arab world in 2011. Part of these efforts included sending Saudi troops, at the request of Bahrain's king, into its neighbor to quell domestic unrest. Saudi leaders feared that a successful revolution in Bahrain would inspire and embolden similar pressures in their kingdom.[26]

---

[23] Friedberg 2012: 49–50.
[24] Li Yuan 2019. The first part of the quotation is the *New York Times'* summary of a January 2019 speech by Li. The last sentences are from the speech.
[25] Ambrosio 2007: 244.   [26] Sanger and Schmitt 2011.

2.1.3   Miscommunications

A third important way in which different ideological worldviews shape politicians' threat perceptions is by increasing the likelihood of misperceptions among them. The greater the ideological differences dividing states' leaders, the more likely they are to attribute different meanings to the same symbols and events, and thus the greater the likelihood of misunderstandings developing. These barriers to effective communication among ideological rivals are not a product of a lack of effort or difficulties of translation, but of different identities that push people to interpret language and other signals in contrary ways. President John F. Kennedy expressed well precisely these points when he wrote to Nikita Khrushchev in November 1961:

I am conscious of the difficulties you and I face in establishing full communication between our two minds. This is not a question of translation but a question of the context in which we hear and respond to what each other has to say. You and I have already recognized that neither of us will convince the other about our respective social systems and general philosophies of life. These differences create a great gulf in communications because language cannot mean the same thing on both sides unless it is related to some underlying purpose.[27]

Among ideological enemies, misperceptions are likely to result in the creation and exaggeration of conflicts of interest as well as missed opportunities for cooperation. In the 1930s, for example, Soviet dictator Josef Stalin tried to communicate to Britain and France that he was interested in forming an alliance against Germany by instructing Western communist parties to support rearmament and by greatly downplaying the role of the Comintern (which was an institution that had been openly dedicated to the fomentation of revolution against capitalism and colonialism). Western conservatives, however, misunderstood Stalin's intent and instead thought Stalin's policy changes were part of a new, more subtle attempt to facilitate ideological subversion.[28] Similarly, British attempts in 1941 to warn Stalin of Hitler's plans to soon attack the Soviet Union were misunderstood by the Soviets, which resulted in the opposite effect to their intent. Stalin and his associates dismissed Britain's warnings as

---

[27] Quoted in Beschloss 1991: 336–37

[28] Viscount Chilston, Britain's ambassador to the Soviet Union, dismissed the Comintern's new policy of creating a "united front" against fascism as "a new-fangled Trojan horse." The shift was "not a change of heart … but a change of tactics." To Chilston, "world revolution remains as ever the ultimate end of Comintern policy." The Northern Department of the Foreign Office agreed, asserting in December 1935 that although the Comintern's activities were "now more underground than open," its "fundamental dogma" remained "world revolution." All quotations are from internal or private documents and can be found in Little 1988: 293.

desperate attempts to embroil the Soviet Union and Germany in conflict. The Soviet ambassador to Britain, Ivan Maisky, even told Foreign Secretary Anthony Eden that British warnings to the Soviet Union about Germany's plans of attack "would not be understood in Moscow and would be resented there."[29] The ironic result of this communications breakdown, according to Gabriel Gorodetsky, was that "Churchill's warning to Stalin of the German deployment [of massive numbers of German troops near the Soviet border] in April [1941], rather than being a landmark in the formation of the Grand Alliance, in fact achieved the opposite. Stalin was diverted from the main danger, suspecting that Churchill was bent on drawing Russia into the hostilities."[30]

2.2   Foreign Policy Worldviews

As we have argued, ideological worldviews influence international events through the three causal pathways of conflict expectations, demonstration effects, and miscommunications. But how important are these ideological factors compared to other variables? In each pathway, ideological variables, or what we call type identities, confront and compete with other causal variables such as power, institutions, and role or social identities. In other worldviews, power interests (realist worldviews), institutional factors (liberal worldviews), and role or social identity factors (constructivist worldviews) may dominate. Relationalist worldviews would argue that none of these factors has any distinct influence on outcomes because all of them are bundled together in the quantum world. They exist only as probabilities, until an investigator asks a question, and then pose a fundamental dilemma for an analysis like this one because they cannot be tested against an objective world. So, let's assume that the specific questions we are asking as investigators trigger the relationist quantum world to yield the Weberian world and specific variables which can be tested against an objective universe. That assumption is not inconsistent with the new relationalism and allows this Weberian analysis to proceed. After all, if Newtonian science is good enough for understanding tennis balls, but not quanta and galaxies (black holes), it may be good enough for the study of politics since the latter operates on the level of tennis balls not quanta or galaxies.

Historically, actors in international affairs have taken four distinct approaches to thinking about the interaction of "type" ideas with other variables. They reflect the four main foreign policy traditions or worldviews of any country: nationalist, realist, institutionalist, and ideological.

---

[29] Quoted in Gorodetsky 1999: 302.   [30] Gorodetsky 1999: 321.

Each tradition implies a different causal relationship between type identities on the one hand and power, institutions, and role or social identities on the other.[31]

The nationalist orientation comes closest to a pure Weberian worldview. Nations, like individuals, are separate and distinct. They have a unique type identity and act, rationally for the most part, to preserve that identity. This imperative to survive shapes in turn the realities of power, relationships/institutions, and social identities. Nations mostly take care of themselves. Independence and unilateralism prevail, not interdependence and multilateralism. Institutions such as alliances are unnecessary, except in extremis. Power balances emerge autonomically. Social or shared identities are thin; type identities matter most.[32] The materialist universe consists of an equilibrium of multiple and roughly equal powers.

The realist worldview is mostly Weberian but adds some interdependent or institutional aspects. Not all type identities matter the same. Great power identities matter more because great powers have more agency (capability) and responsibility to balance power and preserve world order. The balance of power (power) then shapes military capabilities (e.g., arms races), institutional relationships (e.g., the United Nations), and social identities (e.g., great power solidarity). Great powers cooperate and compete regardless of type identity, and cooperation does not narrow ideological differences.[33] Social identities remain thin.

The institutionalist worldview operates between the Weberian and quantum worlds. Interdependent, rather than independent, relationships shape power (e.g., collective security, trade), institutions (e.g., multilateralism), and role or social identities (e.g., common rules, regulations, practices).[34] Actors strive to resolve their geopolitical (realist) and identity differences by negotiations and common rules. They build up international institutions and develop the habit of cooperation, which helps them narrow geopolitical and type identity differences. Over time, role and shared identities take on greater importance, and a world community or "community of nations" emerges.[35]

---

[31] The following analysis draws from Nau, 2002: 43–49; and Nau 2015a: 39–61. For application of this definition of worldviews to countries other than the United States, see Nau and Ollapally 2012.

[32] Hazony 2018

[33] As Kenneth Waltz succinctly explains, to realists "considerations of power dominate considerations of ideology"; Waltz 1990: 31.

[34] Ikenberry expresses these points graphically: "Conflicts will be captured and domesticated in an iron cage of multilateral rules, standards, safeguards, and dispute settlement procedures." See Ikenberry 2009: 16.

[35] On how processes bring about shifts in political loyalties and identities, see Haas 1958.

The social constructivist worldview tacks toward the quantum end of the worldview spectrum. The world is no longer made up of separate Weberian entities or interdependent relationships between separate entities. It is now a holistic world of entanglement in which individual and separate identities disappear into discourses and language games. Communicative practices shape identities, and role or social identities matter more.[36] Social constructivists "bracket the corporate [i.e., domestic] sources of state identity and interests, and concentrate entirely on the constitutive role of international social interaction, exploring how structural contexts, systemic processes, and strategic practice produce and reproduce state identities."[37] Over time, relationships replace identities, as actors merge at higher and higher levels of analysis. The world becomes a whole; actors are diffused rather than distinct.

Let's look at several empirical examples of how "type" ideological variables interact with and at times override materialist, institutionalist, and social constructivist worldviews

2.2.1   When Type Identities Override Geopolitical Realities

Type identities are frequently more determinative of leaders' threat perceptions and foreign policies than material variables, even when geopolitical realities are stark. After World War II, western European countries viewed the United States as less threatening than the Soviet Union even though US troops occupied western European countries and Soviet troops did not. Power balances were not the issue; ideological ones were. Today, US leaders view North Korea as much more threatening than Britain, France, Germany, and Japan, even though the latter are orders of magnitude more powerful (and all have nuclear weapons or the capability to acquire them relatively quickly). During the Concert of Europe from 1815 to 1848, leaders in the monarchical great powers saw weak liberalizing states (such as Naples and the United States) as much more threatening than fellow great powers. Because liberalism might spread (demonstration effect), they viewed liberal revolutions as major threats to their domestic interests.[38]

No better example of how type identities can override profound geopolitical realities exists than the way British and French conservatives and socialists favored opposing alliance policies in the 1930s.[39] Conservatives refused to ally with the Soviet Union despite the massive power threat

---

[36] Wendt 1999: 227–29.   [37] Reus-Smit 1999: 166.
[38] Haas 2005: 93. See also Nelson 2022: chapter 3.
[39] For details, see Haas 2005, chapter 4; Haas 2022, chapter 2.

posed by Germany, whereas most socialists pushed hard for such an alliance to balance Germany. The root source of these clashing preferences was opposing ideological orientations toward Germany and the Soviet Union. Most conservatives viewed the Soviet Union as the greatest ideological danger in the system, Nazi Germany a lesser one.[40] This intense ideological hostility to the Soviet Union prevented an alliance with this state throughout the 1930s. Even after Germany's invasion of Czechoslovakia in March 1939 – when the power-based threat from Germany was reaching extremely high levels – key conservatives continued to emphasize their intense suspicions of the Soviets on ideological grounds. In April that year, Prime Minister Neville Chamberlain wrote his sister, Hilda: "Our chief trouble is with Russia [and thus not with Germany]. I confess to being deeply suspicious of her. I cannot believe that she has the same aims and objects as we have or any sympathy with democracy as such."[41]

British and French socialists reacted ideologically to Germany and the Soviet Union in exactly the reverse way, resulting in opposite alliance preferences. Because socialists viewed Nazi Germany as the greatest ideological threat in the system, the Soviet Union a lesser one, the barriers to an alliance with the Soviet Union were much smaller than they were for conservatives. British Labour Party leaders, according to a summary by William Tucker, argued as early as 1934 that the Soviet Union lacked "aggressive designs toward other states," thus making it "a natural ally of the forces of peace" against the fascist states.[42] There "was no question upon which Labour opinion was more united than the necessity of an [alliance] agreement with the Soviet Union."[43] French socialists concurred.[44] Power variables were identical for British and French conservatives and socialists. Their ideological worldviews, however, were not, and these differences resulted in opposing policies on the most important security issues of the era.

In addition to critically affecting the meaning that individual leaders give to power variables, ideologies can also at times be a direct cause of

---

[40] As Prime Minister Neville Chamberlain's Private Parliamentary Secretary, Alec Douglas-Home, explained: "[T]he main thing to grasp is that Chamberlain, like many others, saw Communism as the major long-term danger. He hated Hitler and German Fascism, but he felt that Europe in general and Britain in particular were in even greater danger from Communism. Hitler was an evil man but in the short term one should – and possible could – do a deal with him." In one example of this thinking, Chamberlain wrote King George VI in September 1938 (the month of the Munich Conference) that his government had "sketched out the prospect of Germany and England as the two pillars of European peace and buttresses against communism." First quotation from George 1965: 220; second quotation from Shaw 2003: 18.

[41] Quoted in Neilson 2006: 285.   [42] Tucker 1950: 233.   [43] Tucker 1950: 232.

[44] Jackson 1988: 191; Greene 1969: 53.

power shifts. Political scientists often treat ideas as a residual variable, exerting only marginal influence after international power and domestic institutional exigencies are accounted for.[45] Ideological leadership is relatively discounted. The historian H.W. Brands, Jr. argues, for example, that President Ronald Reagan's success in the Cold War can be largely explained in terms of events not policy: Reagan "had no policy agenda beyond basic conservative principles. He expected events to furnish direction. They obliged from the start."[46] Yet, it can be argued that events were not moving in Reagan's direction in the late 1970s. The strategic rivalry was moving decisively in the Soviet direction, and the US and world economies were languishing in stagflation. As John Lewis Gaddis notes, "the Nixon-Ford years saw the most substantial reductions in American military capabilities relative to those of the Soviet Union in the entire postwar period."[47] Meanwhile, worldwide inflation rates tripled, growth slowed by 25 percent, and unemployment jumped by 50 percent. Reagan was not favored by structural forces; he had to alter them. In a multivariant and constantly changing world, proving causality is impossible. Yet a plausible case can be made that Reagan's ideas about both strategic relations and the world economy preceded his time in office, mobilized political support to put him into office, informed the policy initiatives he implemented once in office, and ultimately coincided (correlated) with a revitalization of the strategic balance and the world economy.[48] By the early 1990s, the Soviet Union had disappeared, and from 1980 to 2010 the world economy enjoyed average annual real growth of 3 percent plus. In short, ideological factors mobilized a policy agreement (the so-called Washington consensus) that altered geopolitical circumstances.

---

[45] See, for example, Trubowitz 2011.   [46] Brands 2015: 188.

[47] Gaddis 1982: 320–21. Whereas the United States in these years deployed two new strategic weapons systems, the Soviets made operational ten new or updated systems. Between 1970 and 1977, the United States cut deployable ground forces by 207,000 soldiers while the Soviets' armed forces grew by 262,000 men. Washington also cut military expenditures as a percentage of GDP between 1970 and 1977 from 8.2 to 5.2 percent, while Moscow increased theirs from 11 to 13 percent. The shift continued into the 1980s. Soviet defense outlays as a percentage of GDP climbed from 13.5 per cent in 1976 to 18 per cent in 1988, and Soviet nuclear warheads increased from 2,471 in 1961 to 39,000 in 1989, whereas US warheads remained the same, around 22–24,000. While the United States withdrew from Vietnam, the Soviet Union projected force for the first time in Somalia, Ethiopia, Angola, Yemen, and, most significantly, Afghanistan. For additional data, see also Brooks and Wohlforth 2000–01: 24: and Norris and Kristensen 2006: 64–66.

[48] For a full account of this economic story, see Nau 1990; and an update in Nau 2015b: 24–38. For similar accounts, see Samuelson 2008 and Hayward 2009.

2.2.2   *When Type Identities Override Institutionalist Factors*

When ideological identities diverge, leaders are more likely to focus on their competing than their common interests, thereby making it very difficult for institutions and routinized diplomacy to facilitate sustained cooperation.

The failure of détente between the United States and the Soviet Union in the 1970s illustrates these dynamics. President Richard Nixon and National Security Advisor Henry Kissinger adopted realist and institutionalist approaches to US–Soviet relations; they minimized ideological factors. As John Lewis Gaddis summarizes, they believed "that the geopolitical interests of ideologically disparate states could, in certain areas, be congruent. Once diplomacy was purged of its sentimental and emotional [i.e., ideological] components, it should be possible to identify and build upon these common interests held even by previously irreconcilable antagonists: survival, security, a congenial international environment." Sustained "serious negotiations on substantive issues," Nixon and Kissinger believed, was the key to convincing the Soviets to focus not on "the clash of competing interests" but on "the evolution of 'habits of mutual restraint, coexistence, and, ultimately, cooperation.' This, Kissinger insisted, was what was meant by détente."[49] Its goal was the coexistence of great powers, not the eventual triumph or merger of one ideology with another.

The détente process resulted in a number of noteworthy agreements.[50] But institutionalized diplomacy did not succeed in ending the Cold War. The effects of ideological differences, despite Nixon's and Kissinger's beliefs to the contrary, were a major barrier to conflict resolution. As Raymond Garthoff explains, the "foremost" reasons for the collapse of superpower détente in the 1970s were the very different understandings of the meaning and purposes of détente possessed by US and Soviet leaders and their failure to understand these differences.[51] And these differences in conceptions and failures in understanding were rooted in ideological differences. Whereas Nixon and Kissinger hoped that détente would end the Cold War by institutionalizing the pursuit of common interests, Soviet policymakers hoped to use détente to make the superpower rivalry less dangerous while they continued to pursue an intense ideological and military struggle at lower economic cost. As General

---

[49] John Lewis Gaddis 1982: 279, 283, and 289.

[50] The most important of these agreements were the SALT I Treaty, the Basic Principles of Mutual Relations, a comprehensive trade agreement, the Prevention of Nuclear War Agreement, and the Helsinki Accords. For details on these agreements, see Garthoff 1995.

[51] Garthoff 1995: 1069.

Secretary of the Communist Party of the Soviet Union (CPSU) Leonard Brezhnev asserted in 1972:

The CPSU has always held, and now holds, that the class struggle between the two systems – the capitalist and the socialist ... will continue. That is to be expected since the world outlook and the class aims of socialism and capitalism are opposite and irreconcilable. But we shall strive to shift this historically inevitable struggle onto a path free from the periods of war, of dangerous conflicts, and an uncontrolled arms race.[52]

President Reagan took a different approach to détente than Nixon and Kissinger. Like the Soviets under Brezhnev, he emphasized the ideological differences that limited the potential for diplomatic cooperation. He sought not coexistence but an end to the Cold War. As he told Richard Allen, his national security advisor: "my theory about the Cold War is that we win and they lose."[53] Reagan rejected the notion that all ideologies were morally equivalent. As he explained in 1988, "We spoke plainly and bluntly ... We said freedom was better than totalitarianism. We said communism was bad [and] ... made clear that the differences that separated us and the Soviets were deeper and wider than just missile counts and number of warheads."[54] Rather than pursue détente, Reagan armed his diplomacy by reasserting American ideological exceptionalism (distinctiveness) and reviving American economic and military capabilities. He forced the Soviet Union to take negotiations seriously because it could not compete outside the negotiations. As Mikhail Gorbachev told his Politburo colleagues in October 1986, "our goal is to prevent the next round of the arms race. If we do not accomplish it, the threat to us will only grow ... because we are already at the limits of our capabilities."[55] Reagan's approach saw ideological factors driving material realities and determining institutional outcomes.

2.2.3   When Type Identities Override Social Identities

If détente or US ideological superiority did not end the Cold War, did it end by changing social or role identities brought about by changing international practices? Social constructivists might think so. The United States and Soviet Union came together around the shared ideas of Gorbachev's "New Thinking." Social constructivists count on repetitive interactions to influence outcomes, as do institutionalists. The difference is that, for social constructivists, these interactions are communicative and substantive, not ameliorative and procedural. Did

---

[52] Quoted in Gaddis 1982: 312–13.   [53] This discussion draws from Nau 2015a: 174.
[54] Nau 2015a: 174.   [55] Nau 2015a: 181.

the diplomatic discourse in US–Soviet relations change as Gorbachev developed his ideas of glasnost and perestroika and a common European home? This is the social constructivist explanation. Or did type identities shift such that the Soviet Union moved toward liberalism and eventually abandoned communism, and US–Russian institutional and geopolitical relations shifted accordingly from enemies to friends? This is the type identity, agency-oriented explanation.

Efforts by President Reagan and General Secretary Gorbachev to end the Cold War in the mid-to-late 1980s illustrate well these dynamics between type and social identities.[56] Alex Wendt crafts the social constructivist explanation. According to Wendt, Gorbachev's policies are "an example of how states might transform a competitive security system into a cooperative one." Because

> competitive security systems are sustained by practices that create insecurity and distrust … transformational [international] practices should attempt to teach other states that one's own state can be trusted and should not be viewed as a threat to their security. The fastest way to do this is to make unilateral initiatives and self-binding commitments of sufficient significance that another state is faced with "an offer it cannot refuse." Gorbachev [did] this by withdrawing from Afghanistan and Eastern Europe, implementing asymmetric cuts in nuclear and conventional forces, calling for "defensive defense," and so on.[57]

The problem with this analysis is that Gorbachev's much more cooperative international policies from 1985 to 1988 did not convince US leaders that the Cold War was ending. Although US elites acknowledged that Gorbachev's more cooperative international relations were helping to make US–Soviet relations less dangerous, their dominant sentiment was that Gorbachev's initiatives did little to alter the overall adversarial character of the superpowers' relationship. Before 1988, no key American official claimed to believe that the end of US–Soviet enmity was likely in the foreseeable future. For example, on the eve of the Washington Summit in December 1987 when the Intermediate Nuclear Forces (INF) Treaty was signed, Secretary of State George Shultz asserted that "there is nothing in the 'new political thinking' [the name of Gorbachev's domestic and international reform agenda] to date which suggests that the end of the adversarial struggle [between the superpowers] is at hand."[58] The following February, Shultz stated that he found it "difficult to believe that [America's] relations with the Soviet Union will ever be 'normal' in the sense that we have normal relations with most other countries." Thus "it seems unlikely that the US–Soviet

---

[56] This discussion draws on Haas 2007: 145–79; and Nau 2011: 462–74.
[57] Wendt 1992: 420–21.   [58] Shultz 1988b: 7.

relationship will ever lose what always had been and is today a strongly wary and at times adversarial element."[59] A new edition of the *National Security Strategy of the United States*, issued by the President Reagan in January 1988, reached similarly pessimistic conclusions. According to the document, "despite some improvement in US–Soviet relations over the past year, the long-term threat [posed by the USSR] has not perceptibly diminished … There is as yet no evidence that the Soviets have abandoned their long-term [aggressive international] objectives … We must not delude ourselves into believing that the Soviet threat has yet been fundamentally altered."[60]

What pushed the most powerful decision-makers in the Reagan administration to believe the Cold War was ending were not changes in Soviet foreign policies, but proposed changes in Soviet domestic politics (type identity) that convinced key US leaders that the ideological distance dividing the superpowers was narrowing considerably. In April 1988, Gorbachev laid out major new institutional objectives for the Soviet Union that would be voted upon in the Nineteenth Party Conference, which was scheduled for June. These proposals included holding competitive elections involving nonparty members; establishing a new, popularly elected Congress of People's Deputies that would select a standing legislature (a new "Supreme Soviet") that possessed significant power; creating an independent judiciary; and providing protections for freedom of speech, assembly, and press.[61] The conference approved all these initiatives, and the elections for the Congress of People's Deputies was scheduled for March 1989.

Reagan and America's most important policymakers immediately recognized the ideological significance of Gorbachev's 1988 plans. Reagan asserted in a speech in London after the Moscow Summit in June that the Nineteenth Party Conference proposals, which included "such things as official accountability, limitations on length of service in office, [and] an independent judiciary," were "cause for shaking the head in wonder." These proposals convinced Reagan that Gorbachev "is a serious man seeking serious reform." Because of Gorbachev's domestic objectives and their institutionalization, the Soviet Union was very likely now entering a period of "lasting change."[62] Reagan's advisors also took note.

---

[59] Shultz 1988a: 41.   [60] Reagan 1988a: 20.

[61] For details on Gorbachev's proposals for the Nineteenth Party Conference, see Matlock 1995: 122; Adomeit 1998: 351.

[62] Reagan 1988b: 38 and 37. Reagan stated in his memoirs that personal interactions with Gorbachev at the Moscow Summit also helped to build trusting relations, as social constructivists might predict (Reagan 1990: 709, 711–12). This outcome obtained, however, only in the context of Gorbachev's revolutionary domestic proposals.

Ambassador Jack Matlock remarked: "as I read [Gorbachev's proposals] and discovered one new element after another, my excitement grew. Never before had I seen in an official Communist Party document such an extensive section on protecting the rights of citizens or such principles as the separation of powers, judicial independence, and presumption of a defendant's innocence until proven guilty."[63] With these proposals, "what had passed for 'socialism' in Soviet parlance had dropped from sight. What the 'theses' described was something closer to European social democracy."[64] To Matlock, the conference proposals indicated that "Gorbachev was finally prepared to cross the Rubicon and discard the Marxist ideology that had defined and justified the Communist Party dictatorship in the Soviet Union."[65]

It was shortly after the Americans became convinced that Gorbachev was trying to revolutionize the Soviet domestic system that they began to assert that the Cold War was at an end. When Reagan was asked at the Moscow Conference – which was held just weeks after Reagan learned of Gorbachev's goals at the Nineteenth Party Conference – if he could declare the Cold War to be over, the president answered: "I think right now, of course."[66] A few days later, he stated in a speech in London that Gorbachev's revolutionary reforms were possibly ushering in "a new era in human history, and, hopefully, an era of peace and freedom for all."[67] These statements came mere months after Reagan and other leaders had declared that the fundamental threat posed by the Soviet Union remained intact. The night after learning about Gorbachev's new domestic object-ives, National Security Advisor Colin Powell recounts that he "felt a conviction deep in [his] bones ... I realized one phase of my life had ended ... Up until now, as a soldier, my mission had been to confront, contain, and if necessary, combat communism. Now, I had to think about a world without a Cold War."[68]

Gorbachev's domestic policies that indicated a substantial narrowing of the ideological differences dividing the superpowers thus accomplished what changes in geopolitical shifts and international diplomacy could not: they convinced US leaders that US–Soviet enmity was ending. As Nau concludes, "the decisive shifts that ended the Cold War were ideological not material or institutional. The United States and western countries

Previous personal interactions at the Geneva and Reykjavik Summits did not lead the president to believe the Cold War was ending.

[63] Matlock 1995: 122.   [64] Matlock 1995: 122.   [65] Matlock 2004: 295–96.
[66] Reagan 1988c: 32.
[67] Reagan 1988b: 38. The analysis in the preceding paragraphs is drawn from Haas 2007: 159, 166–68.
[68] Powell, with Persico, 1995: 375.

revived confidence in democratic ideals (after the alleged malaise and governability crisis of western societies in the 1970s), while the Soviet Union lost further confidence in communist ideals."[69]

2.3   Conclusions

The point of this chapter is not to argue that worldviews understood as political ideologies and type identities override in all cases other influences on outcomes. There are times when materialist forces exert preeminent influence – for example, when nuclear weapons compel security interdependence;[70] or when institutional forces overcome historical geopolitical rivalries, as in the case of the European Union.[71] Even social and relationalist identities matter increasingly in such issue areas as global warming. It is simply to suggest that our Weberian agency-oriented approach has important advantages that are eviscerated in more relationalist and holistic approaches. In our approach, perspectives are identified with specific actors and objectives. These actors perceive the world differently and contest their differences against an external world which they cannot completely know but which pushes back to tell them if their worldview is not false.[72] They wrestle with moral dilemmas. As Michael Barnett points out (Chapter 5, this volume), Israeli Jews deliberate and decide between nationalist and cosmopolitan worldviews. Whatever they decide, whether they fail or succeed, they are responsible. In debates about the causes of the end of the Cold War, the reader can test different foreign policy worldviews against the evidence and decide which one makes more sense. In holistic worlds, there is no contestation of political or religious perspectives. There is no good and evil. Nothing can be questioned because boundaries are uncertain and everything is in the process of becoming. There are no certainties, no firm truths. Seen critically, the holistic vision is an appeal to disarm intellectually, to abandon the pivot of individual inquiry and insight, to blur any distinction between points of view, and to lose the element of choice which is the very essence of freedom.

Bibliography

Adler, E. and M. Barnett, eds. 1998. *Security Communities*. Cambridge: University of Cambridge Press.

---

[69] Nau 2011: 472.   [70] Deudney 2008.   [71] Ginsberg 2001.
[72] Science never tells us the truth because evidence is always subject to multiple theories (interpretations). It tells us only whether our evidence is not false, meaning consistent with one of these multiple theories. See Nau, Chapter 6, this volume.

Adomeit, H. 1998. *Imperial Overstretch: Germany in Soviet Policy from Stalin to Gorbachev*. Baden-Baden: Nomos Verlagsgesellschaft.

Ambrosio, T. 2007. "Insulating Russia from a Colour Revolution: How the Kremlin Resists Regional Democratic Trends," *Democratization* 14(2): 232–52.

Barnett, M. 1996. "Identity and Alliances in the Middle East," in P. Katzenstein, ed., *The Culture of National Security*. New York: Columbia University Press, pp. 400–47.

Barry, E and S. Myers, 2014. "Putin Reclaims Crimea for Russia and Bitterly Denounces the West." *The New York Times* (March 18).

Beer, C.C., M. Peceny, and S. Sanchez-Terry. 2002. "Dictatorial Peace?" *American Political Science Review* 96(1): 15–26.

Beschloss, M. 1991. *The Crisis Years: Kennedy and Khrushchev, 1960–1963*. New York: HarperCollins.

Brands, H.W. 2105. *Reagan: A Life*. New York: Doubleday.

Brooks, S.G. and W.C. Wohlforth 2000–01. "Power, Globalization, and the End of the Cold War," *International Security* 25(3): 5–53.

Deudney, D. 2008. *Bounding Power*. Princeton, NJ: Princeton University Press.

Easton, D., J. Gunnell, and M. Stein. 1995. "Introduction: Democracy as a Regime Type and the Development of Political Science," in D. Easton, J. Gunnell, and M. Stein, eds., *Regime and Discipline: Democracy and the Development of Political Science*. Ann Arbor, MI: University of Michigan Press, pp. 1–23.

Friedberg, A.L. 2012. "Bucking Beijing," *Foreign Affairs* 91(5): 48–58.

Gaddis, J.L. 1982. *Strategies of Containment: A Critical Appraisal of Postwar American National Security Policy*. Oxford: Oxford University Press.

Garthoff, R.L. 1995. *Détente and Confrontation: American Soviet Relations from Nixon to Reagan*. Washington, DC: The Brookings Institution.

George, M. 1965. *The Warped Vision, British Foreign Policy 1933–1939*. Pittsburgh, PA: University of Pittsburgh Press.

Ginsberg, R.H. 2001. *The European Union in International Politics*. Lanham, MD: Roman and Littlefield.

Gorodetsky, G. 1999. *Grand Delusion: Stalin and the German Invasion of Russia*. New Haven, CT: Yale University Press.

Greene, N. 1969. *Crisis and Decline: The French Socialist Party in the Popular Front Era*. Ithaca, NY: Cornell University Press.

Haas, E.B. 1958. *The Uniting of Europe*. South Bend, NY: Notre Dame University Press.

Haas, M.L. 2005. *The Ideological Origins of Great Power Politics, 1789–1989*. Ithaca, NY: Cornell University Press.

Haas, M.L. 2007. "The United States and the End of the Cold War: Reactions to Shifts in Soviet Power, Policies, or Domestic Politics?" *International Organization* 61(1): 145–79.

Haas, M.L. 2012a. *The Clash of Ideologies: Middle Eastern Politics and American Security*. New York: Oxford University Press.

Haas, M.L. 2012b. Missed Ideological Opportunities and George W. Bush's Middle Eastern Policies. *Security Studies* 21(3): 416–54.

Haas, M.L. 2014. Ideological Polarity and Balancing in Great Power Politics. *Security Studies*, 23(4): 715–53.

Haas, M.L. 2021. When Do Ideological Enemies Ally? *International Security*, 46 (1): 104–46.

Haas, M.L. 2022. *Frenemies: When Ideological Enemies Ally*. Ithaca, NY: Cornell University Press.

Hayward, S.F. 2009. *The Age of Reagan*. New York: Crown Forum.

Hazony, Y. 2018. *The Virtue of Nationalism*. New York: Basic Books.

Ikenberry, G.J. 2009. Introduction: Woodrow Wilson, the Bush Administration, and the Future of Liberal Internationalism," in G.J. Ikenberry, T.J. Knock, A.M. Slaughter, T. Smith, eds., *The Crisis of American Foreign Policy: Wilsonianism in the Twenty-First Century*. Princeton, NJ: Princeton University Press, pp. 1–24.

Jackson, J. 1988. *The Popular Front in France: Defending Democracy, 1934–38*. New York: Cambridge University Press.

Johnston, A. 2008. *Social States: Changes in International Institutions, 1980–2000*. Princeton, NJ: Princeton University Press.

Li, Y. 2019 "China, Some Fear the End of 'Chimerica'," *The New York Times* (May 14).

Little, D. 1988. "Red Scare, 1936: Anti-Bolshevism and the Origins of British Non-Intervention in the Spanish Civil War," *Journal of Contemporary History* 23 (2): 291–311.

Matlock, J. 1995. *Autopsy on an Empire*. New York: Random House.

Matlock, J.F. 2004. *Reagan and Gorbachev: How the Cold War Ended*. New York: Random House.

Miller, B. 1995. *When Opponents Cooperate: Great Power Conflict and Collaboration in World Politics*. Ann Arbor, MI: University of Michigan Press.

Nau, H.R. 1990. *The Myth of America's Decline: Leading the World Economy into the 1990s*. New York: Oxford University Press.

Nau, H.R. 2002. *At Home Abroad: Identity and Power in American Foreign Policy*. Ithaca, NY: Cornell University Press.

Nau, H.R. 2011. "Ideas Have Consequences: The Cold War and Today," *International Politics* 48(4/5): 460–81.

Nau, H.R. 2015a. *Conservative Internationalism: Armed Diplomacy Under Jefferson, Polk, Truman and Reagan. Princeton*: Princeton, NJ: Princeton University Press, paperback with new preface.

Nau, H.R. 2015b. "The Great Expansion," in J.L. Chidester and P. Kengor, eds., *Reagan's Legacy in a World Transformed*. Cambridge, MA: Harvard University Press, pp. 24–38.

Nau, H.R. and D.M. Ollapally, eds., 2012. *Worldviews of Aspiring Powers: Domestic Foreign Policy Debates in China, India, Iran, Japan, and Russia*. New York: Oxford University Press.

Neilson, K. 2006. *Britain, Soviet Russia and the Collapse of the Versailles Order, 1919–1939*. Cambridge: Cambridge University Press.

Nelson, C.E. 2022. *Revolutionary Contagion and International Politics*. Oxford: Oxford University Press.

Norris, R. and H.M. Kristensen. 2006. "Global nuclear stockpiles 1945–2006," *Bulletin of Atomic Scientists* 62(4): 64–66.

Owen, J.M. 2010. *The Clash of Ideas in World Politics: Transnational Networks, States, and Regime Change, 1510–2010*. Princeton, NJ: Princeton University Press.

Powell, C.L. with J.E. Persico. 1995. *My American Journey*. New York: Random House.

Reagan, R. 1988a. "National Security Strategy of the United States," *State Bulletin* 88: 1–31.

Reagan, R. 1988b. "President's Address, Guildhall, London, June 3, 1988," *State Bulletin* 88: 36–40.

Reagan, R. 1988c. "President's News Conference, Spaso House, Moscow, June 1, 1988," *State Bulletin* 88: 31–35.

Reagan, R. 1990. *An American Life*. New York: Simon and Schuster.

Reus-Smit, C. 1999. *The Moral Purpose of the State*. Princeton, NJ: Princeton University Press.

Roberts, H. 1953. "Maxim Litvinov," in G. Craig and F. Gilbert, eds., *The Diplomats, 1919–1939*. Princeton, NJ: Princeton University Press, pp. 344–77.

Samuelson, R.J. 2008. *The Great Inflation and Its Aftermath*. New York: Random House.

Sanger, D. and E. Schmitt. 2011. "US–Saudi Tensions Intensify with Mideast Turmoil." *New York Times*, March 14.

Shaw, L.G. 2003. *The British Political Elite and the Soviet Union, 1937–1939*. London: France Cass.

Shirer, W. 1960. *The Rise and Fall of the Third Reich: A History of Nazi Germany*. New York: Simon and Schuster.

Shultz, G.P. 1988a. "Managing the US–Soviet Relationship," *State Bulletin* 88: 38–43.

Shultz, G.P. 1988b. "National Success and International Stability in a Time of Change," *State Bulletin* 88: 3–7.

Trachtenberg, M. 1999. *A Constructed Peace: The Making of the European Settlement, 1945–1963*. Princeton, NJ: Princeton University Press.

Trubowitz, P. 2011. *Politics and Strategy*. Princeton, NJ: Princeton University Press.

Tucker, W.R. 1950. *The Attitude of the British Labour Party Towards European and Collective Security Problems, 1920–1939*. Genève: Imprimerie du Journal Genève.

Walt, S.M. 1996. *Revolution and War*. Ithaca, NY: Cornell University Press.

Waltz, K.N. 1990. "Realist Thought and Neorealist Theory," *Journal of International Affairs* 44(1): 21–37.

Wendt, A. 1992. "Anarchy Is What States Make of It: The Social Construction of Power Politics," *International* Organization 46(2): 391–425.

Wendt, A. 1999. *Social Theory of International Politics*. Cambridge: Cambridge University Press.

Werner, S. and D. Lemke. 1997. "Opposites Do Not Attract: The Impact of Domestic Institutions, Power, and Prior Commitments on Alignment Choices," *International Studies Quarterly* 41(3): 529–46.

3 Relationality, Post-Newtonian International Relations, and Worldviews

Milja Kurki

The challenges presented today by climate change and ecological collapses, including the ongoing sixth mass extinction,[1] are unprecedented in scale and politically complex. They are also challenging for how International Relations (IR) scholarship and other social sciences have oriented themselves to the world, human and nonhuman. As Audra Mitchell reminds us, in the face of these challenges IR scholars are only just starting to think through how we might orient to questions of survival "as such" rather than simply the survival of individual states or communities.[2] And, as Rafi Youatt suggests, in a rush to "manage" the oncoming crisis, we have failed to consider how interspecies and not just "human" politics is deeply embedded in our responses.[3]

In a way, in the face of the different scale, nature, and temporality of uncertainty implicated in ecological and climate changes, IR, alongside many political and social sciences, has struggled to break free from the conceptual bounds within which we have imagined the world: primarily Newtonian, substantialist, and also often anthropocentric in Katzenstein's terms (see Introduction), and as such also rather narrow in terms of the political imaginations available to think through how we might negotiate the challenges ahead.

So how might we address climate change and ecological collapse differently? How are productive political conversations enabled when human and nonhuman communities adjust to changing ecological and climate conditions on the planet? And how are such questions implicated with the "relational revolution" – the rise of new forms of relational thinking and practice – in the natural and social sciences?

In this chapter I seek to tackle such questions by introducing a set of reflections arising out of "relational cosmology," a reorientation to thought and practice around IR that I have been exploring in recent years.[4] This perspective is aligned closely to the Post-Newtonian, relational, and hyperhumanist ends of the spectra that Katzenstein sets out in

---

[1] Leakey and Lewin 1996.   [2] Mitchell 2017.   [3] Youatt 2020: 4.   [4] Kurki 2020.

the introduction to this work. As a result, as we will see, the perspective here interrogates puzzles around "worldviews," both in scholarly practices and in the "world" at large, in quite a distinct manner vis-à-vis classical paradigms of IR.

The relational perspective explored here suggests that the sciences – natural and social – are undergoing a "relational revolution," moving from Cartesian, Newtonian, and empiricist ways of knowing toward more relational ontologies and epistemologies in line with not only quantum science and relativity theory but also with ecological thought and decolonization of the sciences. Relational cosmology, and Post-Newtonian perspectives more widely, argue that we can and should explore new or different ways of thinking and practicing science, politics, and also questions around agency. These perspectives encourage us to rethink the conceptual parameters and "affective" commitments that structure IR's ways of putting the world together to manage its challenges.

The challenge of the relational perspectives, which are many, is that they do not come with easy answers or straightforward paradigmatic commitments, and they do not often even address the same questions of concern to classical paradigms of liberalism, socialism, or realism: they do not search for a rational individual to ground politics, there is no abstract ethics to justify actions on universal grounds, and there are no clear cut answers to the socialists' favorite question: "What is to be done?"

As such, relational thinking may seem strange, frustrating, and even dangerous perhaps, to some scholars in the field (see, e.g., Nau, Chapter 6, this volume). For example, from this perspective, agents – human and nonhuman – are seen as porous, hybrid, and "distributed," much to the displeasure of many classically Newtonian and humanist emancipatory ideologies, whether liberal or socialist. Relational perspectives – and partially related perspectives such as quantum perspectives[5] – challenge many core conceptions of classical western humanism, its (Newtonian and secular) orientations to science, its habit of separating nature and society, and the

---

[5] Relationalism and quantum perspectives are not subsumable within each other. As I understand relational thought, quantum perspectives contribute to or coalesce in some ways with relational traditions. However, sources of relational thinking can be many and a quantum mechanical base is not required for relational thinking. Also, it is important to note that there are many different answers to questions of agency and politics, for example, that can be derived from different traditions of relational and/or quantum theorising. While here my inclination is to move away from agency as a notion, Wendt's important work on the quantum mind and related works could be seen as steps toward reconstituting agency for a post-Newtonian age. I do not wish to speak for all these perspectives as "one," but simply to introduce one relational perspective which speaks to others in hopefully productive ways while also demonstrating for the purposes of this volume the differential avenues of interrogation that emerge vis-à-vis classical perspectives from a relational viewpoint.

tendency to seek to "manage" people and things. However, in answer, the relational perspectives as explored here also do *not* put forward a single, totalistic "worldview" or an "agent of salvation" (leader, class, rational individual, species), but rather provoke us to find new ways of thinking and feeling the world(s) around us and, through this, also representing the varied agents at stake in IR scholarship of a Post-Newtonian kind.

Relational perspectives, then, encourage a lot of new "theoretical" thinking on agency, politics, international relations, science and religion, and affect. Yet, it is important to note that they are not "theoretical" or "abstract" exercises even as it is tempting to treat them as such. They seek to be intensely practical and put forward new ways of practicing engagement, representation, and, thus, (planetary) politics (see also Duara, Chapter 7, this volume). Indeed, the most significant aspect of the relational perspectives is not (at least in my view) how they "theorize" the world as such, but rather the ways in which they ask us to view, experience, be, and "become" differently in our immediate experiences as well as through our "planetary entanglements."

What this all means for IR scholarship or for climate change is not straightforward to work out – the implications for politics or action are contested (as rebuttals of relational work in this book show; see, for example, Nau, Chapter 6). Yet, the challenge is that, instead of turning back to political ideologies that we have turned to for centuries, political ideologies implicated in the creation of the problems we are faced with in our relationship with the "natural world"[6] as well as in cross-cultural dialogue,[7] we can and should explore the difficult questions emerging from the relational revolution – in the natural and social sciences – in order to develop ways of engaging the "trouble" in the current order and with our conceptions of it.

This relational "end of the spectrum" has in the context of this project been described as "the jungle," and, as such, has been contrasted to the "gardens" or "parks" of more traditional ways of thinking and doing International Relations (Katzenstein, Chapter 10, this volume). There is something seemingly unruly, wild, and "unmanaged" about relational thinking and political practice. And, for others, this perspective appears "cuddly" and "naïve" in somehow assuming that we should love all others around us. Both conclusions, I hope to show, are too easy a response to the difficult questions raised by relational thinking. The relational

---

[6] This notion is used with great caution as it is precisely the notion of a "natural" and "social" world which relational perspectives call into question.

[7] Querejazu 2016; Qin 2018; Ling 2017.

perspectives are many and do not seek a uniform, singular truth. And they have multiple different challenges and questions to navigate themselves. They offer no panacea.

Yet, my belief, in line with Katzenstein's intuition, is that these kinds of perspectives should be explored and debated more in our field precisely because the alternative – to turn back to realism, liberalism, or socialism unreconstructed – also comes with problems in the condition we inhabit. Our ways of conceiving the international and what the focus of IR should be are implicated in a particular ecological and cosmological ordering of the world.[8] The relational perspectives then call on us instead to reimagine how we have historically come to constitute our conception of the world and to shift these imaginations to forms of politics which may seem "new," "radical," and "strange" to some western scholars. Yet, arguably relational qualities, practices, and thoughts, while more present in non-Western traditions, pervade the lives of "western" "individuals" too. As Grove puts it in Chapter 4, if we are all relationally processing in the world, relational thinking and negotiation is of relevance to all. Relational traditions pry open seemingly well-sealed liberal individuals or national communities, and reveal the "other aspects of ourselves," the porosity and comaking, the overlaps, the complex constitution of individuals and communities and species.[9]

In this chapter, I start by reviewing the ways in which authors in and around IR often frame climate and ecological challenges, including the increasing number of critics of IR's way of framing coexistence challenges on the planet. I then explicate what the so-called relational cosmology brings to the table, how it reorients our thinking and being, and, crucially, what introducing it does (in my view) to our orientation to the world (and, indeed, the idea of worldviews as an analytical category). In other words, I seek to explicate what operations of mind (and body!) are required to link relational cosmology to worldviews analysis. This (as Byrnes [Chapter 9] and Allan [Chapter 8] might also lead us to expect) includes reflection on big questions around secularism and religion, the nature of science, and the nature–society dichotomy, as well as the nature of politics and political community. Finally, I seek to show that moving to the conceptual register of relational cosmology entails a shift in how we do politics. While the political implications of relational thinking are not necessarily akin to the usual "policy implications" sought in the study of international politics, they are nevertheless of some import to how

---

[8] Kurki 2020; Burke et al. 2016.
[9] I sense this relational tone also in Barnett's humanist relationalist contribution to this book (Chapter 5).

political praxis can be reoriented in and around IR and in relation to questions of climate and environment.

3.1   Climate Change, Ecological Destruction, and the Problem of International Relations

In the last twenty years, environmental challenges have arisen from the sidelines of the social and natural sciences to present some of the central challenges for theoretical and practical sciences today. This has been precipitated by the materialization of a changing climate and environmental patterns, the communication of a new scientific consensus around challenges presented for human and nonhuman life within the next decades and centuries, and also certain shifts in power relations between human communities and also arguably between key human and nonhuman communities (e.g. farmers and bees). What Timothy Morton calls "hyperobjects" – climatic regimes, planetary circulations, ecosystems ("massively distributed in time and space relative to humans")[10] – are appearing on our horizons, but we do not know what to "do with them": while somehow implicated in our ability to act, and indeed our past actions, they are also not subject to human control but exceed them. They seem to challenge our very conceptions of how to "understand" and "control" the planet and processes on it. As Morton nicely reminds us, they are *"hyper* [in the sense of 'over', 'beyond', in excess] relative to worms, lemons, and ultraviolet rays, as well as humans."[11]

In this section I explore IR ways of attending to these challenges, first within traditional paradigms, and second amongst a series of critical scholars.

3.1.1   Responses to Climate and Environment

While the environment and its use has always stood at the heart of geopolitical origins of IR,[12] and while environmental concerns feature in realist as well as liberal frames in IR theory, the way in which these concerns are addressed reveals crucial aspects of the epistemic, ontological, and thus also political assumptions of these theories.

In realist theory, for example, the "environment" is treated primarily as a resource to be strategized about and utilized to ensure that a state meets its interests (or the interests of its human community). Classically, the realist school would focus on immediate security threats and thus dismiss

[10] Morton 2013: 1.   [11] Morton 2013: 2.   [12] Corry 2017.

climate and ecological change as secondary to the more immediate existential crises human communities face. Yet, this does not mean realists cannot take action on environmental and climate crises: as Sofer argues, "even a hard-nosed realist should support international cooperation on climate change. Due to climate change's impact as a "threat multiplier," the benefits of cooperation now outweigh the potential gap in relative gains between cooperating countries."[13] It is how this action is to be taken that is paramount: key actors on the environment are the state and the international (human communities) and politics involves their human interaction "on" the environment. The sphere of action is the "international." In other words the environment is seen as external to "human" communities' interests, strategies, and intentions. State survival, while dependent on resources, is an abstract problem of human decision-making. States, as human communities, are "lifted off" the planetary negotiations as they determine their own relations to each other and to the "environment."

A classical liberal perspective on environmental change works with similar assumptions, while being more encouraging of "international" negotiation between states and other human communities. Liberal concerns revolve around interdependence and the ways in which environmental risks travel across states (as human communities) necessitating cooperation. To address climate and environmental concerns, then, we must assess how institutional structures could work in creating more sustainable outcomes. Some say liberal democracies can do the work, others call for cosmopolitan arrangements: either way, states have a key role in responding to the moment of crisis presented by climate change – "our political moment," as Beardsworth calls it.[14]

At the heart of liberal approaches is an acceptance of not only states as a key institutional reference point, but also, fundamentally, the *separation of human institutions from the "environment" as a background to be controlled and managed.* To come through the climate challenge, "we" have to manage the environment correctly by redirecting human intentionality and incentive structures. This by and large means working with, but revising, current domestic and global institutional structures. Climate crisis is then ultimately a "human coordination problem," and in dealing with it is essential that we learn from what we have achieved in terms of institutional (re)structuring of global life so far. Rather than challenging the international order, climate change emphasizes the importance of maintaining it and working through it.

[13] Sofer 2015.   [14] See Beardsworth 2018; see also Ward 2008.

But what about the constructivists and critical theorists? Do they not give us useful new ways of thinking on the environment?

For sure. Constructivists call for more detailed engagement with the way in which we construct environmental problems and the discursive parameters of how we can shift how states or communities relate to the problem; on the other hand, critical theorists of various persuasions point to the limits of the underlying assumptions of such perspectives.[15] Governmentality scholars, for example, highlight the environment as a site of creation of liberal governmentality and state power,[16] while feminist political ecologists would call for greater attention to be paid to the ways in which we relate to the environment, via specific conceptions of the human and of the environment.[17] Environmental concerns are constructed, and "we" and our political communities (including their security interests) are constructed with them.

While interesting, here too arguably deeply humanist assumptions often play a key role: it is the discursive and normative construction by humans of the environment which concerns these thinkers. "Our" ideological and normative framings are key in how we come to and act toward the "environment," and new ways of doing politics on it depend on new social constructions among human actors. This is why normative entrepreneurship around environmental sustainability for example matters – domestically and in the international sphere.

This range of perspectives is interesting. Yet, there is arguably an implicit set of "worldviews" – if not a singular, clearly bounded "worldview" – reflected in many of these perspectives. Core assumptions of such could be described as follows.

First, at the heart of this broad worldview stands the idea of the "human," standing over the "environment." A distinction between culture and nature is foundational to much of the social sciences, including IR. As Latour puts it, there is a House of Humans/Politics and a House of Nature that stands at the heart of the modern Western scientific endeavor and political thought.[18] Even political ecologists have reproduced this division of human and nature: "if political ecology poses a problem it is not because it *finally* introduces nature into political preoccupations that had earlier been too exclusively oriented toward humans, it is because it *continues, alas, to use nature to abort politics.*"[19] How we think the human and the natural or the social and the environmental present deep challenges.

---

[15] See e.g. Litfin 1999.   [16] See e.g. Rutherford 2017.   [17] See e.g. Rocheleau 1996.
[18] Latour 2004 (emphasis original).   [19] Latour 2004: 19.

These assumptions are underpinned by even deeper assumptions about there being distinct "things" in the world which work against "backgrounds." Such Newtonian assumptions are fundamental to modern liberalism and realism, which perceive the world as constructed by "things" moving, self-willed and autonomous, but also arguably to many other schools of thought and our everyday language. Indeed, try and think about the world without things and language barriers soon force your mind back to habits of thought with a long legacy in western religious, cosmological, and scientific thought. Yet these assumptions too are particular: that is, framings of basic ontologies of the worlds of Buddhist, Andean, and South Pacific peoples[20] are not in line with these assumptions, but point to different, more relational, ways of framing the very basic orientations to the world and thus our "views on the world." There are not just different worldviews; there are families of worldviews with quite different orientations to substances and relations, the human and the nonhuman, nature and society.

But this is not all: at the heart of how we think the environment also arise deep questions around whose experiences frame the "international" and "global" challenges of environmental or climate change. Indeed, the international is a curious ontological notion in its wedding onto the world of a very particular humanist frame: politics on the planet involves the politics between human communities ("states").

Even the framing of the "global" reproduces this: when we address "global challenges," such as climate change, we are in need of a "universal" human response across political communities. The challenge of how to think the climate, then, is not just how to think common responses but how to think critically about how the international and the global, how human division and commonality, have been imagined. These ways of thinking have not only worked to deprive some human communities of land, rights, and response-ability, but also have embedded into the world a very particular framing of humans and nonhumans. Many of the apocalyptic narratives which drive "global" policy discourses even now have embedded within them racialized and racist assumptions ignorant of experiences of indigenous populations, for example.[21]

It is worth noting the role of these foundational "cosmological" understandings of the world that is at the heart of how we orient to environmental and climate politics (see also Allan, Chapter 8 in this volume, for discussion of cosmology and worldviews). These are sometimes hard to discern but are increasingly unpacked not only in IR[22] but also in the

---

[20] See e.g. Ling, 2017; Querejazu, 2016; Shilliam 2015.
[21] Mitchell and Chaudhury 2020.
[22] Allen 2018; Bain 2020; Kurki 2020; Zanotti 2018.

social and natural sciences more widely. They have also been pointed to by a series of important interventions around the Anthropocene, planet politics, and decolonial thought.

3.1.2   Anthropocene, Planet Politics, and Decoloniality

Although little has shifted in traditional IR vocabularies – or the world-view assumptions underpinning them – as a result of the rise of climate and ecological challenges, this is not the case in the social and natural sciences more widely. Indeed, the "paradoxes of the anthropocene" (arising from the increasing realization of human influence on hyperob-jects while seemingly lacking direct control over them) have been dis-cussed at length in both the natural and social sciences and also increasingly in critical IR in the last decades.[23] Indeed, in recent years there have been many calls in the field for a radical reorientation of the conceptual premises and empirical foci of "International Relations."

Thus, for example, in 2016 a collective of IR scholars released a paper that called for a new turn in IR: a turn toward so-called "planet politics."[24] This manifesto, first, reflected the wider calls in the human-ities and social and natural sciences for scientific disciplines to "deal with" the Anthropocene: the increasing realization of humans" role in structur-ing planetary relations, which also has precipitated calls for overcoming classical notions of "humanhood" as well as the "environment."

Second, this manifesto specifically challenged IR for its fundamental inability to deal with the "social nature" it is implicated in: the embed-dedness of our patterns of international politics, our conceptions of the world and its key actors and all aspects of human life in what used to look to us like an external nonhuman "nature" must be reckoned with, both in policy and in "consciousness" of humans facing ecological disasters around them.

The planet politics manifesto has been critiqued from various angles: for being too conservative and liberal cosmopolitan,[25] for being unclear in meaning,[26] and for how debate around it has been conducted.[27] Yet, nevertheless it indicates an important challenge in IR: that we are coming to the limits of the classical political imaginations on which we have built our ways of dealing with "coexistence challenges" in IR.

Thus, whether it is attempts to build new kinds of democratic orders – a geopolitan democracy,[28] for example – or imaginations of posthuman

---

[23] For a summary of debates on the Anthropocene in IR, see e.g. Harrington 2016.
[24] Burke et al. 2016.   [25] Chandler et al, 2017.   [26] Corry 2020.   [27] Conway 2020.
[28] Eckersley 2017.

politics in complex systems,[29] change is afoot in the study of IR to realign the discipline's conceptual systems and political responses with "planetary realities," as Burke et al would have it.[30] These critics argue that we must look "elsewhere" than the state and the international system to rethink the current order, potential politics, and communities that matter in negotiating the "planetary real."

It follows that not only realism and liberalism but also classical (humanist) traditions of constructivism and critical theory have been left far behind as new types of relationalism have been suggested for IR. At the center of the concern of relational thinkers has been rethinking, as Fishel puts it, "the ways in which we create ourselves, both as individuals and as humans, beyond how the state predefines our identities as citizens."[31] Drawing on critical humanism and posthumanism, analysts have sought to develop ways to think about the human as a historical construction, thus also developing a concern for the way in which the nonhuman has been relegated to a background to "human action" conceived as the center-ground of politics and international relations.[32] Rafi Youatt's important book shows to us how interspecies politics functions in world politics as we know it: just because we have delimited our capacity to understand how politics works does not mean interspecies politics do not already shape our world order and states. We must take on the bias that "species should be a central barrier to who can be part of global politics."[33]

On the other hand, relatedly, building on alternative cosmologies, some relational thinkers have called for a simultaneous turn toward non-Western ideological and cultural sources of rethinking capitalism, communities, and the international.[34] They have argued for engagement with new and old forms of relationalism often not seen from within Western ideological and cultural assumptions wedded to rationalism and individualism.[35]

These kinds of interventions have been termed a "relational turn" in the field.[36] The oncoming ecological changes, alongside attempts to decolonize the social and natural sciences, have brought about a need to think through, far more carefully, how IR scholars have related to the world through very specific conceptual categories. IR has inherited its conceptual bases from specific (often European) cosmologies and

---

[29] Cudworth and Hobden 2011, 2017.   [30] Burke et al. 2016.   [31] Fishel 2017: 11.
[32] Cudworth and Hobden 2011, 2013, 2017; Cudworth, Hobden, and Kavalski, 2018.
[33] Youatt 2020: 4.
[34] Querejazu 2016; Kavalski 2018; Duara 2015; Qin 2018; Shilliam 2015.
[35] Qin 2018.   [36] Kavalski 2018, 2

theological notions, notions later embedded in seemingly secular conceptual order and also disseminated around the world through colonialism. [37]

Relational approaches are of great significance as we tackle the current human and nonhuman predicaments. They challenge more classical ways of conceiving of ecological negotiations in the field of IR, but also crucially start to open up important questions around geopolitical power in knowledge constructions, the nature of science, the relationship between sciences and secularism, and also questions around who make up the "political communities" or "negotiations" that matter. I find them persuasive also because they tap into and question a whole range of underlying assumptions, cosmologies, and worldviews, reflected in the more classical paradigms of IR.

With this in mind, I explore one particular relational frame implicated in the wider relational turn to discern its impacts for reflections on worldviews in IR and ultimately (in Section 3.3) for reorientation of how we might engage questions around environmental and climate politics.

3.2 Relations in a Relational Universe

Instead of trying to reflect the full scope of relational thought in a short chapter, I focus on the implications of relational cosmology, a perspective which I have been working with for some five years now and which (to my mind) expresses relational principles and what is at stake in them rather clearly and also converses with other relational perspectives in interesting way.[38] My focus here is to bring out the core assumptions of relational cosmology and to relate them to the discussion of worldviews and IR theory.

3.2.1 Relational Cosmology

Relational cosmology is developed by Lee Smolin, in conjunction with other physicists such as Carlo Rovelli but also recently, interestingly, in cooperation with social theorists such as Roberto Mangabeira Unger. The core principles of relational cosmology as developed by Smolin come through in texts such as *The Life of the Cosmos* (1997), *Three Roads to Quantum Gravity* (2000), *The Trouble with Physics* (2008), *Time Reborn* (2013), and the coauthored *The Singular Universe* (2015).

---

[37] Bain 2020; Allan 2018; Mitchell 2014; Kurki 2020; Kurki, 2021.
[38] This is developed elsewhere in more detail in Kurki 2020.

Relational cosmology's basic claim is that sciences are telling us to shift our background assumptions, if you like our foundational worldviews or conceptual bases, in some fundamental ways. We must give up on "God's eye views" on the world and get to grips with the thoroughly relational nature of the universe and of us as "situated" knowers within its relationalities. Crucially, this shift is precipitated by experimental and empirical findings of the natural sciences. In the first instance, this arises from relational cosmologists' interest in the theory of general relativity and their development of a specific theory of quantum gravity: Loop Quantum Gravity (LQG). These physical theories, which Smolin and Rovelli are both involved in developing, require, for them, certain shifts in our conceptual universes. The physical theories call on us to "think differently" about "what there is" in the universe.

Crucially, for them, scientific findings are "screaming" for us to realize, and to work through, the fact that there really are no such things as things or backgrounds in the universe. Indeed, space itself is not a background in which things move, but part of the network of relationships in the universe. The loops that make space are "linked to each other, forming a network of relations which weaves the texture of space, like rings of a finely woven immense chain mail."[39] Crucially, these loops are not "anywhere" in space: "they are themselves the space ... the world seems to be less about objects than about interactive relationships."[40]

It follows that what we need to grapple with in the sciences is the need for a thoroughgoing relational, processual understanding of the universe. All "things" and "backgrounds," as we would have it in our everyday discourse derived from Newtonian conceptions of space, are in fact relational processes in the process of relating.[41] Relational cosmology is an extension of what it means to think relationally and has important implications also for the social sciences, for "one of the things that cannot exist outside the universe [and its relations] is ourselves."[42] As Smolin puts it:

relativity and quantum theory each tell us this is not how the world is. They tell us – no, scream at us – that our world is a history of processes. Motion and change are primary. Nothing *is*, except in a very approximate and temporary sense. How something is, or what its state is, is an illusion.[43]

The challenge, then, is how do we think relationally, and how do we follow through with the implications of thoroughgoing relationality? How

---

[39] Rovelli 2014: 41.   [40] Rovelli 2014: 41.   [41] See ch. 4 and 5 in Kurki 2020.
[42] Smolin 2000: 26.   [43] Smolin 2000: 53 (emphasis in original).

do we think without Newtonian configuration space populated by things moving against backgrounds?

With some difficulty. How do we know when the world around us can only be known in ways that are inevitably situated in relations? If nothing in the universe is outside of relational unfolding of the universe – not even the scientists or the laws of the universe, which are also made relationally – how do we think the sciences or the social sciences? This is a challenging situation. As Smolin puts it, "[i]t is not easy to find the right language to use to talk about the world if one really believes that the notion of reality depends on the context of the person who does the talking."[44]

The relational revolution in the sciences extends across the social and natural sciences, and all the sciences, for Smolin, are engaged in a shift of worldview, from a substantialist, Newtonian view toward a processual, relational relative view. A lot is implicated in such a shift. And such a shift has many important implications because a lot is implicated in the shift. Indeed, inhabiting this worldview takes on all kinds of other categories, divisions, and dichotomies that we often work with.

There are at least five key things implicated in such a shift. We need to consider issues with: 1) secularism and religion and their complex relationships in defining conceptual tools; 2) affect and (re)enchantment of the world and science; 3) the categories of human and nonhuman, natural and social; 4) science and democracy, and 5) our conceptions and practices of politics.

1 Science: Not Simply Secular One of the key aspects of relational cosmology and the perspectives of the relational turn more widely is that they necessarily open up questions around religion, secularism, and, indeed, reason and affect in how we engage the world (see 2: Affect: Knowing and Becoming).

This is because at the heart of the critique is a realization of, and, at the same time, a certain discomfort with, (Christian) religious dogmas as they are played out in much of our conceptual systems. Relational cosmology both notices the role of religious thought in science and seeks to point to how this also limits how we can think. It follows that doing science also necessitates thinking on legacies of religion. The comfortable distinction of secularism and religion, then, is not possible within this frame (see also discussions in Byrnes, Chapter 9, this volume).

These concerns come out in different ways. For Smolin, for example, the key concern is the implicit Christian commitments in physical sciences: the ways in which assumptions about Laws of Physics or Nature

---

[44] Smolin 2000: 46.

replay certain unthinkingly religious commitments which prevent us from following through conceptually what empirical findings are telling us. For Carlo Rovelli, the concern is about the inability of man to see itself as part of nature due to a Christian legacy of seeing humans as "lifted" above nature.[45]

Interestingly, these concerns are closely tied up with the interest in political theology in the field of IR.[46] Indeed, both relational cosmology and recent literatures in the field of political theology point to a concern with the hidden religiosity attached to secular humanism and its conceptual basis. Secularism itself is being unpacked for its religious commitments and its particular versions of humanism.[47] The implication is that IR and our own ways of conceiving the world must be probed for their religious undertones, whether in our conceptions of autonomous humans, cosmological origins of notions of anarchy, or improvement or the commitments to the ideas of "laws of nature."

2   Affect: Knowing and Becoming   The foregoing discussion has important implications also for how we try to know, or indeed for the constitution of, "reason." Reason is not disenchanted within this frame, and, strangely, at stake in how we know is not just how we know: it is also how we "are." That is, to know is also to be, to become, in a particular way in and of the world. Indeed, knowing through reason is a particular way of materializing the world, not a universal manifestation of some abstract principles.

As such, to "know" is affective, as well as materially productive of the world's unfolding. That is, we do not simply know through reason, but are materially embodied in the world, which also "cuts" on us.

We are in a very uncomfortable sense not just on the world, trying to know it, but also of it and cutting into it with our concepts and acts. This means that we are never engaged in just knowing about others or their worldviews "in abstract"; we are also ourselves implicated in the world(s) analyzed, and these worlds are dynamic and multiple, partially made up of how we "cut" the world, how we materialize it through our thoughts or actions.

This also pertains to the ways of being of scientists or IR scholars: they are also made of the world's materializations and produce them; they are not "above" them. And scientific knowledges and practices also produce or "cut" the relationalities of the world in specific ways.[48]

---

[45] Rovelli 2014.   [46] Bain 2020; Pasha 2018.   [47] See e.g. Taylor 2008; Mitchell 2014.
[48] See e.g. Barad 2007.

3   The Human and the Nonhuman Agency: Porosity   In the same sense that complexity theorists and posthumanists argue that the modern human is a kind of an invention or a production of relatively recent history with its origins in theological notions of man as well as particular colonial inventions of "humanity," the relational cosmologists allow us to open up or keep looser the idea of the human and its conceptual counterpart, the nonhuman.[49] The idea of the human as "lifted" from its environment, as a manager of its ecology, is a very particular production of life, coincidental with certain religious traditions but also of the rise of agricultural and industrial societies.

From a relational point of view this is not the essence of "the" "human": the human is a processual creation made in relations to and by creating "others," human and nonhuman. When we realize this we come to see that the human is not autonomous but part of a rich set of voices and lifeforms. In the relational universe live, then, not only humans but also the nonhumans which they are entangled with.

Crucially, in this mesh we, "the humans" and others are "strange" in Morton's sense[50] – that is, never fully capturable, partly because "we" are never fully "autonomous"; we are made relationally and know situatedly from relations. That is, the notions of sovereignty of the individual and the state, and indeed of *any* object, is in question in this perspective. There are no beings, there are only relational processes: symbionts relationally processing "across" each other.

In a relational universe, then, we must embrace the "strangeness" required to think and to be, and we see the limits of the Cartesian need to control (and discipline) the human and the nonhuman. And we see the many dialogues which shoot across the "levels of analysis" (natural and social sciences) and dichotomies (nature, society) that structure modern conceptions of the human, of agency, and of the political.

As such, agency, or even prioritization of questions of agency, is not a central concern of this perspective; rather, it is to think through distributed and shared agencies (if that is what one still wishes to call them).

4   Science as Community in Cosmos   The foregoing assumptions also have implications for how we think about science. For Smolin, much like for many posthumanists, science is not abstracted from the world. It is part of becoming, of affective being in the world. What this means is that we do not have clear-cut criteria for good or bad knowledge, much as postpositivists always suspected but now embrace as a key cornerstone of scientific approach itself.

---

[49] Developed in Kurki 2020, ch 5.   [50] Morton 2010.

In this view, knowledge itself is not just knowledge. Instead, curiously, science is more like democracy: it is about openness to and openness about what we assume, think, explore, and interact with. And it is about making relations, cutting the world.

Science is, as Smolin puts it, about a kind of "democratic" being and becoming in the cosmos. It is about probing and thus relating, and rethinking relations and communities that matter. Science is part of the making of a community of relational being becoming the relational cosmos. Science in this perspective, then, is not defined by a "method." As Unger and Smolin put it, "There is no scientific method, science is fundamentally defined as a collection of ethical communities."[51]

5   Conceptions of Politics   Crucially, what is shifted here too are views on politics and what and who count as political agents. There is no classical distinction here between human polities and those polities that do not matter. Communities cross boundaries of "human." This means that in a very real sense we can also think about representing and coexisting in communities with nonhumans, animals, vegetables, and minerals. Or, as Youatt so powerfully puts it, we must start to call into question the "representation of nonhuman life through human speech as a sole point of entry for nonhuman species into the sphere of the political."[52]

How we gather these communities together, and how we process politics without abstracted special human communities, is an intense focus of theoretical and practical research. How do we compose the universe? How do we converse? How do we do democracy when we are more than human?

This is all very well, you might say, but what has this to do with the worldviews frame of this book?

3.2.2   Implications for "Worldviews"

There are (at least) three key implications for the discussion in this book of worldviews – both everyday worldviews and scientific worldviews:
1. *Non-Newtonian alternatives.* There is a kind of (shifted, non-Cartesian, non-Newtonian) worldview reflected in this frame and it appears it challenges a different kind of orientation: a more substantialist orientation with things and agents. It is also a worldview that is seen as part of a much wider, and more varied, relational revolution in arts and the humanities, as well as the sciences. Indeed, Smolin explicitly sees his work as part of a wider relational revolution expressed across western

---

[51] Unger and Smolin, 2015: 363.   [52] Youatt 2020, 4.

culture and science and also beyond it. An interesting aspect of relational cosmology has been its ability to recognize the limits of "western" science and the legitimacy of varied ways of knowing from outside
of the "rationalist" scientific frame. This is in part because of its much
wider understanding of science as situated becoming in relations.

It is then interesting, as Katzenstein suggests, to point to a kind of
a continuum of worldviews from this perspective. Relational cosmology does also suggest that there is a difference between this perspective
and atomist Newtonian ones. And it suggests a more systematic shift
from certain more substantantialist orientations that still play a key
role in the sciences and social sciences such as IR (as well as in
everyday life) to more relational understandings of the world, with
important consequences for our conceptual frames as well as our
engagements with the world.

2. *However, there is a multiplicitous alternative.* It follows that from this
perspective we should be attuned to worldviews and the wide (and
widening?) spectra of them. And we should trace them across communities and across time.

Crucially, within this frame worldviews *can never be understood in
a singular frame.* In this perspective no view, no view of the world, is
ever singular or alone – because no view is lifted "above" the relations
which make it. Even science is based on situated knowledge.

This is not all. All worldviews are also relationally linked. There are
no uniform, autonomous worldviews; there are always just many situated, relationally connected worldviews. Thus, the world, being, and
becoming within it is always polyphonic in speaking, being, and cutting
into the world, and worldviews from this perspective then also thus are
always smeared across each other. That is, they are not pure, or separated, but cut into each other. In Ling's terms, even oppositional worldviews are made of each other; they are off each other relationally.[53] It is
recording this dance, being attentive to the relationalities, which is the
challenge of engaging with worldviews in a relational frame. And this is
in part why they are so interesting to study.

3. *Worlds and Worldviews.* There is another sense in which worldviews"
frames are challenged or pushed by this perspective. As is emphasized
by the so-called ontological-turn authors,[54] worldviews here emerge
less as "views on the world" and more like what we might call "lifeways" or "worlds." That is, since the world does not exist "out there"
to be viewed from the point of view of the special human, and since the
nonhuman makes the human, worldviews too are more like relational

---

[53] Ling 2017.   [54] See e.g. Blaney and Tickner 2017.

paths in the world. They are not "of us" humans but made in relational assemblages with nonhumans. And nonhumans also make of us, our thoughts, frames, relations. Even when we narrate them as others they are in fact in and of relations with us.

Thus, I think we also come to be critical of the "worldviews" frame, for possibly itself embodying certain humanist predilections which may deny some of the ways of thinking through and being "relationally." In this context, exploring the arguments of pluriverse theorists is interesting. They ask us to get beyond thinking about the world as consisting of multiple viewpoints, or perspectives, and to start thinking in terms of multiple worlds, literally: multiple sometimes related worlds of being. As Viveiros de Castro emphasizes, we are not just concerned with multiple "imaginary ways of seeing the world, but real worlds that are being seen."[55] This also implicates our affect, bodies, in knowing – for, literally, how we know is also implicated in our bodily ways of traversing and experiencing.

The challenge, then, is how to deal with multiple worlds without erasing worlds – in thought and action. How do plural lifeways negotiate and collaborate on the planet? While I leave a full explication of this line of thought for another occasion, I think is interesting, potentially, in shifting questions around how we come to questions around worldviews, which may be productive for a project such as this to explore. But what, the reader may ask (and some of the authors in this book have pointedly asked me throughout this project!), are the supposedly concrete, practical implications of this kind of an orientation for where we started: concern around climate and environmental politics?

3.3   Politically Practical, But in a "Strange Way"

> How can we best use our research to stem the tide of ruination? . . . Our hope is that [paying better attention] to overlaid arrangements of human and non-human living spaces . . . will allow us to stand up to the constant barrage of messages asking us to forget – that is, to allow a few private owners and public officials with their eyes focused on short-term gains to pretend that environmental devastation does not exist . . . To survive we need to re-learn multiple forms of curiosity. Curiosity is an attunement to multispecies entanglement, complexity and the shimmer all around us.[56]

First encounters in IR circles with the kind of relational perspectives explored herein often generate responses such as: What does this

---

[55] Viveiros de Castro 2004: 11.   [56] Tsing, Swanson, Gan, and Bubandt 2017: G1, G11.

contribute to *real* resolution of interstate conflict around climate change contributions (requiring, ultimately, state cooperation internationally and human action domestically)? In ignoring basic building blocks of "how we do politics" (between individuals, in states, and on the international stage), does it not in fact undermine our ability to address climate catastrophe? How can we have practice "policy response" in a relational mesh?

The relational perspective examined here, and relational perspectives more widely,[57] do not come to IR or practical politics with disinterest. They come to it with a sense of deep disappointment and a certain level of anger and frustration about how our ways of doing and knowing international politics reproduce ways of "allowing" us to forget about how we must and could shift ways of doing politics. Relational perspectives, then, do not come to IR with a hope for an "invitation" into the IR parlor-game, but with a call for different kinds of dances altogether.

These new dances are not uninterested in the world, nor are they "theoretical," "utopian," or "impractical"; yet, they pull on our sensibilities, ways of being, and lifeways in some strange and uncomfortable ways. If you like, they pull us into the world differently; and encourage us to "commit" to world(s) around us differently. Crucially, within this (set of) worldview(s) who the communities are that matter are shifted, quite fundamentally, and, as a result, so are negotiating sites and modalities of politics. Instead of doing global governance of the humans and for the humans, engagement with politics might *also* entail immersion into marine communities or thinking with trees. And engagement with "humans" here too becomes less about modeling negotiations between abstract, autonomous humans and more about exploring various ways in which "humans" are made and cut the world around them, and not only as (abstract, universal) humans but also as "more-than-humans" (porously processing in mesh).

A couple of points, then, could be noted about "politics" in such a context.

- There is, for sure, interest in *politics beyond states, the international, and the global,* but for somewhat different reasons from classical liberal scholars, say. In this frame, all states, individuals, and communities are porous and worldviews are porous too. Because every "thing" is made in relational processes, they are to be understood as part of relational processes shaped far and wide. Crucially, then, to do "politics" in such a context is not to represent "oneself" or one's "state" – these constructs are just one way to cut the world politically. Rather, the

[57] See e.g. Grove 2019; Kavalski 2018.

aim is to "loosen" actors (at the boundaries) to understand cobeing, entanglement, and conegotiation across "beings," actors, and species. In terms of climate and environment politics this means, for example, that state politics and global responses are not the be-all and end-all of "political" negotiation. Rather, attempts to understand and conduct diplomacy with more-than-human humans and, crucially, plants, animals, and ecosystems becomes a central aspect of politics. Politics is not "only-human." One way of describing this is as a form of *planetary politics*: a process of making kin and doing diplomacy in more-than-human worlds. Or we can understand it as Youatt calls it: as interspecies politics.[58] In this frame we recognize that we must and do negotiate with, on a daily basis, bacteria, fish, and trees as well as humans. They "think" and they "act"; and we represent them even at present, but often badly: we can learn to represent them and ourselves and our symbiotic relations better. As Dutch activists engaged in the Embassy of the North Sea point out, it is difficult but not impossible to learn to represent algae, water, and fish communities.

- Yet, this planetary or interspecies politics – also of interest in different ways for Duara and Grove (Chapters 7 and 4, this volume) – is not "one" and is engaged from different traditions of thought, culturally and in terms of experiences of natural world. Such politics, then, comes with critical sensibility about "crisis environmentalism"[59] or the "planet talking" for us – the environment "dictating" matters[60]. This is in part because the politics of how the "environment" is created, and how the "human" (only) also emerges from this, are key to work through and become animated about in this view. *There is an intense interest in the politics of the human and the nonhuman.* How some migrant populations are made as "less than human," and how mass slaughter of animals is facilitated by constructions of "lifted" humanity, are intense focal points of negotiation politically. These constructions work at the international level, but they are also at play in our daily negotiations.

- As such, there is also a wariness of *"politics" of control, panic, and management*. Relational perspectives point out that much of western political imaginations – including climate change politics – is tied up with forms of control and, simultaneously, many apocalyptic visions of "threats" to humanity (or some humans) and their preferred notions of autonomy and agency. From this perspective, the need to control and manage "the earth" as part of climate change politics is seen as part of the problem, rather than a solution. This does not mean we should not

---

[58] Youatt 2020.   [59] Youatt 2020.
[60] See critique of Burke et al. by Chandler et al. 2017.

take political action on climate change, but it does mean that this action cannot be taken simply to reproduce, in a panic, the same politics of control which are in part to blame for where we have ended up (a deeply hierarchical order of [some humans'] control). These perspectives agree with decolonial and critical perspectives in recognizing that "modern politics" and "international politics" have been not just about representation or coordination only but also, deeply, about discipline, control, and order for some over others. We must therefore watch out for what forms of politics we encourage – politics of negotiation or politics of control – and pay attention to when the one starts to bleed into the other. Implicated in these questions are also questions of colonialism, racism, and species-solipsism.

These kinds of reorientations to politics, and there may be others, may mean different things to different communities in different relational perspectives. For me, "personally" they have provoked important changes in concrete political practice. For example, I have ceased to look to the international order for the "solutions" and have redirected my political action to alternative forms of local and global attempts to understand and represent humans and nonhumans. My academic politics too today revolves around teaching how we might think, "feel," and act differently, thinking carefully with toads, spiders, and plants. Yes, we read "plant theory" in my MA class on the future of IR! And I am pleased my students going into the practice of "classical" politics have written their essays on political leadership of matriarch elephants or how to re-relate to nonhuman life through music. I think their engagement with the world, experientially and politically, has shifted, as has mine, through exposure to relational ways of "loosening" ourselves into the world – even if these political negotiations do not at once overturn the international order and all the cosmological baggage (of classical humanism) it comes with.

Will such politics "save us"? Perhaps not. Indeed, these kinds of perspectives also throw up many difficult questions on which much more reflection is needed. Thus, is relationalism necessarily a good thing, or does relationality mean that "machines," "structures," and "ecologies" can structure our fate to such an extent as to destroy any hope for emancipatory politics?[61] Is there an ethics of relational thinking, and what does it consist of?[62] And how do we assess political action if it is situated and context specific? What happens to structural or collective responses? Are we driven to some sort of weird individualism? What is it

---

[61] Grove implies many important challenges in this regard.
[62] These have been interestingly developed by Zanotti 2018 and Barad 2007, for example.

to represent beyond the human voice? Who are communities if there are no "I"s or "we"s?

These and many other important questions remain unanswered, or different responses to them are being developed. But they are being asked, seriously, and being explored, seriously. This, if nothing else, is evidence of the significant kind of shift in worldviews that is ongoing in the field of IR, along with many others in the context of the relational revolution.

3.4   Conclusion: Of Jungles, Parks, and Cities?

Those who exist in a Newtonian world of things and their patterns and look for order – in the gardens of IR – may not see this kind of intervention as productive. And yet, within the "ruins" of ecological and human chaos we are facing, it is probably best not to pretend that IR or global power management has succeeded in managing these issues. Perhaps we should, as Grove argues, call out the "old white men [who] still strut around the halls of America's best institutions as if they saved us from the Cold War, even as the planet crumbles under the weight of their failed imperial dreams."[63] In the real world there is trouble, much trouble, and we need to stay with the trouble, as Haraway would have it.[64] In a relational universe, perhaps more productive than anything that reproduces the failing orderly IR, with its American hegemony, its colonial impulses, its stubborn state-centrism, its inherent liberal individualism, its alliance with capitalism, is to learn to let go of the special discipline, of the failed paradigms for politics, of the insistent humanism of the social sciences and IR. And we should let go of the measures of success and relevance of those working to a providential plan for human redemption, eventually.

I'm persuaded by the call that we need to get more real. And getting real means also getting real about which kinds of worldviews, or orientations to being in the world, we work with. Relational revolution is here, global ecological collapse is here; "humanity" (as an imagined whole) was never saved and has not saved the world. How do we reckon with this?

The aim of relational thinking is to try to process in and coexist with the world and its rich, real participants, and figure out less brutal ways of living, for more actors. It does not aim to be policy relevant for the "killing machines"[65] of lifeways, cosmologies, and politics that many of our states, democracies, and economic orders are. What we need to "get with" in a relational perspective, then, is a sense of "letting go" of these

---

[63] Grove 2019: 21.   [64] Haraway 2016.   [65] Grove 2019.

orientation points. This letting go is not to give up on politics or community or diplomacy, but it is to give up on imagining political or social
orders as a park, carefully managed, ordered, and eradicating of ecologies
of relationalities.

The spatial metaphor Smolin prefers for a relational form of life in the
universe is a "city."[66] For him, a city is a perfect example of a relational
unfolding of multiplicities of relations. It is not one "thing"; we don't
know where its "borders" are; it is smeared across humans, nonhumans,
and technology and has roots in the rural and the global all at the same
time. States are also smeared, and so are we. To think like this is to let go
of ontological categories that are fixed – a notion of relations with definitions, but it is to gain a way of knowing and being in the world which is
interesting and embedded in the world. In this world, you are made and
you are cutting across others as we speak. And you explore, curiously, the
relations which make you, but which you can never fully capture. Political
being and intra-action is not between defined beings with interests, but
"collaboration across difference"[67] in relations.

It follows that climate change is so many other things than a climate
change problem to be solved by humans in the international politics of the
humans. In a relational worldview it is a process of negotiation of many
actors and relations. It is of the "mesh," and not to be easily tamed or
tackled in a "park" or a "garden." It is a mess of diverse beings cohabiting,
battling for space, transforming and taking over, never uniform, never
singular, never nondynamic or nonlinear. Thus is also world politics.
Relational IR then too is "doutblessly messy," as Kavalski would have
it.[68] That's not a "problem" if the world is also a mess.

What is required in this mess/mesh is constant wariness of the habits of
thought that simplify too much: simplify what it is to think and act
politically, simplify what it is to think and act globally, simplify what it is
to think and act scientifically. And from this perspective what is needed is
fewer new total single global visions – a worldview; rather, what is needed
is "multiplying viewpoints so as to complicate all "provincial" or "closed"
views with new variants."[69]

Thinking carefully on worldviews, then, surely is key in this process.
But we also perhaps need to think on limitations of how we perceive
worldviews. Whose views? Whose worlds? How do worldviews collaborate, conflict, and cohabit? In a relational universe, the key challenge of the
social sciences, and of IR, is to adjust to this inherent and constant
difficulty and also to the limitations of our thought and practice.
Engaging in politics in a relational universe does, then, involve

[66] Smolin 1997.   [67] Tsing 2015.   [68] Kavalski 2018: 101.   [69] Latour 2018: 13.

a different way of engaging uncertainty, as Katzenstein proposes in the introduction. Paraphrasing Morton, engaging politics in a relational universe is "like knowing, but more like letting be known. It is something like coexisting. It is like becoming accustomed to something strange, yet it is also becoming accustomed to strangeness that doesn't become less strange through acclimation."[70]

Bibliography

Allan, Bentley. 2018. *Scientific Cosmology and International Orders*. Cambridge: Cambridge University Press.

Bain, William. 2020. *Political Theology of International Order*. Oxford: Oxford University Press.

Beardsworth, Richard. 2018. "Our Political Moment: Political Responsibility and Leadership in a Globalized, Fragmented Age," *International Relations* 32, 4: 391–40.

Blaney, D. L. and A. B. Tickner. 2017. "Worlding, Ontological Politics and the Possibility of a Decolonial IR," *Millennium* 45, 3: 293–311.

Burke, Anthony, Stefanie Fishel, Audra Mitchell, Simon Dalby, and Daniel Levine. 2016. "Planet Politics: a Manifesto from the end of IR," *Millennium: Journal of International Studies* 44, 3: 499–523.

Chandler, David, Erika Cudworth, and Stephen Hobden. 2017. "Anthropocene, Capitalocene and Liberal Cosmopolitan IR: A Response to Burke et al.'s 'Planet Politics'," *Millennium: Journal of International Studies* 46, 2: 190–208

Conway, Philip. 2020. "On the Way to Planet Politics: From Disciplinary Demise to Cosmopolitical Coordination," *International Relations* 34, 2: 157–179.

Corry, Olaf. 2017. "The 'Nature' of International Relations: From Geopolitics to the Anthropocene." In *Reflections on the Posthuman in International Relations*. E-International Relations Publishing. Available at: www.e-ir.info/publication/reflections-on-the-posthuman-in-international-relations/.

Corry, Olaf. 2020. "Nature and the International: Towards a Materialist Understanding of Multiplicity," *Globalizations* 17, 3: 419–35.

Cudworth, Erika and Stephen Hobden. 2011. *Posthuman International Relations: Complexity, Ecologism and Global Politics*. London: Zed.

Cudworth, Erika and Stephen Hobden. 2013. "Complexity, Ecologism, and Posthuman Politics," *Review of International Studies* 39, 3: 643–64.

Cudworth, Erika and Stephen Hobden. 2017. *The Emancipatory Project of Posthumanism*. London: Routledge.

Cudworth, Erika, Stephen Hobden, and Emilian Kavalski, eds. 2018. *Posthuman Dialogues in International Relations*. London: Routledge.

Duara, Prasenjit. 2015. *The Crisis of Global Modernity: Asian Traditions and Sustainable Future*. Cambridge: Cambridge University Press.

---

[70] Morton 2010: 5.

Eckersley, Robyn. 2017. "Geopolitan Democracy in the Anthropocene," *Political Studies* 65, 4: 983–99.

Fishel, Stefanie. 2017. *The Microbial State: Global Thriving and the Body Politic.* Minneapolis: University of Minnesota Press.

Grove, Jairus. 2019. *Savage Ecology: War and Geoolitics at the End of the World.* Durham, NC: Duke University Press.

Haraway, Donna. 2016. *Staying with Trouble: Making Kin in the Chthulucene.* London: Duke University Press.

Harrington, Cameron. 2016. "Ends of the World: International Relations and the Anthropocene," *Millennium* 44, 3: 478–98

Kavalski, Emilian. 2012. "Waking IR up from its 'Deep Newtonian Slumber'," *Millennium* 41, 1: 137–50

Kavalski, Emilian. 2018. *The Guangxi of International Theory.* London: Routledge.

Kurki, Milja. 2020. *International Relations in a Relational Universe.* Oxford: Oxford University Press.

Kurki, Milja. 2021. "Relational Revolution and Relationality in IR: New Conversations," *Review of International Studies.* E-pub ahead of print. Available at: https://doi.org/10.1017/S0260210521000127.

Latour, Bruno. 2004. *The Politics of Nature.* Cambridge, MA: Harvard University Press.

Latour, Bruno. 2018. *Down to Earth: Politics in the New Climatic Regime.* Cambridge: Polity.

Leakey, Richard and Roger Lewin. 1996. *The Sixth Extinction: Biodiversity and its Survival.* London: Weidenfeld and Nicholson.

Ling, L.H.M. 2013. *The Dao of World Politics. Towards a Post-Westphalian, Wordlist International Relations.* London: Routledge.

Ling, Lily. 2017. "Don't Flatter Yourself: World Politics as We Know It is Changing and So Must Disciplinary IR," in Synne Dyvik, Jan Selby, and Rorden Wilkinson (eds). *What's the Point of International Relations?* London: Routledge, pp. 135–46.

Litfin, Karen. 1999. "Constructing Environmental Security and Ecological Interdependence," *Global Governance* 5: 359–77.

Mitchell, Audra. 2014. *International Intervention in a Secular Age: Re-enchanting Humanity?* London: Routledge.

Mitchell, Audra. 2017. "Is IR Going Extinct?" *European Journal of International Relations* 23, 1: 2–35.

Mitchell, Audra and Aadita Chaudhury. 2020. "Worlding Beyond the 'End of the World': White Apocalyptic Visions and BIPOC Futurisms," *International Relations* 34, 3: 309–32.

Morton, Timothy. 2010. *The Ecological Thought.* Boston, MA: Harvard University Press.

Morton, Timothy. 2013. *Hyperobjects: Philosophy and Ecology after the End of the World.* London: University of Minnesota Press.

Pasha, Mustapha Kamal. 2018. "Beyond the "Religious Turn": International Relations as Political Theology," in A. Gofas, I. Hamati-Ataya, and N. Onuf, eds., *The Sage Handbook of the History, Philosophy and Sociology of International Relations.* New York: SAGE Publishing, pp. 106–21.

Qin, Yaqing. 2016. "A Relational Theory of World Politics," *International Studies Perspectives* 18, 1: 22–47.

Qin, Yaqing. 2018. *A Relational Theory of World Politics*. Cambridge: Cambridge University Press.

Querejazu, Amaya. 2016. "Encountering the Pluriverse: Looking for Alternatives in Other Worlds" *Revista Brasileira de Política Internacional* 59, 2: https://doi.org/10.1590/0034-7329201600207.

Rocheleau, Dianne. 1996. *Feminist Political Ecology: Global Issues and Local Experiences*. Abingdon: Routledge.

Rovelli, Carlo. 2014. *Seven Brief Lessons on Physics*. London: Penguin.

Rovelli, Carlo. 2016. *Reality is Not What It Seems. The Journey to Quantum Gravity*. Trans. by S. Carnell and E. Segre. London: Allen Lane.

Rutherford, Stephanie. 2017. "Environmentality and Green Governmentality," in D. Richardson, N. Castree, M.F. Goodchild, A. Kobayashi, W. Liu, and R.A. Marston, eds., *International Encyclopedia of Geography: People, the Earth, Environment and Technology*: https://doi.org/10.1002/9781118786352.wbieg0111

Shilliam, Robbie. 2015. *The Black Pacific: Anti-Colonial Struggles and Oceanic Connections*. London: Bloomsbury Press.

Smolin, Lee. 1997. *The Life of the Cosmos*. London: Phoenix

Smolin, Lee. 2000. *Three Roads to Quantum Gravity*. London: Phoenix.

Smolin, Lee. 2008. *The Trouble with Physics: The Rise of String Theory, The Fall of a Science and What Comes Next*. London: Penguin.

Smolin, Lee. 2013. *Time Reborn: From the Crisis in Physics to the Future of the Universe*. Boston, MA: Mariner Books.

Sofer, Ken. 2015. "The Realist Case for Climate Change Cooperation, Centre for American Progress." Available at www.americanprogress.org/issues/security/news/2015/11/30/126356/the-realist-case-for-climate-change-cooperation/

Taylor, Charles. 2008. *A Secular Age*. Boston, MA: Harvard University Press.

Tsing, Anna Lowenhaupt. 2005, *Friction: An Ethnography of global connection*. Princeton, NJ: Princeton University Press.

Tsing, Anna Lowenhaupt. 2015. *Mushroom at the End of the World: On the Possibility of Life in Capitalist Ruins*. Princeton, NJ: Princeton University Press.

Tsing, Anna, Heather Swanson, Elaine Gan, and Nils Bubandt, eds., 2017. *Arts of Living on a Damaged Planet (Ghosts)*. Minneapolis: University of Minnesota Press.

Unger, Roberto Mangabeira and Lee Smolin. 2015. *The Singular Universe and the Reality of Time: a Proposal in Natural Philosophy*. Cambridge: Cambridge University Press.

Viveiros de Catsro, Eduardo. 2004. "Perspectival Anthropology and the Method of Controlled Equivocation. Tipití," *Journal of the Society for the Anthropology of Lowland South America* 2, 1: 3–22.

Ward, Hugh. 2008. "Liberal Democracy and Sustainability," *Environmental Politics* 17, 3: 386–409.

Youatt, Rafi. 2020. *Interspecies Politics: Nature, Borders, States.* Ann Arbor, MI: University of Michigan Press.

Zanotti, Laura. 2018. *Ontological Entanglements, Agency and Ethics in International Relations.* London: Routledge.

4   The President as Mascot
Relations All the Way Down

Jairus Victor Grove

The occasion of this collection is the problem of worldviews for the field of international relations (IR). I want to invoke this problem in more than one sense. First, I am interested in how the kinds of worldviews we inhabit change the way we study international relations. In my case, I will try to present the reasoning behind my methodological decision to adopt a relational world view as opposed to a mechanistic world view made up of discrete objects with specific and stable essences. Second, I want to show the way that worldviews function in our relational world – that is, in practice.

In an attempt to create a conversation across the different chapters, I offer an account of what I think relationalism is and its origins within the tradition of international relations. As is often the case of adherents to a particular position, I want to show that we are all relationalists, just some better and more explicit than others. I also want to dispel a few presumptions about what I think relationalism can and cannot do, and give a sketch of what a relational approach could look like in addressing a seemingly straightforward legal or technical question about nuclear authority.

4.1   What is Relationalism, for Me?

First and foremost, relationalism is an *is*, not a *should*. I mean it as a claim to how I believe the world actually works. For me, it comes primarily from the radical empiricist tradition of William James, C.S. Pierce, Alfred North Whitehead, John Dewey, and Gabriel Tarde. Second, the goal of a relational approach is to figure out how things – including people, states, and technological systems – actually work, rather than to make claims about how things should work or predictive claims about how things will continue to work. Therefore, it is in the philosophical sense a *realist* position not primarily interested in questions of representation or interpretation, but also not indifferent to them. Relationalism sees problems of human access to the world (representation) and problems of meaning-making and communication (hermeneutics) as being horizontal with other relations,

124

such as those we think of as biological or technological. This has been described by Manuel Delanda as a "flat ontology."[1] Human observation and interpretation is on the ground floor with everything else, rather than above it, apart from it, or looking down at the world.

Although it certainly has a strong claim to ontology – how things are – relationalism is an ontology of becoming. Process is privileged over structure or fixity in the traditional sense. Highly dynamic and transversal ecosystems are privileged over equilibrium systems such as those imagined by Talcott Parsons or other Hegelian inheritors who see the world as turgid and therefore only open to gradual and often purposive change.

The correlate to an emphasis on becoming or the dynamic evolutionary character of change within systems and of systems directs us to investigate processes – stories about distributed formations and deformations – rather than agents or variables which could be said to be the "effect" of a process. In part, the so-called "flat ontology" of relational worldviews renders distinctions between independent and dependent variables, and agents and structures, somewhat arbitrary. As an aside, arbitrary here does not mean meaningless. It simply means not essential – that is, not bearing an essence. What is causally significant, what is an agent, what is a system instead is most often an effect of investigation. At what scale one asks the question, and the scale of the investigator, radically alters what appears as a part and what appears as a whole. For instance, from this perspective, the methodological individualism of social theory and many other theories is not a natural unit of analysis. Instead, the focus on the individual as a causal principle comes from the unity we "feel" as an "I."

We rarely experience ourselves as disaggregated (although drug-induced effects, bouts of madness, dreaming, etc., are exceptions most people experience over the course of their lives). However, we are disaggregated. From William James' *Principles of Psychology*, in which we are a "bundle of affects and perceptions,"[2] through to contemporary neuroscience investigations of mood-altering gut bacteria, preconscious decision-making, and increasingly compelling philosophical accounts of a subjectless human by Galen Strawson and others, we have strong reason to believe that even this most basic unit quickly begins to come apart at the seams as we zoom in for closer investigation.[3]

---

[1] DeLanda 2005: 47.   [2] James 1995: 107.
[3] Many philosophers of mind, neuroscientists, and political theorists have given compelling, data-rich accounts of human action and will that do not require a knowing, prospective subject. Consciousness is for many contemporary neuroscientists perpetually late to the party. We act and experience and reflect in that order not the other way around. Of the

As we zoom out, the litany of parts reveals more and more wholes. Consider group behavior in the form of riots and crowds, which exhibit flocking behavior even in humans. Extending the view just a little further, communities and then societies appear in which the lack of central planning (and even contrary to central planning) there is repetitive behavior, cooperation, and transactions of all kinds. An aerial view of a major highway system exhibits behavioral phenomena vastly beyond the conscious coordinating capability of individual humans or the technology they are interfacing with. Despite the high number of auto fatalities, that there are not more is astounding. The average daily commute is more than an hour a day of barely conscious muscle memory playing out amongst thousands of actors with little to no communication beyond turn signals and the occasional horn. And what about zooming out much further? If we occupy the space between the earthrise and Carl Sagan's little blue dot, the entire planet becomes something like James Lovelock's *Gaia*. The earth from this perspective is a kind of superorganism of feedback mechanisms, from the carbon cycle to the birth, death, and reabsorption of all of the necessary chemical and mineral components, as well as the creative drive to incorporate them into newly innovative forms of life. Scale as a spacetime, how close and for how long, drives the units of analysis and not the "natural" or "essential" unity of those units. Instead, there are relations at every scale crossing into every other scale. Which relations are most important, most operative, and most determinative of change or stability depends upon the region investigated.

Finally, we have the very strange and exotic wholes which make up much of international relations. So far, the descriptions of parts have been in some sense mechanical, or could be interpreted as such (i.e. brains or weapons, etc.). However, what about Benedict Anderson's imagined communities? Collectivities can feel history and connection with those they have never met, and will show up to fight a war for the injury of those anonymous brethren. Even the strange magic of memory and consciousness scales very differently when considered at different scales. However, we should not separate consciousness or memory from the networks of neurons, perceptions, gut bacteria, print media, and social network

many claims for which Nau is most concerned, this issue raises a serious conundrum for his world view. Nau wants a world of realist, rigorous science to act as a foundation for scholarship and a self-possessed, autonomous scholar to conduct that rigorous science that is in contradiction with the findings of science and much of contemporary philosophy of mind. For me, whether we are free in the way that Nau discusses mind and agency is an empirical question long since discounted by the modernist western scientific culture he seeks to defend. See Strawson 2018; Edelman 2007; Connolly 2002.

platforms that make it possible for consciousness to travel, imitate, innovate, and reaffirm conceptual habits.

At all scales, relationalism describes a multitude of relay and feedbacks constitutive of the processes that give form to what we experience as part–whole relationships in time. Many endure at different scales (plate tectonics for eons, species differences for shorter durations, fashion trends or diplomatic crisis for durations of hours or days) but they only exist, in some sense, solely in their process. When the relations change, the process is over or altered, and the only thing that remains is the impression left on the new arrangement by the arrangements that preceded it. This is true, according to relationalism, from the intimacy of identity all the way to the formation of stars.

While I follow a relational and primarily historical and interpretive approach, I do depart from many other adherents of relationalism in two significant ways.[4] The first involves the assumption of an ethical or normative content to what Milja Kurki calls the "relational cosmology" of the "relational revolution" (Chapter 3, this volume). Kurki believes an ethical impulse is "baked into" a relational worldview. There are a number of examples of this in contemporary theory inside and outside of IR. Two variants are those following Judith Butler and her debt to Emmanuel Levinas and Hannah Arendt, who account for violence as an abrogation of relations and a possibility of nonviolence in relations themselves. Here, violence is in some sense the ignoring of a fundamental relationality among human beings that would, if recognized, create an understanding mutuality opposed to violence. From these accounts, consciousness-raising about the fact of relationality is a solution to global violence just as "realizing" and "experiencing" relationality makes us open or indebted to "the other," to use Levinas' terms. The second variant focuses more on the natural environment and violence against nonhuman others. From this perspective on relationality, environmental destruction and extreme cruelty toward nonhuman animals is, like the Levinasian/Arendtian account, the result of a loss of relationality often attributed to modernist accounts of mind/body and nature/culture dualisms, or, more generally, of anthropocentrism. Like normative relationalism, the environmental strand believes that an awareness of this fact, or a cultivation of an ethos of interdependence beyond the human species, will reduce violence and possibly may make planetary life more sustainable. It is not unusual to take as evidence of this position the confluence of

---

[4] For a more comprehensive history of relational and ecological thought in the social sciences and International Relations, see Grove 2020.

environmental protections by indigenous peoples with relational cosmologies.

Both variants conflate the methodological insights of relationalism with a relational worldview. One is empirical while the other is aspirational. The risk, I believe, in this conflation is a confusion of expectations and a false sense that one has solved more philosophical questions than are possible to solve. It is enough to have an account of the world that integrates ideational and material forces into a single substance and ontology. We ought not expect that this, in addition, restores the world to some perfect order, or that striving for a more universal notion of the good escapes somehow the deep problems of competing interests, relativism, or incommensurable worldviews. Too often the appeal to relationalism's debt to science or fundamental, ancient ontologies is used to depoliticize its normative commitments. However, the ambivalent relationship between relationalism's cosmological and scientific origin stories ought to demand the inverse. Rather than seeing relationality as an ethical exit from particularity and the divisions in politics, it ought to insist upon both as the beginning of inquiry.

While an ethics can be built within a relational ontology, it does not necessarily follow from the ontological insights. After all, seals and great white sharks are deeply relational and aware of each other, and yet could not easily arrive at a common sense of the good. If any interspecies consensus could be reached between predator and prey, it would be minimal (maybe a consensus value on saving the ocean, for instance) and not as a mere result of their relationality, which is mostly characterized by teeth and blood. Could such a relationship be at least free of violence? Even that seems far-fetched given the findings of animal behaviorists that predators *enjoy* their hunt; killing for fun has been observed in orcas, dolphins, and cats.

In fact, rather than say that relationality and violence are opposed, I believe that the opposite claim can and should be made. If everything is relational – from our cells to our consciousness – then certainly violence is relational too. To go a step further, violence – a thoroughly human concept – only distinguishes itself from force or change because of the particular relationships of attention and intimacy which make cruelty possible. What makes an earthquake tragic – that is, unavoidable and indebted to no misanthropy or purposive end – is precisely what makes an act of war violent. Malice, sadism, cruelty, cultivated indifference – all of these extra characteristics are what change the ecological and political relations of actions such that they are violent as opposed to something else.

The second error of many relational approaches is to treat relations as a metaphor, or an independent substance. This is a common error of network theories and assemblage theories. In both cases relations are abstracted from the environment, resulting in an image of "nodes" which fall back into the original trap of agents – that is, unified, essential entities, independent of relations and surrounded by a "web" of connectors. This image is often borrowed from the internet existence we all live amidst. The vast series of "tubes" connecting things are either thought of as an independent substance, like the wires and fiberoptic cables of the network society, or as a kind of metaphor for communication across the ether between nodes.

Either way, treating relations as a "thing" misses the entire point of the ecological approach. We are not constituted *by* relations. We *are* relations. Or, more accurately, everything is an unfolding and refolding process of relations. There are no solid inputs or outputs. All of life is origami. The differences are in the folds, not the substance. A relational approach does not study relations instead of actors or instead of parts. A relational approach studies the folds and processes that make differences, hence the ability to differentiate the therapeutic cut of a scalpel to remove a gangrenous hand, the punitive surgical removal of a hand because someone has been convicted of theft, and the horror of having your hand blown off by an adversary trying to kill you. Mechanistically they are all similar at one level, in that they all involve pain, a missing hand, or another actor creating the condition of losing a hand, a weapon, or a tool. At another level – that of the psycho-social economy, the chances of survival, the character of the trauma, and the feelings of gratitude or revenge – it is the variability of the relations of the process which will be the basis for creating these differences. This is what I mean by an ecological approach. There are not entities *with* relations; it is relations all the way down.

For me, relationalism is an entry point into the complexities of global violence rather than an exit from or prophylactic against it. Similarly, the highly complex and dispersed systems which make violence possible, from breathable air to enmity to the technological systems of enacting violence on larger and larger scales, to the rich histories of national belonging as well as forms-of-life which form the basis of legible differences, suggest to me that a relational approach is incredibly productive for studying such the variable and unstable arrangement of the things that constitute global orders. In what follows, I will present one example of how a relational approach would alter our discussion and research. The example focuses on nuclear weapons, particularly the relationship between constitutional authority and command, and control capability, which are often treated as completely separate questions. My discussion of nuclear weapons command and control is not meant to offer comprehensive accounts of the vast literatures on this question. Instead, I want to show what kinds of questions or research might become visible with a shift to a relational ontology and an ecological research agenda.

4.2   A Relational Approach to Nuclear Authority, or the Insufficiency of Decisionism and Constitutionalism

Broadly speaking, there exist two very different literatures about nuclear weapons. Legal scholars and philosophers spend their time considering whether the American president has the right to use nuclear weapons either constitutionally or morally. A more technical literature on nuclear strategy and capability focuses on policy formulation and implementation. Little if any overlap exists between these two literatures and traditions of inquiry. I want to see what happens when we combine these questions, see how each is shaped by the other, rather than seeing either as primary. Furthermore, what comes of debates over sovereignty and decisionism when we take a more relational or ecological approach?

It is important to keep in mind that an ecological account of security is not simply about connecting technological change with legal and political development internally, but observing the change in the security environment's material conditions – that is, *all of the relations*. For instance, it is difficult to imagine the present state of nuclear weapons development that tended so heavily toward a sovereign model of command and control without taking account, at the most basic level, of the geographic specificity of the Soviet Union during the Cold War. Even a distant competitor such as Japan would have altered the technological development of Intercontinental Ballistic Missiles (ICBMs). A basic feature of the environment like the relatively small size of the Japanese nation-state would probably not have driven the development of MIRV-ed delivery vehicle or even megaton yields entering into the double-digits.[5] The simple fact that

---

[5] There is a tendency toward weapons modernizations driven by war and competition, or what J.F.C Fuller calls the "constant tactical factor," that is the refusal to allow total domination by any actor. However, the kinds of modernizations, and the qualitative and quantitative elements of nuclear weapons, were driven by the geographic and demographic nature of the US opponent. Daniel Deudney's explanation of *security materialism* is a similar approach in that it contextualizes the multivalent relationship between politics, technology, and "nature" for violence capacity: "The forces of destruction are composed of the interaction of nature, particularly geography, and technology, as both the revelation of natural possibilities, and as embodied destructive capability" (Deudney 2000: 88–89). For an in-depth discussion of Fuller's "constant tactical factor," see Grove 2019: 104–15.

Japanese soldiers could not have threatened Western Europe, thus requiring a nonconventional arsenal to even the odds, would have altered the course of nuclear weapons development. But size, geography, competitor – these are *contingencies* of history, contexts for which either the legal/moral or strategic approach could easily account for and does not change how we understand the actors or institutions at work. For an ecological account to be significant (and worth the effort), the nature of change and the actors of the situation ought to appear different (alien, even) to the conceptual tools of methodological individualism presumed by moral legal theory and leadership debates in strategic thought. Otherwise, contingencies such as place, infrastructure, and communication networks are merely details. What is at stake in this section is to consider that these *things* are constitutive, internal actants – that is, details that make a difference in what is and is not possible and what is and is not thinkable. The sovereign is not exterior to the nuclear assemblage nor its command head. Rather, what we understand to be nuclear sovereignty – the final right and capability of nuclear launch of which there is no higher power – is the assemblage itself, by which any particular president is incorporated, habituated, and therefore plugged into. This perspective is in sharp contrast to the individual accountability that is a central value of the humanist Newtonianism that Haas and Nau (Chapter 2) and Nau (Chapter 6) defend so vigorously. As Nau puts it, the discussion of IR and the events we study "would not be possible without individuals."

There exists a fundamental problem in Nau's analysis. His claim of the individual as a basic unit rests on Weber's rich understanding of individual behavior that distinguishes between instrumental rationality, value rationality, emotions, and habits. Nau focuses exclusively on the first two and skips over emotions and habits when he writes "the individual remains primary over structure." Nau thinks that this assertion allows him to move forward with a reading of Weber in which "choice is free, not determined by science or higher norms." What little lip service Nau pays to Weber's rich understanding of structure is subsumed by a deep and abiding faith in a unified and autonomous individual. However, dismissing "structure" does not get us back to a unified individual for one simple reason. The individual is a structure constituted by the deep relationality between the four distinctive Weberian categories on which Nau relies. They are categorically relational even if one were to believe that instrumental rationality is a kind of governing executive function freed from its origins and the processes of perpetual recreation. Values, habits, and feelings (and, I would argue, also instrumental rationality) come from relations that predate the individual even if we want to be humanists. These categories are contingent on early childhood development and learning that are both radically intersubjective before the "I" emerges (as Erikson, Lacan, Piaget, and many childhood developmental psychologists have shown) and radically inter-objective (as the formation of what we recognize as the self comes from the ability to separate from the mother and connect to other people and objects in the formation of independence, as Klein argues).[6] Even if we argue that humans "congeal" at some point late in their teenage years (which is implausible for any teacher of university students and for anyone who thinks that experience induces learning), the four Weberian categories of individual action have to be coordinated by some means other than instrumental rationality, otherwise the others would no longer be categories for behavioral analysis; they would just be a bargain bin for rationality to sift through and choose self-consciously amongst. Of course, this is absurd. Instead, there is a plastic and oscillating intensity of relations between emotional, habitual, rational, and ideational formations of consciousness and sense. This is where structure, affect, intersubjectivity, pedagogy, aesthetics, metabolism, architecture, nonhuman animals, temporality, etc., all come back into play with a vengeance. Nau ignores all of this and moves forward with the rest of his critique of relationism and his defense of human freedom because he black boxes all of these relations in the emergence of consciousness. Put simply, Nau's individualism is Cartesian not Weberian. He thus fundamentally violates the foundational relational assumptions that are embedded in the Weberian model he deploys.

Consider Weber's attention to charisma in *Economy and Society*, applied here to the complex nuclear issue. Weber distinguishes between the power of bureaucracy and the charismatic leadership both in terms of their economy of power and the "rules" of legitimation (or lack thereof) that govern them. Economically, bureaucracy is dependent on a "continuous income" for its functioning.[7] In contrast, Weber writes of charisma that it "lives in, not off this world." Adding a further religious and almost magical tone, he continues: "Because of this mode of legitimation genuine charismatic domination knows no abstract laws and regulations and no formal adjudication."[8] Beyond laws and norms, Weber argues for charisma as a distinctive source of power that differs from the rationalized power of bureaucracy and the less-refined brute force that possess the capability to exercise domination and "transforms all values and breaks all traditional and rational norms."[9] Weber's explanation of charisma deconstructs both the individualist explanation and the casual frame it might suggest – namely, that someone "possesses" charisma and

---

[6] Klein 1984: 50–52.   [7] Weber, Roth and Wittich 1978: 1113.
[8] Weber, Roth and Wittich 1978:1115.   [9] Weber, Roth and Wittich 1978: 1115.

uses it in some instrumental or individualistic way. For Weber, charisma cannot be something that is simply possessed by an individual, for it must *move* the people it inspires in unprecedented ways, often against their own interests. That is, charisma works by neither rational nor habitual means. It breaks rules and creates new values rather than relying on norms or laws. So how does one acquire such a power?

For Weber, for charisma to exist in the first place, charismatic leadership is relationally dependent upon those moved by its power. The self-determination of charisma is not that of the charismatic leader conceived of as a self-possessed individual. Instead, the self-determination of charisma is a co-emergent and semi-autonomous formation resulting from the relation between the leader and the people. In Weber's language: "Charisma is self-determined and sets its own limits. Its bearer seizes the task for which he is destined and demands that others obey and follow him by virtue of his missions. If those to whom he feels sent do not recognize him, his claim collapses; if they recognize it he is their master as long as he 'proves' himself."[10] There is no means by which either the "bearer" of charisma or the will of the followers can be a sufficient cause for charisma. Instead, there exists a deep and variable relationality at the heart of the production of subjects, whom Nau calls individuals. Intersubjectivity creates the condition of possibility for charisma and the catalytic transformation it can deliver. Weber does not offer an individualist account of charisma. And Weber insists that no rational account is on offer as charisma "disrupts all rational rule."[11] It would be fine to ignore just how malleable and coconstitutive humans are if charisma were a rare force in political and geopolitical change. But I concur with Weber that in a "purely empirical and value-free sense charisma is the specifically creative revolutionary force of history."[12] The vision we are given by Weber is one in which all of the agents of change are swept up in a whole that is larger than the sum of its parts, much less any particular individualistic part.[13] For me, Weber's explanation is much closer to what I am trying to develop here in terms of a nuclear sovereign assemblage than is Nau's defense of a substantive or methodological individualism.

What I argue is the precise opposite of Nau. It is only once circulating in the assemblage that the American president can become a significant relay-exchange in the functioning or nonfunctioning of the assemblage, but is never the *final* relay-exchange. While we would likely blame or

[10] Weber, Roth and Wittich 1978: 1112–13   [11] Weber, Roth and Wittich 1978: 1117.
[12] Weber, Roth and Wittich 1978: 1117.
[13] It is worth noting that Weber draws heavily on the charisma of heroes and the ethos derived from heroic acts. However, even the substance and significance of heroism is mutually dependent upon its audience, as in the resonance between leader and crowd.

credit the president in the case of a nuclear launch, much as we did blame or credit George W. Bush with the invasion of Iraq in 2003, such an anthropomorphic image would be a mistake. The command as much as the compliance with the command is not possible without the collaboration of millions of people and countless numbers of things. Nau's image of individual responsibility may satisfy his moral appetite, but it does nothing to reveal how a decision takes place as an event which can unfold across systems and people seemingly as if their dispositions were already decided. How many decisions, infrastructures, years of training, or national identities had to come into formation for a presidential command to make sense, much less be effective in unleashing nuclear war. To put it another way: the decision comes after the potentiality of nuclear war, not before it.[14]

Such a claim, if demonstrated, changes how we understand constitutional constraints of nuclear war. The legal right is less significant, even potentially irrelevant, to the capability to set nuclear war in motion without, for instance, congressional approval. Similarly, in the context of strategic studies, the anthropomorphism that conflates the state and its nuclear arsenal into a single entity, a president, with a structured, individualized rationality driven by victory and survival, becomes self-evident. That is, the sovereign is shown to be a mere stand-in for something vastly more complex than a real, ontological entity. The president, in the most radical reading of this claim, is more like a mascot than a quarterback. In the informatic networks of early warning systems, targeting coordinates, satellite communication, silo commanders, rocket fuel, hangovers, weather balloons, and global ideological competitions, the American president doesn't call the play, the play calls them.[15]

---

[14] Nau's primary critique of relationalism is moral rather than empirical, what he calls a "broadside assault on western rationality" to which Nau attributes the advance of western civilization and its moral progress (Chapter 6, this volume) However, the individualism that Nau clings to does little to empower effective moral action. Consider how many times the effort to blame disastrous foreign policy has been laid at the feet of an individual scapegoat only to be repeated by the scapegoat's successor. The effort to constrain moral thought to the self-possessed, rational agent is efficient in the distribution of blame but does little to impeach the distribution and dispositions of human and technical populations that enable moral catastrophe to become habitual – that is, "just the way things are done."

[15] The chapter refers specifically to the American presidency because the particular history and structure of the US nuclear arsenal is essential to the argument. I suspect that the Russian and Chinese arsenals would be no less assembled than that of the United States, but I do not have sufficient knowledge of their command or infrastructure to make that claim here. I would only say that the level of centralized or decentralized command structure does not alter the claim I am making. As will be detailed later, the permanent possibility of accidental launch or detonation means in the final instance only chance is sovereign. No amount of legal or technical hierarchy changes this fact.

In what follows I will quickly identify the characteristics of the nuclear arsenal that lends itself to a relational or ecological analysis. As I argued in the introduction, relations are the real fabric of existence. They are ontologically real and not a metaphor. Does everything then lend itself to a relational approach? Not necessarily. Not all forms of reductionism – that is. the reliance on unitary actors or instrumental accounts of tools – are useless. Like the case of Newtonian physics, reductions and simplifications can be very powerful despite being in some sense simply inaccurate. However, there are scales of complexity and complexities of causality in which simplifications occlude more than they reveal. I want to argue that there are specific features of the nuclear arsenal that demonstrate the limits of legal-moral and strategic anthropocentrism and anthropomorphism. Furthermore, to understand how war as an event, and nuclear war specifically, requires a relational account to describe the capacity to make wholes out of such disparate parts also goes a long way to discount Nau's belief that relationalism somehow smuggles utopia and peace into its conceptual worldview. Quite the opposite: a relational approach is essential to understanding collective catastrophe as much as it is to any other form of change. What we lose in the shelter of provincial humanist thought is the degree to which global politics depends precisely on the nonindividualistic capacities of human beings. Ought we let political realism off the hook if a president did not "mean" to cause a nuclear war or end civilization, or would the habituation of strategic thinking, nuclear development and deployment, and thousands of hours of drilling officers sitting in bunkers somehow find its way back to the logics of deterrence and escalation dominance that were simultaneously inspired by the vast networks of nuclear capability and that enlivened the circulation and modernization of those nuclear networks? The nuclear world we live in goes well beyond the four-part Weberian schema of social action described by Nau in Chapter 6. Likewise, unfortunately the inhuman and often indifferently autogenocidal character of the nuclear sovereign assemblage calls into question whether becoming part of the connected nature of things leads anywhere in particular, much less to what Kurki calls a "not only human... planetary politics."[16] Instead, relationalism merely is. The fact of the relational world may be as necessary for the possibility of a more humane planetary ethos as it is for the techno-human death cult of the nuclear balance of terror. However, the insight that we live in such a world is not sufficient to explain the inevitability of either outcome.

---

[16] Chapter 3.

4.2.1   *Discovery, Defense, and Design*

Unlike a spear, or even a rifle, nuclear weapons are technics of an entirely different order. For a fission or fusion detonation to take place, sufficient control must exist to alter the common conditions of the physical properties of reality. Fermi's achievement at Chicago Pile-1 on December 2, 1942 is exotic to terrestrial life. The capacity to achieve that feat requires vast cooperation between large numbers of humans, apparatuses, and the rare elements which lend themselves to being pulled apart at the sub-atomic seam. To date, no one can build a nuclear weapon in their basement by themselves. Each and every nuclear artifact is the congealed efforts of hundreds, if not thousands, of human actors and countless technical, mathematical, and elemental entities. And this is all before we have considered how to target, deploy, or scenario-plan the use of nuclear weapons.

Nuclear weapons have no earthbound correlate and are only possible because of a vast scientific-technical-socio-political order encountering the special properties of a relatively rare material rather than the genius of a few individuals. Methodological individualism fails entirely at understanding even one component of the nuclear arsenal: nuclear weapons. The novel or exotic properties of radioactive material and the near-accidental discovery of radiation by Marie Curie, the subsequent fits and starts on the pathway to develop a sustained chain reaction, and the hundreds of different mathematical, physical, chemical, and geographic discoveries that accumulated to make possible the now refined high-yield ICBM all challenge a simple, linear, explanation of the current state of affairs as being the result of planning or decision-making as we would understand it within the frame of the moral or strategic individual.

But that is just history. Can we not begin with the individual once a president has inherited the vast assemblage of the nuclear weapon? However, the basis on which that individual emerged as an American president for which a nuclear weapon makes sense, or is at one's command, is no less complex. The security environment and the necessary interpretation of the environment that made nuclear weapons desirable is outside the decisional character of the president. In time, the security environment preceded the president. Practically speaking, the relevant nuclear knowledge is not present or directly under the jurisdiction of a president. Furthermore, the decision to launch or not launch is the result of hundreds of daily security briefings, which are each the result of the interpretation of thousands of analysts, which are the result of intelligence and data collected, sorted, coded, and processed by myriads of individuals. And what of the frame by which each of these analysts comes to understand the significance of what they see?

Therefore, the origin story, or what others have called an onto-story, of the nuclear president is neither a legal-moral history, a strategic history, nor a technical history – it is all of these at once. If the nuclear assemblage is all of these things, there is not one place, or a first place, to identify as an origin; instead, the preference for an onto-story is to think about how something emerges not for the first time but again. We start in the middle because there is no beginning of an assemblage, there is only the tangle of its relations.[17] In short, despite the fact that they appear to be built more uniformly from human things such as perceptions, representations, ideas, and stories, the strategic environment and the legal-moral environment are no less assembled and distributed than the highly inhuman technics of nuclear weapons.

Because of its significance to both legal-moral history and strategic thinking, I will focus here on the Cuban Missile Crisis. For the missile crisis to take place, we need to track and understand the missile as another highly complex technical component of the nuclear assemblage.[18] Before the missile, the American Strategic Air Command was rapid and destructive by prenuclear standards of warfare, but the increasing desire to centralize decision-making and the state's destructive capacity at a distance follows the course of the missile not the airplane. To achieve the transformation from air-power to missile power, teams had to be assembled. Codenamed Operation Paper Clip, the United States employed Werner von Braun, the leading Nazi scientist, to develop rocket technology for production in the United States by extending the capability of the V2 rocket developed and deployed by the Third Reich during World War II. The first two designs, the Redstone IRBM and Jupiter IRBM, were relatively clumsy Intermediated Range Ballistic Missiles. The first actually *Intercontinental* Ballistic Missile was the Atlas, which was made operational in 1959. The Atlas was cumbersome, slow, and subject to attack because of its above-ground launch pad. The first SLBM went underwater in the USS George Washington, on November 15, 1960.[19] The SLBM locked in Second Strike capability because of the inability to target and kill submarines in a decapitating first-strike. The first generation of ICBMs that fit the sovereign image of intercontinental

---

[17] For extended discussion and methodological defense of starting in the middle or "in media res," see Bousquet, Grove, and Shah 2020: 99–118.

[18] For a relational account of how the missile becomes a dominant form of warfare, see MacKenzie 2001.

[19] Norris, Kosiak, and Schwartz 1998: 136–37.

exchange, the Minuteman, was deployed two years after the first SLBM was put on alert, on October 27, 1962.

These technological achievements gave contour to the Cuban Missile Crisis. The technological achievement of the Minuteman created the violence capability for a truly intercontinental conflict. Despite the name, the nuclear sovereign assemblage is not primarily radioactive. Its sensory and informatic character is equally important. If you cannot see anything or know anything, what then? Therefore, the reliability and clarity of U2 photographs were also essential to the crisis in Cuba and how the nuclear sovereign assemblage defined the model of executive leadership and sovereign control that emerged from those fourteen October days.

Kennedy's minute-by-minute crisis-management decision-making was a highly complex system of institutional organization, technological capacity, ideology, and leadership, each constituted by and feeding back into the other. What emerged was a new conception of time and warfare that only escalated and consolidated sovereign power and technological development further, but neither sovereignty nor technological development, nor even geopolitical competition, would fit primacy or firstness, much less exogenous characteristics of what scientifically we would call a "cause."

From the perspective of those witnessing the event in real time, at no other time did the American president seem as significantly in charge. From Arthur Schlesinger's front row seat, the Cuban Missile Crisis was the very paradigm of a methodological individualism: "the management of the great foreign policy crisis of the Kennedy years – the Soviet attempt to install nuclear missiles in Cuba – came as if in proof of the proposition that the nuclear age left no alternative to unilateral presidential decision."[20]

And yet, immediately after this statement, Schlesinger points out that Kennedy did not make his decision alone: "Kennedy took the decision into his own hands, but it is to be noted that he did not make it in imperial solitude" Instead, he created and relied upon a special executive committee.[21] While commendable and imperative to the situation, there is nothing democratic or republican about such a committee. Nor is there any means of review or accountability for the committee's actions. As Schlesinger succinctly puts it, "Congress played no role at all."[22] While I take Schlesinger's point that the procedures of the US constitutions were made obsolete, it was not the replacement of Congress – a collective body – by the president – a single individual – that took

---

[20] Schlesinger 2004: 173.   [21] Schlesinger 2004: 173.   [22] Schlesinger 2004: 174.

place. Instead, one collectivity – Congress – was replaced by another collectivity – the nuclear sovereign assemblage. One may be less democratic than the other, but not because of its unitary nature.

The question, then, is what enabled a president and a single room of advisors 1,200 miles from the potential battlefield to take command? President Kennedy may have been commander-in-chief in this situation, but he was not in any sense in control or even in charge in the way Schlesinger imagined it. The ability to implement extensive networks and organizational changes such that presidential authorization from one mobile source could predictably command the whole of the US strategic nuclear forces creates a new kind of executive authority resting with the network rather than with the messages in the network.

As compared to an actual command, where the charisma and respect of the leader may be at play, or legal authority relying on institutional legitimacy, in the nuclear arsenal the bully pulpit is replaced by the "football." Presidential authority becomes more significantly a question of signal fidelity. By April 1967, less than five years after the Cuban Missile Crisis, 1,000 Minuteman ICBMS were built and deployed.[23] Following the Cuban Missile Crisis and the new nuclear force structure and capability, "the football" – aka "the button" or "trigger" – was always with the president. Although technical more than political, the football is not a literal button, but contains a SIOP decision handbook and the codes so that the president can authenticate that he is indeed the president. The actual "go" codes are decentralized and housed at secure facilities throughout the country.[24] The incredible breadth of telephone coverage and its redundancy established by AT&T by the 1950s made it possible for the president to communicate from any location to virtually any other location. The result is what Paul Bracken calls a "self-healing network," depriving the Soviet Union of central communication targets.[25] By the 1970s, Command, Control, Communications and early warning networks (intelligence) (C3I) accomplished the goal of bringing "the individual pieces of a defense system together into a coherent overall structure."[26] From the perspective of a strong advocate of the system, Bruce Blair, this is meant to be total; "once deterrence fails, it fails completely." Blair's only concern is to maintain an "undeniable capacity to destroy the Soviet target base in a retaliatory strike."[27]

In terms of presidential consolidations of sovereignty, deterrence made it possible for one human being to be the head of the forces from almost

---

[23] Norris, Kosiak and Schwartz 1998: 131.
[24] Blair, Pike and Schwartz, 1998: 222. Ford 1986.   [25] Bracken 1983: 207–8.
[26] Bracken 1983: 179.   [27] Blair 1985: 5.

any location, facilitating the already desirable centralization of nuclear-war-making authority in the president. Neither the sovereign nor sovereignty are simply *present* or *absent* in a decision or the ability to make decision. The sovereignty or authority of the president must be *built* out of wire, telephone poles, hardened targets, rapid transport, and early warning systems. Authority is coterminus with capability, and the possibility of a decision is coterminus with the sensory infrastructure that makes that authority possible, further routinized by the targeting which was determined by scenario planning and war gaming that both influenced the development of technical capability and were influenced by the limits and capacities of technical capability. In this relational account, individual accountability is submerged in a variety of assemblages and relationships.

4.2.2   From Presidential Powers to the Nuclear Sovereign Assemblage

The very effort to secure the survivability and centrality of the American president's decision and the effort to build a sovereign that could command a nuclear arsenal created the very techno-strategic ecosystem in which the American president became a mascot rather than a quarterback. Here I will try to theorize how to understand the ambiguous role of the sovereign in the assemblage of nuclear sovereignty. Furthermore, I will argue that the anthropocentric image, or Schmittian ideal, of one *human* in charge is insufficient for understanding how the event of a nuclear war would take place.[28]

In Schlesinger's account of nuclear decision-making we have a stark image of nuclear weapons as the totalization of sovereignty rather than the end of the sovereign. The nuclear state of emergency sidesteps democracy because it is possible for a single individual to decide and to go to war and to finish that war in 30 minutes. At first glance, this apocalyptic diagnosis seems accurate. Nuclear weapons at current numbers could destroy the condition of human life as we know it. And, given the structure of the US nuclear command, any Congressional or popular attempts to stop the process of nuclear launch would likely be in vain. Politics and a democratic balance of power require time: time to react, time to respond, time to debate, time to strategize, time to implement. ICBMs nullify time. Nuclear decision-making is, as Deudney says, "dominated by the dogma of speed."[29]

---

[28] Consider how indebted International Relations is to a sovereign that is a single individual. Carl Schmitt's vision of the political as they who decide on the exception is common well beyond those who cite Schmitt 2007 explicitly.

[29] Deudney 1995: 26.

While the nuclear state of affairs runs contrary to the possibility of democracy, it does not favor the autocrat – at least, not as we would understand it as an all-powerful individual. The threat of the *extreme case* has obscured the actual case that presents opportunities for intervention as well as a very different image of decision-making and the decider. Politics, whether micro or macro, does not begin and end with the sovereign decision; the sovereign decision emerges from a relay of forces, connections, and other previous decisions, resonances, and actants that are presupposed in each subsequent iteration of the sovereign decision, each layered into multiple streams of time, perception, and medium of relation. Even an increasingly automated nuclear arsenal requires the participation of millions of people and countless networks, objects, tectonic stability, stable solar flare activity, and on and on. Focusing on individual accountability, as does Nau (Chapter 6), does not help us explain how we got to such a vulnerable and contingent state of things any more than it tells us how to get out of it. The decision and the decider only appear singular when we truncate time and space to the moment the president "pushes the button." Or, to put it another way, the president as nuclear sovereign only appears if we are primed by methodological individualism to look for an already constituted, single decider, in space and time, to explain a nuclear event. Here, I think we can see precisely what Kurki means when she writes "At the heart of liberal approaches is an acceptance of not only states as a key institutional reference point, but also, fundamentally, the *separation of human institutions from the 'environment' as a background to be controlled and managed.*"[30] While I am not sure there is the tight connection Kurki sees between the relational perspective and a particular political ethos, I am fully in agreement that analytically we cannot understand the complex arrangements of the world and the novelties that emerge from them if we hide in a Newtonian reductionism or narrowly Weberian humanism. What we do with that understanding is unfortunately also beyond the scope of humanism as much as it is the individual. What the knowledge will become, what processes it is folded into and intensifies exceeds the control of an individual or even collective of individuals. To put it another way, the capacity of the nuclear sovereign assemblage and its resilient cybernetic network was also indicative of a relational worldview that displaced unitary command structures and more ancient ideas about the unity of the executive.

So, while real danger exists, the destructive capacity of the system does not rest with the president. To illustrate this point, I want to keep the president as sovereign in torsion with the assemblage of sovereignty. In so

[30] Chapter 3 .

doing, I want to consider how an alternative image of sovereignty – that is, the nuclear sovereign assemblage – accounts for the discrepancy between nuclear authority and capability. The goal is to provide a more-than-human account of the nuclear-predicament account that sees beyond the moment of nuclear decision to the broader landscape of atomic politics, and to take one further step down the relational rabbit hole.

The goal of an ecological approach is not to replace sovereignty with its assemblage. Certainly, the sovereign decision is a powerful, expressive, performative act of individuation, and is highly effective in mobilizing populations of things. A sovereign nuclear decision even more so, but such a decision is not self-constituted or self-causal. The processes of individuation and mobilization require a field of relations and resonances from which the sovereign decision emerges. The decision itself is also not decisive. The sovereign – in so far as they are constituted by the enunciation of decisions – is a condensation point for a national ethos, affect, and institutional individuation. Each decision is constitutive not of the "sovereign" alone, as is the case in Schlesinger's observation, but of a sovereign point of identification or reified consistency which can become habitual but need not – and in fact cannot – remain static or immobile.

What I hope is becoming clear is that a focus on the ecology or assemblage of nuclear sovereignty need not supplant or ignore a degree of human involvement in the signification of actors and events. Rather, the point is that *real* networks or fundamental entanglements of things are further complicated by the way humans participate in meaning-making in those entanglements. The task here is to demonstrate the degree to which the emergence of a discourse of sovereignty ought not to be mistaken for the actual nuclear sovereign assemblage that amplifies and makes possible the event of nuclear war. We see only the effects which we correlate to the sovereign, often through secondhand accounts or the personality politics of media streams.

The impersonal character of the presidential position in the nuclear sovereign assemblage could in part explain why there is so little transition time between each sovereign and so little variation in the intensifying breadth of war powers. The sovereign is a reference point or index for a history of actions and events made more complex by the function it is believed to serve – a body, but not the body in the sense of an individual. It is a body that is built from the matter of decisions. It is the titular focal point of an assemblage, a mascot not a quarterback.[31]

---

[31] Fuller 1998.

By way of a crude time line one could say that sovereignty in the United States has been characterized by three periods. 1. The republican model, whereby the inherent advantage or tendency toward centralization through war plays out as a juridical struggle between the three branches of government. Prior to an intensely mediated society the role of the American public is limited but not nonexistent. 2. The autocratic model, whereby the development of nuclear weapons enables the president to ignore the other two branches because war can begin and end without a single soldier putting their boots on. 3. The assemblage model, whereby the means of war becomes dispersed such that the sovereign's function becomes more like a refrain to give consistency to a dispersed, pluripotential network with each strand on the cusp of escaping or disrupting the state/military apparatus.

The transition from each stage is roughly cybernetic in so far as it is periodized by the evolution of "codes." In the first model we have a code of conduct or an expectation of behavior: the gentleman sovereign. In the second there is the attempt to centralize the C3I of nuclear war through a centralization of codes vested in the president. Lastly, there is the dispersal of codes such that the system can maximize survivability but the result is a system that can no longer secure hierarchy or sovereignty in relation to war. Instead, the sovereign survives as an expressive point of identification. War then becomes more obviously emergent. Resonances and relations throughout the nuclear sovereign assemblage exist in a continuum between nonwar and war, depending on the necessity for testing, alert, or accidental machinic statements provoked by weather balloons, reactor meltdowns, or acute paranoia.

One danger of continuing to sustain the individualist fiction that the nuclear arsenal can be wielded by the president directly is that it undermines the capacity to resist and steer nuclear politics. A new constitution, more Congressional oversight, more or less automation, or electing a president who is more moral or strategic would not be sufficient to alter how highly distributed and deeply embedded the assemblage of the nuclear arsenal is. A nuclear crisis reduced to the personality or authority of a president tells us little about the nature or possibility of a nuclear conflict. Behind the curtain of the American presidency lies a vast machine-like vista well beyond the control of any *one* person, or even any one ideology or system of governmentality.

4.3   Conclusion

In the case of nuclear command and its ambivalent relationship to sovereignty as imagined in our habitual descriptions of presidential authority,

I have tried to show how a relational approach to nuclear sovereignty as opposed to either a materialist or ideational approach is necessary to understand how embedded and at times perpetual the infrastructure of nuclear violence has become. What is presented here is not sufficient to make that case indisputably or lay out what new mode of political action would be equivalent to the complexity of each problem. That is beyond what can be done in one chapter. However, I hope that the slightly different account of the problem that more fully accounts for the relational complexity and inhuman character of nuclear command as ecological problems can open up practical questions about how purely individualist approaches or purely discursive approaches blunt our understanding of how these problems work. To craft from that a way forward would need to center in some sense on the very practical and material condition by which territories, spaces, and habits of each encounter are built and repeated, often below the radar of anything we would call a decision.

However, the deadlock of arms-reduction treaties and even contemporary efforts at threat reductions, are, from a relational point of view, much easier to understand. When the more concrete assemblage of nuclear power becomes part of the discussion the interests of the strategic actors seemingly wielding the weapons, as well as tired narratives about the failure of "political will" or "leadership," can be displaced in favor of the nuclear infrastructures which are in some sense more durable than our political systems. The nuclear sovereign assemblage has a momentum and a trajectory well beyond the intentions or agency of those who thought themselves its maker. In a sense, then, Nau may be right that "individual freedom is at stake," but not because relationalism somehow "dissolved it" – although wouldn't it be a neat trick if the ontological framework of the universe could be altered by a compelling argument? Instead, individual freedom, in the way conceived by Nau's reading of Weber, may be at risk precisely because it never existed in the first place, and that is precisely why the predicaments we find ourselves in, from a nuclear armed world to an imploding ecosystem, come to pass in the first place.

Bibliography

Blair, Bruce. 1985. *Strategic Command and Control: Redefining the Nuclear Threat*, Washington, DC: Brookings Institute.

Blair, John Pike and Stephen Schwartz. 1998. "Targeting and Controlling the Bomb," in Stephen I. Schwartz, ed., *Atomic Audit: The Cost and Consequences of US Nuclear Weapons since 1940*. Washington, DC: Brookings Institution Press.

Bousquet, Antoine, Jairus Grove, and Nisha Shah. 2020. "Becoming War: Towards a Martial Empiricism," *Security Dialogue* 51, 2–3: 99–118.

Bracken, Paul. 1983. *The Command and Control of Nuclear Forces*. New Haven, CT: Yale University Press.

Connolly, William E. 2002. *Neuropolitics: Thinking, Culture, Speed. Theory out of Bounds*. Minneapolis: University of Minnesota Press.

DeLanda, M. 2005. *Intensive Science and Virtual Philosophy*. Continuum Impacts Series. London: Bloomsbury Academic.

Deudney, Daniel. 1995. "Nuclear Weapons and the Waning of the Real-State," *Daedalus* 124, 2: 226. www.jstor.org/stable/20027303.

Deudney, Daniel. 2000. "Geopolitics as Theory: Historical Security Materialism," *European Journal of International Relations* 6, 1: 77–107.

Deudney, Daniel. 2007. *Bounding Power: Republican Security Theory from the Polis to the Global Village*. Princeton, NJ: Princeton University Press.

Edelman, Gerald M. 2007. *Second Nature: Brain Science and Human Knowledge*. New Haven, CT: Yale University Press.

Fuller, J.F.C. 1998. *Armament and History: The Influence of Armament on History from the Dawn of Classical Warfare to the End of the Second World War*. 1st ed. New York: Da Capo Press.

Grove, Jairus. 2019. *Savage Ecology: War and Geopolitics at the End of the World*. Durham, NC: Duke University Press.

Grove, Jairus. 2020. "Bringing the World Back in: Revolutions and Relations before and after the Quantum Event," *Security Dialogue* 51, 5: 414–33.

James, William. 1995. *The Principles of Psychology: In Two Volumes. Vol. 1. Fascism* [1890]. Ed. Henry Holt. New York: Dover.

Klein, Melanie. 1984. *Love, Guilt, and Reparation, and Other Works, 1921-1945. The Writings of Melanie Klein, vol. 1*. New York: Free Press.

MacKenzie, Donald A. 2001. *Inventing Accuracy: A Historical Sociology of Nuclear Missile Guidance*, Cambridge, MA: MIT Press.

Norris, Robert, Steven Kosiak, and Stephen Schwartz. 1998. "Deploying the Bomb," in Stephen I. Schwartz, ed., *Atomic Audit: The Cost and Consequences of US Nuclear Weapons since 1940*. Washington, DC: Brookings Institution Press.

Schlesinger, Arthur M. 2004. *The Imperial Presidency*. Boston, MA: Houghton Mifflin.

Schmitt, Carl. 2007. *The Concept of the Political*. Expanded ed. Chicago, IL: University of Chicago Press.

Strawson, Galen. 2018. *Things That Bother Me: Death, Freedom, the Self, Etc.* New York Review Books Classics. New York City: New York Review Books.

Weber, Max, Guenther Roth, and Claus Wittich. 1978. *Economy and Society: An Outline of Interpretive Sociology*. Berkeley: University of California Press.

5   Jewish Questions and Jewish Worldviews

Michael Barnett

Why study worldviews? What does the concept add that is not covered by kindred concepts such as civilization, paradigm, ideology, and discourse? Each incorporates the values, knowledge, practices, and identities that bind the members of a community and organize social relations; shape meanings; craft narratives of the past, present, and future; define and justify ethical action; and establish the background conditions that form habit and the subconscious. You say civilization, I say worldview. Following the observations of Stephen Kalberg and others, my view is that worldviews do something these others do not: blend the worldly and the heavenly.[1] They are tantamount to an "ethical universe" that links the here-and-now to the transcendent, and the practical and metaphysical.[2] In line with Katzenstein's discussion in Chapter 1, they consider how a community addresses the "ultimate" questions of meaning, purpose, suffering, and injustice.[3] What is the place of the community in the cosmos and the relationship to the universal? What is the relationship to outsiders? What duties and obligations does it have to them? How do they cope with suffering and evil? How is suffering related to salvation and redemption? To the extent that worldviews address these fundamental questions that often can strike terror and panic in the hearts and minds of humans, they help create order out of the chaos.[4] The world is a jungle, but worldviews provide a transcendental canopy.

This chapter considers the multiple and changing worldviews of western Jewry in search of ontological and physical security in a post-Enlightenment world of nation-states. Because the volume provides multiple worldviews on worldviews, and Chapter 1 situates worldviews in relationship to forms of relationalism and humanism, I should begin by briefly explaining why I occupy the cell of humanist relationalism. I adopt a sociological relationalism that does not venture into quantum-style relationalism or hyper-humanism. Although I have been informed by others in the project that quantum-style relationalism subsumes sociological relationalism because it is the mother of all relationalisms, which it might be, but I have not been persuaded that the

---

[1] Kalberg 2004.   [2] Kalberg 2004: 140–41.   [3] Kalberg 2004: 141.   [4] Berger 1969.

former's high level of abstraction is either necessary or can be sufficiently grounded to capture the changing meanings and practices of worldviews. Moreover, although there are communities, religious and otherwise, whose worldviews incorporate relationality with nonhuman forms, at best this is a minor feature of Judaism and the Jewish people.[5]

My sociological position also distances my argument from substantialism in ways that follow from constructivist international relations. Actors, whether they are individuals or groups, are social constructions. Said otherwise, they are not natural but rather are social kinds. This sociological position can and does incorporate the possibility that groups can be more than aggregates of individuals and can have a collective identity, and that these collectives can have enduring features, including identities, beliefs, interests, and practices. But this differs from substantialism's tendency toward essentialism and reification. Instead, worldviews "do not have a life of their own, apart from their human carriers."[6] As Katzenstein writes in his discussion of Weber and Dilthey in Chapter 1, the interpretive tradition works at the individual and group levels of analysis to access the cultural meanings and significance that individuals and groups give to the world; however, these worldviews are not the byproduct of psychology, but rather of a culture with an integrity. Worldviews, in this way, provide a "causal impulse" akin to the conditions of possibility discussed by constructivists.[7] As social constructions, worldviews can be settled or unsettled, and they can be unsettled by internal developments and contradictions or by external shocks and disturbances.

These dimensions of humanist relationalism inform my narrative of the changing worldviews of western Jewry in response to the Enlightenment and the rise of the nation-state. All groups are social kinds and thus are constructed. Most groups that make an impression have a history, and in the case of the Jews it is 5,782 years and counting. And, similar to all social kinds, Jews have debated what defines them as a people, what is their purpose, how to make sense of suffering, what are their core tenets, how to interpret and give meaning to their central texts, who is and can be a member, and what are the boundaries between themselves and others and what should be their relationship to them. Jews have managed to maintain a collective identity despite having lived most of their history in exile and, in the modern period, in pockets of isolated communities strewn across the Christian and Muslim worlds. Yet there is diversity within unity, which is always the case for any community or cultural grouping, and especially so for a people that are diasporic, dispersed, and, historically speaking, have lived in relative isolation from each other. Ashkenazi and

[5] See, for instance, Povenilli 2016.   [6] McNeill 1998: 1.   [7] Kalberg 2004.

Sephardic Jews share a unity, but also a diversity. So, too, do many western Jewish communities. As the punchline to several Jewish jokes goes: two Jews, three synagogues.

Jews are both a certain and an uncertain people. They are a certain people to the extent that they have a strong collective and transnational identity with mutual obligations. They are an uncertain people with regard to their survival. As a barely tolerated and often hated minority, Jews have experienced all kinds of oppression, violence, forced migration, and genocide. Jewish history and important religious events are often narrated by moments of considerable suffering. Indeed, suffering is so central to the Jewish historical narrative that, according to the eminent historian of Jewish history Salo Baron, they possess a "lachrymose" view of their history.[8] And, according to various other scholars, this reading of history shapes their worldviews and anxiety about their physical and ontological survival.[9] The consequence is that suffering and survival enter worldviews in two ways. Suffering must be explained, and in a way that provides meaning. And the threat of destruction is part of their worldview.

The historical period I examine – a post-Enlightenment world of nation-states – posed threats to and presented opportunities for western Jews that, in turn, led to a change in worldviews. Although worldviews have various dimensions, I focus on what is called the "Jewish Question." The theologically stylized formulation is: are the Jews are a people apart, or are they a light unto nations? Should they emphasize and preserve those laws, customs, traditions, and rituals that make them distinctive, or should they accentuate and cultivate what they share with humanity? How should they balance and navigate the relationship between particularism and universalism?[10]

These theological questions began to have practical importance with the rise of the Enlightenment and the nation-state in Europe in the eighteenth century. The urgent question became: how can the Jews, a diasporic, transnational community, find a secure place in a world with universalizing tendencies and that is carved up into different territories that are expected to circumscribe identities and loyalties?[11] The Enlightenment and nationalism compelled Jews to reconsider how they classify themselves as a people, their place and purpose in the world, and

---

[8] Baron 1963.   [9] Katz 2008; Benbassa 2010.

[10] On the relationship between particularism and universalism in Jewish political thought, see Cohen 2003; Eisen 1983; Lundgren 2001; Slezkine 2004; Walzer 2001.

[11] Gottlieb 2006: 10 (quoted in Pianko 2012). On a similar note, see Batnitzky 2011: 169–79.

their relationship to non-Jews. The universal threatened to remove the boundaries that distinguish Jews as a separate people, and inclusive forms of nationalism expected the Jews to transfer their loyalties from their fellow brethren to their fellow citizens.[12] Under such conditions, the Jews might possibly cease to exist as a people, cut off from other Jews and their history. But if they refused the invitation, they would potentially signal that they were a separate and possibly threatening people. At least they had a choice. Other countries, shaped by counter-Enlightenment and chauvinistic nationalism, treated Jews as the quintessential "other," an outsider worthy of exclusion, persecution, and violence. Different worldviews began to emerge in relationship to these different circumstances. There is a larger history lesson here: if you want to understand how different Jewish communities have answered the Jewish Question, start by looking at the gentiles. This piece of advice is attributed to Heinrich Heine, the great nineteenth-century poet and writer who was born a Jew and then converted to Christianity. A Yiddish proverb offers a similar, though more fatalistic, conclusion: *Vy es kristit zikh, azoy yidlt zikh* – "As the Christians go, so go the Jews."[13]

The responses by Jewish communities to these challenges and opportunities provided by the Enlightenment also were mediated by political theology. Whether Jews are primarily a religious, national, or ethnic community is a post-Enlightenment debate that underscores how Judaism has become less important to Jewish identity for many western Jews. But even when it appears to have receded, it still figures prominently. An ongoing challenge for any religious community is the translation of theological concepts rooted in text into political choices shaped by context.[14] In short, political theology is the process and result of connecting the transcendental to the imminent. The search for a "usable past" is central to this exercise. There is no one, true, original meaning or interpretation. Religious texts do not speak for themselves; there is an active

---

[12] Elazar 2000; Lundgren 2001; Miller and Ury 2010; Sznaider 2007.

[13] Cited in Mendelsohn 1993: 37.

[14] There is no single definition of political theology. For a menu of choices, see Cavanaugh and Scott 2007; Kerr and Labreche 2018; and Kessler 2013. For Lilla (2007), conversations about political authority, the ends of politics, and the human condition often venture into the divine. Cavanaugh and Scott (2007) define it as "The analysis and criticism of political arrangements (including cultural-psychological, social, and economic aspects) from the perspective of differing interpretations of God's ways with the world." Their definition touches upon Carl Schmitt's (2005:36): "All significant concepts of the modern theory of the state are secularized theological concepts not only because of their historical development – in which they are transferred from theology to the theory of the state – but also because of their systemic structure." Following Emile Durkheim's concept of religion, others define political theology as the infusion of political concepts with the sacred.

human process of interpretation that occurs at the individual and collect-ive levels. Consequently, all religious communities debate the meaning of texts and which elements are most urgent and salient. History and politics channel this search for a usable past, and mold this past into the ingredi-ents that shape a worldview. The recognition that religion shaped how Jews understood the meanings, and responded to the challenges, of the Enlightenment and nationalism underscores that worldviews are never hermetically sealed but are constantly rubbing shoulders with, absorbing, and reacting to other worldviews, a point raised by other chapters in this volume.

These unsettled times underscored how worldviews are simultaneously background and foreground. Whereas Chapter 1 focuses on the back-ground, I shift the angle to the foreground. Western Jews are engaged in backward- and forward-looking debates about how to respond to current circumstances and challenges in ways that connect the past to a possible future that addresses their ontological and physical security. There is no single answer to these debates. However, if a proposed solution is to find an audience, it must satisfy the need for both physical and ontological security. And while there have been multiple answers, they are *Jewish* responses. But the fact that responses are in the multiple, and that differ-ent responses can become hegemonic in different national and trans-national contexts, highlights how a single community can have multiple worldviews and how any community's worldview, just like its culture, has both unity and diversity.[15]

The rest of the chapter is divided into two sections organized around two periods, from the 1800s through 1948, and from 1948 to the present. Global structures and world-turning events provided the stimulus for the transformation of Jewish worldviews. The first section describes how variations in the Enlightenment and nationalism, and the perceived necessity of Jewish sovereignty and statehood for survival, led to the emergence of four Jewish worldviews: a diaspora nationalism, which mixed nonterritorialism and particularism; a rooted cosmopolitanism, which combined nonterritorialism and universalism; an ethnonational Zionism, which blended territorialism and particularism; and a prophetic Zionism that contained territorialism and universalism. The second sec-tion examines how the Holocaust and the creation of the State of Israel led the two largest Jewish communities in the world, the American and the Israeli, to develop two distinct worldviews: American Jews continued to orbit around a rooted cosmopolitanism; and Israeli Jews migrated from a

---

[15] Kalberg 2012: 74.

prophetic Zionism to ethnonationalist Zionism. The conclusion draws out the lessons of this story for humanist relationalism.

5.1   Jewish Worldviews: Nationalism and Cosmopolitanism

Except for the brief slice of history when they had political power in ancient Israel, Jews have been a minority people in exile that operated with a nearly singular worldview that pivoted around isolation in and exclusion from the world. Jewish life and religious practice varied regionally and historically, but this was diversity within unity. However, after centuries of relative isolation, two yoked transformations forced Jews to reconsider their worldview.

The first major transformation was the Enlightenment. By privileging reason over superstition, change over tradition, science over religion, and, most importantly, humanity over discrimination, Enlightenment thought held that people should be judged as individuals and on their achievements, not their religion or other discriminatory factors. Because the Enlightenment made it less defensible to treat some people as inherently inferior and undeserving of equal treatment and respect, it represented the beginning of the emancipation of the Jews and other minorities and the possibility of having rights and citizenship.[16] This was a revolutionary moment in the history of the Jews. As Salo Baron, pronounced more than ninety years ago, "The history of the Jews in the last century and a half has turned on one central fact: that of Emancipation."[17] Two decades ago, David Vital similarly concluded that: "The principal engine of change in the modern history of the Jews of Europe was the revolutionary idea that it might be after all right and proper for them to enjoy full and equal civil and political rights with all other subjects of the several realms they inhabited."[18] In his monumental history of Jewish emancipation, David Sorkin reviews how the variable of the emancipation nearly determined differences in the conditions of European Jews since the eighteenth century.[19] In any event, with the possibility of their emancipation, the debate about their relationship to the particular and the universal spilled out of the *yeshivot* and into politics. Yet not all states and polities embraced Enlightenment; indeed, most European Jews lived in places where counter-Enlightenment flourished and Jews were defined as less than human.[20]

---

[16] Katznelson and Birnbaum 1995.   [17] Baron 1928: 515 (cited in Sorkin 2019: 2–3).
[18] Vital 1999: 29 (cited in Sorkin, 2019: 3).   [19] Sorkin 2019.
[20] Bethencourt 2016; Stuurman 2017.

Similar issues emerged because of the second major transformation: the rise of nationalism. A nation, generically speaking, is a political community that is bound by a common history, language, religion, spirit, or sense of fate. What gives the nation something of a special status in modern politics is the project of nationalism and its goal of statehood. In short, nationalism consists of a nation with a collective identity and interests, and with the belief that its interests and self-determination are advanced by gaining or maintaining sovereignty or authority over a homeland. In many instances, the nation replaced God as the sacred.[21]

As self-defined nations went about their business of nation- and state-building, some had open clubs while others were restricted. The classic distinction is that between civic and ethnic nationalism, which, not coincidentally, was coined by a Zionist and Jewish scholar of nationalism, Hans Kohn.[22] In ethnic nationalism, membership is determined by blood, lineage, kinship, and tribe. As Michael Ignatieff famously described, in this brand of nationalism "an individual's deepest attachments are inherited, not chosen."[23] States that subscribe to this form of nationalism favor one group over another. In those countries where ethnic nationalism took root, Jews did not have to consider which features of their Jewishness they were prepared to surrender to become part of the nation because they were, for all intents and purposes, automatically disqualified from membership. An alternative form of nationalism is based not on blood or heritage, but on a shared civic character. "This nationalism," Ignatieff argues, "is called civic because it envisages the nation as a community of equal, rights-bearing citizens, united in patriotic attachment to a shared set of political practices and values."[24] In the early days of nation- and state-building, this meant transforming regional, religious, and ethnic identities into a unifying national identity.

The rise of nationalism alongside the first wave of globalization helped to create the rise of cosmopolitanism. There are many kinds of cosmopolitanism, but most modern forms trace their origin to the Enlightenment and include several core tenants. There is a belief that each person is of equal worth an a subject of moral concerns. Relatedly, individuals and communities have duties and obligations to all other humans near and far and that transcend existing territorial, political, cultural, gender, racial, and religious boundaries. And, humans should strive to transcend "particularism in order to achieve a more complete understanding of that experience."[25] These modern forms, moreover,

---

[21] Smith 2004.   [22] Kohn 2005. Also see Mosse 1997; Tamir 2019.
[23] Ignatieff 1995: 3–5.   [24] Ignatieff 1995.
[25] Hollinger 1985: 59. Also see Appiah 2007; Beck and Sznaider 2009; Calhoun 2008; Cheah, 2006; Gilroy 2005; Waldron 2000; Alevi 2015; Greene and Viaene 2012.

became more desirable with the simultaneous rise of the nation-state and the internationalization of the world; whereas the former demanded that individuals circumscribe their identities and duties, the better encouraged individuals to transcend borders.

There has been a spirited philosophical and political debate regarding the relationship between nationalism and cosmopolitanism ever since they emerged as projects and aspirations around the mid-nineteenth century.[26] As should be apparent by comparing how Duara in Chapter 7 and I approach the topic of cosmopolitanism, the relationship between it and nationalism is hard to pin down because neither has a fixed meaning, and the boundaries between them have evolved in relationship to each other and in response to the historical times. And, to further complicate matters, the boundaries between them are not only historically fluid but also community dependent. Different communities in historical and spatial proximity can have very different views of the relationship between nationalism and cosmopolitanism. To go deeper down the rabbit's hole, as I will soon do, the same community can have contending views about this relationship. That said, the debate tends to orbit around whether nationalism and cosmopolitanism are competing or complementary.

The zero-sum view is that they are rivals and that when one is up the other down, a view that derives from the belief that national and cosmopolitan identities, like oil and water, cannot mix. During the era of nationalism in the nineteenth and early twentieth centuries, nationalism was in and cosmopolitanism was out. This was an era of state-building, in which society was expected to not only defer to the state but also to identify with it and no others. Movements that imagined an alternative political project that directly challenged the authority and purpose of the state, such as socialism, and those peoples who were viewed as incapable of shifting their loyalties, such as the Jews, were viewed as enemies of the nation. This nineteenth-century perspective appears to be making a comeback, as current trends exhibit a retreat from forms of internationalism and cosmopolitanism and the return of a self-centered nationalism.

Alternatively, cosmopolitanism and nationalism might have a positive-sum and symbiotic relationship. Nations have common interests that can only be individually and collectively advanced with the presence of a cosmopolitan spirit. In this regard, forms of cosmopolitanism can stabilize, not undermine, a world organized around the nation-state. Many nations and nationalisms present themselves as serving not just the

---

[26] Sluga 2015.

nation-state but also the international community, and such presentations and their associated practices can help legitimate the nation-state. Cosmopolitan beliefs and practices can deepen while maintaining the legitimacy of the state. For instance, Immanuel Kant imagined a historical unfolding whereby states developed a pacific relationship while maintaining their sovereignty.[27] There have been historical periods when such sentiments developed into dominant trends and practices in the world order. For instance, World Wars I and II discredited egoistic nationalism and created a space for the development of internationalism with islands of cosmopolitanism. Lions and lambs could not only coexist, but also enjoy a platonic consummation.

The rise of nationalism and the Enlightenment profoundly impacted how Jewish communities answered the Jewish Question and pursued their ontological and physical survival in an era of the rise of nation-states. After centuries of having little choice but to be a people apart, the emergence of nationalism and the nation-state meant that Jews were judged according to whether they were perceived to be capable of shifting their loyalties from each other to the state. Whether nationalism was, on balance, more positive than negative depended on which form prevailed. In the emerging folk nationalisms of Eastern Europe in the nineteenth century, Jews were defined as outsiders because of their heritage, dress, religion, and Yiddish tongue. Under such circumstances Jews had very limited choices, including immigrate to the West, join movements such as socialism that aspired to remove all differences between peoples, or become Zionists.

In situations of civic nationalism Jews were welcome – on the condition that they shed any transnational identity in favor of their new state-bounded identity. For instance, in 1789, Count Stanislas de Clermont-Tonnerre famously declared: "To the Jews as a nation – nothing; to the Jews as human beings, everything."[28] If the Jews wanted to be a nation, then they could not be French, and if they wanted to be French then they had to forget any thoughts of being a nation. Jews decided to become French. A similar process occurred in other liberal-oriented nations, as Jews became Germans, Dutch, British, and Americans. But if the Jews were not a nation, then what were they? Either a religious community or an ethnic group, or some combination thereof, but in any case this was a private and not a public concern. Complicating their claims, though, were the eastern Jews, who had been excluded from membership and

---

[27] Kant 1784.
[28] French National Assembly, December 23, 1789 (cited in Mendes-Flohr and Reinharz 1995, 114–16).

were now increasingly claiming that the Jews were a nation that deserved their own homeland or state. If the eastern Jews were right about the Jews being a nation, then western Jews were trying to con their Christian neighbors.

The Enlightenment and civic nationalism also placed new demands on Jewish communities. Jews had the opportunity to be granted equal rights and accepted as citizens of the nation-state – but only if they abandoned those features that gentiles found offensive and believed sustained their clannish tendencies. It was not enough to pledge loyalty to the nation – they had to fit in. Accordingly, Jews began to reconsider their way of life, traditions, and religious laws and customs, attempting to reform or remove those that Christians found contemptible and that Jews believed would hinder their bounded integration into a modern, civilized society.[29] They removed any claims to be a "chosen people" or that they were in exile, each of which communicated the view that Jews were both superior and just passing through. But how much of a makeover was too much? At what point did altering their practices to win acceptance turn into an assimilation that was a euphemism for cultural suicide? The *Haskalah* movement in the nineteenth century was one of the first important attempts to provide an answer.[30] Centered in Germany, it advanced the simultaneous solidarity of the Jews and their integration into Christian societies. In the United States, a Judaism that once had no need for adjectives now began to acquire them – reform, conservative, and Orthodox. Reform Judaism became the primary vehicle for allowing Jews to remain Jews while also fitting into a modernizing and liberalizing society. It was this prophetic theology that helped to nurture a cosmopolitanism and universalism among western, and especially reforming, Jews.[31]

Reform Judaism drew much of its inspiration from prophetic Judaism.[32] Prophetic Judaism refers to the sayings of the prophets who lived between the seventh and eighth century BCE, a period in which the Jewish tribes were having difficulty sustaining themselves, religiously and politically. They had formed a monarchy, an unusual move for a people that believed that only God was a true king. The monarchy became corrupt and arguably blasphemous as it used faith to mask its many indiscretions. In response to these transgressions, dozens of prophets, including Amos, several Isaiahs, Hosea, and Micah, professed that God had spoken directly to them, commanding them to exhort the Jews to return to a path of righteousness, to reaffirm that there was only one, invisible, God, to choose good over evil, and to work for justice. God's

[29] Batnisky 2011; Meyer 1990.   [30] Litvak 2012.   [31] Barnett 2016.   [32] Barnett 2016.

message was clear: to be righteous requires more than unthinkingly following commandments, reflexively holding ceremonies, and performing rituals to be righteous – it also demands an ethical life, treating others kindly, and working for justice. A house of worship that becomes a "den of thieves" is not pious. Reform Judaism drew from the prophetic tradition as it emphasized the importance of ethics and justice – themes that did not require Jews to spend hours in prayer and that made them appear more acceptable to non-Jews.

The combination of the kinds of emancipation and nationalism split the Jewish community into four stylized worldviews distinguished by the intersection of nonterritorial/territorial and particular/universal. Particularity regards whether Jews are a people apart and universality whether they are part of a common humanity. Deterritoriality captures whether Jews can (and should) exist without a home or state of their own. Judaism and the Jewish people are attached to the ancient land of Israel, reflected in and reinforced by religious texts, songs, prayers, and expressions. But this attachment does not necessarily demand either immigration to their ancient homeland or the belief that Jews require an exclusive homeland or state in order to survive and thrive.[33]

Territoriality concerns whether Jews need a homeland or state of their own that allows them to control and defend their lives. Zionism is the chief example of territoriality.[34] It originated in the nineteenth century in Europe and as a response to Jewish ontological and physical insecurity; if Jews became part of other nations they might assimilate to the point of disappearance, and Jews needed a state of their own for self-determination and self-defense. In this respect it tracks with many other nationalisms at the time, but as a latecomer it drew from the various existing nationalisms. But in almost all versions Zionism was intended to do more than provide protection and self-determination; it was also intended to provide a break from and a return to history. Centuries of living in exile had led the Jews to acquire many unsavory characteristics: obsequious, weak, compliant, cowardly, passive, and willing to obey even the most suicidal of commands.[35] According to mainstream Zionist thought, diaspora Jews do not get respect from gentiles because they do not deserve it. By returning to Palestine and working the land, by building a state and defending it with courage, muscle, and power, Jews will recover their dignity and Christians will treat them with the respect they have earned. Zionism was a twelve-step program that

[33] Alroey 2011; Boyarin and Boyarin 2002; Dubnov 2007; Pianko 2010; Smith 1995.
[34] For a sampling of this rich menu and vast literature, see Aveniri 1981; Hertzberg 1979; Lacqueur 2003; Linfield 2019; Meyers 1995; Selzer 1970.
[35] Luz 2008: 50–52; Eisen 1983; Zerubavel 1995.

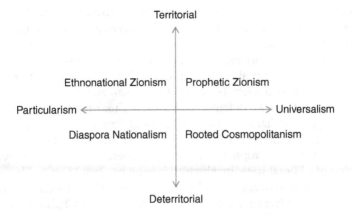

Figure 5.1 Worldviews of Western Jews

would help Jews become "normal" and make an awe-inspiring return to history.

Three caveats before describing each worldview. Because subcommunities can have their distinct worldviews, there could be as many worldviews as there are subunits. I am including those Jewish worldviews that want to maintain the physical and ontological survival of Jewish people. There were Jews who were quite tired of the "disaster" of being Jewish, as Howard Kallen undiplomatically put it, wanting to shed any sign of their Jewishness, and who felt no love for or obligation to the Jewish people.[36] Some assimilated into society either by rejecting Judaism and/or converting to Christianity. Many Jews also joined socialist and communist movements, which held that anti-Semitism would end with the arrival of a socialism that would choke off the supply of opium that turned the masses into religious dopes.[37] Second, I am examining those Jewish worldviews that are political to the extent that they are attempting to address the social organization of the Jewish people in a world carved into nation-states. There are religiously oriented sects that, for all intents and purposes, have withdrawn from the secular world. Third, these stylized views are ideal-types.[38] In other words, their purpose is not to reflect a granular reality, but rather to help identify different kinds of, and measure change in, worldviews. There might be three synagogues for every two Jews, but it also might be theoretically and empirically advantageous to compare all three to two different ideal-types. In this regard, they are sociological

---

[36] Kallen 1921: 37–38.   [37] Marx 1844.   [38] Kalberg 2004; Swedberg 2018.

categories because they identify distinctive attributes that distinguish between types, and historical categories because they can help trace change in and across Jewish communities.

Prophetic Zionism emerges from the interplay of territorialism and universalism. It is territorial because it demands a homeland or state for the Jews in the land of ancient Israel where they can enjoy self-determination and marshall their own defense. This form of Zionism also had a universal or cosmopolitan character, both in terms of how it imagined organizing state–society relations and the state's place in the world. There were two major branches of prophetic Zionism. A liberal Zionism imagined the creation of a liberal state, in which all inhabitants would enjoy liberty and equality. It would become a light unto nations. This was the Zionism of Herzl, many leaders of the Zionist movement such as Chaim Weizmann, and the prevailing form in western countries such as the United States. There also was a Labor or Socialist Zionism. This Zionism emerged as a critique of capitalism and bourgeois nationalism, aspiring to create a socialist state that would provide the foundation for genuine equality and justice and become a role model for the world until a global socialism emerged that would remove the need for a world divided by sovereignty. This was the Zionism of Moses Hess, Ber Borochov, David Ben-Gurion, the Jewish leadership in Palestine, and the Mapai government that ruled Israel for three decades. Both liberal and labor Zionism, though, confronted the limits of egalitarianism when having to create a *Jewish* state with a significant Arab minority in a hostile environment: as a Jewish state, would Jews enjoy special privileges, and would the state provide room for non-Jews in its national identity? And as a Jewish state, how would it respond to the potential threat posed by the Palestinians and Arabs? Importantly, liberal Zionists tended to be highly secular and labor Zionists quite hostile to religious authority.

Ethnonational Zionism ascribes to the idea that a state for the Jews should be by and for the Jews. There are two major branches. One follows from revisionist Zionism.[39] Spearheaded by Ze'ev Jabotinsky, it began less as a rejection of Zionism than as a critique of the Zionist leadership in Palestine and abroad. Although he never rejected liberal values, his nationalism had a strong ethnic and racial component. He also admired those European nationalisms that wanted to flex their muscle and militarize, even going so far as mimicking some of Italian nationalism's fascist elements. Unlike the labor and liberal Zionists. who exhibited some flexibility in their territorial demands, he imagined a Jewish majority on both sides of the Jordan River. He passed away in exile in 1940, and his

[39] Zouplna 2008.

legacy continued with Menachem Begin and others, often venturing from a minimalist to a more maximalist revisionism.[40] Alongside revisionist Zionism is religious Zionism, which blends nationalism and Orthodox Judaism. Of the many important intellectual figures, Rabbi Abraham Isaac Kook was among the most influential, interpreting the Jewish return in messianic terms and advocating for the establishment of a Jewish state that followed religious law on all of ancient Israel.[41]

Diaspora nationalism refers to a Jewish people dispersed across different lands that see themselves as a nation with a shared identity, history, and common fate.[42] As responses to the emerging European nationalism, diaspora nationalism developed alongside, and in ways as a counterpoint to, Zionism.[43] The primary point of differentiation between it and forms of Zionism is the necessity and possible function of a Jewish state. The Jewish people would benefit from common, transnational institutions, and even be members of multilateral institutions and international organizations, but these features of political life could be accomplished without a sovereign state. Perhaps most critical in this regard was cultural, religious, and physical survival. Many diaspora nationalists advocated a two-front campaign – develop forms of autonomy at home and global norms and institutions to protect them from their domestic enemies. Also, while diaspora nationalists tended to reject the idea of a state, they nevertheless favored a Jewish homeland to provide a fertile ground for a Jewish renaissance and to anchor Jews in a universalizing world. Not only did they believe that a Jewish state was impractical, but many also thought that living in the diaspora was ethically superior to political sovereignty. Whereas Zionists saw exile as producing abnormalities and deformities in the Jewish character, some diaspora nationalists believed that it nurtured a cosmopolitanism and more easily merged the particular and the universal, developed a multiperspectival view, and integrated the best of different cultures. For some non-Jews, this diasporic character became a major explanation for the purported genius of the Jews. Living on the margins enabled Jews to create something world-turning from loose and disparate ends; Marx, Einstein, and Freud became the paradigmatic examples.[44]

Rooted cosmopolitan sits at the intersection of nonterritoriality and universality.[45] It overlaps with diaspora nationalism in terms of its

---

[40] Shimoni 1995: 209.   [41] Kaplan 2005.   [42] Anderson 1992.
[43] Brenner 2018; Devine 2018; Gertz 2018; Rabinovitch 2012; Shunsky 2018.
[44] Veblen 1919.
[45] The label "rooted cosmopolitanism" has a checkered history because of its association with Stalin's anti-Semitic campaign against Jews. For a quite different usage that I follow, see Tarrow 2005 and Loeffler 2018.

rejection of the necessity of Jewish sovereignty for a meaningful and secure Jewish life. But whereas diaspora nationalism often imagined forms of geographic, legal, and political autonomy in order to maintain the Jewish cultural identity, rooted cosmopolitans tended to root themselves in the individualism of liberal, democratic societies. Relatedly, while diaspora nationalism tended to hope for various forms of national and international protections to secure their cultural and physical existence, rooted cosmopolitans tended to rely on a strategy of acceptance and a liberalism of equality. Consequently, diaspora nationalism flourished in eastern Europe, and rooted cosmopolitanism in Western liberalizing democracies. Rooted cosmopolitanism's liberal, democratic roots also account for its suspicion of Zionism because of its exclusionary nationalist character. Consequently, while Zionism might be necessary for securing the physical and cultural existence of some Jews, they are fine where they are.

Rooted cosmopolitanism's universalism stems from a political theology and humanism that accentuates the liberal and pluralist character of modern (international) society. In this way, its domestic political culture shapes its international and cosmopolitan orientation. Accordingly, rooted cosmopolitans tend to have the sort of orientation associated with liberal internationalism, and for two major reasons. One is that their universalism crosses borders. Their values of liberalism, democracy, equality, and liberty are not tied to the nation-state but rather are part of global justice. As Jews they could play a role in bringing these values to the rest of the world, and many of them did, as evidenced by their role in the creation of international human rights. The other reason owed to Jewish survival and security. The same humanistic values that brought security and acceptance to them in Western liberal democracies could also help bring security to Jews in non-Western lands. As such, advocated internationalism and civilizing missions.[46] And, it just so happened that those western countries where Jews were becoming accepted and enjoying access to political power were also the West's major powers, creating, at times, a relationship between Jewish interests and imperialism.

5.2   Profiles in Changing Worldviews

These four primary worldviews that crystallized in the early twentieth century had different answers to the Jewish Question and Jewish ontological and physical security in the context of changing kinds of

---

[46] Leff 2006; Green 2008; Wistrich 1998: especially 64.

Enlightenment processes and nationalism. As I argued in the opening pages, worldviews can change because of internal and external developments. In the first half of the twentieth century, Jewish worldviews were shaken by a series of violent ruptures that culminated in the Holocaust. In the second half of the twentieth century the worldviews of the two largest Jewish communities, the American and the Israeli, followed their environments: among American Jews it remained part of rooted cosmopolitanism, with shades of particularism; in Israel, a prophetic Zionism became replaced by an ethnonational Zionism.[47] Once again, for the sake of simplicity and because of space constraints, nuance is an unaffordable luxury.

5.2.1   1900–1948

The first half century of the twentieth century constituted a downward spiral of the destruction of European Jewry. Pogroms cycled and recycled through Russia and Eastern Europe until the outbreak of World War I. The war had a disproportionate effect on the Jews, the end of the war continued the killing spree, and the new states of eastern Europe maintained their well-earned reputation for anti-Semitism. The combination of counter-Enlightenment forces and chauvinistic nationalism fed into a rabid anti-Semitism, beginning in Nazi Germany but then spreading to other parts of Europe; at times, the Germans and the local populations appeared to engage in one-upmanship regarding who could be cruelest to, and kill the most, Jews. Nazi Germany might have lost the war against the allies, but they almost won the war against the European Jews.

The Jews of Europe had few (if any) protections or exit options. Following in the footsteps of diaspora nationalism, following WWI many eastern Jewish leaders proposed the construction of semi-autonomous provinces and specialized rights for the Jews to provide security and preserve their cultural identity. Because these new states could not be trusted, they and various western Jewish leaders, including the relatively influential American Jewish delegation, proposed internationalizing these rights and creating protections lodged in the new League of Nations. Predictably, the new leaders of Eastern Europe opposed the idea of carving out a state within a state, Western states were hesitant about establishing robust enforcement mechanisms that would dispense with the principle of sovereignty, and so states created the unprecedented international minority rights treaties – but without enforcement

---

[47] Much of this section draws from Barnett 2016.

mechanisms. Unsurprisingly, these rights had little protective value when they were most needed over the next two decades.

The only other option was immigration, and while Germany and other countries were prepared to see their Jews flee at the appropriate price, there were few countries prepared to accept them. The United States had been a principal destination point for European Jews before World War One but it all but closed its doors in 1924. Palestine was the other alternative. Britain's Balfour Declaration of 1917 pledged to create a Jewish homeland in Palestine, which was subsequently endorsed by the League of Nations, and Britain became its mandatory authority. From the very start the British had to try and accommodate two competing nationalisms, and became increasingly resistant to allowing substantial Jewish immigration for fear of triggering unrest and possibly civil war. But because Palestine was the only possible option, and because the violent anti-Semitism in Europe proved the fundamental point that Christians would never figure out how to protect or stop killing Jews, the Zionists' demands became more urgent and forceful; Britain, though, refused to do anything that might distract from its focus on Nazi Germany or cause the Palestinians to rebel or become allied with Germany.

The destruction of European Jewry had an immediate impact on which worldviews were seen as either practical or utopian to the point of suicidal. Because diaspora nationalism could not address how to protect the Jews' physical security, it retreated to the steam rooms, cafes, and other places where Jewish intellectuals debated utopian solutions. Rooted cosmopolitanism in many Western states, and especially in the United States, began to warm to Zionism for several reasons. Arguably most important in the United States was the emergence of an American culture that provided space for hyphenated identities.[48] Against this welcoming possibility, American Jewish leaders such as Louis Brandeis, who would become the first Jew appointed to the US Supreme Court, began reassuring American Jews that they could be part of the Jewish and the American nation, and that their Zionism did not diminish but rather strengthened their American identity. But all the while theirs was an *American* Zionism: Jews needed a homeland and not a state; and any homeland had to recognize the rights of the Arab population. In short, many early-twentieth-century American Zionists favored forms of binationalism in Palestine – not partitioning Palestine, but rather finding a formula for Jews' and Palestinians' coexistence.[49] Importantly, although anti-Semitism was also on the rise in the United States, American Jews doubled down on liberalism and universalism, emphasizing how America was their home and Zionism

---

[48] Barnett 2016.   [49] Ben-Israel 2018.

was a solution for other Jews. Not until 1942 did American Jewish organizations finally accept that Jews needed a "commonwealth" – that is, a state, of their own.

Labor and revisionist Zionism, which represented prophetic and ethnonational worldviews, battled each other for influence and power in the Yishuv and in world Zionist organizations; but, in the end, ideology mattered a lot less than whose strategy and tactics for creating an independent state seemed most compelling and practical. Labor Zionism, led by David Ben-Gurion, which was busily creating a proto-state and placing facts on the ground, controlled the major Jewish institutions in Palestine and, for all intents and purposes, represented the Jewish community in relations and negotiations with the British authorities. The Revisionists' charismatic powerhouse Ze'ev Jabotinsky died in exile in 1940, and their other leaders, including future Prime Ministers Menachem Begin and Yitzhak Shamir, lived underground as a consequence of their acts of terrorism against Palestinians, British mandatory authorities, and the occasional Jewish rival.

The Holocaust followed by the miraculous return of Jewish sovereignty after 2,000 years combined evils and dreams beyond imagination. Catastrophe then renewal. It is impossible to overstate the magnitude of their impact. The Holocaust and Israel became historically and metaphysically connected through death and rebirth. And their combination helped Jews, across these worldviews, make sense of the suffering and provided a way to cope. The Holocaust caused Jews to turn dark and to wonder how it was possible that God could have allowed such horrors to happen. What had they done to warrant such a punishment? What did this evil say about the world? Jews responded to these religious, spiritual, and existential challenges in various ways. Some turned their backs on religion, God, and the very idea that it was possible to explain the Holocaust. The Holocaust, like all events of such horror, destroyed the conceptual resources available to make sense of evil and suffering.[50] Indeed, to try to even make sense of the Holocaust represented an obscenity.[51] As Theodore Adorno famously wrote, "There can be no poetry after Auschwitz."[52] Not the creation of the Jewish state, or anything else, could ever explain, justify, or give meaning to the destruction of the European Jews while the world stood by and let it happen.[53]

---

[50] Neiman 2002: 256.   [51] Neiman 2002: 250–58, 261–62.
[52] Adorno 1949: 34 (cited in interview with Herbert Marcuse on Adorno).
[53] Bauman 2001.

Many others, however, invested Israel with a significance and a meaning that enabled them to cope with the horrors of the Holocaust and have reason to hope. This can be interpreted as a form of theodicy.[54] The eighteenth-century philosopher Gottfried Leibniz introduced the concept to a modern audience, and then Max Weber illuminated the concept as it became central to his sociology of religion. Different religions and ethical communities have offered different responses to the existence of evil, sin, and disappointments in a transcendental and divinely ordered world, but the need to do so is powerfully felt in those religions that believe in a loving and all-powerful God.[55] As Max Weber wrote, "The more the development [of religious ideas] tends toward the conception of a transcendental unitary god who is universal, the more there arises the problem of how the extraordinary power of such a god can be reconciled with the imperfection of the world."[56] Although many Jews, religious and secular alike, refused to try and find meaning in the Holocaust, Israel provided a blessed stand-in. It gave them a reason for belief. The Holocaust became part of the sacred, and, by extension, so too did Israel.

5.2.2   1948–2020

The destruction of European Jewry and the creation of Israel meant that the United States and Israel became the two largest Jewish communities in the world. Both began building their lives. In the United States, anti-Semitism became unacceptable (though it still occurred) and Jews became integrated into what was now referred to as a Judeo-Christian America. There was not the same need for Jewish country clubs, hospitals, community centers, and the like as Jews were increasingly allowed to join more inclusive institutions. Many Jews also became involved in various civil rights and empowerment movements, seeing their own struggles in those of others. In hindsight, the surprise is not that the Holocaust impacted the outlook of American Jews, but that its impact was so minimal at the outset and that American Jews continued onward with a cosmopolitan ethic.

Israel began with a prophetic streak, but this principle became compromised as a matter of politics; or, alternatively stated, Israel wanted to be both particular and universal, but the former ranked above the latter in terms of the hierarchy of needs.[57] In his speeches and writings at the time, Ben-Gurion often referenced the prophetic tradition and Israel's rightful

---

[54] Fuller 2011; Neiman 2002; Weber 1963.
[55] Berger 1969: 59–80; Leibinz [1710] 1998; Weber 1948.
[56] Weber 1963: 138–39 (cited in Morgan and Wilkinson 2001: 201).
[57] Lieblich and Shachar 2014.

place as a light unto nations. But the prophets had never dealt with the harsh reality of gathering Holocaust survivors and Jews from Arab lands in numbers that equaled the existing population in Israel, and developing an economy under dire circumstances and without natural resources. Nor could Israel beat swords into ploughshares surrounded by enemies that pledged its destruction; instead, necessity suggested just the opposite. In the document declaring Israel's independence, Ben-Gurion reassured that all citizens, regardless of religion, race, gender, or creed, would be treated as equal.[58] Liberal democracy was not twaddle, but this was a Jewish state, and while Israeli Arabs were formally equal and had the right to vote, this potential fifth column did not enjoy the same rights or freedom of movement as Jews.

The 1967 and 1973 wars had a significant impact on the worldviews of American and Israeli Jews, though with slightly different effects. For many Jews, the major plot lines of the wars tracked each other. In both cases Arabs waged war and the world stood by. In 1967 the Arab states mobilized their armies and marched them to their border with Israel with speeches predicting Israel's coming destruction. Israel went to the United Nations, France, and the United States for help, but found none. Instead of waiting to be attacked, it struck preemptively, and in six days demolished three Arab armies and captured the Sinai, the West Bank and Jerusalem, and the Golan Heights, flipping the standard narrative of Jewish weakness on its head. Six years later, Egypt and Syria launched a surprise attack on the holiest day in Judaism, and once again the world stood by and did nothing. Even the United States hesitated to resupply an Israeli army that was on the ropes. Israel turned near-defeat into victory, but a pyrrhic one.

This is also a period that coincides with the construction of the "Holocaust." The Holocaust was no stranger to American Jewish life, but it was relatively minor compared to what it would become. Beginning in the 1970s the Holocaust gained prominence in the United States and around the world, aided by the collective effort of well-placed individuals and organizations, and especially Jewish leaders and associations, who determined it must become more central to Jewish and global consciousness. The increased emphasis on the "Holocaust" resulted from accidental and intentional activity, sincere and strategic action, and the conjunction of forces beyond anyone's control. The wars of the Middle East and the sanctification of the Holocaust bonded to form a single experience for American Jews.[59] By the mid-1970s it was near impossible to think about Israel without also conjuring up the Holocaust, and vice

[58] Cited in Walzer 2012: 74.   [59] Woocher 1986: 132.

versa. The Holocaust was an immediate reminder that Jews are never safe and can never rely on others for their existence, and that a self-reliant, strong Jewish state is the only guarantor of the Jewish people. Israel is a Jewish state dedicated to ensuring the survival of the Jews, in the here and now, in the future, in Israel, and in the diaspora. The Holocaust reminded Jews that forces would rise, from time to time, to destroy the Jewish people, and Israel reminded them that Jews would persevere.

Because of the wars and the growing salience of the Holocaust, the balance between particularism and universalism among American and Israeli Jews shifted from the latter to the former. Israel became part of the American Jewish identity.[60] For many American Jews, Israel became a form of idolatry, and to be a Jew in good standing depended more on supporting Israel, right or wrong, than keeping Shabbat. There was an increase in American Jewish immigration to Israel, but American Zionism continued to mean American Jews providing financial and political support from the United States. Alongside Israel, the Holocaust also helped to reinforce the more particularlistic aspects of the American Jewish identity and create a greater attachment to Israel. But they remained rooted cosmopolitans with strong universalistic tendencies.

In Israel a new form of nationalism began to develop, much less prophetic and much more ethnonationalist and messianic in character. When Israel's borders were limited to the 1949 armistice, there was little room for religious and revisionist Zionism to expand. But the capture of the territories, and especially those seen as part of biblical Israel, provided an outlet for their visions of a Greater Israel. And those Israeli Jews who might not see the ideological value of the territories could appreciate adding to Israel's strategic depth. Israeli settlement activity began soon after 1967, and then accelerated with the 1977 election of Menachem Begin, whose Likud Party had strong roots in revisionist ideology. The Labor and Likud parties continued to vie for control, but the ground was shifting to the right. The Holocaust also became more fully intertwined in Israeli Jewish identity, though in a context of a growing ethnonationalism that amplified Israel's particularism.[61]

Like what happened in the United States, the Holocaust also became central to Israeli identity beginning in the 1960s. In the first decades of the Israeli state, the Holocaust victims were treated as a living example of life in the galut; many Israeli leaders held to myths of Jews going to their deaths like sheep, and occasionally referred to survivors as "soaps." The 1961 trial of Albert Eichmann was one of the first showcase events in

---

[60] Barnett 2016; Ben-Moshe and Segev 2007.   [61] Zertal 2005.

Israel, and, beginning with the 1967 war, Israel began using Holocaust analogies to refer to the conflict with Arab states and the Palestinians.

Despite these shared experiences that swelled feelings of Jewish precarity, their preexisting worldviews offered different ways to respond to such feelings, creating a growing difference in worldviews between American and Israeli Jews. American Jews retained a strong attachment to Israel, but began to increasingly question their relationship to an Israel that appeared to contain a different set of values than them. American Jews remain both Americans and Jews. They retain a strong sense of their Jewish identity, but it is a Jewish identity that continues to be profoundly shaped by an American experience that retains strong connections to humanism and cosmopolitanism. The Israeli Jewish identity, on the other hand, is defined by its ethnic and religious character. There is little remaining of prophetic Zionism in Israeli politics as ethnonational Zionism has become hegemonic.[62] The consequence is that Israeli and American Jews have become brothers from different planets. And while these brothers maintain relations, these relations are fraught with tension and opposition. The Jewish Question remains.

5.3   Conclusion

I want to conclude with two observations regarding the relationship between Jewish worldviews and relationalism. The first is the recognition that while worldviews presume a permanence, they also are susceptible to change. To distinguish between change *in* a worldview and change *of* a worldview requires some measure of distinction. In other words, what aspect of a worldview is being isolated and used to mark a transformation? There is no gold standard, in part because there are various elements of worldviews. My account of Jewish worldviews, though, has focused on the relationship between the community and their relationship to outsiders and their place in the world, otherwise known as the Jewish Question. But, as many of the major European intellectuals, who also happened to be Jewish, observed, you don't have to be Jewish to experience the Jewish Question. The relationship between the particular and the universal, as Marx, Durkheim, Simmel, Levi-Strauss, Berlin, and Arendt, and other eminent Jewish scholars noted, is a central feature and experience of modernity. And for a Jewish community defined by religion and ethnicity, the universalizing properties of the Enlightenment and modernity threatened extinction.

---

[62] Gertz 2018; Weingrod 2018.

Accordingly, the central question for many Jewish communities became how to retain some semblance of their Jewish identity while integrating in an increasingly humanistic world. There were many factors that shaped how different Jewish communities answered this dilemma, including what their non-Jewish neighbors might think of them. And if their non-Jewish neighbors were not pleased, there was the chance that their toleration might wear thin. As such, this was a debate that was shaped by historical context and the search for security mediated by the desire to retain features of a religious and secularized Jewish identity. And the very fact that there was not one answer but multiple answers, all formed under the rubric of the Jewish Question, highlights how a single community can have distinguishable worldviews.

The second point is more directed at hyper-humanism. As I stated at the outset, my sociological relationalism incorporates not just a humanism but also a recognition that while all groups are socially constructed, they also can have enduring properties and see themselves as having a history and memory that links them from the past to the present to the future. When Jews began debating the Jewish Question in the late eighteenth century, they did so with a belief that they shared a common history and set of religious texts that provided the wellspring of memory and belonging. Being and becoming were part of a dialectic process, and neither could exist without the other. There must be a there there – a desire to maintain some semblance of belonging even as they choose different paths for becoming. Jews might not have agreed on the basis of their belonging, but they agreed on the necessity of keeping belonging alive. The particular required a permanence, even if at the level of metaphysics, with the danger that humanism might turn into a version of hyper-humanism. What would be the consequence? Jews, and all communities would become ever-changing things (or things that are not things) that have little basis of existence. Their sense of self would have no basis in history, culture, or belief. Individuals would experience alienation and anomie. They would cease to have hopes or ways of coping with disappointment and suffering. Do humans long for this deracinated existence? Communities are often criticized for the burdens and obligations they impose on their members, but a world defined by highly mutable and constantly disappearing things sounds like another form of imprisonment.

The questions posed in this volume are reminiscent of Martin Buber's struggle to find a comfortable relationship between humanism and relationalism. Born in Vienna in 1878, he moved to Germany as a young man, rose to considerable prestige, and then fled Nazi Germany for Palestine in 1938 at the age of 60, where he taught at the Hebrew

University of Jerusalem. In a recent biography, Paul Mendes-Flohr underscores how Buber eventually committed to a relationalism to try and align the particular and the universal. As Mendes-Flohr tells it, there were three stages to Buber's intellectual development.[63] In Stage One he worried that the Enlightenment would lead to the erasure of the supernatural Jew, who is deeply connected to thousands of years of tradition, history, and practice, and rooted in Torah and rabbinic tradition, and to the rise of the "natural" Jew, who aspires to become part of humanity. This shift owes partly to the attraction of Enlightenment thought and to the desire to mute anti-Semitism by doing everything to avoid offending Christians. But at what cost? Humanism, Bubor warned, would lead to the disappearance of the Jewish people and offer nothing but emptiness.

In his effort to recover the supernatural Jew, Buber turned to Hasidism, which he believed represented a sort of "pure" Judaism. However, Buber hoped not for a return, but rather a rebirth – a Jewish renaissance. In Stage Two Buber entered into Jewish politics, embraced Zionism, and worked for Herzl. What attracted Buber to Zionism, though, was not the idea of imitating European politics or establishing a Jewish state, but rather the possibility of promoting a Jewish cultural renewal in which Jewish rebirth and humanity were in dialectical relationship. Indeed, he feared that a Jewish nation that became a sovereign state would cease to have the ability to enjoy a real Jewish renewal; European nationalisms were hardly attractive role models. Buber championed binationalism, broke from organized Zionism, and concluded that renewal did not require living in Palestine but rather could occur in the diaspora.

Stage Three begins when he moves to Berlin, continuing his Judaic learning, and becomes mentored by Wilhelm Dilthey and Georg Simmel. He now adopts a relationalism that is steeped in both the imminent and the transcendent and the particular and the universal. Such commitments provide the metaphysical foundations for a fluidity between being and becoming and his magisterial *I and Thou*. He retains an abiding belief that the Jews are rooted in a primordial covenant whose life in faith is mediated through religious texts. But there is always the danger that a people might become cloistered and unable to engage in genuine dialogues with those outside the community. He wanted a Jewish people that were able to realize their "commitment to a larger family of humankind" and worried that Jewish nationalism in Palestine might develop in a way that disregarded the genuine needs and aspirations of non-Jews.[64] Such a nationalism would not only harm Palestinians, but would also lead to a damaged Jewish people in Israel. Jews, like all peoples, need to be able to establish

[63] Mendes-Flohr 2019: 164–65.   [64] Mendes-Flohr 2019: 238–39.

relations that recognize others and allow the possibility of being changed through dialogue. Buber's worldview was both Jewish and humanistic. In this regard, he wanted to avoid the dangers of substantialism and hyper-humanism and locate an ethical humanism and a form of politics that recognized the intrinsic relationship between being and becoming.

Bibliography

Adorno, Theodor. 1949. "An Essay on Cultural Criticism and Society," *Prisms*, p. 34. Cited from interview with Herbert Marcuse on Adorno. www.marcuse.org/herbert/people/adorno/AdornoPoetryAuschwitzQuote.htm Accessed March 27, 2020.

Alevi, Seema. 2015. *Muslim Cosmopolitanism in an Age of Empire*. Cambridge, MA: Harvard University Press.

Alroey, Gur. 2011. "Zionism without Zion? Territorialist Ideology and the Zionist Movement," *Jewish Social Studies* 18, 1: 1–32.

Anderson, Bendict. 1992. "Long-Distance Nationalism: World Capitalism and the Rise of Identity Politics," The Wertheim Lecture. Amsterdam: Centre for Asian Studies.

Appiah, Anthony. 2007. *Cosmopolitanism*. New York: Norton.

Aveniri, Shlomo. 1981. *The Making of Modern Zionism: The Intellectual Origins of the Jewish State*. New York: Basic Books.

Barnett, Michael. 2013. "Cosmopolitanism: Good for Israel? Or Bad for Israel?" in Emanuel Adler, ed., *Israel in the World*. New York: Routledge Press, pp. 32–50.

Barnett, Michael. 2016. *The Star and the Stripes: A History of the Foreign Policies of American Jews*. Princeton, NJ: Princeton University Press.

Baron, Salo. 1928. "Ghetto and Emancipation: Shall We Revise the Traditional View?" *Menorah Journal* 14, 6, June: 515–26.

Baron, Salo. 1963. "Newer Emphases in Jewish History," *Jewish Social Studies* 25, 4, October: 235–48.

Batnisky, Leora. 2011. *How Judaism Became a Religion: An Introduction to Modern Jewish Thought*. Princeton, NJ: Princeton University Press.

Bauman, Zygmunt. 2001. *Modernity and the Holocaust*. Ithaca, NY: Cornell University Press.

Beck, Ulrich and Natan Sznaider. 2009. "New Cosmopolitanism in the Social Sciences," in Bryan S. Turner and Robert J. Holton (eds.), *The Routledge International Handbook of Globalization Studies*. New York: Routledge Press, pp. 659–676.

Benbassa, Esther. 2010. *Suffering as Identity: The Jewish Paradigm*. New York: Verso Press.

Ben-Israel, Hevda. 2018. "Bi-Nationalism vs. Nationalism: The Case of Judah Magnes," *Israel Studies* 23, 1, Spring: 86–105.

Ben-Moshe, Danny and Zohar Segev, eds. 2007. *Israel, the Diaspora, and Jewish Identity*. Portland, OR: Sussex Academic Press.

Berger, Peter. 1969. *The Sacred Canopy*. New York: Anchor Books.

Berlin, Isaiah. 1972. "The Bent Twig: A Note on Nationalism," *Foreign Affairs* 51, 1, October: 11–30.

Bethencourt, Francisco. 2016. "Humankind: From Division to Recomposition," in F. Klose and Mirjam Thulin, eds., *Humanity: A History of European Concepts in Practice from the Sixteenth Century to the Present.* Gottingen: Vandenhoeck & Ruprecht, pp. 29–50.

Boyarin, Jonathan and Daniel Boyarin. 2002. *Powers of Diaspora: Two Essays on the Relevance of Jewish Culture.* Minneapolis: University of Minnesota Press.

Brenner, Michael. 2018a. "A State Like any Other State or a Light Unto Nations?" *Israel Studies*, 23, 3, Fall: 3–10.

Brenner, Michael. 2018b. *In Search of Israel: History of an Idea.* Princeton. NJ: Princeton University Press.

Butler-Smith, Alice. 2009. "Diaspora Nationality vs. Diaspora Nationalism: American Jewish Identity and Zionism after the Jewish State," Israel Affairs 15, 2: 158–79.

Calhoun, Craig. 2008. "Cosmopolitanism and Nationalism," *Nations and Nationalism* 14, 3: 427–48.

Cavanaugh, William and Peter Scott, eds., 2007. "Introduction," in *The Blackwell Companion to Political Theology.* Malden, MA: Blackwell, pp. 1–5.

Cheah, Pheng. 2006. "Cosmopolitanism," *Theory, Culture & Society* 23, 2–3: 486–496.

Cohen, Mitchell. 2003. "A Preface to the Study of American Jewish Political Thought," *Jewish Social Studies* 9, 2, Winter: 1–27.

Cohen, Naomi. 1975. *American Jews and the Zionist Idea.* New York: KTAV Publishing House.

Devine, Donna. 2018. "The Gods that Failed in Israel," *Israel Studies* 23, 3, Fall: 42–51.

Dubnov, Arie. 2007. "Between Liberalism and Jewish Nationalism: Young Isaiah Berlin on the Road towards Diaspora Nationalism," *Modern Intellectual History* 4, 2: 303–26.

Eisen, Arnold. 1983. *The Chosen People in America: A Study in Jewish Religious Ideology.* Bloomington: Indiana University Press.

Eisen, Arnold. 1998. "Israel at 50: An American Jewish Perspective," in *American Jewish Year Book.* New York: American Jewish Committee, pp. 47–71.

Elazar, Daniel. 2000. "Response: A Reinvented Jewish Polity in a Globalized World," in Allon Gal and Alfred Gottschalk, eds., *Beyond Survival and Philanthropy: American Jewry and Israel.* Cincinnati, OH: Hebrew Union College Press, pp. 228–35,

French National Assembly. 1789. "Debate on the Eligibility of Jews for Citizenship," December 23; cited in Paul Mendes-Flohr and Jehuda Reinharz, eds. 1995. *The Jew in the Modern World: A Documentary History,* 2nd ed. New York: Oxford University Press, pp. 114–16.

Fuller, Steven. 2011. "Theodicy Sociologized: Suffering Smart in the Twenty-First Century," *Irish Journal of Sociology* 19, 1: 93–115.

Gertz, Nurith. 2018. "Ethical and National Redemption," *Israel Studies* 23, 3, Fall: 52–60.

Gilroy, Paul. 2005. "A New Cosmopolitanism," *Interventions*, 7, 3: 287–92.

Gottlieb, Michah. 2006. "Interview with Michael Walzer," *AJS Perspectives*, Fall: 10–14.

Green, Abigail. 2008. "The British Empire and the Jews: An Imperialism of Human Rights?" *Past and Present* 199, 1: 175–205.

Greene, Abigail and Vincent Viaene, eds., 2012. *Religious Internationals in the Modern World*. New York: Palgrave.

Halperin, Ben. 1956. *An American Jew: A Zionist Analysis*. New York: Schocken Books.

Halperin, Ben. 1983. "America is Different," in Marshall Sklare, ed., *American Jews: A Reader*. New York: Berhman House, pp. 25–46.

Herzberg, Arthur. 1979. *The Zionist Idea*. New York: Antheum Press.

Hollinger, David. 1985. *In the American Province*. Baltimore, MD: Johns Hopkins University Press.

Ignatieff, Michael. 1995. *Blood and Belonging*. New York: Farrar Straus and Giroux.

Kalberg, Stephen. 2004. "The Past and Present Influence of World Views: Max Weber on a Neglected Sociological Concept," *Journal of Classical Sociology* 4, 2: 139–63.

Kalberg, Stephen. 2012. *Max Weber's Comparative Historical Sociology Today*. Farnham: Ashgate.

Kallen, Horace. 1921. *Zionism and World Politics*. London: William Heinemann.

Kant, Immanuel. 1784. "Idea for a Universal History with a Cosmopolitan Purpose." www.marxists.org/reference/subject/ethics/kant/universal-history .htm. Accessed March 24, 2020.

Kaplan, Eran. 2005. "A Rebel with a Cause: Hillel Kook, Begin, and Jabotinsky's Ideological Legacy," *Israel Studies* 10, 3, Fall: 87–103.

Katznelson, Ira and Pierre Birnbaum, eds., 1995. *Paths of Emancipation: Jews, States, and Citizenship*. Princeton, NJ: Princeton University Press.

Kerr, Jason and Ben Labreche. 2018. "Introduction: The Varieties of Political Theology," *Journal for Early Modern Cultural Studies* 18, 2, Spring: 1–10.

Kessler, Michael John, ed., 2013. *Political Theology for a Plural Age*. New York: Oxford University Press.

Kohn, Hans. 2005. *The Idea of Nationalism: A Study in Its Origins and Background*. New Brunswick, NJ: Transaction Press.

Kurz, Nathan. 2021. *Jewish Internationalism and Human Rights After the Holocaust*. New York: Cambridge University Press.

Lacqueur, Walter. 2003. *A History of Zionism*. New York: Schocken Books.

Leff, Lisa. 2006. *Sacred Bonds of Solidarity: The Rise of Jewish Internationalism in Nineteenth-Century France*. Stanford, CA: Stanford University Press.

Leibinz, Gottfried [1710] 1998. *Theodicy: Essays on the Goodness of God, Freedom of Man, and the Origin of Evil*. Lasalle, IL: Open Court.

Lieblich, Eliav and Yoram Schahar. 2014. "Cosmopolitanism at a Crossroads: Hersch Lauterpacht and the Israeli Declaration of Independence," *British Yearbook of International Law*, 84, 1, 1–51.

Lilla, Mark. 2007. *The Stillborn God: Religion, Politics, and the Modern West*. New York: Knopf.

Linfield, Susan. 2019. *The Lion's Den: Zionism and the Left from Arendt to Chomsky.* New Haven, CT: Yale University Press.

Litvak, Olga. 2012. *Haskalah: The Romantic Movement in Judaism.* New Brunswick: Rutgers University Press.

Loeffler, James. 2018. *Rooted Cosmopolitans: Jews and Human Rights in the Twentieth Century.* New Haven, CT: Yale University Press.

Lundgren, Svante. 2001. *Particularism and Universalism in Modern Jewish Thought.* Binghamton University: Global Publications.

Luz, Ehud. 2003. *Wrestling with an Angel: Power, Morality, and Jewish Identity.* New Haven, CT: Yale University Press.

Marx, Karl. 1844. "On the Jewish Question," www.marxists.org/archive/marx/works/1844/jewish-question/. Accessed March 18, 2020.

McNeill, William. 1998. "History and the Scientific Worldview," *History and Theory* 37, 1: 1–13.

Mendelsohn, Ezra. 1993. *On Modern Jewish Politics.* New York: Oxford University Press.

Mendes-Flohr, Paul. 2019. *Martin Buber: A Life of Faith and Dissent.* New Haven, CT: Yale University Press.

Mendes-Flohr, Paul and Jehuda Reinharz, eds., 1995. *The Jew in the Modern World: A Documentary History.* 2nd ed. New York: Oxford University Press.

Meyer, Michael. 1990. *Jewish Identity in the Modern World.* Seattle: University of Washington Press.

Meyers, David. 1995. *Reinventing the Jewish Past: European Jewish Intellectuals and the Jewish Return to History.* New York: Oxford University Press.

Michels, Tony. 2011. "Is America Different? A Critique of American Jewish Exceptionalism," *American Jewish History* 96, 3, September: 201–24.

Miller, Michael and Scott Ury. 2010. "Cosmopolitanism: The End of Jewishness?" *European History Review* 17, 3, June: 337–59.

Morgan, David and Iain Wilkinson. 2001. "The Problem of Suffering and the Sociological Task of Theodicy," *European Journal of Social Theory* 4, 2: 199–214.

Mosse, George. 1997. "Can Nationalism Be Saved? About Zionism, Rightful and Unjust," *Israel Studies* 2, 1, Spring: 156–73.

Naor, Arye. 2005. "'Behold, Rachel, Behold': The Six Day War as a Biblical Experience and Its Impact on Israel's Political Mentality," *Journal of Israeli History* 24, 2: 229–50.

Neiman, Susan. 2002. *Evil in Modern Thought: An Alternative History of Philosophy.* Princeton, NJ: Princeton University Press.

Peleg, Ilan, ed. 2019. *Victimhood Discourse in Contemporary Israel.* New York: Lexington Books.

Pianko, Noam. 2010. *Zionism and the Roads Not Taken.* Bloomington, IN: Indiana University Press.

Pianko, Noam. 2012. "'Make Room for Us': Jewish Collective Solidarity in Contemporary Political Thought," *Journal of Modern Jewish Studies* 11, 2, July: 191–205.

Povinelli, Linda. 2016. *Geontologies: A Requiem to Late Liberalism.* Durham, NC: Duke University Press.

Rabinovitch, Simon, ed., 2012. *Jews and Diaspora Nationalism: Writings on Jewish Peoplehood in Europe and the United States*. Waltham, MA: Brandeis University Press.

Scham, Paul. 2018. "'A Nation That Dwells Alone': Israeli Religious Nationalism in the 21st Century," *Israel Studies* 23, 3: 207–15.

Schmitt, Carl. 2005. *Political Theology*. Chicago, IL: University of Chicago Press.

Seltzer, Michael. 1970. *Zionism Reconsidered*. New York: McMillan Company.

Seltzer, Robert and Norman Cohen, eds., 1995. *The Americanization of the Jews*. New York: New York University Press.

Shelef, Nadav. "'Both Banks of the Jordan' to the 'Whole Land of Israel': Ideological Change in Revisionist Zionism," *Israel Studies* 9, 1: 125–48.

Shimoni, Gideon. 1995. *Zionist Ideology*. Waltham, MA: Brandeis University Press.

Shunsky, Dmitry. 2018. *Beyond the Nation-State: The Zionist Political Imagination from Pinsker to Ben-Gurion*. New Haven, CT: Yale University Press.

Sluga, Glenda 2015. *Internationalism in an Age of Nationalism*. Philadelphia: University of Pennsylvania Press.

Smith, Anthony. 1995. "Zionism and Diaspora Nationalism," *Israel Affairs* 2, 2: 1–19.

Smith, Anthony. 2004. *Chosen People: Sacred Sources of National Identity*. New York: Oxford University Press.

Sznaider, Natan. 2007. "Hannah Arendt's Jewish Cosmopolitanism: Between the Universal and the Particular," *European Journal of Social Theory* 10, 1: 112–22.

Sorkin, David. 2019. *Jewish Emancipation: A History Across Five Centuries*. Princeton, NJ: Princeton University Press.

Stuurman, Siep. 2017. *The Invention of Humanity: Equality and Cultural Difference in World History*. Cambridge, MA: Harvard University Press.

Swedberg, Richard. 2018. "How to Use Max Weber's Ideal-Types in Sociological Analysis," *Journal of Classical Sociology* 18, 3: 181–96.

Slezkine, Yuri. 2004. *The Jewish Century*. Princeton, NJ: Princeton University Press.

Tamir, Yael. 2019. "Not So Civic: Is There a Difference Between Civic and Ethnic Nationalism?" *Annual Review of Political Science* 22: 419–34.

Tamir, Yael. 2019. *Why Nationalism?* Princeton, NJ: Princeton University Press.

Tarrow, Sidney. 2005. *The New Transnational Activism*. New York: Cambridge University Press.

Traverso, Enzo. 2016. *The End of Jewish Modernity*. New York: Pluto Press.

Urofsky, Melvin. 1975. *American Zionism: From Herzl to the Holocaust*. Lincoln: University of Nebraska Press.

Veblen, Thorsten. 1919. "The Intellectual Pre-Eminence of the Jews in Modern Europe," *Political Science Quarterly* 34, 1, March: 33–42.

Waldron, Jeremy. 2000. "What is Cosmopolitanism?" *The Journal of Political Philosophy* 8, 2: 227–43.

Walzer, Michael. 2001. "Universalism and Jewish Values," May 15, Twentieth Annual Morgenthau Memorial Lecture on Ethics and Foreign Policy. New York: Carnegie Council on Ethics and International Affairs.

Walzer, Michael. 2012. "Michael Walzer Responds," *Dissent* 59, 4: Fall.

Weber, Max. [1920] 1963. *Sociology of Religion*. London: Metheun.

Weber, Max. 1948. "The Social Psychology of the World Religions," in H.H. Gerth and C.W. Mills, eds., *From Max Weber*. New York: Routledge Press, pp. 267–301.

Weingrod, Alex. 2018. "The Two Israels Revisited," *Israel Studies* 23, 3, Fall: 132–40.

Wistrich, Robert. 1998. "Zionism and Its Jewish 'Assimilationist' Critics (1897–1948)," *Jewish Social Studies* 4, 2, Winter: 59–111.

Woocher, Jonathan. 1986. *Sacred Survival: The Civil Religion of American Jews*. Bloomington: Indiana University Press.

Vital, David. 1999. *A People Apart: A Political History of the Jews of Europe, 1789–1939*. Oxford: Oxford University Press.

Zertal, Idith. 2005. *Israel's Holocaust and the Politics of Nationhood*. New York: Cambridge University Press.

Zerubavel, Yael. 1995. *Recovered Roots: Collective Memory and the Making of Israeli National Tradition*. Chicago, IL: Chicago University Press.

Zouplna, Jan. 2008. "Revisionist Zionism: Image, Reality, and the Quest for Historical Narrative," *Middle Eastern Studies* 44, 1: 3–27.

Part II

Accountable Agents and Epistemic Engines

6 Weberian and Relationalist Worldviews: What Is at Stake?

Henry R. Nau

This volume challenges us to stretch our imagination and rethink the world of international relations. It engages modern substantialist, Weberian approaches to social science with new postmodern, relationalist or quantum approaches and concludes that substantialist views which emphasize the individual are outdated.[1] This conclusion is premature. Stretching our imagination is one thing; tearing it up is another. As we proceed, we need a clear picture of what we are stretching and potentially tearing up; it could be the reasoning individual and the human capacity to imagine itself.

This chapter offers a full-throated (albeit limited) exposition and defense of the Enlightenment/Weberian worldview that underlines modern social science. The Enlightenment worldview gave form to the aspiration for individual freedom and choice. It rescued humanity from the stultifying clutches of mysticism (Nature) and religion (the Divine). It dethroned philosopher kings and papal elites and empowered ordinary, individual human beings, equipped with reason, spirit (emotion, faith), and education, to create, assess, debate, and pass judgment on alternative worldviews. Natural science exploded under Isaac Newton's vision of an orderly universe fixed in time and space following predictable laws. And social science spawned a virtual cornucopia of modern worldviews, both individualistic and authoritarian. Liberalism (John Locke), capitalism (Adam Smith), humanism (Max Weber), communism (Karl Marx), and fascism (Friedrick Nietzsche), among others, competed (and fought)

[1] These terms have shifted several times in the course of this project. Substantialist may be a better term than rationalist because it implies substance (entities) rather than just method (practices). But to juxtapose substantialist with relationalist implies that relationalism has no substance, when of course it does. That substance lies in the content of relationships rather than individuals. I use the terms relational-ist and relational-ism rather than relational to acknowledge the relationalist claim that it is a holistic worldview more than relationships or interdependence. And I use the terms Enlightenment (seventeenth–nineteenth century) and postmodern (twentieth century and beyond) to address the relationalist claim that the Enlightenment view is obsolete.

179

to organize and direct social and scientific life.[2] In the West, through struggle, humanist and capitalist worldviews prevailed, fueling material progress, the spread of republican institutions, and gnawing anguish about minorities left behind.

Now, postmodern worldviews of relationalism and hyper-humanism (unity of human beings and nature) challenge Enlightenment worldviews. They reject the individualistic ontology of human affairs in favor of a wholistic or cosmological one. Milja Kurki writes: "The relational perspective explored here suggests that the sciences – natural and social – are undergoing a 'relational revolution,' moving from Cartesian, Newtonian, and empiricist ways of knowing toward more relational ontologies and epistemologies in line with not only quantum science and relativity theory but also with ecological thought and decolonization of the sciences."[3] Relationalist views envision a world of intense and entangled relationships deeply embedded in historical and cosmological context, in which substantialist things such as individuals and institutions do not exist or exist only in emergent form when they are investigated. In this holistic and processual universe, individual human beings have no location (position), no alternative (choice), and no escape (only one observed universe). The relationalist worldview draws from quantum science, in which reality is not fixed in time or space but appears simultaneously and unpredictably in multiple places and dissolves the distinction between the observer (individual) and the observed (universe).

These different worldviews not only reflect different ontologies, they prescribe different world politics. As Kurki infers, the relationalist turn entails a political agenda – a broadside assault on western rationality (reason), individuality (freedom), capitalism (growth), and colonialism (control/hierarchy).[4] In place of Enlightenment goals, relationalism advocates a future agenda of environmentalism that prioritizes climate change, hyper-humanism that relinquishes human control of nature, and egalitarianism that flattens material and moral differences. Much more is at stake than abstract intellectual discourse. The relationalist turn may imperil the very notion of free, reasoning individuals capable of self-conscious thought and choice in human affairs.

This chapter insists that individual human beings remain at the epicenter of social science inquiry. Quantum science does not mandate an epochal transformation of worldviews from rationality and individualism to relationality and cosmology.[5] Modeling the social sciences after the

---

[2] See Duara, Chapter 7. Hereafter, unless indicated otherwise, chapter cross-references refer to chapters in the present volume.
[3] Chapter 3.   [4] Chapter 3.   [5] Katzenstein, Chapter 10; Wendt 2015.

natural sciences is, in fact, a cardinal mistake. Relationalists highlight that mistake when they argue that Enlightenment science under Newton hijacked the social sciences and created a disenchanted modernity of atoms (individuals) and laws (causality) devoid of spirit and meaning. Now they make the same mistake by modeling the postmodern world after quantum science. But the Newtonian world was never just a billiard ball world of fixed entities, time and space. It was inspired and limited by Christian beliefs that the divine did not roll dice (a predictable world) and human beings were made equally worthy in the image of the divine. And the quantum worldview today is not just a mathematical model of entanglement and uncertainty; it is also a social vision to reimagine the political world as harmonious, contingent, and relationally or group-based (identity politics, multiculturalism, etc.), rather than as competitive, progressive, and individually based (markets, individual human rights, etc.).

The Enlightenment produced good and evil. This chapter does not claim otherwise. The Enlightenment's crown jewel, however, was the emancipation, for better *and* worse, of the individual human being as a reasoning, responsible, and rights-seeking agent in society. On balance, this secular, individually driven humanist worldview was progressive, materially and socially. Despite all of its wars and warts, the Enlightenment era superintended unparalleled expansion of material prosperity, human longevity, public education, political freedom (yes, more democracies than ever before), and global equality (yes, half of the world's population is now middle class).[6] Any post-Enlightenment worldview that challenges the individualist ontology of the Enlightenment has a high bar to meet.

The chapter proceeds in four parts. The first part explores the relationship between the individual and the whole, the timeworn conundrum of agency and structure. It contends that the individual remains primary over structure in several principal ways: as a source of endless diversity, a repository for the capability of reason, a portal of entry for human conversation, and the only species thus far that practices science and is capable of representing and studying itself. Individuals are not autonomous, but they have space in their embedded situation for choice and change. The main issue between this chapter and others in this volume is *how much* space they have and where that space *resides*. Relationalist

---

[6] Among many accounts of this progress, see Pinker 2011; Pomeranz 2000; Maddison 1991; Landes 1999; Nau 1990; and Mokyr 1990. On recent progress in race relations in America, see Thernstrom and Thernstrom 1997. By contrast, relationalists argue that the Enlightenment is the cause of everything retrograde about modern life: environmental degradation, systemic racism, white supremacy, oppression of minority cultures, unrelenting material inequality, and so on.

accounts tend to discount agency at the individual level, Weberian accounts at the structural level. We risk a lot by disregarding either.

The second and third parts address the content and juxtaposition of competing worldviews. How do we compare and test them? This part holds fast to the notion of a *universal capability* of individual human beings to reason and a *universal method* of science to test alternative propositions (worldviews) by experiment against an outside physical and social world. To be sure, the *content* of reason and science is *parochial* and differs by culture. In some worldviews, rational and individualistic factors play the larger role, in others nonrational (e.g., emotion, intuition) and holistic factors.[7] If these multiple worldviews are incommensurable, however, we have no way to evaluate and test them. Worldviews become religious not scientific undertakings, adopted by faith not reason. On the other hand, if we retain science as a common method (mathematics, experimentation), we can compare and evaluate worldviews across different cultures. In this section I assume that all worldviews incorporate two elements: *content*, or their relative emphasis on rational vs. nonrational factors; and *scale*, or their relative emphasis on individualistic vs. structural levels of analysis.[8]

The fourth part addresses the ethics of different worldviews. Worldviews have consequences – some horrific, such as the Holocaust. Who or what is accountable for these outcomes? If Weberian worldviews have moral shortcomings – and they do – relationalist worldviews do as well. Calling for openness and multiple worldviews (modernities), relationalist views are at times quite dogmatic. They pass judgment on worldviews as "right" or "wrong" not as "false" or "not false," and speak of the pursuit of "truth" against which, they claim, resistance is futile.[9] They downplay individual agency and emphasize entangled relationships, conjuring up a "totalizing" worldview that marginalizes individual rights and privacy. They blur distinctions between science and religion and argue that worldviews "are inescapably normative."[10] Yet, curiously, relationalists say little about the substance of relationalist norms. They pass over the question of how a relationalist world, in which all possibilities are welcomed, defends itself against the barbarity of an Adolf Hitler or a Joseph Stalin; they infer that other religions (Hinduism, Buddhism) are more in tune with nature than Christianity; they refrain from spirited criticism of worldviews that

---

[7] See for example, Duara's discussion of the Chinese imperial world order: Chapter 7.

[8] In this sense, content (relative weight of rational vs. nonrational factors) and levels of analysis (relative weight of agency vs. structure) are "common" elements that individuals mix and match to create worldviews, analogous to the way historical elites or "creative agents" mix and match "cosmological" elements in Allan's account. See Chapter 8.

[9] See Byrnes, Chapter 9.   [10] Katzenstein, Chapter 1.

discriminate against women (Saudi Arabia, India) or Muslims (China); and they blame America and the Enlightenment for elevating European worldviews and marginalizing others. Weberian worldviews, by contrast, with their individualistic and disaggregated ontology, accommodate alternative worldviews as long as these worldviews submit to objective falsification and do not claim that their world is the only world which cannot be tested or resisted.[11]

6.1   The Individual and the Whole

As noted, Enlightenment worldviews are multiple. Where do we start? Michael Barnett provides a pretty good definition of liberal Enlightenment worldviews: "By privileging reason over superstition, change over tradition, science over religion, and, most importantly, humanity over discrimination, enlightenment thought held that people should be judged as individuals and on their achievements, not their religion or other discriminating factors."[12] In this world, individuals are not only real and significant, they are morally and ethically accountable! They do not disappear, along with other "things," from a Newtonian/Weberian world of "essence and identity" to join a relationalist world of "different kinds of dances."[13]

Where did this emphasis on individualism come from? In the early Enlightenment, it came from Isaac Newton and his application of individual reason to the study of nature. "Think of it," Gale Christianson writes, "a lone human being bent low over a desk, supplied with nothing more than a quill pen, a pot of homemade ink, and countless sheets of blank paper, calculating precisely how the cosmos goes."[14] In the late Enlightenment, Max Weber generalized this application of reasoning to the study of human as well as natural sciences. Individual human beings, not the divine or prophets, interpreted reality. In Weber's sociology, according to Stephen Kalberg, "individuals are genuine actors capable of interpreting their social realities and of initiating creative action."[15] (Note the word "creative": the capacity to imagine something that is

---

[11] In the Weberian account, the working world of science as method is closed in the sense that a single, objective but unknowable universe exists to adjudicate across worldviews, while the imagined world of reason is open in the sense that no specific worldview is excluded. This is the opposite of relationalism and quantum science, in which the imagined world is closed (the only world is the observed world), while the working world is open, accommodating many different localized, nongeneralizable methods. See Katzenstein, Chapter 10. On the closing of imagination in the quantum world, David Waldner (2017: 208) writes: "we must, however difficult as it is, refrain from imagining that we know what is going on prior to the act of measurement: the principle [of uncertainty] prohibits us from asking 'what is really going on.'"

[12] Chapter 5.   [13] Kurki, Chapter 3.   [14] Christianson 2005: xiii.
[15] Kalberg 1994: 25.

neither embedded in the past nor represented in the present.) Kalberg continues: "Weber welcomed emphatically the freedoms and rights the modern world bestowed upon the individual[16] ... Individuals act, for Weber, not social organisms or collectivities ... meaning is found only in the consciousness of human beings."[17] In their introduction to *From Max Weber: Essays in Sociology*, Gerth and Mills concur: "His [Weber's] point of departure and the ultimate unit of his analysis is the individual person."[18] In Weber's own words, "action in the sense of a subjectively understandable orientation of behavior exists only as the behavior of one or more *individual* human beings."[19]

Weber considers four types of social action rooted in individual behavior: means–ends rational action (rational choice), value-rational action (idealistic or ideological), affectual action (feeling or emotional), and traditional or customary action (habitual).[20] Only one, means–ends rationality, is materially based. He does not conflate the social world with the natural world. Reality is not dead matter, disenchanted. It is both material (means–ends) and ideal (value-rational), emotional (affectual) and habitual (practices). Enchantment persists. It just doesn't rule human minds at the expense of reason, as it did in pre-Enlightenment thought.

Per Weber, ideal and material interests intersect to yield patterning action. This patterning action is shaped by both individuals and structure. Structures exist, to be sure. Weber speaks of "value spheres" which prescribe obligations in various life spheres and "are not created by individuals."[21] But value spheres conflict; there are no universally valid value spheres; and the individual adjudicates among them: "Torn between conflicting obligations derived from different value spheres, the individual must simply choose."[22] For Weber, this choice is free, not determined by science or higher norms. As Gerth and Mills write, "He [Weber] felt that freedom consists not in realizing alleged historical necessities but rather in making deliberate choices between open alternatives."[23] For Weber, "choice is the task of life itself."[24] While Weber accords a role to structure, he warns against the holistic, all-encompassing notion of structure that Grove emphasizes in relationalism. As Kalberg writes, "organic theories, according to Weber, are helpful and indeed indispensable, yet, if utilized other than as a means of facilitating

---

[16] Weber 2009: x.   [17] Kalberg 1994: 25.
[18] Introduction by Gerth and Mills, in Weber 1958: 55.
[19] Quoted in Kalberg 1994: 25 (emphasis original).
[20] Kalberg 1980: 1147–49; Kalberg 1994: 63–66.   [21] Brubaker 1984: 72.
[22] Brubaker 1984: 72.   [23] Introduction by Gerth and Mills, in Weber 1958: 70.
[24] Brubaker 1984: 72.

preliminary conceptualization, a high risk of 'reification' arises: 'society' and the 'organic whole' rather than the individual may become viewed as the single important level of analysis"[25]

Relationalists reject this Weberian view of individualism. They indict individualism as "the inability of man to see itself as part of nature due to a Christian legacy of seeing humans as 'lifted' above nature."[26] The original sin is hierarchy, "the 'human' standing over the 'environment',"[27] free and separate from nature (animals, plants) and other human beings (society), able potentially to surmount heritage and context, dethrone the architects of authority (church and state), and shape, in part, the world of the future. As Kurki suggests, this heresy of hierarchy derives from the Protestant worldview that human beings are called upon by reason and faith to explore, master, and grow the natural universe around them. By fostering such heresy, Christianity did not unleash freedom; it unleashed the master-less man, the rapacious capitalist, and the relentless colonialist.

Relationalists minimize the role of individual reason in human affairs and categorically reject any universal principles derived from reason. As Kurki writes, "knowing through reason is a particular way of materializing the world, not a universal manifestation of some abstract principles."[28] Nevertheless, the *capability* of individual human beings to reason and give meaning to the world around them *is* universal, even if the *content* of reason and its multiple manifestations are parochial and differ by culture, religion, and other factors. As Allan points out,[29] the application of reason or rationalization takes many localized forms. Individuals are endlessly diverse and wrapped up in many parts: heritage, race, class, nationality, emotion, psychology, intuition, charisma, character, reason, religion, civilization, cosmology, and so on. Many of these parts are deeply embedded and constitute the historical antecedents or "inheritance" that Allan

---

[25] Kalberg 1994: 27. In remarks submitted too late in our deliberations for a full response (Grove, draft of Chapter 4), Grove asserts that Weber is totally relationalist and "deconstructs" individualism. As my brief response suggests, that is an overreach. In the passages Grove cites, Weber is discussing charisma as "a balancing conception for bureaucracy" (i.e., for rational behavior) not embracing it as an overriding reality "in which," as Grove writes, "all of the agents of change are swept up in a whole." The value spheres remain independent of one another, and the individual remains the indispensable fulcrum of human (moral) choice among them. Wilhelm Dilthey also insists on the separation of the individual and society: "The individual is on the one hand an element in the interactions of society, a point of intersection of the various systems of these interactions, reacting to the influences of that society with conscious intentions and actions; but on the other he is an intellect contemplating and investigating all of this"; Dilthey 1989: 89.
[26] Kurki citing Rovelli, Chapter 3.   [27] Kurki, Chapter 3.   [28] Chapter 3.
[29] Chapter 8.

emphasizes; they anchor individuals in place. Reason, however, is the one part that offers the human being a potential escape from this procrustean embeddedness.[30] Incorporating self-consciousness, reason "lifts up" the individual human being to investigate, organize, study, and influence nature and society. Reason facilitates reflection, discussion, and *self-study*, offering a portability across differing worldviews that emotion, intuition, and religion do not. In some worldviews, reason plays a bigger or prior role; in others, intuition or religion does.[31] But in all cultures reasoning is present if individuals choose to apply it. To argue otherwise is to discriminate, to endow a particular individual or culture with a capability of reason that other individuals and cultures do not possess. And to ascribe reason to nonhuman beings (plants and animals) ignores the obvious fact that they do not have that capability yet, at least not in sufficient measure to permit self-study. When they do, they will join the world of humans and represent themselves. Hyper-humanism will have arrived.

In a sense, the capability to reason is the agency of modern human life. This agency is distributed at all layers or scales of human activity, individual and collective. It is perhaps most accessible on the individual scale; but without the structures of schools and free societies that educate and protect it, reason soon withers, locked up in monasteries, gulags, and samizdats. Thus, individuals and the groups they form are never completely autonomous from society. Indeed, at birth, they are relationally constituted without choice. But subsequently, based on the Weberian worldview, individuals may be educated by reason and reasoning communities (that's us, the academy) to determine meaning for themselves and to choose practices and communities that meet their standards of reality and morality. Relationships are important, but relationships, unlike individuals, are not self-conscious and do not exercise reason. Somewhere in the relationalist world, therefore, agency – by which I mean self-conscious, reasoning individual human beings and the *inter*-actional (not *intra*-actional as in relationalism) communities they join and leave – is the starting and enduring point of reflective inquiry. For

---

[30] As Robert Nozich writes: reason is "a means whereby ... humanity is able to correct and rise above personal and group bias." See 1993: xiii.

[31] Notice I am not claiming the dominance of reason in all worldviews. In some, as Grove suggests, intuition comes first: "I have an intuition of what makes sense ... and then I begin the reasoned process of discounting the other positions to build a defensible image of a judgement" (quote from Grove's memo exchanged among authors before Zoom Sessions, June 8, 10, 12, 2020.) In others, such as the Weberian approach, one starts with reason and peels off the layers of intuition and other nonrational factors that don't make sense.

Weberian thought, the bottom line is that human agency, at whatever level it may exist, is sufficient *enough* to provide *meaningful* choice.[32]

Individualism is indispensable for several other reasons. First, individual human beings are the only actors that can represent themselves. The kind of discussion we are having in this volume would not be possible without individuals. Notice there are no institutions authoring a chapter, no representatives of the embedded world we inhabit – no community practices, background or tacit knowledge, cosmological elements, religious communities, relationalist bundles or folds, quantum worlds, or any other holistic entity. Not even AI (artificial intelligence) – that is, no robots equivalent to the individual human being, at least not yet.[33]

Second, individualism is the source of endless diversity in human affairs. No two reasoning individuals are exactly the same! This is a remarkable feature of human evolution and distinguishes "human" particles studied by the social sciences from "natural" particles studied by natural scientists. Being "unlike," human beings do not equate with "like atoms" in a Newtonian world or "like particles/waves" in a quantum world. To impose the natural science model on the social sciences commits the second sin of Aristotle's understanding of equality: it treats unequal things – natural particles and human beings – equally.[34]

Third, human particles seem to be, again so far, the only specie that can conceptualize and study themselves, the only specie that is self-conscious and can practice both natural and social science.[35] If nonhuman beings (animals) were included in this exercise, how would they communicate and represent themselves? They would have to depend upon human beings. But who gave human beings that right? As Kurki acknowledges, "we represent them even at present, but often badly: we can learn to represent them and ourselves and our symbiotic relations better."[36] Maybe so, but isn't the presumption that we can represent them at all without their consent an exercise of hierarchical or colonial control? I'm not arguing against speaking out for animal rights. It's a good thing, in my worldview, when human beings take care of all living things and nurture

---

[32] Relationalists contend that agency is a consequence not a choice: "agency is already relationally constituted in the sense that it was made possible by the configuration of historical inheritance and interactions with other actors" (Allan, Chapter 8).

[33] Even AI and robots depend upon causal (agentic) as well as contextual (structural) reasoning: "AI will stall if computers don't get better at wrestling with causation" (Bergstein 2020: 63)

[34] The first sin is the one we usually think about, treating equal things (two human beings) unequally. See Aristotle, Politics, translated by Benjamin Jowett, book 5, part 1, http://classics.mit.edu/Aristotle/politics.5.five.html.

[35] Except occasionally, this volume pays little attention to consciousness. See Katzenstein, Chapter 1 and Chapter 10; Wendt 2015: Part II.

[36] Chapter 3.

nature. I'm suggesting instead that human beings are the only creatures that raise these questions. Nonhumans are not yet at the table or, as far as we know, clamoring for a seat.

Finally, even if individuals are totally entrapped in the embedded features of their environment (that is, not autonomous *at all*), they are still the only channels by which we learn about worldviews, including holistic ones that deny individuality. Worldviews don't emerge out of the ether. They emerge from the mind and experience of a single individual.[37] *We can get to the "real" world of relationalism or any other "real" world only by starting in an individualist world.* The individual remains the *portal of entry* for worldviews and intellectual discourse about them.

6.2   Multiple Worldviews

There seems to be, at least to me, a consensus in this volume as to what worldviews are. They are a combination of values together with methods by which we navigate the world around us.[38] Without methods, worldviews become pure ideals or truth. They cannot be tested; they can only be accepted, like religion. And without values, worldviews become meaningless methods leading to anomie, the ultimate disenchantment. Critics like to characterize Weber's approach as "methodological individualism," but they ignore the prior value he placed on the reasoning individual. The individual was not a tool of analysis; it was the valued agent that gave meaning to analysis.

One way to compare worldviews, therefore, is to examine the relative content of worldviews – that is, the relative role of rational (reason) vs. nonrational (religion, emotion, etc.) factors in various worldviews, and the relative level of analysis being emphasized (i.e. individual vs. structure). Weberian worldviews tend to be heavy on reason and the individual level of analysis, relationalist worldviews on nonrational factors and the holistic level of analysis.[39]

In this volume, Milja Kurki, Peter Katzenstein, and Jairus Grove make the case for a strong relationalism that minimizes rational factors in human behavior and adopts a deeply historical and holistic level of analysis. Katzenstein highlights the nonrational aspects of reality: "The

---

[37] We acknowledge that when we celebrate events such as Kuhn's Aristotle experience, in which the pieces of an intellectual puzzle suddenly fall into place in the mind of a single human being. See Katzenstein, Chapter 10.

[38] Katzenstein, Chapter 1.

[39] By comparing worldviews, I am not insisting that worldviews are rivals or assuming that they are nested harmoniously inside a single preeminent worldview. I am simply suggesting that there is more than one valid worldview that is potentially falsifiable against an assumed objective world. See Katzenstein, Chapter 10.

interpretation of reality as consisting only of risk is not readily open to rational reconstruction or refutation."[40] Kurki emphasizes the interconnectedness of everything: "nothing in the universe is outside of relational unfolding of the universe – not even the scientists or the laws of the universe which are also made relationally."[41] Grove prioritizes intuition over reason (see footnote 31) and, while acknowledging that some layers or scales of agency may exist within the holistic structure, argues that such agency does not equate with a rational subject or individual human being. Instead, agency is relational at all scales: "We are not constituted *by* relations. We *are* relations." The individual "comes from the unity we 'feel' as an 'I'." Actors become assemblages, ensembles, and folds that exceed the particular human subject and appear depending on "at what scale one asks the question." "The scale of the investigator," Grove adds, "radically alters what appears as a part and what appears as a whole."[42]

Bentley Allan's worldview is slightly less holistic and more attentive to creative elites, albeit still acting at a deeply embedded level of analysis. He starts with cosmological elements – ontology, episteme, temporality, cosmogony, and human destiny – that provide the ingredients for worldviews and exist outside worldviews in the sense that they come first.[43] Then, according to Allan, "creative actors" mix and match these elements in various ways to produce worldviews or "local stabilizations of cosmological elements." The content of these stabilizations is not universal and depends on the history and experiences of different cultures. In the case of western thought, rationalization produced a localized worldview of "materialism" and "object-orientation." This combination gave rise to "modernist values of rationality, control, and growth which serve as the basis of world politics today."[44] In other civilizations, rationalization created nonmaterialist and "subject" oriented worlds (Haitian *Iwa*, Buddhism). Allan creates more space for individual agency: "Agency is always possible but never omnipotent. Creative agents must work with and against the cosmological and institutional resources at hand."[45] The question is whether contemporary elites can interpret or reinterpret their inherited experience and alter it in any way that significantly affects the future. Who are the creative elites today that become the embedded historical elites tomorrow?

---

[40] Chapter 1.
[41] Kurki Draft, International Studies Association, Toronto, Canada 2019: 3.
[42] Grove, Chapter 4. This formulation preserves a rather critical, agentic role for the investigator, which is also true in quantum science. See discussion later in this chapter.
[43] Can these elements change? Can we add or subtract a cosmological element? If so, who or what does that?
[44] Chapter 8.   [45] Chapter 8.

Presenjit Duara takes one element of Allan's cosmological menu, namely temporality, and links it, via the "epistemic engine" of the nation-form, with the Enlightenment worldview of modernity. Like Allan, he is sensitive to the multiple content of Enlightenment modernity – autocratic, emphasizing nonrational and holistic factors, as well as liberal, emphasizing reason and individualistic factors – and regards agency as weak even at collective scales. That leads him to wonder if the agentic force of civil society, which he sees as the most hopeful challenger of the Enlightenment nation-form, is ultimately too weak, too diffused to succeed.[46]

Timothy Byrnes drops down below the cosmological level of analysis and starts with religions, not cosmological elements, as foundational to worldviews. Religions have moral content, are multiple, and are concerned with truth not just process, interaction, or inanimate cosmological elements. He raises the interesting question of how we can know separate religions. Because religion is not only a way of *seeing* the world but also a way of *being* in the world, how do we bridge different worlds of *being*? He advocates a path of "informed empathy."[47] You stand outside other religions and become informed, and then you try to imagine that other religion by moving as close as you can to it without assuming or usurping its identity. But how close is too close? When do you invade or take over the other religion? Here Byrnes acknowledges a role for agency. Religions exist separately; they do not smear into one another like wave functions. On the other hand, religious communities are deeply embedded in the historical process. They are mutually constituted with other factors like politics, such that "a separation of religion and politics is a chimera."[48]

Michael Barnett disaggregates the analysis still further. Unlike Byrnes, he does not see religion and politics as mutually constituted (holistically entangled) and thus explores a critical possibility – rooted cosmopolitanism – in which the two variables are separated – namely a Jewish community in America committed to a cosmopolitan theology and humanism, but rooted in a non-Jewish territorial state. By moving to a lower level of analysis, he retrieves a variable and a degree of freedom that is otherwise lost when variables are mutually constituted.[49] For Barnett, Jewish worldviews derive from independent forces of religion and politics (territoriality) and have distinctive qualities that define "who is and can be a member, and what are the boundaries between themselves and others." These worldviews

---

[46] Duara, Chapter 7.   [47] Chapter 9.   [48] Chapter 9.

[49] The methodology of mutual constitution locks up separate variables at higher levels of analysis and takes them out of play at lower levels of analysis. The higher the level of analysis, therefore, the fewer the variables that can be isolated and act as agents. In this way, more holistic worldviews necessarily diminish human agency and choice.

worry about borders where entanglement may threaten security. They also have "core tenets." A worldview may change not only from external entanglements but also from internal tensions when members of the community begin to debate its core characteristics.[50] To be sure, external circumstances still matter. Interacting in America, the Jewish community by and large favored an open, civic nationalism of cosmopolitanism; interacting in the Middle East, it chose a closed, ethnic nationalism of separateness. Yet value commitments or agency may hold the key to future outcomes. Barnett speculates that Jews in America and Israel may drift apart "if American Jews continued to orbit around a rooted cosmopolitanism; and Israeli Jews migrated from a prophetic Zionism to ethnonationalist Zionism."[51]

In adopting a Weberian worldview, Mark Haas and I accord the greatest emphasis to the role of reason and the individual level of analysis. To some significant degree, leaders (elites) act independently in the present both to reinterpret the past and to shape the future. While they form groups and adapt to social circumstances, they also change those circumstances and ultimately create over time the structures that define a particular historical experience.[52] Some structures may be harder to change than others. Some may never change – in most cases not because they are unchangeable, but rather because human actions and interactions have not yet become aware of them or mobilized sufficient effort to engage and transform them. From the perspective developed by Haas/Nau, most structures are susceptible to change, not by one action or one human being (or even by one generation or one nation) but by a train of actions and interactions moving across time in a similar direction. Agency is distributed across all levels and time but it is strongest at lower levels and contemporaneously where it constantly "stirs the pot" to inhibit, shape, or diffuse subsequent structures at more holistic levels.[53]

I entered the investigation of worldviews by trying to find a framework to compare foreign policy debates in aspiring powers (China, India, Iran, Japan, and Russia) and determine whether those debates were moving away from or toward the foreign policy debates in the United States.[54]

---

[50] Barnett, Chapter 5.   [51] Barnett, Chapter 5.

[52] If "creative" elites have enough agency to create or change worldviews in the past, as Allan, Duara, and others in this volume argue, why can they not do so also in the present? This argues for a broader conception of elites, not just deeply embedded historical elites.

[53] See Chapter 2. There is evolution in this approach, as Ernst Haas (1990) persuasively argues, but there is no determinism (see also Nau 2008). And structure and agency, as in Weber, are both material and ideological (Mark Haas 2005, ch. 1; Nau 2002, ch. 1).

[54] For example, was the center of gravity of the Chinese foreign policy debate moving away from isolation toward more involvement in the world, while the center of gravity of the US debate was moving in the opposite direction? And, if so, were these shifts motivated

I was reaching for a structural level of analysis that would go beyond individual events and leaders (the focus of quotidian foreign policy) but not ossify in incommensurable cultures and civilizations. I created a framework of four schools of foreign policy thought – nationalist, realist, liberal internationalist, and conservative internationalist. To be as objective as possible, I defined these schools in neutral terms of scope (limited, expansive), means (military, diplomatic/economic), and ends (accept or transform world) of foreign policy, rather than ideological or substantive terms of liberalism, fascism, Islamism, communism, culture, and the like. I started, in short, with a set of rationalist categories (science as method) presumed to be accessible to all cultures through a universal human capacity to reason (reason as universal). The country specialists in the study said the framework could not be applied across cultures. Categories don't mean the same thing in different cultures. Well, we persuaded them to try anyway, and they were surprised at the extent to which it did illuminate the respective movement of debates among the countries.

Thus, it is possible, I concluded, to study the behavior of alternative cultures/religions/worldviews without either essentializing those worldviews (danger of the Weberian approach) or shackling them in a structure that can be challenged, if at all, only from within (danger of the relationalist approach).

6.3   Worldviews and Science

To do this, however, we need standards. The Enlightenment gave us the standard of science as a universal method: mathematics, experimental practice. That method depends upon the assumption of a real "objective" world even if we can never know that world. We ask and test how that world works, based on the values we hold (e.g., world is predictable or uncertain), and the real world pushes back against our experimental inquiries and tells us which worldviews are consistent with it and which are not. Notice science as method tells us only which worldviews are not false (i.e., not inconsistent with reality); it never tells us which worldviews are true (i.e., the actual reality).

This is a crucial point, at least for me. Truth lies not in the universal method of science but in the multiple values that inform science as method. Newton's Christian views led him to expect and practice a "predictable" science; Weber's human-centric views led him to anticipate a "progressive" science; the values held by Weber's critics led them

primarily by rising and declining power or by ideological competition? See Nau and Ollapally 2012.

to expect a "disenchanted" science; Hitler's fascist and Stalin's communist worldviews led them to promote "racist" and "pseudo" sciences (Mengele and Lysenko). Relationalists value conjunctive relationality (not individuals) and pursue a science of local not universal knowledge. Values inform all worldviews, but science as method tells us which worldviews fare best against an assumed objective world.

Strong relationalists reject science as a universal method of testing against an objective reality. They talk about "different sciences"[55] and argue that "science ... is not defined by a 'method'."[56] Quoting Roberto Unger and Lee Smolin, Kurki concludes: "There is no scientific method, science is fundamentally defined as a collection of ethical communities."[57] Here we come very close to worldviews as pure values (ethical communities) with methods being anything – scientific, magical, religious – that values dictate. Each community defines its own value and methods, and presumably the "real" world accommodates them all because there is no common method to determine which worldviews are not consistent with an assumed "real" (i.e., objective) world.

There are three layers of uncertainty involved in this issue of scientific objectivity (universality). Newtonian science studies the natural (nonhuman) world: objects such as planets and particles which cannot change their characteristics and which scientists neither like nor dislike. Laws are fixed and cannot be affected by the scientist. The human observer is also situated outside and independent of the natural world. In Newtonian science, the observer can be mostly objective even though scientists still operate in an intersubjective, ethical (social) community (for Newton, the Church of England) that defines what is or is not to be investigated and expected.

Weberian science studies not only the natural but also the social world in which human beings are involved and can change their minds. Laws are no longer fixed, and the observer, though still distinct, studies things it likes and dislikes, such as churches, trade unions, markets, political parties, etc. While Weberian scientists assume they can strip their social preferences from their scientific pursuits, they are human, not superhuman, and can succeed only up to a point. Objectivity is more elusive.[58]

---

[55] Katzenstein, Chapter 10. Katzenstein clings to the notion of a common mathematics which comprises "a world external to each agent that is not solely dependent on human minds." But he argues that that reality is not an "objective entity" but a "mathematical abstraction" tied more to beliefs than facts.

[56] Kurki, Chapter 3.   [57] Chapter 3.

[58] When relationalists make the claim that "first and foremost, relationalism is an *is*, not a *should*," they would be more accurate to say that relationalism is a "might be," how the world "might be" and "might be expected" to work, not how the world actually "is" or "should" work. See Grove, Chapter 4.

Quantum science adds a third level of uncertainty.[59] It assumes that the human observer is not only studying itself but is now inextricably entangled with the world it is studying. The observer, the observed, and the background exist only together (there is no separate individual, observation, or background), and emerge only when a particular question (measurement) is asked (made). Observation triggers or collapses the entangled quantum world and reveals the only world we can know. There is no world behind the observed one. Objectivity, in short, is now out of the question. The world depends entirely on the questions the observer asks.

Relationalism in general pushes us toward this quantum level of uncertainty. But a strong relationalism goes beyond quantum science in two ways: it drastically reduces (if not eliminates) the role of the observer (the individual investigator), and it gives up the universal method of experimental science in favor of a localized and diluted method of "trial and error."[60] Quantum science does neither. In the case of the observer, it elevates, not eliminates, the significance of the observer (individual). Through the act of measuring, the observer now literally "creates" ("gives meaning to") the world we observe, which is the only world we can know.[61] As Steven Weinberg muses, "Man may indeed be the measure of all things."[62] That seems to reinforce the Weberian worldview that individuals are a significant location of agency. But in quantum physics the observer now has no way to test observations against an objective world because there is no objective world. The universal scientific method is no longer available, and we have to settle for a localized form of experimentation based on trial and error, yielding results which cannot be generalized. That point seems to reinforce the relationalist worldview.

But wait a minute. Some Newtonian (classical) physicists still contest the quantum proposition that there is no objective world. They argue that wave collapse is going on all the time objectively in a real but unknown world behind the observed world. They seek evidence of such "objective" wave collapse, independent of "subjective" measurement.[63] Interestingly, in

[59] Henderson 2020.
[60] Referencing Albert Hirschman, Katzenstein explains "trial and error" methods as "learning by doing, listening rather than preaching, humility, and the capacity to adjust and adapt to changing circumstances." There is no systematic experimentation: "we stumble into progress rather than plan for it" or literally, "fall from error into truth" (Chapter 10). All knowledge is contingent and cannot be generalized from specific case to specific case.
[61] As Bob Henderson puts it (2020): "This makes human beings, who are after all the only ones making the observations, in essence responsible for conjuring the reality we experience out of a murky nether world that quantum mechanics implies is simply unknowable."
[62] Weinberg 2013.
[63] As Henderson 2020 writes, this research involves "a class of theories called 'objective collapse models' that doesn't rely on human observation to collapse a wave function's

these efforts, Newtonian and quantum scientists use the same methods of science, mathematics and experiments, but derive very different content from those methods. Neither, however, has given up on the idea of science as a universal method. Quantum science may still prevail, but if it does it won't prevail forever, any more than Newtonian science did. Science advances from one falsified theory to another "not yet" falsified theory, not from false to true (at which point science ends).[64] And, since scientists tell us that we know only about 4 percent of the universe as we see it, the real world that we don't see is likely to remain elusive for a very long time to come. Scientists therefore should not speak about "the reality" let alone "the truth" of their findings, only about a method that tells them which findings are not false or not *yet* false.

In the meantime, quantum science raises some harrowing ethical issues when applied to the human world: the potential of unhinged human observers playing the role of creator, and the absence of any common moral standard by which to hold varying worldviews accountable.

6.4 Worldviews and Ethics

Having downsized if not eliminated the role of the reasoning individual in shaping worldviews, and having adopted a quantum view that the world we see is the only one there is, relationalism in this volume has surprisingly little to say about ethical and moral responsibility, either individual or collective. This neglect follows from relationalist logic. Because the world is holistic and incorporates all possibilities, there is little or no choice, and hence little or no responsibility. We have removed practically all degrees of human freedom to act and change the world. What's left are different values or religions and related methods of science which are compatible but not commensurable, harmonious but not integral, and equivalent but not competitive. Katzenstein writes:

both science and religion are variegated practices of different ways of knowing ... Both inquire into the possibility that the world might be different than it appears. Both are instances of us living in multiple realities and thus are examples of the profound human capacity of meaning-making ... Religious and scientific practices are rooted in the world of play.[65]

Play is an interesting term, implying a game or imaginary reality. In that game, however, what are the rules, and who makes them? Maybe no rules are needed. Science and religion are drawing closer together: "the border

---

possibilities to a single outcome, but that invokes instead an objective, physical process to do the job whether anyone's looking or not." See also Powell 2015.
[64] Weinberg 2013; Kuhn 1962.   [65] Chapter 10.

between quantum mechanics and religion is porous."[66] Religious values and scientific methods do not collide, they resonate. Multiple beliefs and realities cut or "smear" into one another like quantum waves. They blend, harmonize.

Such a harmonious concatenation of multiple worldviews expresses an aspiration that we all share. If relationalism is nothing more than an appeal for curiosity, openness, and tolerance, it is welcomed. But what if multiple worldviews do not harmonize? What if some worldviews condone slavery, deny individual human rights, justify genocide, discriminate against women (Islam in Saudi Arabia) or minorities (Uighurs in China), wage holy war against the infidel, and so on? In the flattened ontology that relationalists advocate, are all worldviews "true" or "moral"?

The issue here is not whether human beings are entangled but what *the content* of that entanglement is. The content of entanglement is what Haas and I try to get at with the concept of "ideological distance," whether worldviews are converging or diverging.[67] According to relationalists, the quantum social world is cooperative; ideological distance is always at or near zero. Conversely, the Weberian world is conflictual; ideological distance is always positive and sometimes large. As Alexander Wendt explains:

If your starting premise for thinking about social life is atomistic, then conflict is the natural starting point for life – every organism is out for itself, they're all selfish, it's all about survival of the fittest. Cooperation is very difficult because we're all separate and all trying to survive and do our own thing. On the other hand, if your starting point is holistic, where everything's entangled, then cooperation may be much easier to achieve. It may even be the default situation, and conflict is the exception. So it turns upside down a lot of the foundational assumptions, I think, of mainstream social science.[68]

Whether social life is atomistic or entangled, however, does not tell us much about outcomes. The master–slave relationship is entangled but not cooperative. The relationship between liberal states in the democratic peace is separate but not conflictual. No conflict in either case may mean no freedom to challenge slavery or democracy, and therefore no moral accountability – a *totalitarian* entanglement for which no one is responsible and which, apparently, no one can change.

Over time, of course, the content of social entanglement does change. Outright slavery is no longer acceptable. Communism, at least in the Soviet form, is gone. How does such change occur, and who is responsible for the original conflict and its eventual outcome? Katzenstein writes: "Divergent worldviews do not get resolved by appeals to logic and

---

[66] Katzenstein, Chapter 10.   [67] See Chapter 2.   [68] Wendt 2019.

evidence but through individual experiences and social processes."[69] So, how do "individual experience" and "social processes" accomplish this resolution? If logic and evidence are ruled out, what are the means of resolution – emotion, habit, intuition, etc.? Are these means peaceful or violent? Practically everyone agrees that Nazism had to be defeated by rationalist instruments (Grove might say assemblages) of power; Nazi ideology could not be blended or accommodated by relationalist effects of norms.

The relationalist worldview lacks any ethical standard for evaluating or resolving divergencies in the content of alternative worldviews. Everything is local and specific even though the world itself is holistic and entangled. And all events are uncertain even though the quantum model itself is certain and can't be challenged. The combination of the loss of objectivity (no real world behind the observed one) and the multiplicity of incommensurable but equivalent worldviews leaves almost everything up for grabs. A flattened ontology leads to a flattened ethical landscape as well.

Kurki seeks a relational ethic of *response-ability*: an ability to respond sensitively, openly, and thoughtfully to human and nonhuman relationships.[70] It is an appealing insight. But in a world in which there are no things (individuals) or backgrounds (objective world), where exactly is this responsibility located, and what is its substance? Grove, for example, sees violence as relational but not easily overcome by consciousness-raising.[71] You can become aware of relations, he points out, without coming to a sense of the common good. Kurki ponders the same point about knowledge: science "is part of becoming ... what this means is that we do not have clear criteria for good or bad knowledge."[72] The substance of ethics or knowledge, what is good and what is bad, is hard to pin down. Even harder to pin down is the location of ethical responsibility. In Grove's examination of presidential powers and nuclear weapons, he admits that the president is ultimately unaware of who or what is in control."[73] And if no one is in control, no one has responsibility.

Responsibility is not merely the "ability to respond." It's the ability to respond "by someone or something" in a "substantive" way toward some moral "end." Weber distinguished between an "ethic of responsibility," which Kurki's formulation might capture, and an "ethic of ultimate ends," which Kurki does not consider.[74] Perhaps this is because an

---

[69] Chapter 1.
[70] Kurki Draft, International Studies Association, Toronto, Canada, 2019: 15.
[71] Chapter 4.   [72] Chapter 3 .   [73] Chapter 4.   [74] Weber 1958: 120–128.

ethic of ultimate ends requires more than a relationship; it requires a direction, an arrow, not simply a flat surface or "fold."

As noted earlier, Grove suggests that "the scale of the investigator ... radically alters what appears as a part and what appears as a whole." If that's the case, the individual investigator, the individual, is back at the heart of a quantum-based social science model.[75] The Weberian commitment to the individual human being as the source of meaning and morality in a multiscalar world remains indispensable. That does not rule out agency at other levels. Relationalist factors are multiple, real, and often confining. But, to a meaningful extent, they form out of the interpretations and interactions of reasoning individuals, they change because of individual initiatives, and they dissolve because individuals leave and join other relationships. *The only "authenticated" actors beyond the individual in a Weberian worldview, therefore, are those groups, institutions, classes, etc., that are chosen or affirmed voluntarily by the consent of individual human beings acting in a setting where they have a meaningful degree of choice.* Holistic worldviews diminish that degree of choice and consent, however well-meaning they may be by embracing all possibilities.

The Weberian view judges and chooses. That is neither easy nor pleasant. No one wants to be accused of being judgmental. But we all do it.[76] Indeed, how does one avoid it? The Holocaust was a monstrous act of evil. How do we understand it in a world that blends religion and science? As Barnett (Chapter 5) shows, the Holocaust poses a wrenching question of existence, not just a vague smearing of relationships and "response-ability" to change or becoming. If such a question can be answered only in a specific situation (when the quantum wave function collapses), then we have abandoned both our humanity and our influence on world affairs.

Am I forcing everyone into a Weberian worldview?[77] Possibly, but I am not saying that the Weberian view is the *only* view. I am saying that I can

---

[75] Katzenstein (Chapter 10) describes it this way: "Agents act on their personal experiences and beliefs and, based on their measurement practices of the world, they make wholly personal experiences. This does not mean that the theory is only about Self and not about Other. Anyone can use the theory. And in using it each one assures themselves that beliefs about the consequences of their encounters with the world are consistent." Thus, the theory is universally available to anyone, like reason in the Weberian approach, but deeply relationalist based on measurement practices, which assures beliefs are consistent (harmonious), unlike the Weberian approach based on reason which allows for "inconsistent" beliefs.

[76] In this volume, for example, relationalists indict the Enlightenment; and Grove wants to call out the "old white men [who] still strut around the halls of America's 'best' institutions as if they saved us from the Cold War, even as the planet crumbles under the weight of their failed imperial dreams." Quoted in Katzenstein, Chapter 1.

[77] Weber sensed this tension when he wrote: "if we are competent in our pursuit [of teaching] we can force the individual, or at least we can help him, to give an *account of the ultimate meaning of his own conduct*" (italics original). See Weber 1958: 152.

find a location in the Weberian universe to host an alternative point of view (and do so when I compare the worldviews in this volume; see earlier in this chapter); I cannot find such a location in a relationalist universe. At the beginning, this project postulated a revolution in natural and social science thought rejecting Enlightenment and Newtonian worldviews. In later stages, Katzenstein emphasized complementarities among Newtonian and Post-Newtonian worldviews.[78] By complementarity, however, Katzenstein forces the Newtonian view into the relationalist universe where "the determinist or probability-inflected Newtonian world can be thought of as a special case that reveals itself when the quantum world of infinite possibilities and radical uncertainty collapses."[79] Bottom line? There is no location in the relationist world for dissent. Alternatives either fit into the quantum world or are patently false.

Moreover, understanding another worldview does not mean accepting it or making it equivalent. Would the world be better off today if the Reformation and Enlightenment had not occurred, or if the Haitian *lwa* not the Weberian worldview had dominated world politics after 1600?[80] Best, you say, if neither dominated? OK, but spell out the global consequences of the Haitian worldview or the specific parameters of equal coexistence which makes all worldviews (fascism, communism) acceptable and worth learning from. Unless we specify "what" we learn from "which" worldview, we are simply treating worldviews like souvenirs, collecting and trivializing them. Worse, we are opening the floodgates to any worldview with no standard for judging good and bad. Maybe the relationalist turn pops open an irresistible, new window of a more harmonious world that we have missed because of the atomistic and competitive frame of western modernism. But maybe it doesn't. And if it doesn't, not only material progress but individual freedom is at stake.

Which leads to a final question: where do relationalist cosmologies place the divine? What lies behind the Big Bang? Relationalists are eager to unify the human and natural worlds and see a growing commonality between science and religion. The obstacle to unifying the human and natural worlds, however, is an understanding of consciousness which humans have and nonhumans do not. And the obstacle to uniting the scientific and religious (*supra*natural) worlds is an understanding of the soul, the human capacity to imagine the divine.[81] Separating these three worlds – nature, humanity, and the divine – has led to abuse: humanity

---

[78] Chapter 10.   [79] Chapter 10.
[80] This question does not disrespect the Iwa; it takes it seriously.
[81] This is what Niebuhr (1949) called the "transcendence" of the human being.

masquerading as gods (the Church before the Enlightenment) or humanity "lifted up" to control nature (the critics' view of the Enlightenment). But uniting them may lead to even worse abuse. What stands in the way of a science that poses as a religion or a nature that restrains prosperity?[82] By blurring the distinction between religion and science, nature and humanity, relationalism weakens Enlightenment institutions that separate state and church, markets and feudalism. It enables potentially powerful new gods of unchallenged expertise and science to take the stage (because, remember, there is no objective universe). We could wind up again in a pre-Enlightenment world wherein scientists and their authoritarian enablers usurp the power of privilege to suppress the rights of reasoning individuals. Resistance would be anti-science and futile, as it was anti-God and heresy in pre-Enlightenment times. As Timothy Byrnes writes, "if a relational cosmology is grounded in faith or in the pursuit of what is 'really real,' then the unknown itself is the basis of Truth and the human propensity to resistance is ultimately futile."[83] And if the unknown is truth and cannot be resisted, the Dark Ages may be upon us once again.

6.5   Conclusion

I come back to the need, therefore, to maintain a Weberian worldview, whatever the debate in physics, if only to retain a "critical" perspective on the totalizing tendencies of the relationalist school of thought. As Mike Barnett concludes, "Without worldviews we would not know how to go on, and would be lost in the wilds until a charismatic leader arrived to provide guidance."[84] In the barren "wilds" of relationalism (the jungle), that charismatic leader would probably be a totalizing ideology, one admitting of no alternatives – radical Islam under the Caliphate, Medieval Christianity under the Inquisition, totalitarian atheism under fascism and communism, or scientific elitism under a relationalist banner that substitutes expertise for politics and human choice. The Weberian worldview is still a necessary defense against that sort of evil.

Bibliography

Aristotle, *Politics*, book 5, part 1, translated by Benjamin Jowett: http://classics.mit.edu/Aristotle/politics.5.five.html

---

[82] For a nature that restrains prosperity, see Duara, Chapter 7 and Katzenstein, Chapter 10, anticipating that "pandemics and other natural disasters may become more effective brakes than the competition between states."
[83] Chapter 9.
[84] Barnett Draft, International Studies Association, Toronto, Canada 2019: 1.

Barnett, Michael. 2019. "A World of Worldviews? Draft Paper." Roundtable: Worldviews and World Politics, International Studies Association Annual Meeting, Toronto, March 27–30.

Bergstein, Brian. 2020. "AI Still Gets Confused about the Way the World Works," *MIT Technology Review*, 123, 2 (March/April): 62–65.

Brubaker, Rogers. 1984. *The Limits of Rationality: An Essay on the Social and Moral Thought of Max Weber*. London: George Allen and Unwin.

Christianson, Gale E. 2005. *Isaac Newton: Lives and Legacies*. Oxford: Oxford University Press.

Dilthey, Wilhelm, 1989. *Wilhelm Dilthey, Selected Works, Volume 1: Introduction to the Human Sciences*, edited with an introduction by Rudolf A. Makkreel and Frithjof Rodi. Princeton, NJ: Princeton University Press.

Haas, Ernst B. 1990. *When Knowledge is Power: Three Models of Change in International Organizations*. Berkeley: University of California Press.

Haas, Mark L. 2005. *The Ideological Origins of Great Power Politics, 1789–1989*. Ithaca, NY: Cornell University Press.

Henderson, Bob. 2020. "The Rebel Physicist on the Hunt for A Better Story than Quantum Mechanics," *The New York Times Magazine* (June 25). www .nytimes.com/2020/06/25/magazine/angelo-bassi-quantum-mechanic.html

Kalberg, Stephen. 1980. "Max Weber's Types of Rationality," *American Journal of Sociology*, 85, 5 (March): 1145–79.

Kalberg, Stephen. 1994. *Max Weber's Comparative-Historical Sociology*. Chicago, IL: University of Chicago Press.

Katzenstein, Peter. 2019. "Worldviews in World Politics: Draft Paper." Roundtable: Worldviews and World Politics, International Studies Association Annual Meeting, Toronto, March 27–30.

Kuhn, Thomas. 1962. *The Structure of Scientific Revolutions*. Chicago: University of Chicago Press.

Kurki, Milja. 2019. "International Relations in a Relational Universe: Draft Paper." Roundtable: Worldviews and World Politics, International Studies Association (ISA) Annual Meeting, Toronto, March 27–30.

Landes, David S. 1999. *The Wealth and Poverty of Nations*. New York: W. W. Norton & Company.

Maddison, Angus. 1991. *Dynamic Forces in Capitalist Development: A Long-run Comparative View*. New York: Oxford University Press.

Mokyr, Joel. 1990. *The Lever of Riches: Technological Creativity and Economic Progress*. New York: Oxford University Press.

Morgenthau, Hans J. 1946. *Scientific Man vs. Power Politics*. Chicago: The University of Chicago Press.

Nau, Henry R. 1990. *The Myth of America's Decline: Leading the World Economy into the 1990s*. New York: Oxford University Press.

Nau, Henry R. 2002. *At Home Abroad: Identity and Power in American Foreign Policy*. Ithaca, NY: Cornell University Press.

Nau, Henry R. 2008. "The Scholar and the Policy-Maker," in Christian Reus-Smit and Duncan Snidal, eds., *The Oxford Handbook of International Affairs*. Oxford: Oxford University Press, pp. 635–648.

Nau, Henry R. 2013. "Review of *Sinicization* by Peter Katzenstein," *Perspectives on Politics* 11, September 3: 997–99.

Nau, Henry R. and Deepa M. Ollapally, eds. 2012. *Worldviews of Aspiring Powers: Domestic Foreign Policy Debates in China, India, Iran, Japan and Russia.* New York: Oxford University Press.

Niebuhr, Reinhold. 1949. *The Nature and Destiny of Man,* volumes 1 and 2. New York: Charles Scribner's Sons.

Nozick, Robert. 1993. *The Nature of Rationality.* Princeton, NJ: Princeton University Press.

Pinker, Steven. 2011. *The Better Angels Of Our Nature: Why Violence Has Declined.* New York: Penguin Books.

Pomeranz, Kenneth. 2000. *The Great Divergence: China, Europe and the Making of the World Economy.* Princeton, NJ: Princeton University Press.

Powell, Corey S. 2015. "Relativity vs. Quantum Mechanics: The Battle for the Universe," *The Guardian,* November 4. www.theguardian.com/news/2015/no v/04/relativity-quantum-mechanics-universe-physicists#maincontent

Thernstrom, Stephan and Abigail Thernstrom. 1997. *America in Black and White: One Nation Indivisible.* New York: Simon and Schuster.

Waldner, David. 2017. "Schrödinger's Cat and the Dog That Didn't Bark: Why Quantum Mechanics is (Probably) Irrelevant to the Social Sciences." *Critical Review,* 29, 2 (June 23): 199–233.

Weber, Max. 1958. *From Max Weber: Essays in Sociology,"* translated, edited, and with an introduction by H.H. Gerth and C. Wright Mills, A Galaxy Book. New York: Oxford University Press.

Weber, Max. 2009. *The Protestant Ethic and the. Spirit of Capitalism,* translated and introduced by Stephen Kalberg. New York: Oxford University Press.

Weinberg, Steven. 2013. "Physics: What We Do and Don't Know," *The New York Review of Books* (November 7). www.nybooks.com/articles/2013/11 /07/physics-what-we-do-and-dont-know/

Wendt, Alexander. 1999. *Social Theory of International Politics.* Cambridge: Cambridge University Press.

Wendt, Alexander. 2015. *Quantum Mind and Social Science.* Princeton, NJ: Princeton University Press.

Wendt, Alexander. 2019. Interview on *Quantum Physics and Social Science,* Sept. 1. www.youtube.com/watch?v=qEZGjdIqL7c&t=2s

7   Oceans, Jungles, and Gardens
World Politics and the Planet

Prasenjit Duara

As a historian attentive to global trends, I have appreciated the opportunity to participate in the workshops leading to this volume on World Politics and Worldviews. The recent decades appear, as in several other fields, to have witnessed an explosion of methods and scope in the study of International Relations. Going well beyond the study of state-to-state and the varieties of cross-national relations, these approaches take on the vital issue of agency, common to all sciences. Do we conceive of agency as human activity, whether individual, collective, or sensory (especially visual media), or should we adopt a more distributed concept of agentive beings, human and nonhuman? Since the latter have significant demonstrated effects on world politics, they are legitimate fields of inquiry. Particularly concerned by the Anthropocene as I am, I explore how worldviews and cosmologies do or do not, can or cannot, help us understand not only the politics of the world, but also of the planet.

The same relational, processual, and widened scope to be found in Kurki, Grove and Allan in the volume has also prompted me to inquire about the relationships between worldviews and cosmologies.[1] Committed philosophically to a processual perspective, I develop a schema of layered and interactive temporalities to grasp the mediations that result in world politics and to probe the possibilities of alternative worldviews and cosmologies. To prefigure the argument: Enlightenment ideas, assumptions, and projects have constituted temporally the most durable *cosmology* underlying world politics over two hundred years. These assumptions and associated historical processes have generated a dynamic, circulatory system of nation-states driven by what I term the epistemic engine of the nation-form. In turn, this engine has had globally transformative consequences, but also generated colossal counterfinalities on the planet. Worldviews derive from the epistemic engine, but also from historical, religious, and personal and collective experiences not reducible to the engine. A principal goal of this chapter is to explore the

---

[1] See Chapters 3, 4, and 8, respectively.

extent to which, and how, experiential worldviews can penetrate or negotiate the epistemic engine to influence the world order and world politics.

In the Section 7.1 I develop a conceptual framework around the
"epistemic engine" which organizes and circulates the cosmological
dimensions of Enlightenment modernity, usefully described by
Bentley Allan (Chapter 8, this volume). In Section 7.2, I explore how
the imperial Chinese world order – functional until at least the late
nineteenth century – reveals a different cosmology shaping a different
"world" order and politics. I go on to explore the contemporary PRC
view of the world order, probing the extent to which its historical
experiences can be seen to reshape the hegemonic epistemic engine. In
Section 7.3, I draw from a paradigm of "oceanic temporality" to grasp
counterfinalities generated by the epistemic engine on the earth and the
ocean itself. Can the counterflows of social movements allow us to
imagine what Katzenstein calls a post-Enlightenment, hyper-humanist
cosmology?

7.1   The Epistemic Engine and the World Order

Regarding the ontological and epistemological conditions described by Allan,
Newtonian physics furnishes the conception of nature as governed by mathematically apprehended laws.[2] Based significantly on the Cartesian conception of duality of the mind and the external world, humans are capable of
knowing and using these laws. Regarding temporality, the Newtonian view
holds an absolute conception of time as linear and irreversible and space as an
empty container within which movement occurs. We are reminded of
Benedict Anderson's application of Walter Benjamin's "empty, homogenous
time" to the nation.[3] Post-Newtonian cosmogony does not seem to have
significantly affected the worldview of global political actors or of mainstream
IR scholarship beyond the operative principle of the disenchantment of the
world.

The Enlightenment was, like all powerful historical developments,
a complex one with important alternative currents – such as Spinoza's
monism or Humean skepticism – that challenged some of the cosmological underpinnings. Moreover, as Katzenstein shows, quantum physics and evolutionary complexity cannot be seen to operate within this
paradigm.[4] Most of all, the bulk of the world's population can scarcely be
said to subscribe to such a disenchanted cosmology. Yet the alternatives
have not yet figured as a major force in world politics. For much of the
social sciences, and especially for the major actors in world politics, the

---

[2] Chapter 8, this volume.   [3] Anderson 1991.   [4] Chapter 1, this volume.

cosmology bequeathed by the Enlightenment remains the hegemonic doxa of our time.

Arguably, the greatest complexity arises when we consider the conception of human destiny. The optimistic view of human progress celebrated by Enlightenment thinkers was subject to a more pessimistic view in the late nineteenth and early twentieth centuries, represented in scholarship – perhaps iconically – by Max Weber's recognition that science could no longer be universal but would have to yield ground to the determination of ultimate values by forces beyond rationality, by a certain polytheistic re-enchantment. "Fate, and certainly not 'science,' holds sway over these gods and their struggles. One can only understand what the godhead is for the one order or for the other, or better, what godhead is in the one or in the other order."[5] In other words, rationalization cannot overcome the politicization – beyond individualization – of values.

The philosophical deflation of the optimistic stance reached a peak toward the end of World War I – Weber's speech "Science as a Vocation" was penned in 1917– when thinkers around the world railed against the barbarous consequences of modern technological civilization. The roughly simultaneous advent of relativity theory and quantum mechanics also displaced Newtonian science as the reigning paradigm within scientific and philosophical circles. But even as the moral and cosmological foundations of the Newtonian Enlightenment project begins to come apart, conventional knowledge of world leaders and mainstream social sciences continues to function within that paradigm. Just as most of the world continues to follow a cosmology founded on enchantment, so too do world politics and its scholarship follow a paradigm that may be out of synch with further advances in scientific philosophy. At the same time, let us remind ourselves that cosmologies are themselves chartings through unknowable planetary processes.

If we take the Newtonian Enlightenment project to be the cosmology of modernity, I view the world order that derives from – and is legitimated by – such a cosmology to be the evolving Westphalian–Vatellian–UN order as, perhaps, what Carl Schmitt called the European *nomos*.[6] This world order has been cultivated as a garden, patchily and erratically over the centuries, keeping at bay the ever-encroaching jungle both from within and without. The relationship between Enlightenment cosmology and the world order and world politics is mediated by an epistemic engine.

---

[5] Weber 1918: 15; see also Weber 2004: 23 for a different wording of the translation.
[6] Schmitt 1976.

I draw the category of the episteme from structuralist and post-structuralist ideas, but add the term "engine" to denote its dynamic and circulatory temporality. By circulatory I don't mean circular, but a process whereby not all aspects of the nation-form are equally adopted but are successively adapted and recirculatated. The epistemic engine is structured by conventional economic and political power driven by accumulation strategies and state territorialization following Arrighi's diagnosis that global capitalism is made possible "by the capture of mobile capital for territorial and population control, and the control of territories and people for the purposes of mobile capital."[7] At the same time, the epistemic engine embeds Foucauldian forms of power within knowledge and as knowledge (power/knowledge). Foucault's notion of the episteme is the "apparatus" or "regime" which governs the separation not of the true from the false, but of what may from what may not be characterized as acceptable knowledge – the conditions of possibility.[8] We might say that it is this epistemic dimension of modern (secular) cosmology that works to bracket religious and nature-centric views from occupying center-stage in the world order.[9]

How might we grasp the vehicle or vector by which the episteme circulates and functions globally? I suggest that the vector is none other than the nation, or, more precisely, the nation-form.[10] The nation is the epistemic engine that powers the circulation of the cosmology embedded in world-views and generates the legitimacy of the world order. The nation-form embeds the relatively durable ideas of popular sovereignty, militarized territoriality, and Enlightenment progress. Temporally, it is expressed in a linear and teleological history of self-same subject which realizes its glory through struggle and competition. The Subject is exemplified in the Spartan song "We are who you were, we will be who you are."[11] The nation is able thus to reconcile its requirement for a timeless essence (to claim territory and sovereignty) while promising progressive change. As the ur-form of all identity politics, the foundational sense of the Self in nationalism requires a strong sense of the Other, and under certain circumstances, like the present, flares up with extraordinary virulence.

There is an isomorphism, and perhaps homology due to shared ancestry, between this conception of the nation and the individual and methodological individualism discussed by Henry Nau in this volume.[12] While

---

[7] Arrighi 1994: 32–33.   [8] Foucault 1980: 197, 109–15.

[9] Arguably, we can think of Newtonian cosmology as a worldview that acquires a doxic status – at least in geopolitics– through the dominant institutions of power and knowledge production.

[10] For "nation-form," see Balibar 1991.   [11] Cited in Renan 1990: 19.

[12] See Chapter 6.

Enlightenment liberalism enshrined individualism as a value through notions of equality and inalienable rights of "life, liberty and the pursuit of happiness," the rights-bearing individual also came to be the model of the subject or agent in society. This individual is abstracted from the processual relationships through which identity evolves. Although Weber sought to distinguish individualism as a value from the abstracted idea of methodological individualism as the model of rational human action, the latter presupposes an ontological and normative individualism as a prerequisite of sociology.[13]

The point I want to make here is not about the rationality of individual action, but the transfer of this mode of individualization to transform a society into the singular collective of the nation. Note that Article III of the French Revolution's Declaration of the Rights of Man and Citizen deposits the ultimate right – of sovereignty – hemming all others, in the Nation. Since then, the rights of "nations" over two and half centuries may well have been asserted more than the rights of individuals. The presumption of so much IR work that world politics is conducted by personified nations reflects this kind of methodologically individuated nationalism and reproduces the engine of the nation-form.

The epistemic engine, grounded in the cosmological dualism between subject (human) and object (nonhuman/nature), is propelled by the goal of conquering nature. Historically described as "progress," the goal is to be achieved within the nation largely in competition with other nations over the control of global resources. The engine references both the material and the epistemic. It absorbs and reproduces Enlightenment axioms; it thus allows the unlimited consumption of energy and nature while discharging its exhaust on environment and society. Note that the history of twentieth-century socialism reveals that it was not only capitalism but the Enlightenment idea of the progressive mastery of nature that drives increasing control over nature.

The circulation of the nation-form is equally propelled by notions of competitive efficiency – in the manner of contemporary corporate firms – learning, copying, adapting, and stealing from nations that are more successful in the productivity of its population and in garnering global resources. The history of the twentieth century in Asia is one of the overhaul of older empires and polities to build nations because it seemed to them to be the only means of resisting imperialist competition and domination. They could only lick 'em by joining them. In the process, the epistemic engine has generated a runaway global technosphere with cascading consequences and counterfinalities described herein.

---

[13] Weiss 2015: 228.

Nations are also interdependent for economic and other purposes, and rules are created to save them from mutual destruction (as almost happened during the two world wars). The Westphalian–Vatellian system, the League of Nations, and the United Nations have been tasked with maintaining those rules and protocols. This nation-state system that frames the world order sustains the nation-form, which is a condition of political participation. Of course, the interests of individual and groups of powerful nations can and do supersede those rules.

While the nation-form perhaps dates to the French and American revolutions, it also has European roots in what Carl Schmitt called the "*nomos*": a long-durée historical conception of the spatial, political, and juridical principles and rules of a political community governing land appropriation (including by conquest), division, and distribution.[14] The *nomos* was adapted from Greek and Christian conceptions, but its global significance arose from its refiguration as a project of order and domination after the 1648 Treaty of Westphalia.

For Schmitt, the *nomos* refers to the interstate system organized in Europe, which served at once as the anchor of and the blueprint for modern international law. By bracketing certain spaces of war and domination between these powers, it sought to regulate relations among the European states. It represented the means to contain this violence from becoming anarchic, as, for instance, through the Treaty of Tordesillas.[15] As a doctrine that only applied to European lands, the *nomos* also enabled these states to dominate, occupy, and ravage the people, the resources, and the open seas beyond the European *nomos*. Schmitt remained avowedly Eurocentric in *Nomos of the Earth*, published in 1950, mourning the loss of its European character as it was being overtaken by America and the United Nations.[16]

The nation-form of the epistemic engine drives the world order as it recruits and organizes the different forces and factors making the modern world. Its leaders and representatives pursue their goals through modes of knowledge whose conditions of possibility are governed by the ontology and epistemology of the Enlightenment and, more particularly, the Newtonian worldview. What is the relationship between other worldviews and the epistemic engine? Katzenstein draws on Dilthey to describe a worldview as a combination of ideas, values, faith, dispositions, morals, and, not least, historical and lived experience.[17] In this volume, Tim Byrnes and Michael Barnett make a strong case for showing how religious worldviews shape world politics.[18] Worldviews are clearly also of great

---

[14] Schmitt 1976: ch 4.   [15] Reilly 2009: 174–75.
[16] Schmitt 1976: 51–52, 87–88. Blanco and Valle 2014: 7–8.   [17] Chapter 1, this volume.
[18] Chapter 9 and Chapter 5 in this volume, respectively.

significance to human concerns and political priorities and are not reducible to other imperatives. I argue that since the epistemological engine is
hegemonic (not totalistic) and simultaneously drives the episteme and the
levers of the global political economy (such as the IMF, the WHO, the
WTO, the US military, and financial corporations), worldviews tend to
be expressed in world politics in negotiation with or through the filter of
the hegemonic engine.

There has been a proliferation of nonstate actors on the global stage
and media in the last few decades. The recent movement of young people,
frequently below the age threshold of citizenship, protesting the inactivity
of world leaders regarding climate change, may well represent such an
intervention based on their collective experiences and expectations. To be
sure, they too have to rely on the stage of world politics underwritten by
the epistemic engine to have their voices heard. I think here of the young
Greta Thunberg, whose career trajectory we might follow. In the last
section of the chapter I will assess the possible pathways whereby social
movements, old and new, seek to forge a practical vision for a new order.

To date, no nation has been able to challenge or function successfully
outside the prescriptive nation-form, which involves among its central
features territoriality, the self–other binary, progress, competition, and
the pursuit of increasing control over natural forces. The Panchashila
movement of the decolonizing nations presented a brief flash of alternative visions of a new order, but rapidly gave way to territorial and identitarian competition. To be sure, its religious and historical experience and
vision has made the Islamic Republic of Iran an outlier in the
Enlightenment-based epistemic engine, but Iran conforms to the principal precepts of the territorial identitarian state, including a competitive
modernization agenda. The same could be said of Saudi Arabia.

Perhaps the imperial Chinese world order, which emerged from
a different cosmology and functioned in a radically different way from
the Newtonian world of politics, represented the most powerful alternative since the rise of the Western order. I now turn to it and its successor
state, the People's Republic of China.

7.2   The World Orders of Imperial and Contemporary China

The world order of late imperial China (circa tenth–nineteenth centuries)
was another kind of garden that it is difficult to characterize, in significant
part because our terminology is suffused by the contemporary assumptions of international relations. This order represented a complex set of
Chinese imperial tribute practices which I treat as a Wittgensteinian "language game" that is distinguished from the idea of a system which

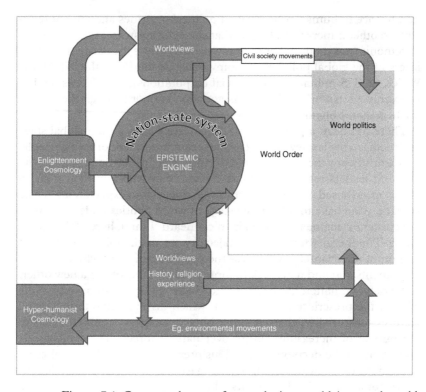

Figure 7.1 Conceptual map of cosmologies, worldviews and world politics

presupposes rules, abstract principles, and essences.[19] Language games are not well-bounded systems constituted by a single principle or doctrine – say, of sovereignty or the nation-form – but open-ended. Norms, rituals, and codes (which are learned) are provisional, capacious, and flexible.

The Qing imperial order was not one of theoretically equal states, but a paternalistic, hierarchical order, principally based on tribute. The Westphalian system was formulated theoretically on equality and noninterference between *recognized* states; in practice, these states were highly intrusive in each other's affairs, territorially competitive, and globally expansive. Through Schmitt's *Nomos*, we see that with the discovery of the Americas, the jurisdiction of European international law produced an extra-European frontier which became the outside – a space of exception for their European masters. Imperial Chinese rulers were largely

---

[19] Wittgenstein 2009: §6, 23, 65 and passim; Biletzki and Matar 2020.

uninterested in ruling or controlling spaces beyond the imperial frontiers, whether for accumulation, conversion, or political power.

In the imperial Chinese rhetoric, tribute, paid by states and communities peripheral to China, was an expression of the subordination of these groups to the imperial state. In return, the emperor bestowed gifts – including the all-important license to trade – upon the tribute bearers. In practice, it represented a wider web that did not involve merely the relationship between China and the tribute bearer, but a host of "several other lesser or satellite tribute relationships not directly concerning China and forming a considerably more complex system of reciprocal relationships."[20]Through most of the second millennium, trade became the most prominent feature of the tribute system.

Different games do not have the common essence of "games" but are recognizable by *family resemblances* of overlapping codes and practices. Thus, for instance, when the Qing emperors performed the roles of both the Boddhisattva Manjusri as well as the patron who descends to meet his spiritual mentor, the Dalai Lama, half-way, the Tibetans and Qing were engaged in overlapping language games (the ambiguity of which would become problematic in a different epistemic context of sovereign states). All this is, of course, different from his role as the Son of Heaven or having treaties signed on his behalf (such as the Treaty of Nerchinsk in 1689, which approached the principle of Westphalian sovereignty). We may think of the East Asian tribute order as a complex language game which incorporated various modes of ritual and other performative procedures with diverse and changing roles for the players. For instance, the Chinese Song dynasty (tenth–twelfth centuries) also had to deliver large values of tribute to the Khitan (Liao) and the Tanggut (Xi Xia), although it profited more from its trade surpluses with these states.[21]

Military violence was not absent. Most famously, the Ming naval expeditions led by Admiral Zheng He in the first third of the fifteenth century, forced tribute, captured slaves and even a king in Sri Lanka in a bid to demonstrate the power of the Chinese emperor. However, such military authority over the sea route was not maintained beyond a brief window in the fifteenth century. Nor did China control the land routes over Central Asia. Rather, one might say that Chinese military power outside the empire was mostly an equilibrating operation. Expeditions were undertaken as punitive measures against bordering states, including Korea, or tribes who often harassed and threatened the empire at its periphery. For example, during the eighteenth century, the Burmese Konbaung state conducted raids along the southwestern frontier. This

[20] Hamashita 1994: 92.   [21] Shiba 1983: 98.

prompted several punitive military expeditions, with mixed results. Military campaigns were expensive and were designed principally to stabilize the tribute order and manage the bordering states, rather than for colonial and territorial expansion beyond the empire.[22]

The contemporary Chinese state operates under the obviously very different conditions of capitalism, nationalism, and statism. At the same time, its own historical narrative and rhetoric has been deeply mindful of the violence and plunder wreaked by imperialist nation-states. In recent years, it has also glorified its historical relations with neighboring states and kingdoms as an alternative order, conducted harmoniously under the ideals of *tianxia* (all under heaven) and *wangdao* (the kingly way). This rhetoric of harmony or "win–win" has been extended to the Belt and Road Initiative (BRI) publicized with much fanfare as the revival of the landed and maritime Silk Roads connecting China with the world. To what extent does the historical experience and rhetoric of China – its worldview – challenge the world order undergirded by the epistemic engine? Does it merely replace or supplement one great power with another?

The most publicized scholarly position on the relevance of *tianxia*, related to the tribute order, to the contemporary world order has been developed by the philosopher Zhao Tingyang. Historically, he argues the *tianxia* worldview emerged in the transition from the Shang to the Zhou at the beginning of the first millennium BCE. A limited power that succeeded a much larger empire, the Zhou devised the worldview to control the larger entity by making global politics a priority over the local. As such, it was a strategic act that eventuated in a long peace governed by a global worldview harmonizing differences in the world.[23]

The contemporary extension of the *tianxia* model would involve a "world institution" controlling a larger territory and military force than that controlled by the autonomous substates. These substates will be independent in most respects, except in their legitimacy and obligations for which they depend on the recognition of the world institution. Rather than being based on force and self-interest, the cultural empire would use ritual as a means to limit the self and its interests. *Tianxia* is a hierarchical worldview which prioritizes order over freedom, elite governance over democracy, and the superior political institution over the lower levels.[24]

The anthropologist Wang Mingming presents us with a different view of *tianxia*, which he argues cannot be grasped in a singular manner. He differentiates the historical role of *tianxia* before and after the first

---

[22] Zhou 2011: 172.   [23] Zhao 2009: 6–8.   [24] Zhao 2009: 11–18.

unification of China by the Qin in 221 BCE. In the classical pre-Qin period, *tianxia* represented a religious cosmology without strict demarcation of the human, natural, and divine order. *Tianxia* encompassed the different kingdoms or *guo* according to a theory of concentric circles around a cosmic–moral core of closeness to a transcendent Heaven. The Zhou emperor himself, as the Son of Heaven, was subordinated to Heaven in the name of *tianxia*, and order was sustained by a reciprocity of ritualized relationships within this concentric world.[25]

After the imperial unification, Wang argues that *tianxia* cosmology became subordinated to the centralized imperial state (*guo*), and the earlier distinction between the Zhou state and the realm of *tianxia* began to disappear as *tianxia* became effectively a project of imperial order and control. Imperial *tianxia* was also creatively deployed to create a Sino-centric order of hierarchy in the empire and superiority to manage foreign tributaries and vassals, as described earlier. Access to the transcendent power of Heaven became increasingly monopolized by the imperial center through its elaborate and synchronized system of official sacrifices and rituals in authorized ceremonial centers through the world. The concept of "all under Heaven" now became manifested in the idealized perfect union between Heaven and Earth by the central role of the Son of Heaven in it.[26]

While Zhao acknowledges that the post-Qin ideal of *tianxia* is transformed, his conception still offers a top-down method of political ordering as the essence of the *tianxia* system. Zhao believes that political leadership must emanate at the highest level – the *tianxia* political institution – which must then be "transposed" to the lower levels (how the top controls the bottom is not clear) and not vice versa. This is a thus a descending order from "all under heaven" to nation-states to families. At the same time as political order or control descends, an ethical order ascends from families to states to *tianxia*. Thus, this results in a relationship of mutual justification, but would presumably also act as the system of mutual checks.[27]

I do not find this model to be a suitable alternative. Do we not presuppose a highly idealized conception of humanity and a literalist reading of rhetoric if we think that ritual-familial order alone will restrain the politically superior to act benevolently? If it did work well in the Zhou, we will need to consider a multiplicity of factors, including kinship ties, a differentiated control of resources, and a complex balance of power. With regard to the contemporary utilization of *tianxia*, it seems rather odd to be applying an ancient system quite so mechanically to an entirely

[25] Wang 2012: 343–47.   [26] Wang 2012: 351–54.   [27] Zhao 2006: 33.

changed world. Moreover, since the political system is not based upon democratically elected leaders, we don't know how world government will be constituted. Yet, it may not be unreasonable to see in it strong elements of a future Chinese-dominated world order.

The other, more recent historical past is the modern Chinese revolutionary experience. The communist revolution in China produced a mighty party-state and a revolutionary sense of purpose and agency that not only defied the world order but also broke away early from Soviet dependence and became a nuclear power by 1964. The People's Republic of China was not represented in the United Nations until 1971. But even as its worldview challenged the world order of capitalist states, it remained a child of Enlightenment modernity and was bound in myriad ways to the epistemic engine of the nation-form. Particularly evident, these bonds were the imperative to conquer nature for human ends and, more complexly, the self–other form of national identity.

Communist ideology and Maoist thought were committed to the liberation of the world, but the ideology of class conflict and the imperatives of state power (particularly in a hostile world) converted class identity into a nationalist one. To be sure, the Maoist revolution always had a strong nationalist component, but in this worldview the nation was seen as a necessary step toward a nationless and classless communist utopia. During the Cultural Revolution, the Chinese nation came to be seen as the only revolutionary proletarian nation (barring Albania) confronted by bourgeois and revisionist nations around the world. Class and nation became one. Today, of course, as communist ideology has ebbed in China, nationalism has become the overwhelming form of identity expression in China.

Let us consider the rise of China, a nonliberal, authoritarian state power, to superpower status in the world order. I do not believe that China will necessarily erode the cosmological foundations of Enlightenment modernity. Enlightenment thought has always contained a significant strain of nondemocratic thought. Rooted in rationality, science, the ideal of progress, natural law, human rights, and humanitarianism, the Enlightenment was characterized just as much by what one author calls "proto-totalitarian" ideas of politics and governance as by what we would today call liberalism and individual rights. The possibility of rationally channeling and even coercing humans to follow scientific laws of behavior (eg. Rousseau's *morale sensitive*) encouraged many continental Enlightenment thinkers to support enlightened despotism.[28] The

[28] Crocker 1985: 225.

ideas of Machiavelli, Hobbes, and Voltaire, as well as John Adams and James Madison, also shaped the Enlightenment project.

Many Chinese thinkers look to this tradition, and particularly to the more recent ideas of Carl Schmitt and Leo Strauss, to trace their affiliation with a nonliberal Enlightenment project.[29] Chinese thinkers are also attracted to Joseph Nye's idea of soft power or a "win–win" strategy of engaging the world. These ideas would be quite compatible with Zhao's proposed blueprint of *tianxia*, and one could conceive of a Chinese world order that was formed from a mix of authoritarian Enlightenment rationality with an affective – if not quite fictive kinship – model of hierarchical loyalty and reciprocity. We do not have space here to explore such a strategic mission, but I will undertake a brief analysis of BRI, which may be viewed as a practical expression of the worldview of the Chinese state possibly informed by its historical experiences.[30]

As is well known, BRI represents a massive expansion of Chinese economic investments in infrastructure partnerships, including high-speed railroads, telecommunications, new ports, energy cooperation, and, indeed, the technosphere. Chinese investments abroad – whether state-owned or private – have been driven by the search for outlets for excess capital, labor, and older, especially coal-mining, technology within China. The investments also tend to be extractive and energy hungry. Many countries engage with the BRI because they require capital for infrastructure development not easily available to them. Moreover, they can also partake of advanced digital technologies such as 5G, Beidou, the Chinese geophysical positioning system, and other technology connected with the Digital Silk Road that is accompanying infrastructure building.

The BRI is publicized as inspired by principles of harmony and authority that are noncontentious and not liberal. Chinese state policies follow the Panchashila principles of noninterference in the internal matters of sovereign states. Hence, in its dealings with governments in Asia, Africa, and elsewhere, it responds to the kind of regime that is operative. Where civil society groups are well developed, the Chinese representatives *can* be responsive to demands made by them. Where civil society is weak, Chinese investors are willing to deal with governments regardless of issues of transparency and corruption. A Chinese rhetoric of affective, historical relations and loyalty – including some instances of debt forgiveness– are very much in evidence in these relationships.

While there are functions and dimensions of the BRI that are useful and palatable to the countries engaged with the projects, BRI projects and contracts are not subject to the protocols and procedures of Western

[29] Marchal et al. 2017.   [30] For a fuller analysis, see Duara 2019.

principles of international commercial contract and legal regimes. BRI policies privilege development and order at the expense of transparency and the rights of people. "Asian-style mediation" and customized arbitration mechanisms are preferred. This modality, given the vast scale of BRI projects (more than 300 billion US dollars already invested) and the complexities of Chinese decision-makers, goals, and interests, has generated tensions and problems not only in host societies but also for the Chinese side in the contemporary world. I identify three sets of issues that represent fields of power and contestation.

The first of these is debt. African countries' debt to Chinese loans and investments is more than $140 billion, and a similar amount is owed by Latin American and Caribbean countries. The debt of Asian countries is probably higher still; Sri Lanka's inability to repay China the high costs of constructing the Hambantota port has led to the leasing of the port to a Chinese company for 99 years. While many Chinese investments are productive, the Center for Global Development's report concluded that eight countries are at risk of debt distress on the basis of available data on debt-to-GDP ratios.[31] Although debtor countries certainly suffer, the creditor countries also bear considerable pressure from resistance and instabilities in the debtor countries and pressure from international agencies.[32] More recently, China has had to redraft many BRI contracts under terms less favorable to it, and will presumably confront more severe problems due to the current COVID-19 crisis.

The second is the problem of environmental degradation and distress. Between 2014 and 2017, six Chinese banks participated in US$143 billion worth of syndicated loans to the BRI region's energy and transportation sectors. Almost three-quarters of the total volume of this finance went to the oil, gas, and petrochemical industries.[33] While China has recently emerged as a leader in the production of renewable energy, and still more recently in environmental conservation, it is doing so by outsourcing its natural resource requirements. Civil society movements in many parts of the globe are responding by applying pressure on their governments and the projects.

Finally, there is the matter of "digital power." Artificial Intelligence, 5G networks of intermechanical communication and action, sophisticated geo-satellite navigation equipment, and new ways of combining surveillance technology with social credit systems are part of this digital power. To be sure, all major powers are developing digital technology for military purposes. However, China is a global leader in civil surveillance

---

[31] Hurley et al. 2018; Takata 2019.   [32] Ghoshal and Miller 2019.
[33] Zhou et al. 2018: 12–13.

and has been selling its pioneering technology to authoritarian regimes abroad, who will seek to use it to deter popular movements against unpopular projects.[34]

What does this highly provisional assessment of the BRI tell us about China as the most prominent global power with an alternative, nonliberal worldview? First, by provisioning development finance to countries disregarded by the West, it demonstrates anti-imperialist solidarity. Just as important is the rhetoric of Silk Road historical and affective ties. However, I believe that, as a capitalist and firmly nationalist power, it is deeply implicated in the epistemic engine and invested in the nation-state system. As such, it also faces challenges from the nationalisms of states and/or their populations. But the dimension that could most destabilize the global order is the state's capacity of digital power to surveil, disrupt, and hijack civil society. This has profound consequences not only for the world order, but also on the channels through which civil society seeks to bring about a more just worldview based on an alternative cosmology. In my view, while a Chinese world order could mitigate some and exacerbate other features of the Enlightenment, it appears to be too highly invested in the epistemic engine to be able to develop a more capacious alternative order.

We do not know what channels another worldview might give us to address our deepest problems, but the channel of social activism – with all its faults – is one we know. At same time, the present epistemic engine – whether liberal or not – is ill-equipped to address the crisis of the Anthropocene – the greatest challenge human society has known.

7.3   Oceanic Temporality and Alternative Worldviews

Enlightenment cosmology may have nurtured orderly gardens so humans may develop their potential ultimately, even universally. But the epistemological engine that conditions this order fueled by strategies of accumulation, appropriation, and creative destruction has produced counterfinalities – and not only through fossil-fuel consumption – of an order that human society as a whole has perhaps not witnessed before. According to some, it has led to an autonomous global "technosphere" comprised of human and technological systems, including infrastructure, transportation, communications, power production, financial networks, and bureaucracies, to name a few.[35] The epistemic engine drives this accelerating technosphere at a pace where it is not human agency that serves as a brake, but rather pandemics such the current COVID-19

---

[34] Polyakova et al. 2019.   [35] Haff 2019.

outbreak, and, more certainly, the climate crisis that is ravaging the planet.

If the prevalent cosmology has played a major role in this global crisis, it is not the metaphor of the jungle but that of the ocean that is more compelling. The raging oceans today incarnate the unknowable planetary processes that challenge our cosmology. We can say that this unknowability is swelled by cascading counterfinalities of our interventions. Jean-Paul Sartre described counterfinalities thus: "*in* and *through* labour Nature becomes both a new source of tools and a new threat. In being realized, human ends define a field of counter-finality around themselves."[36] We have possibly tamed the jungle sufficiently, so that it appears in pockets, patches, and periodic conflagrations. Not so the ocean, which through ocean-atmospheric activity has the capacity to destroy the conditions of life as we know it.

Elsewhere I have tried to show that oceanic and ocean-atmospheric flows and circulations represent a paradigm for natural and even historical processes. For most of human history, conceptions of time were continuous with natural flows or, at least, did not severely disrupt the designs of natural flows. At a fundamental level the historical process engaging humans is also natural. Intertemporal connections and communication among humans both resemble and are indissolubly linked with other beings – organic and inorganic.[37]

Biological organisms are constantly registering and responding to environmental changes. The Star Moss Cam is a sensor technology that does not merely sense mosses over time but observes how the moss itself is a sensor that is detecting and responding to changes in the environment – to which humans have contributed.[38] More directly, Timothy LeCain describes how ecologically careful breeding of silkworms in Japan and cattle in Montana as coevolution between creature and human over generations were destroyed by arsenic released from modern copper mining in both areas.[39] Intentional processes generate other processes. Some die away or confluence with other generative processes, others produce deadly counterfinalities.

Communities more directly dependent on nature developed cosmologies that were more attuned to natural patterns even in large-scale empires such as the pre-modern Chinese or Indian polities. Gargantuan projects of imperial ambition such as the Great Wall of China still followed natural contours seeking to demarcate the steppe from the sown. To be sure, these ideals could not prevent their violations, but without the ideal we can scarcely hope to be sustainable. Communities that lived and

---

[36] Sartre 1976: 164.   [37] Duara 2021.   [38] Gabrys 2016: 63–64.   [39] LeCain 2017.

worked on the oceans, whether on coastlands or small islands, were of course more adaptable to oceanic forces. The early oceanic travelers, most famously the Polynesians, reveal how their techniques could generate great and sustainable achievements by following the movements of the oceans.

Today, we know better how oceans condition life on the terrestrial landscape. The route of the Gulf Stream explains why Canada's east coast is frozen much of the winter whereas England's is not, and why Western European shores, including the Norwegian coast, are milder than similar latitudes to the East and West.[40] The slowing of the thermohaline, deep-ocean conveyer belt due to polar ice melt is now contributing to colder European winters.[41] Asian agriculture remains heavily dependent on the monsoon rains. Scientists have reported that the monsoons in Asia and Africa appear to correlate with reversals in the pressure gradient across the Pacific Ocean. Accelerated global climate change has destabilized the monsoon, and there are dire predictions of desertification across south and west Asia.[42]

Well into the twentieth century, Carl Schmitt believed that the European *nomos* could not be conceived to extend over the oceans. After four centuries of deep-sea navigation, Schmitt continued to describe the "antithesis of land and sea as an antithesis of diverse spatial orders."[43] In contrast to the territorial sovereignty over land, the sea was free: "It could be freely exploited by all states . . . it had no borders and was open. Naturally, it was decisive that the freedom of the sea also meant the freedom to pursue wars."[44] In other words, the seas were beyond the pale of civilization.

Even if it was beyond the pale, the bloody contests on the ocean not only produced conquest and colonies, but also underwrote conceptions of sovereignty in Europe. In this new watery wilderness, pirates and navies were difficult to distinguish. Privateers such as Sir Francis Drake commanded warships in the service of the Queen of England. One's status on the seas depended on the backing of power. Laurel Benton has suggested that as royal commission holders, adventurers, and pirates staked claims over territories and waters in the New World and in Africa and Asia against other European claimants, they made sovereignty claims in the name of the king in legal courts in Europe, thus circling back to consolidate conceptions of sovereignty in the new order.[45]

Unsurprisingly, the conception of history as linear and tunneled, and of a progressing Subject, whether religious, imperial, or ultimately national,

---

[40] Miaschi 2017.   [41] Lozier 2010.   [42] Amrith 2019.   [43] Schmitt 1976: 54
[44] Schmitt 1976: 179, 352. See also Raschke 2019.   [45] Benton 2010: 280–81.

arose roughly simultaneously with Newtonian cosmology and growing confidence about oceanic control toward the end of the eighteenth century. The epistemic engine concresces the process where ideas of sovereignty, overseas conquest, scientific advances, and the idea of progress coalesce.[46] The circulatory idea of the nation expressed through a roughly isomorphic historical form was picked up across much of the world by the end of the nineteenth century. Most national histories were constituted by a sequence of ancient, medieval, and modern periods, with some kind of "renaissance function" that enabled the recovery of an ancient past to join the modern. In this way, the nation was ancient or timeless while also launched on a modern progressive future. At the same, the bracketing of the medieval or the intermediate as alien, often both aesthetically and ethnically, spurred the self–other tribalism of the nation.[47]

Between World Wars I and II, this Eurocentric *nomos* of the earth ended. In the Panama Declaration of 1939, the United States was the first to declare its specific security zone extending 300 nautical miles into the Atlantic and the Pacific. The theorist of Lebensraum, Friedrich Ratzel, declared that space had protruded into the expanse and evenness of the sea. Technological developments such as submarines and airpower added to the spatialization or, as we say today, the "territorialization" of the oceans and have robbed it of its elemental character.[48] Although Schmitt ends his inquiry with the hope of a new global *nomos*, the thrust of his final chapter, written during the Cold War, was not promising.

If oceanic violence was restricted mainly to surface waters and seacatch until the end of the nineteenth century, in the twentieth century and our present time humans are penetrating the volume and depth of the ocean, leaving us with a predictable disaster scenario. The colonization of the ocean over the last hundred years or so has been an industrial and technological colonization, battering it with massive commercial traffic and fishing, nuclear testing, constant bombardment for oil and gas explorations, and militarized island buildings, among other invasions. Not least, it is being strangled as the dumpsite of the terrestrial planet.

Meanwhile, the epistemic engine has continued to propel the territorialization of the ocean. In 1982, the majority of the nations agreed on a nation's extension of its exclusive economic zone (EEZ) to 200 nautical

---

[46] Concrescence is the process philosopher A. N. Whitehead's term for actual entities and actual occasions (whether an electron or any other happening) to produce the "novel togetherness." Concrescence *is* the process of growing together into a unified perspective on its immediate past. Note that subjects in process philosophy become objectified for other subjects (Whitehead 1979: 21, 31, 211–12).

[47] Duara 1995, 2015.   [48] Schmitt 1976: 284.

miles (nm). It has been estimated that should every coastal state make this national jurisdictional claim, it would cover 43 million square nautical miles, or approximately 41 percent of the oceanic area. Not satisfied with this, coastal states demanded that EEZ of 200 nm be extended from the edge of the coastal state's continental shelf, leading to further jurisdictional cover. Not only is this new edge difficult to measure, the extensions have also led to overlapping national claims generating potential and real conflicts.[49] Other principles evoked by the states, such as the (contestable) claims of "historical" maritime jurisdiction, make the fraught situation more warlike. The contemporary cases of China in the South China Sea and Russia in the Arctic Circle are simply the most prominent of these.

The hubris that human activity can destroy, negate, and transcend the medium of its sustenance is the mad thought that we face. The modern idea of the conquest of nature and the institutionalized and technological modes of exhausting it are unprecedented. Whether or not human agency can prevent the "slow death" facing much biotic life on the planet, it is not likely to happen without radical changes in the epistemic engine and the cosmology that have contributed significantly to it. Indeed, adaptations and changes to the cosmology which are perhaps not intrinsically impossible are made much more difficult by the entrenchment of the epistemic engine.

Over recent decades there has been considerable civil society activism regarding the environment that is converging – albeit from radically different and even conflicting perspectives and interest – upon a holistic philosophical attitude that rejects the God–world, subject–object, human–nature dualistic assumptions of the Enlightenment project. These movements represent widely different communities and civic associations, from the world's marginalized precariate whose livelihood is most directly threatened by climate change, to modern civic, religious, and scientific groups and agencies committed to environmental protection and justice. Forest dwellers, indigenous peoples, small island societies, and threatened rural communities, among others, often turn to their more holistic cosmologies and religious resources and leaders to resist corporate and state expropriation of the commons upon which they depend. They are often joined by – or coalesce with – NGOs and other civic groups of professionals, scientists, and various local and transnational agencies in the effort to protect the environment. While this is a weak historical force, it is poised on something globally significant.

---

[49] Schofield 2012.

I have argued that this coalescence converges on a loose notion of the sacrality of nature with social, discursive, and legal underpinnings. While for many of the threatened subaltern communities this sacrality is part of the ecology of life and livelihood, for the more disenchanted moderns, the sacrality of nature is expressed through the notion of legal protection as the "common heritage of humankind." Legislation and judicial decisions of this kind have often been initiated, advocated, and pushed through by civic groups. I call these natural spaces sacred because they represent an *inviolability* arising from the elemental urge to protect the sources of life. There are more than 160,000 legally protected areas in the world (national and international), including almost 1,000 World Heritage sites (cultural and natural), which cover over 12 percent of the land area of the world. On several occasions, these expressions have begun to converge – for instance, in the Eastern Himalayas protected zone in Yunnan, which is the home of many minority groups as well as the cradle of NGO activism in China. In India, New Zealand, and Ecuador, to name just a few countries, indigenous communities have initiated movements to protect the commons that have succeeded in securing legal "rights of nature" sanctioned by the highest courts in the land.[50]

As is evident, this conception of sacred nature mobilizing older conceptions, fragments, and inventions is an *emergent* one and depends to a considerable degree on the contemporary framework of the epistemic engine. Not only does it depend on national and transnational legal institutions, it also mobilizes the classic Enlightenment ideal of rights. What we find, and what I believe, is that we cannot ignore the past to build the future. Whitehead tells us "The novel entity is at once the together of the 'many' which it finds, and also it is one among the disjunctive 'many' that it leaves; it is a novel entity, disjunctively, among the many entities which it synthesizes. The many become one and are increased by one."[51] Hence, it is necessary to join the most ethically defensible elements of Enlightenment cosmology with the alternative futuristic visions to arrive at the novel entity.

To be sure, this is easier said than done. There are debates among these groups over whether the argument of rights negates the religious and ethical worldviews of many groups in the world. One such debate is reported from the Buddhist groups in Taiwan, and particularly in the view of the philosopher-nun Shih Chao-hwei. For Venerable Shih, the most fundamental principle of environmental conservation is the equality of *all* life because all life is interdependent (dependent arising) and because suffering, not necessarily "rights" reasoning, is the standard for

---

[50] Duara 2015: 266–287.   [51] Whitehead 1979: 21.

ethical consideration.[52] Empathy and compassion for suffering is a basic element of many religions, not least in the figure of Christ. Arguably, it is (or can be) the ethical baseline for worldviews.

However, Venerable Shih's worldview about all sentient life is not shared by the indigenous hunter communities in Taiwan. The latter have objected to the Wildlife Protection law, which Buddhist groups have supported, on the basis of their *human* rights. Nonetheless, the indigenous groups continue to be interested in natural and environmental rights. Noting that rights of nature have been legislated and implemented in several parts of the world, Jeffrey Nicolaisen suggests that a space of agreement or compromise between the two groups and their political representatives has opened up.[53] A fundamental task for the environmental, civil rights, and religious groups is to generate a sustainable planet by mediating between the biocentric and anthropocentric views.

It is clear that those worldviews and historical cosmologies invoked to create an alternative world will likely need to pass through the channels of the epistemic engine. To what extent can the rights discourse be turned against some of the most fundamental functions that have made it the privileged instrument of the engine – that is, private property rights and sovereign rights? And if it can, can the civic activists who are the most important agents of its transformation play the role when their human – individual and collective – rights are weakened or abolished? In the end, there is work to be done on both ends: protecting human rights, and protecting our world where it is endangered by the very engine of these rights. Perhaps this is the *multiverse* that we will have to learn to work in.

Bibliography

Althusser, Louis. 1971. "Ideology and Ideological State Apparatuses," in *Lenin and Philosophy and other Essays*. Translated from the French by Ben Brewster. New York: Monthly Review Press [2001], pp. 121–76.

Amrith, Sunil. 2019. "When the Monsoon Goes Away." *Aeon*, March 4. https://aeon.co/essays/the-life-and-possible-death-of-the-great-asian-monsoon.

Anderson, Benedict. 1991. *Imagined Communities: Reflections on the Origins and Spread of Nationalism*. London: Verso Press.

Arrighi, Giovanni. 1994. *The Long Twentieth Century: Money, Power, and the Origins of Our Times*. New York: Verso Press.

Balibar, Etienne. 1991. "The Nation Form: History and Ideology," in Etienne Balibar and Immanuel Wallerstein, eds., *Race, Nation, Class: Ambiguous Identities*. London: Verso Press, pp. 86–106.

[52] Shih 2014.   [53] Nicolaisen 2020.

Benton, Lauren. 2010. *A Search for Sovereignty: Law and Geography in European Empire, 1400–1900*. Cambridge: Cambridge University Press, pp. 280–81.

Biletzki, Anat and Matar, Anat. 2020. "Ludwig Wittgenstein," *The Stanford Encyclopedia of Philosophy* (Spring Edition), Edward N. Zalta (ed.). https://plato.stanford.edu/archives/spr2020/entries/wittgenstein/.

Blanco, John D. and Ivonne del Valle. 2014. "Reorienting Schmitt's *Nomos*: Political Theology, and Colonial (and Other) Exceptions in the Creation of Modern and Global Worlds," *Politica Comun* 5: 7–8. http://dx.doi.org/10.3998/pc.12322227.0005.001

Callahan, William A. 2008. "Chinese Visions of World Order: Post-Hegemonic or a New Hegemony?" *International Studies Review* 10: 749–61.

Cobb, John B. and David Ray Griffin. 1976. *Process Theology: An Introduction*. Philadelphia, PA: The Westminster Press

Crocker Lester, G. 1985. "Interpreting the Enlightenment: A Political Approach," *Journal of the History of Ideas*, 46, 2 (Apr.–Jun.): 211–30

Duara, Prasenjit. 1995. *Rescuing History from the Nation: Questioning Narratives of Modern China*. Chicago, IL: University of Chicago Press.

Duara, Prasenjit. 2015. *The Crisis of Global Modernity: Asian Traditions and a Sustainable Future*. Cambridge: Cambridge University Press.

Duara, Prasenjit. 2019. "The Chinese World Order in Historical Perspective: The Imperialism of Nation-states or Soft Power," *China and the World: Ancient and Modern Silk Road* 2, 4: 1–33 World Scientific Publishing Company, Singapore. https://doi.org/10.1142/S2591729319500238

Duara, Prasenjit. 2021. "Oceans as a Paradigm of History," *Theory, Culture and Society*. https://doi.org/10.1177/0263276420984538

Foucault, Michel. 1980. "Truth and Power," in Colin Gordon, Ed., *Power/Knowledge: Selected Interviews and Other Writings, 1972-1977*. New York: Pantheon Books, pp. 109–13

Gabrys, Jennifer. 2016. *Program Earth: Environmental Sensing Technology and the Making of a Computational Planet*. Minneapolis: University of Minnesota Press.

Ghoshal, Sayantan and Marcus Miller. 2019. "Introduction to the Special Issue on Sovereign Debt Restructuring," *Oxford Economic Papers* 71, 2: 309–19. https://doi.org/10.1093/oep/gpz020

Haff, Peter. 2019. "The Technosphere and its Physical Stratigraphical Record," in Jan Zalasiewicz, Colin N. Waters, Mark Williams, and Colin Summerhayes, eds., *The Anthropocene as a Geological Time Unit: A Guide to the Scientific Evidence and Current Debate*. Cambridge: Cambridge University Press, pp. 137–55.

Hamashita, Takeshi. 1994. "The Tribute Trade System and Modern Asia," in A. J.H. Latham and H. Kawakatsu, eds., *Japanese Industrialization and the Asian Economy*. Routledge: London and New York, pp. 91–103.

Hurley, John, Scott Morris, and Gailyn Portelance. 2018. "Examining the Debt Implications of the Belt and Road Initiative from a Policy Perspective," CGD Policy Paper No. 121 (Washington, DC: Center for Global Development), pp. 1–39. www.cgdev.org/publication/examining-debt-implications-belt-and-road-initiative-a-policy-perspective

LeCain, Timothy J. 2017. *The Matter of History: How Things Create the Past.* Cambridge: Cambridge University Press.

Lim, Darren J., Michalis Moutselos, and Michael McKenna. 2019. "Puzzled Out? The Unsurprising Outcomes of the Greek Bailout Negotiations," *Journal of European Public Policy*, 26, 3: 325–43, https://doi.org/10.1080/1350 1763.2018.1450890

Lozier, M. Susan. 2010. "Deconstructing the Conveyor Belt," *Science* 328, 5985: 1507–11. http://science.sciencemag.org/content/328/5985/1507

Marchal, Kai and Carl K. Y. Shaw, eds. 2017. *Carl Schmitt and Leo Strauss in the Chinese-Speaking World: Reorienting the Political.* Lanham, MD: Lexington Books.

Miaschi, John. 2017. "How Do Ocean Currents Affect Climate?" *WorldAtlas*, Apr. 25. www.worldatlas.com/articles/how-do-ocean-currents-affect-climate .html.

Nicolaisen, Jeffrey. 2020. "Protecting Life in Taiwan: Can the Rights of Nature Protect All Sentient Beings?" *ISLE: Interdisciplinary Studies in Literature and Environment* 27, 3: 613–32.

Polyakova, Alina and Chris Meserole. 2019. "Exporting Digital Authoritarianism: The Russian and Chinese Models." Democracy and Disorder series, *Foreign Policy at Brookings*, Washington DC. August. www.brookings.edu/wp-content/ uploads/2019/08/FP_20190827_digital_authoritarianism_polyakova_meserole .pdf

Raschke, Carl. 2019. "What Is The New 'Nomos of the Earth'? Reflections on the Later Schmitt," *Political Theology Network.* https://politicaltheology.com/what-is-the-new-nomos-of-the-earth-reflections-on-the-later-schmitt-carl-raschke/

Reilly, John J. 2009. "Carl Schmitt, The Nomos of the Earth in the International Law of the Jus Publicum Europaeum," *Comparative Civilizations Review* 60, 11: 172–76.

Renan, Ernest. 1990. "What is a Nation?" in Homi Bhabha, ed., *Nation and Narration.* New York: Routledge, pp. 8–22.

Sartre, Jean-Paul. 1976. *Critique of Dialectical Reason: Theory of Practical Ensembles* transl. by Alan Sheridan-Smith, ed by Jonathan Rée. London: Verso Press.

Schmitt, Carl. 1976. *The Nomos of the Earth in the International Law of the Jus Publicum Europaeum.* New York: Telos Press.

Schofield, Clive. 2012. "Parting the Waves: Claims to Maritime Jurisdiction and the Division of Ocean Space," *Penn State Journal of Law & International Affairs.* 40. https://elibrary.law.psu.edu/jlia/vol1/iss1/3

Shiba, Yoshinobu. 1983. "Sung Foreign Trade: Its Scope and Organization," in Morris Rossabi, ed., *China Among Equals: The Middle Kingdom and Its Neighbors, 10th–14th Centuries.* Berkeley: University of California Press.

Shih, Chao-hwei. 2014. *Buddhist Normative Ethics.* Taoyuan, Taiwan: Dharma-Dhatu Publication.

Takata, Yoichi. 2019. "The Vanishing Illusion of China's Financial Might," *NikkeiAsian Review*, May 13, https://asia.nikkei.com/Spotlight/Comment/The-vanishing-illusion-of-China-s-financial-might.

Wang, Mingming. 2012. "'All Under Heaven' (tianxia):Cosmological Perspectives and Political Ontologies in Pre-modern China," *Hau: Journal of Ethnographic Theory* 2, 1: 337–83.

Weber, Max. 1918. "Science as a Vocation" [Wissenschaft als Beruf], from *Gesammlte Aufsaetze zur Wissenschaftslehre* (Tubingen, 1922), Originally delivered as a speech at Munich University, 1918; published 1919, Munich: Duncker & Humblodt. www.wisdom.weizmann.ac.il/~oded/X/WeberScience Vocation.pdf

Weber, Max. 2004. "Science as a Vocation," in David Owen and Tracy B. Strong (ed. and intro), *The Vocation Lectures*; translated by Rodney Livingstone. Indianapolis, IN: Hackett Publishing Co, pp 1–31.

Weiss, Johannes. 2015. "Weber's Limits: Value and Meaning, Rationality and Individualism," *Max Weber Studies* 15, 2: 214–31.

Whitehead, Alfred North. 1979. *Process and Reality*, ed. David Ray Griffin and Donald W Sherburne. New York: Free Press.

Wittgenstein, Ludwig. 2009. *Philosophical Investigations*, transl. G. E. M. Anscombe, P. M. S. Hacker, and Joachim Schulte. Revised 4th ed., P.M.S. Hacker and J. Schulte (eds.). Sussex: Wiley Blackwell.

Zhao, Tingyang. 2006. "Rethinking Empire from a Chinese Concept 'All-under-Heaven'(Tian-xia)," *Social Identities: Journal for the Study of Race, Nation and Culture* 12, 1 (January): 29–41.

Zhao, Tingyang. 2009. "A Political World Philosophy in terms of All-under-heaven (Tian-xia)," *Diogenes* 56, 5: 5–18.

Zhou, Fangyin. 2011. "Equilibrium Analysis of the Tributary System," *The Chinese Journal of International Politics* 4: 147–78. https://doi.org/10.1093/cjip/por005.

Zhou, Lihan, Sean Gilbert, Ye Wang, Miquel Muñoz Cabré, and Kevin P. Gallagher. 2018. "Moving the Green Belt and Road Initiative: From Words to Actions," Working Paper. Washington, DC: World Resources Institute, pp. 1–44.

Part III

Science and Religion

8 Scientific Worldviews in World Politics
Rationalization and the Cosmological Inheritance of the Social Sciences

Bentley B. Allan

In the Weberian tradition, worldviews "imply a coherent set of values" that provide "answers to the broader questions of meaning, purpose, suffering, and injustice."[1] Worldviews imbue the lives of their holders with "direction, organization, and unity."[2] Weber distinguishes worldviews from other collections of beliefs and values in two ways. First, analytically, the coherence and comprehensiveness of worldviews distinguish them from organizational cultures or ideologies. Second, worldviews are distinct from myths or cosmologies to the degree that they form a system of rationalized beliefs and claims. They contain explicit values that tend to produce regularized conduct.[3]

In this chapter, I differentiate worldviews from other collections of fundamental beliefs about the universe: cosmological ideas. I define cosmology as a configuration of ideas and practices that relate humans to the nature of the world and the universe. Cosmologies weave together a variety of fundamental claims about humanity and reality. In previous work, I have distinguished between five kinds of cosmological elements:[4]

ONTOLOGY: fundamental units of matter, the forces that govern them, and categories of representation.
EPISTEME: modes and procedures likely to produce reliable or true knowledge of the universe.
TEMPORALITY: the nature and direction of time.
COSMOGONY: the origins and history of the universe.
HUMAN DESTINY: the role or place of humanity in the cosmos.

---

[1] Kalberg 2012, 74. See Katzenstein, Chapter 1, this volume. [2] Kalberg 2012, 75.
[3] In the implicit Weberian theory of action, worldviews generate behaviors through their institutionalization in routines and organizations. It is worth noting that in this volume (Katzenstein, Chapter 1), worldviews and actions are at the very least in a recursive relationship in which they express repetitive habits and emotions, which in turn perform and reproduce those worldviews.
[4] Allan 2018, 11.

On this conception, cosmologies are not fully coherent doctrines that all members of a social group internalize and understand.[5] Rather, we should imagine that cosmological elements circulate in and through texts, memories, rituals, institutional rules, organizational procedures, and so on. They are available as resources for the creation of more or less coherent cosmologies in particular contexts. However, there is little basis for assuming that all individuals within social groups share a single set of beliefs about the universe.

On my account, worldviews are local stabilizations of cosmological elements. They draw together fundamental ideas about the universe into a coherent package of values, identities, and beliefs. In order to frame certain values as meaningful and natural, worldviews depend on ontological presuppositions about what exists and epistemic notions of how we know which values are worth pursuing. A worldview cannot exist without cosmological elements. But again, not all actors have a worldview. To use the concept wisely, we have to theorize the conditions under which worldviews can be produced and stabilized by individuals.

In this chapter, I use this distinction between cosmological elements and worldviews to renarrate the story of rationalization. On Weber's account, rationalization processes make worldviews possible by creating abstract systems of beliefs that are instilled in individuals, orienting them to the fulfillment of universal values. At the same time, the rationalization embodied in scientific ideas threatens the cohesiveness of worldviews by accelerating disenchantment. This undermines our orientation to universal values and threatens to eliminate ethical constraints on action. Weber's great insight here is to historicize the elements of action. I contend he did not take this far enough and that we can benefit from a deeply empirical tracing of the grounds of action.

My argument is that the rationalization narrative is better understood as a more specific historical process: the rise and spread of cosmological ideas from the Western scientific tradition. Specifically, I trace the history of two cosmological elements: materialism and object-orientation. Taken together, these cosmological elements create a backdrop for action in which subjects are separate from a material world of objects. The process of folding materialism and object-orientation into political discourses did not disenchant worldviews, draining them of meaning or eliminating value-orientations. Rather, it formed the basis of new modernist values of rationality, control, and growth which serve as the basis of world

[5] On this, see Barth's (1987) study of ritual variation within cosmological traditions.

politics today. I suggest that worldviews centered on the values of "civilization" (in the colonial era) and "economic growth" (in the postwar era) rested on materialist presuppositions and object orientations.

With this history in hand we can better examine the scientific worldviews that appear in the social sciences today. My goal here is to show that the cosmological inheritance of the social sciences, materialism and object-orientation, must be examined. With Katzenstein and Kurki, I trace the desire to control the world back to scientific ideas, but I hope to add value by identifying some of the specific ideas involved.[6] I suggest that materialism and object-orientation make the social sciences susceptible to colonial modes of analysis. But, rather than reject social science, I defend a pluralist field and present the possibility of a re-enchanted social science that reflexively grounds itself and its worldviews in cosmological traditions.

8.1   Worldviews and Cosmologies in Process

Following Katzenstein, worldviews are local, temporary sets of connected beliefs that express a strong sense of how the world works.[7] On my conception, worldviews are local and temporary enactments. By temporary, I mean to highlight that the formation of a coherent, politically effective worldview is an achievement. Worldviews are the result of individuals expressing and refining collections of beliefs. Worldviews must be forged by weaving cosmological materials together with habits, emotions, values, and identities into relatively coherent frameworks. Their political effectiveness is always the result of sustained effort.

For this reason, worldviews are local. By local, I mean that worldviews are held, or enacted, by specific individuals, social classes, and professions. We should not ascribe them, as Weber seems to do, to entire societies or regions. On this view, worldviews are not likely to be deeply structural elements of the international.[8] But they are often necessary to explain the actions of particular individuals and groups.[9] For example, if we want to explain why Keynes acted the way that he did in the Bretton Woods negotiations, or why the neoconservatives in George W. Bush's administration sought war with Iraq, we need to understand the

---

[6] Katzenstein, Chapter 1; Kurki, Chapter 3, this volume.   [7] Chapter 1.
[8] That said, I consider this to be an empirical question. In principle, someone could demonstrate the operation of a coherent set of values operating across states. But I think rigorous studies of the international distribution of ideas find more difference than similarity. See Hopf and Allan 2016.
[9] Haas and Nau, Chapter 2, this volume.

worldviews of these participants. But not everyone has a worldview, and not every important event in world politics is shaped by worldviews.

The backdrop here is a world of processes in which actors, organizations, rules, values, and cosmologies are in motion.[10] The values and principles underlying international order, for example, are not simply static lines of text written in charters and treaties. Those lines must be meaningful to a community of interpreters that consists of state officials, international organization bureaucrats, global civil society members, and epistemic communities. These actors carry and reproduce sets of beliefs and values. They creatively engage with them, pushing and pulling them to help solve problems. Thus, the ideas that underlie world politics are dynamically negotiated and in flux. Nonetheless, we cannot abandon the task of trying to specify the ideas that structure world politics. But to do so, we need to think about how ideas are stabilized in a processual world.

8.1.1   *Modes of Stabilization*

To explain stability in a world of process, we need to theorize the modes of stabilization that underwrite persistence and continuity. I want to highlight just a few modes of stabilization: social groups, anchoring practices, and what I call complementarities. First, stability can be underwritten by social groups that carry and reproduce relatively stable ideas. Consider the role of scientists, experts, and professionals. These groups carry and reproduce professional values, scientific models, and epistemic tools. Powerful processes of technical and professional socialization can impart similar representations, beliefs, values, ethoses, and desires. But even individuals shaped by coherent groups may drift apart unless their socialization is reinforced by anchoring practices. Anchoring practices are "repeated interactional patterns" that pull individuals to deploy the same actions and meanings.[11] In professions and expert groups, anchoring practices are usually premised upon an epistemic tool, such as clinical diagnostics for medical professionals or cost–benefit analyses for management consultants. These practices draw actors into similar contexts where they reproduce similar values, models, and desires over time.

Reaching for a general mechanism here, we might say that stability can be achieved by forging complementarities between ideas and practical, social, institutional, and political contexts.[12] Complementarities are alignments between ideas and contexts, such that the elements reinforce

---

[10] Whitehead 1978; Abbott 2016.   [11] Swidler 2001: 85.   [12] Allan 2019: 189.

one another. Complementarities are forged by creative actors around the key purposes or anchoring practices of groups and organizations. They operate when ideas and practices lead actors to move back and forth within a set of categories, actions, and values.

For example, officials in the World Bank have disbursed loans on the basis of financing gap models.[13] These models serve as an anchoring practice to help staff solve the epistemic and political problems that arise in their work. But those models also have to be aligned with the social norms and institutional rules that help officials execute their tasks in a complex organization. Beyond the Bank, financing gap models were legitimated and reinforced by academic growth theory. Growth theory was complementary to financing gap models, desired increases in national income, and institutional rules that promoted large loans. The complementarities across these elements helped stabilize each element. Nonetheless, the drawing together of disparate elements always forms a dynamic nexus that is shifting and evolving, even if it exhibits continuities.

Complementarities are not preexisting or functional entities. They are forged by creative actors that seek to align ideas and contexts. Creative actors must yoke together practices, rules, and beliefs, forging the connections that underwrite stability. There is play and contingency in the process of alignment. The form and content of social life emerges from the coming together of elements that each have their own contingent history.

The forging of complementarities is essential to the challenges of political mobilization. In a processual perspective, politics is about moving people.[14] Moving people requires ideas, but also opportunity, resources, and organization. It requires creative work to align ideas with the necessary contextual factors. Constructing a stable, politically potent worldview is precisely this kind of creative act. But this local creativity is always suffused by multiple and intersecting structural processes that operate in similar – which is not to say the *same* – ways across space and time. Agency is always possible but never omnipotent. Creative agents must work with and against the cosmological and institutional resources at hand.

8.1.2 *Worldviews in World Politics*

In order to see how powerful worldviews are forged in world politics, consider the emergence of economic worldviews in the twentieth century.

---

[13] Allan 2019: 192–93.   [14] Tilly 2001; Tilly 2003.

Recall that worldviews draw on cosmological elements such as onto-logical categories and epistemic claims about good knowledge. Since the late nineteenth century, the ontological categories of Western politics have been dominated by representations of epistemic objects like society, public health, labor, the economy, human rights, and the climate. These objects were constituted as distinct entities by scientists, experts, and professionals who defined, measured, and codified them. But they were not merely "constructions": they reflected, and constituted, changes in practice.[15] New practices, transactions, and flows brought together individuals into fields of action that could be demarcated from others.[16] Thinkers and practitioners forged complementarities between the philo-sophical distinction between subjects and objects and a new set of epistemic tools for representing and intervening in objects.

Objects depend on both the modes of stabilization introduced earlier. Objects are stabilized by social groups of experts and professionals. Economists, for example, help produce and naturalize the economy. Objects are stable to the extent that they are embedded in practical, social, institutional, and political contexts. As Daston puts it, "scientific objects ... grow more richly real as they become entangled in webs of cultural significance, material practices, and theoretical derivations."[17] In the terms of this volume, embedding economic objects in worldviews gives them a place in the political projects of actors. From there, elements of worldviews are institutionalized in policy statements, organizational procedures, rules governing exchange, capital investments of firms, and so on. The economy is made rather than imagined.

In the twentieth century, a number of important groups in the United States and the Soviet Union developed economic worldviews. In the United States, for example, the economy was the basis for Rostow's worldview, in which American liberalism would establish a world order wherein all societies would modernize into liberal democracies.[18] In the Soviet Union, the Communist Party articulated a worldview in which "The New Soviet Man" would embody the modernity of an economic order led by the revolutionary class.[19] The expansion of production through economic planning in the Soviet Union would usher in a new communist world modernity.[20] Thus, the postwar international economic order came to be structured by two competing superpowers, both of which enacted economic worldviews.

These worldviews were premised on cosmological elements. First, they relied on an ontology in which "the economy" is designated as an isolated

---

[15] Mitchell 2002.   [16] Daston 2000.   [17] Daston 2000: 13.   [18] Gilman 2003.
[19] Hopf 2002.   [20] Rindzevičiūtė 2019.

social object in a field of social objects (alongside politics, society, public health, households, etc.). These worldviews were simply not possible before the 1950s and the 1960s because there was no concept of "the economy" before the 1930s. According to Mitchell, prior to the 1930s, references to "economy" denote the old, eighteenth-century principle of prudent management or frugality.[21] It is only with the advent of a new epistemic tool, national accounting statistics, that the economy became a delimited object. A new concept and a new tool could then be aligned with diverse developments, such as the increase in financial flows, to create a genuinely new social sphere. That is to say, the economy is not merely a social construct, but is the product of the rearrangement of the world. As such, it provides a stable basis for the construction of new values and state practices of intervention.

Second, as Scott argues, both Cold War worldviews were premised on an epistemic basis he calls "high-modernism": "self-confidence about scientific and technical progress, the expansion of production, the growing satisfaction of human needs, the mastery of nature (including human nature), and, above all, the rational design of social order commensurate with the scientific understanding of natural laws."[22] High-modernism is epistemic in the sense that it relies on assumptions about how knowledge can be used. It rests on an ontological depiction of the universe as a law-governed order. And it has a clear relation to values including the desirability of rationality and the imperative to dominate nature. In this way, high-modernism merges cosmological elements and the kinds of specific values that structure worldviews.

So, the contending worldviews of the Cold War were in part built upon a set of common cosmological elements which were creatively combined into different worldviews. What I want to suggest in the next section is that none of this was natural. It did not emerge from a universal process of development, modernization, or rationalization. Instead, it was the product of a more uncertain channeling of cosmological elements from the natural and social sciences into political discourses. Thus, the worldviews that circulate in world politics and social science are products of a particular history of cosmological change.

8.2   Rationalization: The History of Scientific Worldviews

Weber's theory of rationalization offers an entry point to consider the history of worldviews in the West. Although Weber does not distinguish between worldviews and cosmological ideas, drawing the distinction

---

[21] Mitchell 2005.   [22] Scott 1998: 4.

helps reframe Weber's theory of rationalization. Taken together, *The Protestant Work Ethic* and *The Sociology of Religion* argue that worldviews are a product of the rationalization of myths and religions.[23] Rationalization creates a world of external values that can structure subjectivity and motivate individuals.

By pushing the historical thrust of Weber's argument further, we arrive at a conception of the self as constituted by cosmological elements.[24] This conception of a self that is relationally constituted by cosmological ideas helps us to unbundle the concept of rationalization and its supposed product, Western modernity, into more historically specific processes. My argument is that we can better understand the history of Western worldviews by tracing two cosmological developments: the emergence of materialism and the production of a world of objects. As we shall see, these developments provide resources for the construction of worldviews in world politics. Moreover, these ideational configurations were stabilized through their relations to one another (complementarity) and the economic and colonial contexts in which they were developed (anchoring). Finally, we shall see that they comprise part of what I call the cosmological inheritance of the social sciences. This inheritance orients us to control and makes it easy to slide into colonial modes of analysis.

8.2.1   Rationalization in Weber

Weber's theory of rationalization is a key part of his overall theory of modernity, which aimed to explain the distinctiveness of the West. Weber placed so much importance on rationalization because he felt it was necessary to account for the emergence of capitalist development in the West.[25] This, in part, serves as a legitimation of the superiority of the German nation and Protestant value-orientations.[26] There are now a number of literatures that call into question the distinctiveness of the West and the need for a theory of Western exceptionalism.[27]

---

[23] My exegetical focus here is on the latter text, which represents Weber's later views on the matter.

[24] This can be read as a complement to Grove's relational reading of Weber in this volume (Chapter 4).

[25] Schluchter 1985: 9–12.

[26] Boatça 2013; Shilliam 2008; Zimmerman 2006. I am grateful to Robbie Shilliam for conversations on this point.

[27] On the importance of the East in the development of the West, see Abu-Lughod 1991; Hobson 2004. On the importance of colonialism see, Pomeranz 2000; Findlay and O'Rourke 2007. On the importance of the salutary European climate offered by the Medieval Warming Period, see Fagan 2008.

Nonetheless, working through Weberian rationalization can help us reconsider the role of scientific ideas in Western worldviews.

Weber uses the term "rationalization" to apply to wide variety of processes: the systematization of religious belief, the increasing precision of military procedures, the legalization of political life, and so on. It refers broadly to the standardization, abstraction, and quantification of behavior in any social sphere. I want to focus on two effects of rationalization processes.[28] First, substantive rationalization produces *value-oriented* individuals and systems of ethics. Second, practical and formal rationalization increases instrumental rationality and pure means–ends action. For Weber, the rise of science intensifies the disintegration of ultimate values and the domination of formal means–ends rationality.

In *The Sociology of Religion* all the major world religions undergo substantive rationalization. Weber argues that the rationalization of religions results in prophets making increased ethical demands upon the gods. Over time, prophets tended to produce more complex and systematic theoretical accounts of the universe that depicted it as a "harmonious and rational order."[29] These demands rested on "the increasing scope of a rational comprehension of an enduring and orderly cosmos."[30]

Furthermore, in salvation religions, prophets draw together the cosmological and the social, infusing everyday life with cosmological strictures and practices. This orients the religious individual to "a unified view of the world derived from a consciously integrated meaningful attitude toward life."[31] Since salvation depends on "both social and cosmic events," individuals must pattern their conduct in a meaningful way. That is, systematized religion produces individuals that are oriented to impersonal and universal values. Integrated, rationalized worldviews cultivate a new kind of person oriented "to a cosmos of obligations."[32] Such people then act in more predictable or calculable ways – their action is formally rationalized.

In effect, Weber historicizes the basis of action itself. He provides an account of how people come to orient their action to a set of values that are not present or inherent in everyday life. Thus, the degree to which individuals pursue a cosmologically oriented life within a "meaningful, ordered totality" is itself the product of rationalization processes.[33]

This is the basis of Weber's explanation for the differences between the West, which produces capitalism, and other societies, which do not.[34] Weber's argument is that only Protestantism produced the right

[28] Weber 1978, 585, 1186. Cf. Kalberg 1980: 1151–58; Kalberg 2012: 39.
[29] Weber 1978: 431.   [30] Weber 1978: 430.   [31] Weber 1978: 450.
[32] Weber 1978: 430.   [33] Weber 1978: 451.   [34] Schluchter 1985: 156–66.

combination of theocentrism (orientation to a transcendent god), ascetism (control of self as the path to salvation), and this-worldliness (desire to realize God's will in this world):

> Only ascetic Protestantism completely eliminated magic and the supernatural quest for salvation, of which the highest form was intellectualist, contemplative illumination. It alone created the religious motivations for seeking salvation primarily through immersion in one's worldly vocation . . . For the various popular regions of Asia, in contrast to ascetic Protestantism, the world remained a great enchanted garden . . . No path led from the magical religiosity of the non-intellectual strata of Asia to a rational, methodical control of life. Nor did any path lead to that methodical control from the world-accommodation of Confucianism, from the world-rejection of Buddhism, from the world-conquest of Islam, or from the messianic expectations and economic pariah law of Judaism.[35]

This revision of the argument of the *Protestant Ethic* represents the culmination of Weber's work from 1905 to 1920.

In short, rationalization produces individuals who are meaningfully oriented to values. Moreover, those values fulfilled what Weber saw as the highest ideals of Western civilization: "autonomous yet compassionate and community-oriented individuals" that lived their lives in the pursuit of meaningful values.[36]

The rise of science enters the story here as one of a variety of sources that threaten values. In the Vocation lectures, Weber argues that scientific rationalization has profound effects on worldviews. Science teaches us that "we are not ruled by mysterious, unpredictable forces, but that, on the contrary, we can in principle *control everything by means of calculation.*"[37] This knowledge leads to "the disenchantment of the world," culminating in the withdrawal of "the ultimate and most sublime values" from public life.[38] Science, for Weber, cannot replace those values because it cannot answer Tolstoy's questions: "What should we do? How shall we live?"[39]

The consequences of this, for Weber, are widespread and significant. The disintegration of ethical worldviews threatens the sociological basis of Western civilization. As Kalberg concludes:

> Weber could not discover an organization, class, or social stratum firmly anchored in modern Western societies capable of replacing ethical salvation religions as an institutionalized carrier of ethical rationality and value-rationalization processes . . . devoid of the personal dimension, the realms of economy, law, and science, as well as all bureaucratic rulership, now developed solely in relation to

---

[35] Weber 1978: 630.   [36] Kalberg 2012: 41.
[37] Weber 2004: 12–13 (emphasis original).   [38] Weber 2004: 13, 30.
[39] Weber 2004: 17.

external necessities and impersonal rules, laws, and regulations. These arenas thus remained outside of – and unrestrained by – all ethical claims.[40]

This led Weber to advocate a form of German nationalism in which moral obligation to the *Volk* would replace the passive instrumental rationality of the people.[41]

8.2.2   History

In this reading, Weber's account of rationalization is not grounded in a careful history of how ideas produced rationalizing elements. Rather, it is situated in Weber's attempt to make sense of Western distinctiveness in a world of difference.[42] The result is a totalizing and abstract image of rationalization as a universal and inevitable process. However, as Joas points out, we should not treat all the phenomena Weber identifies together under the umbrella of a single, universal process.[43]

Instead, we can unbundle modernity into a set of ideational and practical shifts linked together through contingent yet powerful complementarities. This may allow us to retain some sense of the overarching narrative of rationalization, in which the ground of action is transformed by long-term historical processes, without positing the necessity and unavoidability of disenchantment. My approach to this unbundling is to show how cosmological elements from the scientific tradition were incorporated into European and American political traditions. On this account, rationalization is the folding of cosmological elements (materialism and object-orientation) into social and political discourses where they formed the basis of worldviews based on control.

Starting in the sixteenth century, early modern natural philosophy in Europe was dominated by a materialist and mechanist ontology.[44] A materialist ontology posits that the fundamental building blocks of the universe are physical entities. A mechanist ontology posits a world that is governed by formal and efficient causes.[45] Forged together in a system of discursive complementarities, early modern materialism and mechanism offered a vision of the universe as lifeless matter in motion.

---

[40] Kalberg 2012: 41.   [41] Shilliam 2008: 157–58.   [42] Shilliam 2008: 159–62.
[43] Joas 2017: 1.
[44] I am using the term broadly and somewhat anachronistically to include progenitors of the natural sciences such as "natural philosophy," which was a distinct and broader set of practices in early modern knowledge production. See Shapin 1996; Shapin and Schaffer 1985.
[45] Collingwood 1945: 97–99.

Materialist and mechanist ontological claims developed in opposition to a variety of vitalist and organicist views. Vitalist writers depicted a pluralist world of living entities in which nature operated as an agent.[46] Organicist thought emphasized not the power of interacting corpuscles, but the holistic representation of nature and the world as living entities. A pluralist world of living organic wholes was far messier and less predictable than the rationally legible world of mechanically interacting matter. Perhaps this explains why Calvin himself, who was so central to Weber's story of rationalization, joined natural philosophers in opposing the "filthy dog Lucretius" and other vitalists.[47] Calvin admired the "exact diligence" of the astronomers because it revealed the "cunning workmanship" of God's providence.[48]

Other religious scholars attacked mechanism on the basis that it restricted God's will and depended itself on a form of vitalism. Henry More, a seventeenth-century Cambridge philosopher, argued that mechanists implied that matter had "freedom of will" and the "knowledge and perception" necessary to act.[49] Instead, More suggested, "an Immaterial Being" was responsible for making matter move. Along these and other lines of contestation, materialism and mechanism were disputed ontological claims through the seventeenth century and into the eighteenth century. As such, materialism and mechanism did not fully displace existing traditions of thought and practice. They had to be worked into creative networks of complementarities alongside existing discourses and practices.

The broad acceptance of Newton's view of the universe finally achieved in the eighteenth century can largely be explained by the fact that it was compatible with and could be drawn into religious worldviews.[50] Newton's image of a rational, law-governed cosmos was consistent with the Christian belief in an omnipotent God that had created an ordered universe. Moreover, Newton, consistent with his own theological impulses, left room for God in the mysterious operations of gravity. This was consistent with More's immaterial mover. It was also the reason Newton was denounced for relying on "occult forces."[51] The Newtonian view of the universe was not disenchanted. And it was stabilized through its relation to Christian ritual and political power.

Although strict materialism has been contested since its emergence, it has dominated scientific views of nature for centuries. A sure sign of its power is that even those, such as Newton, Kant, and Weber, who argued

---

[46] Boaistuau 1581.   [47] Calvin 1561: 16.   [48] Calvin 1561: 15.
[49] Henry More, quoted in Shapin and Schaffer 1985: 211.   [50] Gaukroger 2007.
[51] Crombie and Hoskin 1970: 49–51.

against materialism had to adopt the dichotomous division of the world into material and ideational forces.

The material–ideational division played an important role in the development of the colonial social sciences in the nineteenth century.[52] In the shadow of Darwin, social anthropologists in Britain and elsewhere grounded their understanding of the new object "society" in a biological conception of humanity. Famously, Darwinism contributed to the rise of scientific racism in late colonial Europe. However, in British colonialism, scientific racism was less influential than social anthropology. Early anthropologists such as John Lubbock and Edward Burnett Tylor espoused a theory of sociocultural evolution on which peoples, conceived as distinct entities, developed along a linear sequence from savagery to civilization.[53] This formed the basis of the British Colonial Office's position that colonialism was necessary to shepherd primitive societies through the process of development. Scientific racism was unsuitable for this doctrine because it suggested that inferior races could never attain civilization. Instead, British colonial officials believed in their own racial superiority and that their native charges could progress toward civilization.[54]

Malinowski and his students later came to dominate British anthropology and played a central role in British colonial policy.[55] Such connections to colonial practice were not incidental, but an integral part of the network of complementarities that stabilized and supported Malinowski's work. Malinowski's "functionalist" anthropology posited a system of basic institutions that served to fulfill basic human needs.[56] The task of the anthropologist was to understand what function otherwise mysterious behaviors served. So Malinowski and other functionalists advocated for anthropologists to deeply immerse themselves within the social fabric to discern the true meaning and purpose of basic institutions, rituals, and beliefs.

The sociocultural and functionalist conceptions of society were not materialist in a reductive sense. Anthropologists in Malinowski's tradition did not posit that race or biology was destiny. But it was materialist, and disenchanted, in a different sense. On the functionalist view, the basis of society is an aggregate of material bodies, and the only forces legible to social science are ones that register for those bodies. To be sure, societies are formed by bringing together individual bodies in a set of institutions, bound together by ideas and practices. But, as Malinowski and the

---

[52] This follows Allan 2018: 156–202.   [53] Kuklick 1978: 98.   [54] Lorimer 2009: 194.
[55] Mills 2002.   [56] E.g. Malinowski 1922.

functionalists made clear, the ideas were not really considered to be constitutive of peoples.

In colonial anthropology and imperial practice, ideas had only a functional relation to peoples: they help groups solve practical problems. Culture was a means of satisfying "basic individual biopsychological needs," and was merely a generalization of kinship relations and economic structures, not a "systemic milieu" in which relationships were constituted.[57] Thus, any set of ideas which resolves the material problems of existence or Darwinian survival are just as good as any other. Hence, the normative value of colonialism and assimilation: they provide a better set of ideas to meet material needs in superior ways. In an ontological sense, this theory separated cultures from peoples. Doing so justified colonialism as a system for guiding peoples to better, more functional sets of beliefs. We can see here how colonial worldviews could draw sustenance from scientific cosmological elements.

That separation was related to a broader ontological and epistemic shift: the proliferation of "epistemic objects" after 1830.[58] These objects – society, labor, public health, the economy, and so on – divided the world into distinct spheres of action. The emergence of "society" was important because it made possible the rise of the social sciences generally.[59] It was first conceptualized in the eighteenth century as an "aggregation of human beings that have come together for a certain purpose," as in a society of engineers. But by the end of the century, it emerged as a third sphere between households (the subject of the moral sciences) and the state (the subject of political economy).[60] Once created, the concept had a profound effect on social practices. An autonomous society could have effects on individuals and institutions, legitimating ideas like the "social welfare state." The concept also initiated a process of demarcating other spheres and subspheres, proliferating the objects of the social sciences.[61]

Once demarcated, such spheres could be measured with statistical techniques. In the early decades of the twentieth century, these objects were conceptualized as cybernetic systems governed by law-like mechanisms. The social sciences promised to uncover these mechanisms. This altered the basic terms of government which were now responsible for managing these objects.[62] The proliferation of object-experts enabled government interventions designed to change the dynamics of the objects.

---

[57] Stocking 1987: 321.   [58] Daston 2000; Wagner 2003.   [59] Wagner 2000: 133.
[60] Wagner 2000: 134.   [61] Wagner 2000: 140–48.   [62] Foucault 2007: 68–79.

Kusch argues that the roots of this phenomenon lie in the merger of Kantian thinking with technological advances:

This revolution consists in installing and mobilizing a world of objects *outside* a subject. That is why, from simple sickness to the vicissitudes of our physical and spiritual life, we always find the solution or the *reason in this outside*. And an *outside* is always given: from the simple *reason* that explains to me the cause of my sorrow to a large administrative issue that could become concretized in an Agricultural Extension Office.[63]

Understanding and action are premised upon the separation between the inside of the subject and the outside of the world of objects. And, as we have seen, that outside is defined in material terms as dead matter in motion.

It is this separation that makes Weberian value-orientation possible and natural. As in functional anthropology, we as subjects are separate from the world of ideas and artifacts. We can pick up and use elements of the outside as we choose. This basic frame fuels the valorization and naturalization of reason. Reason could now be conceptualized and defined in means–ends terms as knowledge of the outside for the manipulation of the outside in the service of internal ends. Rationality itself is a value-orientation.

This shift underlies the scientific forms of rationalization identified by Meyer and his coauthors. They argue that on the dominant culture of world society, "salvation lies in rationalized structures grounded in scientific and technical knowledge."[64] The widespread authority of science underwrites and benefits from a process of rationalization in which all actors are expected to use scientific and technical knowledge to solve problems.[65] But it is important to precisely state the effect of science here: it established a discourse in which the world is populated with material objects that can be defined in scientific terms.

Reason is then the task of gaining understanding and exerting control over these objects through means–ends rationality. The desire to control the world through experiment and action is also not natural. It too emerges from this history in which a materialist world of dead matter is displayed as a series of manipulable entities. The image of the scientific experiment, in which nature is carefully controlled to produce reliable information and outcomes, is part of a broader constellation of ideas that are incorporated into the Newtonian worldviews of the social sciences and the modernist worldviews that shape world politics.

---

[63] Kusch 2010: 12–13.   [64] Meyer et al. 1997: 174. Cf. Meyer 2010.
[65] Meyer et al. 1997: 166.

In my retelling, Weber's idea of rationality itself is a product of history. Kant of course assumed the existence of an a priori reason. But multiple subsequent traditions in social theory have sought to show that the grounds of rationality are themselves embedded in history. This is precisely what defenders of rational worldviews miss.[66] Indeed, Weber himself built a worldview on the concept of rationality. On the one hand, Weber valorized rationality-as-value-orientation under Protestantism. On the other hand, he critiqued rationality-as-disenchantment. His desire to diagnose the distinctiveness of the West led him here.[67]

From here, we see that the concept of rationality deployed by Weber is not a natural object but a product of the history of rationalization that he himself identified. The systematization and standardization of action across spheres reflects the emergence of cosmological elements from the natural sciences in political and social discourses. Further, it reflects a long process of forging complementarities between materialism, mechanism, object-orientation, and other ideas. These ideas draw strength from one another to form powerful and persuasive networks of meaning. These networks can then be variously mobilized in specific worldviews.

Moreover, once we conceptualize the process of rationalization at this level of detail we can see why it does not eliminate values or value-orientation amongst individuals by draining discourses of meaning. Scientific rationalization provides a different set of ideational elements through which values can be constructed. Newtonian and Darwinian representations of the cosmos and humanity became the basis of many political worldviews.

In sum, rationalization processes change the conceptual material from which worldviews are made. This constrains and influences worldviews, but does not determine them. This balances the roles of structure and agency as laid out in Section 8.1. Structural processes like the movement of scientific ideas into political discourses have broad effects, but those effects leave room for creative action to forge worldviews and the networks of complementarities necessary to stabilize and mobilize them.

8.2.3   Rationalization in the Social Sciences

Katzenstein's opening to this volume argues that we social scientists are stuck within Newtonian worldviews.[68] This section develops a related theme: materialism and object-orientation are part of the broader cosmological inheritance that enframes the social sciences today.[69] Further,

---

[66] Haas and Nau, Chapter 2 .   [67] Boatcă 2013.   [68] Chapter 1.

[69] To be precise, however, as my discussion of Newton suggests, Newton himself was not a materialist in the early modern sense. Nonetheless, he worked within the dichotomous discourse that movement produced.

building on Shilliam, I want to argue that the social sciences rest on rationalized, disenchanted discourses. The disenchantment of social science, which Weber himself struggled with, makes it harder to represent nonmaterialist elements and to take seriously the power of religion and cosmology.[70] From here, we can see how the coloniality of the social sciences in its functionalist, object-oriented mode separates peoples from cosmology at a basic level.

In Shilliam's retelling, the story of the Haitian revolution usually notes two events in the build-up to the insurrection on August 22, 1791. On August 14, there was the "properly-political" meeting of slaves and workers at the Lenormand de Mézy estate. Ostensibly it was here that the revolution was born as creoles, drawing inspiration from the French Revolution, plotted anticolonial rebellion.[71] On August 21, after two estates were prematurely set ablaze, there was a hastily arranged meeting of chiefs at Bwa Kayiman. There, Dutty Boukman, an early leader of the revolution, presided over a ritual with Cécile Fatiman, a Vodou priestess. The next day, the revolution began, and 184 sugar plantations were destroyed in the ensuing weeks. This second meeting is generally considered to be "merely a religious Vodou ceremony" that provided a signal to initiate the rebellion.[72]

Shilliam argues that the colonial nature of social science excludes the possibility that the meeting at Bwa Kayiman exerted a real effect on the revolution itself. To do so, he highlights the importance of what he calls "African retentions" in Haiti. In 1791, half of the 500,000 slaves in Saint Domingue had arrived in the previous five years, and two-thirds had been born in Africa.[73] These people carried with them diverse cosmological traditions from the African continent. Thus, the meeting at Bwa Kayiman reflected African cosmologies, political hierarchies, and national groupings.[74] Shilliam describes how the meeting brought together chiefs of African nations with *lwa* (spiritual agents).

At Bwa Kayiman, Cécile Fatiman "is ridden by the *lwa* Ezili Kawuolo," the patron of secret societies.[75] The Vodou conception of the self is radically relational and not reducible to conceptions of a closed subject. In Vodou, a person's "seat of agency" can be "mounted" by a *lwa*. Via this mediation, a *lwa* can become an agent in the world, serving as a channel for cosmic forces. One of these forces is justice. In the context of a slave colony, mediation with the *lwa* is a means of bringing justice into the profane world:

Mediating with the *lwa* allows the profanely enslaved to channel forces from the spiritual hinterlands that bypass and exceed the control of their downpressors.

[70] Shilliam 2017.   [71] Shilliam 2017: 10, 2.   [72] Shilliam 2017: 10.
[73] Shilliam 2017: 6.   [74] Shilliam 2017: 6–7.   [75] Shilliam 2017: 3.

The community is re-sanctified by gaining cosmic force and direction in the pursuit of justice: The *lwa* and the chiefs, moved to arms, gathered at Bwa Kayiman.[76]

In this account, Shilliam presents the *lwa* as agents of the revolution: "If the *lwa* were not gathered at Bwa Kayiman with the chiefs, then there would have been no revolution."[77] Shilliam asks, what moved the people? "If the people did not *know* that the *lwa* were riding (with) them to burn down the plantations, then they would not have moved their feet."[78]

The problem is not only that social science cannot capture the power of the *lwa*. That is certainly the case: the secular terms of colonial social science must declare the *lwa* "supernatural" and thereby render them inert and absurd.[79] But regardless of whether or not one is willing to entertain the possibility of *lwa* agency, Shilliam's argument makes an important point: the colonial bias of social science makes the analyst privilege the causal significance of (white) legal-juridical acts over (black) cosmological ones.

Moreover, Shilliam's argument shows us what is at stake in the social scientific representation of ideas as separate from peoples. As Shilliam puts it, "colonial science seeks to segregate peoples from their lands, their pasts, their ancestors, spirits and agencies."[80] That is, by denigrating cosmological ideas as "super-natural" and "super-stitious," social science denies the constitutive element that ideas and spirits play in the formation of peoples.

This may seem like a counterintuitive critique of constructivists and ideational theorists a century removed from Malinowski. After all, cultural theorists argue that ideas make a "people" distinct from a set of biological individuals. But in colonial science ideas form peoples only in a shallow sense. The functionalism of materialist colonial science posits that a people is merely a set of biological bodies appended to a set of ideas. Those ideas fulfill functional, practical purposes. But functionally equivalent ideas are all interchangeable. There is no regard given to the specific cosmological heritage of peoples. Such ideas, and therefore peoples, have no specific ontological status as unique, or culturally valuable, entities in and of themselves. Diversity and pluralism refer not to the products of specific complex histories which form distinct cosmological-geographical-biological entities. Rather, diversity and

---

[76] Shilliam 2017: 14.   [77] Shilliam 2017: 23.   [78] Shilliam 2017: 23.

[79] Shilliam (2017) points out that colonial science needs the category "supernatural" to distinguish itself from myth. Further, Shilliam refuses to give in to this colonizing move, declaring "the *lwa* are not super-natural, they are other-wise" (2017: 23).

[80] Shilliam 2017: 8.

pluralism are mere numerical terms, referring to the proliferation of traditions, each with the same status within social science.

8.3   Interlude: On Parks in Social Science

On Saturdays, my daughter plays soccer in Druid Hill Park, a short drive from my home in Baltimore. The park opened in 1860, just two years after Central Park in New York. Druid Hill is similar in size to Central Park and is also surrounded on all sides by the city. But unlike Central Park, Druid Hill is not contained within Manhattan's rigid grid. From above, Druid Hill looks more like the head of a dinosaur in profile. The park features the usual amenities: biking paths, soccer fields, and pools (which used to be segregated). But large sections of the park are left as forest, having never been landscaped.

I am happy in the park – between a rationalist, ordered garden and a relationalist forest – if it means I value and pursue a kind of general social science despite my processual and historicist commitments. But I don't think parks should be monocultured. They should have a plurality of places to allow for a plurality of activities, all of which reflect the diverse and changing needs of a city.

Some theorists might suggest that taking history, process, and coloniality seriously means we must jettison any pretense to social scientific explanation.[81] On such a view, a project which posits worldviews as a force in world politics is misguided. The inherent instability and undecidability of meanings implies that any attempt within International Relations (IR) to fix a meaning to the world is an act of power.[82] As such, it tells us more about the productive power of IR as a discipline than it does about the world we purport to explain. Many theorists are unwilling to be complicit in the modernist productions of IR theory, and thus they adopt a critical stance against general or middle-ground theory.

Working from similar ontological premises, I draw a different conclusion. Social science theory in a processual mode can still strive to create general or middle-ground theories. But the purpose of those theories is not to create a catalogue of laws. Rather, it is to provide an agile base for an experimental approach to politics.[83] Theories, like worldviews, orient us in an uncertain world, allowing us to juggle multiple causal factors, see trade-offs, appraise opportunities, and engage with the world in novel ways. General theory need not be modernist, nor strive to disembody its objects from their contexts. Rather, by mapping the complexity of social

[81] See Doty's (1997) critique of structuration theory in IR.   [82] Doty 1997: 387.
[83] See Katzenstein, Chapter 1.

worlds within legible frameworks, we can provide a flexible starting point for understanding and action without the dream of control.

Moreover, precisely because IR wields productive power, IR needs scholars who are willing to draw critical and modernist traditions together. Rather than leave the mainstream safe to ignore the importance of structural power, creative agency, history, and relationality, at least some of us should work to destabilize and change the conventional wisdom.[84] A starting point here is to use social science concepts to narrate and understand the complexity of social reality. But our concepts have to be located within a deep history alive to its contingencies and instabilities. Take for example the concept of worldviews. If we take Weber's arguments about the emergence of worldviews seriously, it does not make sense to apply the concept without historical and social scope conditions. We cannot simply interpret history such that every actor has a worldview or value-orientation. But under the right conditions, worldviews are a useful tool for explaining the actions of individuals and groups.

Moreover, with Shilliam, we need to turn from the critical interrogation of concepts back to history. Decolonizing our concepts allows for new interpretations that more vividly capture the differences that mark the social world. Placing our own work in the colonial history of social science allows us to see without the constraints imposed by the coloniality of our discipline. From there, we might be more open to the values and commitments offered by other worldviews, cosmologies, and modes of life.

From this vantage point, Haas and Nau's defense of individualism in this volume is unpersuasive because it ignores the history of the concepts they themselves deploy. They argue that "individuals can be educated liberally to become self-critical and eventually form and change their worldviews on rational and accountable grounds."[85] There is much to admire in their defense of agency and liberalism. However, it is important to note that their rationally ascertained liberal individualism is itself the product of the historical conceptual developments partially outlined earlier. Any choice of worldview is itself highly structured by historical inheritance. And if the choice is considered rational, the room for agency has been delimited further. Choice is never complete. Choice of worldview is itself is a negotiation of relational connections to history, education, and other agents in our lives.

But, more deeply, Weber would say that we, as products of rationalization, are the inheritors of a rationalized frame of action which orients us to

---

[84] See Katzenstein, Chapter 1 on locating this conventional wisdom in the terms of this volume.

[85] Chapter 2, this volume.

certain kinds of values and exposes us to the risks of disenchantment. We do not have "natural" worldviews. As much as we may want to go back to unquestioning enchantment, we cannot. This is precisely the challenge Shilliam presents us with: even if we try we cannot, from within social science, posit the agency of the *lwa*. So, the idea that we can and should rationally choose a worldview expresses a cosmological development we cannot undo. But we can grapple with and bring the tensions of our own rationalized history into our practice as critical, yet theoretically ambitious social scientists.

In the end, the difference between Haas and Nau and myself lies not in whether we acknowledge the fact of agency, but in where we locate it. Haas and Nau show agency at the surface: connecting up variants of the modernist, economic worldviews across the lines of the Cold War. Their argument is convincing, but it misses the cosmological backdrop which constrained the actors by placing them within a particular political landscape. This is not to say the actors did not exhibit real human agency – they did! But that agency is already relationally constituted in the sense that it was made possible by the configuration of historical inheritance and interactions with other actors.

In Druid Hill, the landscape upon which the children play is already ordered by history (and its messy configurations of knowledge, power, and agency). I cannot look at the swimming pools there without seeing the ongoing and present legacy of segregation and apartheid in my city. Whatever I do today does not erase that inheritance. Power is present in the landscape.

8.4   Conclusion

I take inspiration from processual and critical perspectives that offer relational views of the world, but I think we can put relational concepts to use in the world. I realize any attempt to assert knowledge is a play of power – one that could fall into colonial ways of thinking. But I personally feel a responsibility to act anyway, to fix meanings that I think are accurate and will have good effects on the world. This implies the necessity of a reflexive perspective. This reflexivity should be grounded in history.

My own historical work implies that our knowledge as social scientists acts as a channel for cosmological elements to enter political discourses.[86] Inspired by this, part of my intellectual project is to draw on alternative ontologies and epistemes and use them to refigure social science concepts to make more room for creativity, contingency, and change. In bringing

---

[86] Allan 2018.

processualism and history into the social sciences I seek to weaken the hold that materialism and object-orientation have on the social sciences today. This is not the same as advocating a worldview, but I do think that this work is important to the goal of deflating modernism and increasing ecological sensibilities in the long run. This supports the gambit that Katzenstein, Kurki, and others make: alternative scientific knowledges, such as quantum mechanics or ecology, could be harnessed to rework existing material and object-based conceptions of reality. This would provide a new platform for relating worldviews and cosmologies, as well as producing new ones. Staging this conversation in a nonhierarchical, decolonized manner is an urgent need in the social sciences, and in world politics more broadly.

Perhaps in a relational social science we could consistently enact a vision of selves and peoples that are deeply constituted and transformed by cosmological ideas. But that, I think, would require not just a different ontology but an earnest grappling with the basic colonial categories and impulses that still shape social science. After all, the social sciences are oriented, albeit inchoately, to social control. We still strive to create models of objects that allow the state and other actors to make targeted interventions. Moreover, the social sciences are poorly suited as a guide to the kind of inter-cosmological conversations that would help us relate different groups in nonhierarchical ways. Thus, we need to bring in resources from other traditions to work with our colonial past.

One promise of a decolonized, relational social science is that it might help us rethink the central problem of politics in a processual ontology: moving people. Tilly's flattening of power into mobilization could be put to use by a social science that no longer reduces motivation to material, rational interest.[87] An alternative model of social change would take seriously that we need confidence in our actions – we need to *know* the *lwa* are with us. More than a proper map of the world, a social science which sought to intervene in the world would have to be a creative response to the world that cultivated faith in justice and collective action. However, to do that social science would have to recover some sense that action is more directly tied to cosmological inheritances, acknowledging that we are part of more complex relational wholes than our science allows us to admit right now.

Returning to Weber, this insight from Shilliam provides an alternative reading of disenchantment in the West. Perhaps disenchantment is a loss of faith in cosmology itself. And perhaps we can reclaim cosmology without resorting either to tongue-in-cheek spiritualism or to nationalist

[87] Tilly 2003.

proxies (per Weber). Instead, we can posit that history is cosmological. The histories of peoples are histories forged within and through cosmological elements that leave their traces in stories, institutions, and family traditions. This creates a real cosmological inheritance that cannot be abandoned.

In this framing, we do not choose a cosmology, but inherit cosmological traditions that place various resources for meaning-making at our disposal. It is the creative act of weaving cosmologies from these resources that provides the promise of mobilization with some element of enchantment. Cosmology can be treated as a real source of enchantment while being seen as the product of history.

From this vantage point, we can take cosmology seriously while maintaining a reflexive and critical stance in regard to cosmological inheritance. This reflexivity can help us guard against unreflective nationalisms and racisms that may creep alongside the valorization of cosmological tradition. Grounding ourselves in a relational and processual understanding of history, without reducing people's histories to pure function, could enable us to reclaim vivid and meaningful cosmologies.

Bibliography

Abbott, Andrew. 2016. *Processual Sociology*. Chicago, IL: University of Chicago Press.

Abu-Lughod, Janet L. 1991. *Before European Hegemony: The World System AD 1250–1350*. Oxford: Oxford University Press.

Allan, Bentley B. 2018. *Scientific Cosmology and International Orders*. Cambridge: Cambridge University Press.

Allan, Bentley B. 2019. "Paradigm and Nexus: Neoclassical Economics and the Growth Imperative in the World Bank, 1948–2000," *Review of International Political Economy* 26, 1: 183–206.

Barth, Fredrik. 1987. *Cosmologies in the Making: A Generative Approach to Cultural Variation in Inner New Guinea*. Cambridge: Cambridge University Press.

Berger, Peter and Thomas Luckmann. 1966. *The Social Construction of Reality*. New York: Anchor Books.

Boaistuau, Pierre. 1581 [1558]. *Theatrum mundi*. Available at: http://eebo.chadwyck.com/.

Boatcă, Manuela. 2013. "'From the Standpoint of Germanism': A Postcolonial Critique of Weber's Theory of Race and Ethnicity." In Julian Go, ed. *Postcolonial Sociology*. Bingley: Emerald Group Publishing, pp. 55–80.

Calvin, Jean. 1561 [1536]. *The institution of the Christian religion ...* Available at: http://eebo.chadwyck.com/

Collingwood, R.W. 1945. *The Idea of Nature*. Oxford: Clarendon Press.

Crombie, A.C. and Michael Hoskin. 1970. "The Scientific Movement and the Diffusion of Scientific Ideas." In J.S. Bromley, ed. *New Cambridge Modern History, Vol. 6: The Rise of Great Britain and Russia*. Cambridge: Cambridge University Press, pp. 37–71.

Daston, Lorraine. 2000 "The Coming Into Being of Scientific Objects." In Lorraine Daston, ed. *Biographies of Scientific Objects*. Chicago, IL: University of Chicago Press, pp. 1–15.

Doty, Roxanne Lynn. 1997. "Aporia: A Critical Exploration of the Agent-Structure Problematique in International Relations Theory," *European Journal of International Relations* 3, 3: 365–92.

Fagan, Brian. 2008. *The Great Warming*. New York: Bloomsbury.

Findlay, Ronald, and Kevin H. O'Rourke. 2007. *Power and Plenty: Trade, War, and the World Economy in the Second Millennium*. Princeton, NJ: Princeton University Press.

Gaukroger, Stephen. 2007. *The Emergence of a Scientific Culture: Science and the Shaping of Modernity 1210–1685*. Oxford: Clarendon Press.

Gilman, Nils. 2003. *Mandarins of the Future: Modernization Theory in Cold War America*. Baltimore, MD: Johns Hopkins University Press.

Hobson, John M. 2004. *The Eastern Origins of Western Civilisation*. Cambridge: Cambridge University Press.

Hopf, Ted, and Bentley Allan, eds. 2016. *Making Identity Count: Building a National Identity Database*. Oxford: Oxford University Press.

Hopf, Ted. 2002. *The Social Construction of International Politics*. Ithaca, NY: Cornell University Press.

Joas, Hans. 2017. "Max Weber and the Dangerous Nouns of Process," *Interview with Max Planck Institute for Social Anthropology*. 4 December. Available at: www.eth.mpg.de/4637825/Joas_Interview_2017_12_EN.pdf

Kalberg, Stephen. 1980. "Max Weber's Types of Rationality: Cornerstones for the Analysis of Rationalization Processes in History," *American Journal of Sociology* 85, 5: 1145–79.

Kalberg, Stephen. 2012. *Max Weber's Comparative-Historical Sociology Today: Major Themes, Mode of Causal Analysis, and Applications*. Farnham: Ashgate.

Kuklick, Henrika. 1978. "Sins of the Fathers: British Anthropology and African Colonial Administration," *Researches in Sociology of Knowledge, Sciences and Art* 1: 93–199.

Kusch, Rodolfo. 2010. *Indigenous and Popular Thinking in America*. Durham, NC: Duke University Press.

Lorimer, Douglas. 2009. "From Natural Science to Social Science: Race and the Language of Race Relations in Late Victorian and Edwardian Discourse." In Duncan Kelly, ed. *Lineages of Empire*. Oxford: Oxford University Press, pp. 181–212.

Malinowski, Bronisław. 1961 [1922]. *Argonauts of the Western Pacific*. New York: Dutton.

Meyer, John W., John Boli, George M. Thomas, and Francisco O. Ramirez. 1997. "World Society and the Nation-State," *American Journal of Sociology* 103, 1: 144–81.

Mills, David. 2002. "British Anthropology at the End of Empire: The Rise and Fall of the Colonial Social Science Research Council, 1944–1962," *Revue d'Histoire des Sciences Humaines* 1, 6: 161–88.

Mitchell, Timothy. 2002. *Rule of Experts: Egypt, Techno-politics, Modernity.* Berkeley, CA: University of California Press.

Mitchell, Timothy. 2005. "Economists and the Economy in the Twentieth Century." In George Steinmetz, ed. *The Politics of Method in the Human Sciences: Positivism and its Epistemological Others.* Durham, NC: Duke University Press, pp. 126–41.

Pomeranz, Kenneth. 2000. *The Great Divergence: China, Europe, and the Making of the Modern World Economy.* Princeton, NJ: Princeton University Press.

Rindzevičiūtė, Eglė. 2019. "Systems Analysis as Infrastructural Knowledge: Scientific Expertise and Dissensus under State Socialism," *History of Political Economy* 51, 6: 204–27.

Schluchter, Wolfgang. 1985. *The Rise of Western Rationalism: Max Weber's Developmental History.* Berkeley, CA: University of California Press.

Scott, James C. 1998. *Seeing Like a State: How Certain Schemes to Improve the Human Condition Have Failed.* New Haven, CT: Yale University Press.

Shapin, Steven and Simon Schaffer. 1985. *Leviathan and the Air-Pump: Hobbes, Boyle, and the Experimental Life.* Princeton, NJ: Princeton University Press.

Shapin, Steven. 1996. *The Scientific Revolution.* Chicago, IL: University of Chicago Press.

Shilliam, Robbie. 2008. *German Thought and International Relations: The Rise and Fall of a Liberal Project.* New York: Palgrave.

Shilliam, Robbie. 2017. "Race and Revolution at Bwa Kayiman," *Millennium* 45, 3: 269–92.

Stocking, George W. 1987. *Victorian Anthropology.* New York: Simon and Schuster.

Swidler, Ann. 2001. "What Anchors Cultural Practices." In T.R. Schatzki, K. K. Cetina, and E. von Savigny, eds. *The Practice Turn in Contemporary Theory.* London: Routledge, pp. 83–101.

Tilly, Charles. 2001. "Mechanisms in Political Processes," *Annual Review of Political Science* 4: 21–41.

Tilly, Charles. 2003. *The Politics of Collective Violence.* Cambridge: Cambridge University Press.

Toulmin, Stephen. 1990. *Cosmopolis: The Hidden Agenda of Modernity.* New York: The Free Press.

Wagner, Peter. 2000. "'An Entirely New Object of Consciousness, of Volition, of Thought': The Coming into Being and (almost) Passing Away of 'Society' as a Scientific Object." In Lorraine Daston, ed. *Biographies of Scientific Objects.* Chicago, IL: University of Chicago Press, pp. 132–57.

Wagner, Peter. 2003. "The Uses of the Social Sciences." In Theodore M. Porter and Dorothy Ross, eds. *The Cambridge History of Science, Volume 7: The Modern Social Sciences.* Cambridge: Cambridge University Press, pp. 535–52.

Weber, Max. 1946. *From Max Weber: Essays in Sociology.* Trans. H. H. Gerth and C. Wright Mills. Oxford: Oxford University Press.

254 *Bentley B. Allan*

Weber, Max. 1978. *Economy and Society: An Outline of Interpretive Sociology.* Ed. Guenther Roth and Claus Wittich. Berkeley, CA: University of California Press.

Weber, Max. 2004. *The Vocation Lectures.* Trans. Rodney Livingstone. Indianapolis, IN: Hackett.

Whitehead, Alfred North. 1978. *Process and Reality.* New York: Free Press.

Zimmerman, Andrew. 2006. "Decolonizing Weber," *Postcolonial Studies* 9, 1: 53–79.

Timothy A. Byrnes

In the Preface to this book, Peter Katzenstein cites religion as one of our contemporary era's "foundational worldviews," indicating the degree to which religion is implicated in the concept and category of "worldview" that all of the contributors to this volume are seeking to define, explicate, and draw attention to. Indeed, this entire collaborative examination of worldviews and their role in International Relations (IR) relies, in part, on religious belief, religious practice, and religious modes of being as paradigmatic examples of the ways in which human beings throughout history have made sense of the world and their place in it. Katzenstein notes in Chapter 1, for example, that "worldviews contain arguments about the ontological building blocks of the world, the epistemic requirements of acceptable knowledge claims, and the origin and destiny of humanity." This construction could almost serve as the definition of the kind of "arguments" that varied religious traditions have provided for millennia in response to fundamental questions related to existence and meaning. What is the nature of being? What is the role of faith in constructing systems of knowledge? Where did the world and human life come from? How definitive is human experience on Earth? And what awaits humanity, both at the end of an individual life, and at the end of human history, as we know it? For many individuals and communities over time, religion has provided the most relevant and most meaningful answers to these perennial questions. For many individuals and communities over time, in other words, religion has resided at the very center of encompassing and foundational worldviews.

My central goal in this chapter, then, is to emphasize the depth to which – and the diversity with which – religion is *still* implicated in many of the worldviews that characterize our contemporary era. Modernity dawned. But, to the surprise of many social theorists and behavioral analysts, religion did not just fade away. As a way of making sense of basic reality, human experience, and communal belonging, religion has stubbornly and pervasively survived. In terms of the categories being used in this volume, the religious worldviews that continue to provide meaning and grounding for so many people can often be quite mechanistic in operation. These worldviews constitute, at their core, meticulously tended "gardens," with well-marked walkways and the promise of draconian sanctions for wandering off the prescribed path. But in other contexts and from other perspectives, religious worldviews can also be deeply relational. Relational religious worldviews are grounded in the intricate interconnections between humanity and the divine, between humanity and nature, and within humanity itself as the cocreative force of a world that is always in the process of becoming. In addition to constructing "gardens," in other words, religious worldviews can also acknowledge the density of the "forest," and even celebrate the uncertainty and inscrutability of the "jungle."

Whatever metaphor one wishes to use in order to categorize them, however, I will argue here that religious worldviews – because they attach meaning to human experience and establish social order (or at least ascribe meaning to disorder) – are always deeply grounded simultaneously in both religion and in politics. In fact, I will go further and also argue that the category of worldviews points us to the way in which religion and politics relate to each other not as separate, distinct variables, but rather as coconstitutive elements of coherent, cohesive ways of being in the world.

9.1   Neglect of Religious Worldviews in the Analysis of Global Politics

A simple acknowledgment of the role that various forms of religion play in constructing worldviews relevant to contemporary global politics draws our attention to one of the great mysteries of modern scholarship in the field of IR: the relative paucity of reliance on religion as an underlying factor in explaining political outcomes on the global stage. To be sure, some IR analysts in recent years have responded to the unavoidable prominence of apparently religiously motivated actors on the world stage by acknowledging religion as a potential source of politically relevant identity, and a potential grounding for politically relevant interest formation. Nevertheless, recent examinations of research and publishing patterns reveal IR to have been slow to rethink the assumptions arising out of secularization theory and to reassess the role that religion might play in relations between states and among the broad array of nonstate actors engaged in contemporary world politics.[1]

This myopia is particularly notable given how foundational religion, broadly defined, was in the very construction of the central theoretical

---

[1] Wald and Wilcox 2006: 523–529.

schools of International Relations in the first place. Realism, after all, was originally grounded in a conception of self-interested humankind that was derived from religious understandings of sin and the "fallen" nature of humanity's relationship with God.[2] Liberal institutionalism, alternatively, reflected a belief that relationships between and among states – as between and among individuals – could be based in the recognition of mutual benefit and the building of mutual trust. Some prominent early proponents of these notions were driven explicitly by their religious beliefs,[3] and some viewed the role of international organizations from a decidedly religious perspective. Constructivism, in at least some of its iterations, relied from the start on the political meaning of identity – a category that for many (most?) human beings is grounded, at least in part, in religious belief, practice, and community.

The central reason that IR has resisted a recognition of religion's enduring importance is the same misapprehension that has plagued social science more generally: an overreliance on a deeply problematic secularization theory holding that "modernization necessarily leads to a decline of religion, both in society and in the minds of individuals."[4] This overly simplistic understanding of the complex processes of secularization mistook the functional differentiation characteristic of modern life – the decline of totalistic social structures based solely in religion – for a much less certain diminution of actual religious belief and practice. Relatedly, the presumption of religion's decline led many social scientists to discount the prevalence of what José Casanova has called the "deprivatization" of religion in our modern era.[5]

IR was perhaps especially susceptible to this analytical limitation because of how deeply the very founding of the field itself was grounded in the ostensible marginalization of religion in the arena of European power politics. In what has been variously called the "Westphalian presumption,"[6] the "Westphalian synthesis,"[7] or the "Westphalian legacy,"[8] International Relations theory has long been laboring under the assumption that religion and religious motivations had been rendered insignificant to "modern" world politics by the Peace of Westphalia in 1648. The seventeenth century princes of Europe (disingenuously) declared that religion was too dangerous, too unpredictable, and too prone to conflict to serve as a meaningful grounding for their relations with one another. And so modern students of the state system that those princes created (inaccurately) presumed that they could safely ignore

[2] Thomas 2005; Niebuhr 1953.   [3] Burnidge 2016.   [4] Berger 1996/97: 4.
[5] Casanova 1994   [6] Thomas 2005: 54.   [7] Philpott 2002: 66.
[8] Carlson and Owens 2003: 1

religion, at least as it related to the definition of state interest or the trajectory of interstate interactions.

Unfortunately, the theoretical echoes of the Westphalian "synthesis" endured long after the modern evidence ceased supporting the historical "presumption" on which the "legacy" was based (indeed, if the evidence ever did support it in the first place). But as Scott Thomas has phrased it, using purposefully religious terminology: the secularizing effects of the "Westphalian settlement established a *political theology* for modern IR . . . a *doctrine* that prescribes what the role of religion and political authority should be in domestic and international politics that has lasted for 300 years."[9] As rejection of religion settled into the "genetic code of the discipline of International Relations,"[10] several generations of analysts grew to intellectual and professional maturity almost completely ignoring religion, either because they explicitly deemed it not relevantly present in the field of study they were advancing, or because they were simply ill-disposed to notice it. Peter Berger, manifesting the zeal of the epistemo-logical convert, went so far as to argue that "the difficult-to-understand phenomenon [was] *not* Iranian mullahs, but American university professors."[11]

Some who have sought to account for so many IR scholars and other social scientists remaining so blind for so long to the effects of religion on world politics have speculated that part of the reason might simply be that these scholars tended not to be religious themselves. We know that religion is nothing more than antediluvian superstition, the thinking went. So, surely, such outmoded thinking cannot authentically motivate the behavior of our research subjects. I have lately begun to wonder, however, whether the presumption of irreligious identity on the part of contemporary scholars might itself be a form of the secularization myth. During a lunch discussion among a number of the contributors to this volume, for example, it became clear that each attendee had a personal "religious story" to tell. Some of these stories included continued mem-bership in explicitly religious communities. Some, to be sure, did not. But all of these stories and the significance that the participants readily granted to them suggested that each participant in that discussion had emerged from a personal background that prominently included religious experience in one form or another. Might it be reasonable, therefore, to consider the possibility that many of my colleagues' "worldviews" – the "basic ideas that shape the questions [they] ask or fail to ask, provide [them] with explanatory and interpretive concepts, and suggest hunches

---

[9] Thomas 2005: 23 (emphasis added)   [10] Petito and Hatzopoulos 2003: 1
[11] Berger 1996/97: 3 (emphasis in original).

or plausible answers"[12] – have been shaped in part by their own exposure to religion?

One of the problems, I suspect, with acknowledging this dynamic in personal terms, and applying it analytically, is that emphasizing the widespread role of religion in contemporary politics in general and in the construction of worldviews more specifically runs counter to the deep commitment that most IR scholars have to reliance on scientific explanations that can be uncovered and specified according to the generally acceptable theoretical paradigms and methodological applications of the field. But Bentley Allan, in a chapter that focuses precisely on the sources and ramifications of this epistemological commitment, shows us just how limiting and distorting that reliance can be. Allan conjectures late in Chapter 8 that a full explanation for the Revolution in Haiti might have to include motivations and preferences related to the religious beliefs and predispositions of the revolution's participants. Meaning no disrespect to Allan's discovery or to his straightforward reporting of it, my response upon reading an early draft of his contribution was: of course! Given the widespread religious beliefs and practices of that place and time, why would our default position be to presume that religion was *not* a factor in the genesis and conduct of political phenomenon such as the Haitian revolution?

9.2   The Relevance of Religious Worldviews in Global Politics

Phrased more generally, given that huge swaths of the world's population have (and still do) define their personal and collective identities and commitments in religious terms and in their relationship to "ultimate reality," why in heaven's name should we be surprised that many people ground their political commitments and political activities in their religious beliefs and worldviews? One central reason for our surprise, I suppose, is our headstrong insistence on the dominance of supposedly parsimonious explanations for complex and multilevel social dynamics that resist parsimonious explanation. To be clear, I don't mean to suggest here that religion should be relied on as a totalistic explanatory factor in a simplistic or facile understanding of IR. We shouldn't replace an unfortunate ignorance of religion with an equally inappropriate overreliance on it. What I do wish to suggest, however, is that it ought to be relatively uncontroversial to proceed under the presumption that, to cite a few examples: Islamists are grounded, in part, in their experience of Islam;[13] Christian dominionists are grounded, in part, in their experience

---

[12] Katzenstein, Chapter 1, this volume.   [13] Mandaville 2020; Hamid 2016.

of Christianity;[14] and the Dalai Lama is more than just a grandfatherly avatar of compassion and self-knowledge.[15] These are all examples of highly consequential political worldviews (or spokespersons for them) that in my judgment one would have to be willfully blind not to acknowledge as profoundly, explicitly, and (dare I say it?) obviously grounded in religion.

Michael Barnett's examination in Chapter 5 of the ways in which Judaism serves as the foundation of variable political worldviews in both Israel and the diaspora is a good example of the kind of analysis that takes seriously the religious concepts and categorizations that I argue are so foundational to modern worldviews. In my view, however, Barnett doesn't go far enough in acknowledging the depth of the relationship between religion and politics in the construction of Jewish worldviews. Indeed, part of the problem in this connection is our continued insistence on positing a "relationship" between two "factors" that are so deeply intertwined and so mutually constitutive that the analytical distinction between them may be hard to sustain. The above-cited examples make this point. Islamism, Christian dominionism, and Tibetan nationalism are not merely the political manifestations of underlying religious worldviews. I would argue, instead, that they *are* in a foundational sense worldviews themselves: ways of being in the world that have been mutually constituted through the profound interconnectedness of religious commitments and political interests.

This is why it is so futile, by the way, to try to convince Evangelicals in the United States that their enduring support for the manifestly un-Christian Donald Trump is, itself, un-Christian. The version of Christianity practiced by many Evangelicals in the United States today is actually at its core Trumpist, or at least reliably Republican in nature. And it has been for at least the last several decades. Church (or mosque or temple) and state can surely be legally and constitutionally separated. But a separation of religion and politics is a chimera. Religion and politics are not so much distinct realms of human experience as they are, often, mutually constituted and mutually re-enforcing elements of a single internally coherent worldview.

American voters whose personal identities are firmly grounded in such a cohesive worldview can no more be expected to readily separate their religion from their politics than members of the Bharatiya Janata Party can be expected to separate Hinduism from Indian nationalism. In "Hindutva," we have an example of the ultimate grounding of a politically consequential worldview in a religious identity.[16] It is not

[14] Goldberg 2006   [15] Mehrotra 2005.   [16] Savakar 1923.

that a "religious" identity competes with or supersedes the "political" in this construction of a distinctively Hindu/Indian worldview. Instead, there is in this case a true fusion, or mutual construction, of the religious and the political in the formation of a distinctive worldview that today defines the dominant articulation of Indian nationalism.

This example – and this way of understanding religion's role in constructing worldviews – highlights the frequency with which religious beliefs, practices, and communities are implicated in fundamentalist political projects that epitomize the order, conformity, and predictability of the "garden." Reacting to the kind of unsettling cosmological uncertainty described by Milja Kurki in Chapter 3, many people apparently rely on religion to provide the clarity of divine and human authority, the certitude of clearly delineated ethical frameworks, the comforting promise of eternal life, and the succor of likeminded hands to clasp onto in the frightening darkness. These religious worldviews often define themselves precisely around the conjuring of an omnipotent and omniscient God who casts a judge's eye on humanity while maintaining a direct line of communication with a clerical caste of one form or another who then authoritatively interpret the divine will and intention. Those interpretations are, in turn, transformed by an earthly priesthood into "dogma," which is used to justify political power of the most unassailable sort. Polish Popes, Iranian mullahs, and Israeli ultra-Orthodox rabbis all claim exclusive access to God's Truth, and all have constructed exquisitely detailed "gardens" that provide ordered meaning based in religious worldviews that drive non-negotiable political commitments.

As powerful as this gardening imagery is, however, it is not the only way of conceptualizing religion's potential role in the construction of ways of being in the world. Religious beliefs, practices, and systems of meaning are far more diverse than the garden metaphor implies. Radical openness to uncertainty, after all, and to the relational fundaments of human experience are deeply foundational to nondogmatic traditions such as Buddhism and Hinduism. In systems of spiritual practice explicitly based in values such as detachment, the negation of the self, and the pursuit of wakefulness to the real, the metaphor of religious worldviews as "gardens" is difficult to maintain.

However, the potential grounding of relational worldviews in religious belief and practice is a broad phenomenon that stretches well beyond merely those traditions that are based more in practice than in dogma. In fact, on close examination it turns out that even the most dogmatic of religious traditions can define themselves in deeply seated forms of relational theology. For example, if "God is love" – as Roman Catholic children have been taught to believe from time immemorial – then the divine presence that lends ultimate meaning to human experience is not merely an anthropomorphized celestial "person," but is instead the relational dynamic of creation itself. The very existence of the human race, in other words, is not merely a *sign* of God's love. The mysterious reality of existence is, rather, the very expression and actualization of that love. Individual men and women, created "in the image and likeness of God," are not enjoined to follow a detailed set of moral and religious laws simply as a kind of cosmic test or challenge by a distant self-interested judge. Instead, these moral and religious laws exist, in the first place, for the deeply relational purpose of knitting the human family together into a Church, into the "mystical Body of Christ." This identity with the Christ, enacted in the sacramental experience of the Holy Eucharist, is a personal relation with the embodied "Word" of God, sent forth in order to reconcile God's people to an eternal unity with the deeply benevolent Creator of the universe.

Looked at in this way, even one of the most dogmatic of religions does more than command its adherents to climb a ladder of ontological certainty toward a "God's eye" vision from which order, conformity, and oppression can be imposed. A religion such as Roman Catholicism is inviting its members into intimate Communion with their God, and thereby challenging its adherents to embrace a form of courageous faithfulness in the face of an apparently inscrutable reality. Those climbing the ladder of religious belief, practice, and commitment may seek to convince themselves that they are heading ever upward to the safety of dogmatic certainty. But the ladder might more accurately be understood as the uncertain and rather treacherous upward path toward the life-defining act of leaping, faithfully, into the unknown.

One could argue, I suppose, that relational worldviews imply their own kinds of "Gods" that pose a threat to human freedom because we don't really possess the capacity to truly know or resist their effects. But if a relational cosmology is grounded in faith or in the pursuit of what is "really real," then the unknown itself is the basis of Truth and the human propensity to resistance is ultimately futile. We are, some religious worldviews might suggest, in the act of "becoming" through our relationships not only with each other, but also with that which we cannot measure, define, or know through Newtonian scientific methods.

I will leave others to argue over whether or not the "forest" or the "jungle" are appropriate metaphors for deepening our understanding of relational worldviews. But whatever metaphors we turn to, it seems that religious worldviews can and do span the categories that this volume was designed to highlight and compare. I would say that in this regard much depends on whether, in the words of novelist Sue Monk Kidd, one worships "the God of rescue" or "the God of presence."[17] But the central point is that a broad-based examination of the role of worldviews in global politics ought to have the welcome effect of clarifying our acknowledgment that religion, in all its diversity, often defines what Katzenstein calls in Chapter 1 the "basic ideas that shape the questions we ask or fail to ask, provide us with explanatory and interpretive concepts, and suggest hunches or plausible answers."

9.3   Methodological Atheism and Informed Empathy

The stunning diversity of religion as a category of human experience is a central and straightforward reason why religion is implicated in such a broad array of worldviews. However, the analytical use of the category of religion may have been hindered in some ways by the complexity and controversy that can surround the very act of defining the term. Sociologist Christian Smith, for example, offered that "religion is a complex of culturally prescribed practices, based on premises about the existence and nature of superhuman powers, whether personal or impersonal, which seek to help practitioners gain access to and communicate or align themselves with those powers, in hopes of realizing human goods and avoiding things bad."[18] Got all that? Looking forward to "operationalizing" it as a "variable"?

William Cantwell Smith ascribes the definitional challenge associated with "religion" not only to the complexity of the object of study, but also to the fact that religion is so often seen by the analysts themselves as a system of ultimate meaning in one form or another. Given that "what a man thinks about religion is central to what he thinks about life and the universe as a whole," the meaning that "one ascribes to the term is a key to the meaning that one finds in existence."[19] I have noted over the course of my own career in this field that scholarly communities engaged in the study of religion often include members who are themselves explicitly motivated by their own religious commitments. Controversy over the serving of liquor was a prominent feature of the initial meetings in the 1980s of the "Religion and Politics" Special Section of the American Political Science Association. Tying the complexity of the subject matter directly to the diversity and predilections of those examining it, W.C. Smith concludes that "to hope to reach any agreement . . . is perhaps to look for a consensus on ultimate questions of man, truth, and destiny."[20]

[17] Kidd 2020: 470.   [18] C. Smith 2017: 22.   [19] W.C. Smith 1962: 18.
[20] W.C. Smith 1962: 18.

This definitional problem has bedeviled everyone from theorists trying to specify the role of religion in society to Supreme Court justices trying to identify what qualifies for protection (and limitation) under the free exercise and anti-establishment clauses of the US Constitution. But for our examination of religion's relationship to (and embodiment of) world-views, a lack of clear conceptual consensus is itself an indication of the depth of religion's place in the category under examination. Definitional disputes among theorists writing about religion revolve mainly around the degrees to which varying approaches to the subject focus on the communal and institutional aspects of religion, or on its functional properties, or on its ethical or theological precepts. The disputes, in other words, are largely about the very question of exactly how religion and religions constitute and articulate various ways of being in the world, and of understandings of "how the world works."

Religious traditions vary so extravagantly, one from the other, that some theorists even resist the category and argue that it is "a distorted concept not really corresponding to anything definite or distinctive in the objective world."[21] I don't think we need to go that far in response to religion's empirical variance, but it is advisable to steer clear, whenever possible, of sweeping pronouncements about the nature of "religion" per se. But again, such a caution serves our purposes well. If we acknowledge that worldviews are variable, then the degree to which, and the ways in which, religion is implemented in the construction of those worldviews can quite appropriately be expected to be variable as well. Even within a broadly defined religious tradition such as "Christianity" or "Buddhism," diversity of structure, system, function, and ethos can also be significant, in the sense of both large and important.

Given this diversity, and given how often these various traditions rely on mutually exclusive truth claims, one is tempted (I am tempted!) to reject the authenticity of all of the claims and to retreat into rationalist justifications about which interests (presumably materialist) are *really* being served through religious means. In our examination of religious worldviews, however, it is best to suspend judgment about the validity or even the authenticity of religious claims and assume for the sake of argument that people actually believe – or strive to believe – that which they say they believe. Seth Kunin provided a helpful guide on this point when he extolled "methodological atheism," or the idea that for social scientists "the claims made by believers themselves about the status of their religion or religious objects should be seen as data to be studied

---

[21] W.C. Smith 1962: 17.

rather than as an authoritative statements about the nature of the object under study."[22]

Some scholars have preferred the term "methodological agnosticism" as a somewhat less dismissive way of approaching the religious beliefs of research subjects.[23] But whether adopting a methodological posture of atheism or agnosticism, "the analyst must assume [for the sake of the analysis] that the object being studied is a social rather than divine product."[24] And, at the same time, social scientists seeking to make sense of religion's place in social and political settings ought also to heed Ninian Smart's advice to adopt a method of "phenomenology ... that tries to bring out what the religious acts *mean to the actors.*"[25] "This implies," Smart says, "that in describing the way people behave, we do not use, so far as we can avoid them, alien categories to evoke the nature of their acts and to understand those acts."[26]

This posture of "informed empathy"[27] seems particularly apposite in the context of specifying religious worldviews. A simple set of thought experiments, involving the three Abrahamic religions, should be enough to make the point. Imagine for a moment that you actually believed as a matter of undoubted fact that Yahweh had purposefully selected the Jews as His chosen people and that a central identifying feature of this unique Covenant was the Jewish people's right to live perpetually in the Land of Israel. Would that conviction not have powerful effects on how you interpreted the sweep of human history, the appropriate place of the Jewish people in that history, and the very nature of regional conflict and IR?

Imagine for a moment, alternatively, that you actually believed as a matter of undoubted fact not only that Jesus of Nazareth was the unique incarnation of The One True God into human history, but also that this same Jesus would return at the end of time to judge the living and the dead so as to reward the worthy with eternal salvation and consign the unworthy to eternal damnation. Would that set of convictions not have powerful effects on how you judged the nature of human sovereignty over worldly affairs, the finality of physical death, or the role of sin and virtue in human affairs?

Finally, imagine for a moment that you actually believed as a matter of undoubted fact that there is no God but Allah, that Mohammed is His messenger, and that the Qur'án is the direct word of the sole Supreme Being who created the universe, and who calls His followers to follow His mandated law in all aspects of human life. Would that set of convictions

[22] Kunin 2003: 74.   [23] Smart 1973.   [24] Kunin 2003: 74.
[25] Smart 1996: 2 (emphasis added).   [26] Smart 1996: 2.   [27] Smart 1996: 2.

not have powerful effects on how you understood the role that this body of law ought to play in human experience and how you might react to the efforts of outsiders to control the social structures and legal systems under which your community of believers ought to live?

To repeat, the adoption of this "empathetic" perspective does not mean that one accepts, in the sense of sharing, the truth of the cosmic, sweeping, and (often) mutually exclusive claims being made by the individuals and communities under examination. To the contrary, it means maintaining a "position of neutrality"[28] that allows one to credit in experiential terms the depth of the convictions under study without judging their theological validity. And in so doing, it becomes rather obvious how central religion is in a dizzying variety of contexts to the construction of worldviews. Religion is often at the heart of the processes through which a community's shared "truth" is enshrined as a kind of epistemological consensus in a given social context. Religion, in all its complexity, can provide the indispensable common knowledge that allows a community to live together with meaning and confidence in what otherwise might present itself as a deterministic or risky world. Perhaps this is why so many social theorists who include religion in their analyses explicitly rely on the concept of "worldview" in order to capture what religion so often comprises and provides.

9.4   Weber and Geertz

Max Weber, to cite perhaps the most prominent of these theorists, grounded his notion of worldview in the individual's relationship to specific elements of society, prominently including religion. Positing a dynamic relationship between religious ideas and economic behavior, Weber argued that different religious traditions would have different relationships with economic structures and practices, particularly those associated with capitalism. This dynamic was laid out most expansively (and most famously) in *The Protestant Ethic and the Spirit of Capitalism*, where Weber starts with the observation that "a glance at the occupational statistics of any country of mixed religious composition brings to light with remarkable frequency ... the fact that business leaders and owners of capital ... are overwhelmingly Protestant [as opposed to Catholic]."[29] Weber ascribes this finding to "the permanent intrinsic character of [the two Christian communities'] religious beliefs."[30] And then, as the heart of his argument, he asserts that the characteristically Protestant imperative to provide outward indications of one's

---

[28] Kunin 2003: 117   [29] Weber 1976: 35.   [30] Weber 1976: 40.

membership in the select and saved requires a form of asceticism and industrious work ethic that is well suited to the spirit of capitalism.

Weber argues, in so many words, that religious beliefs at the individual level have variant relationships with modern capitalist practices, and that out of these particular relationships very different worldviews arise. Attitudes toward worldly economic matters such as thrift, industriousness, investment, trust, and the rest are closely related to religious belief. And those economic values, in turn, deeply influence other aspects of an individual's (or a religious community's) worldview, from ideas about appropriate family and social structures, to the setting of political priorities and interests, to convictions concerning the proper ordering of global relations.

These considerations bring to mind the several semesters I have spent over the years in Geneva, Switzerland, leading groups of undergraduate students as they performed academic study of the many international organizations that are housed there. Each and every semester, students would articulate in informal conversations with me a kind of visceral, vulgar Weberianism as they tried to make sense of the stark distinction between their living and working environment in (Calvinist) Geneva and the recreational opportunities afforded to them on weekend sojourns to, say, (Catholic) Barcelona. The students recognized immediately that the all-night adventures of The Ramblas were simply unavailable – virtually unthinkable, really – within the early-rising ethos of Geneva, whose skyline along Lac Leman is dominated by the imposing edifices and twinkling lights of ... banks and insurance companies.

Weber's disquisition on the relationship between Protestantism and capitalism, of course, is one of the founding building blocks of modern sociology. Less well known, perhaps, is the fact that he applied this same method to other religious traditions as well, finding, in the words of Reinhard Bendix, that "some had an accelerating and others a retarding effect upon the rationality of economic life."[31] Turning from Europe to China, for example, Weber argued that the "Confucian man's ... cardinal virtue was to fulfill the traditional obligations of family and office."[32] Embedded in a cultural system of kinship networks grounded in filial piety, followers of the Confucian ethic were at one and the same time sheltered from the potential hardship that provides incentives within capitalism, and oriented toward a form of harmony and social order that discourages the economic stratification that characterizes capitalism. As Bendix sums up the comparison: "the Puritans combined their ascetic conduct with an intensity of belief and an enthusiasm for action that were

[31] Bendix 1977: 83   [32] Bendix 1977: 136.

completely alien to the esthetic values of Confucianism." "It was this difference," he concludes, "that contributed to an autonomous capitalist development in the West and the absence of a similar development in China."[33]

Weber performed a similar comparative analysis concerning Hinduism in India. I don't need to detail that analysis here beyond noting his emphasis on the ways that the caste system and a transient understanding of an individual's relationship to personal identity and worldly achievement militated against "the incorporation of the acquisitive drive in an inner-worldly ethic of conduct."[34] I should stress, I suppose, that in laying out Weber's arguments I am not endorsing his views on the relationship between religion and economics – and that relationship's role in constructing worldviews – any more than I am endorsing any other way of conceptualizing the role of religious belief and practice in establishing what is "really real" about "how the world works."

Indeed, Weber's theory seems particularly susceptible to oversimplification (see, for example, my earlier mention of my students' attempts to account for their personal experience of Europe's cultural variations). And all of Weber's statements about how "Protestants" behave, how "Confucian" families operate, and how "Hindus" construct identity are exquisitely open to the charge that he essentializes very complex social phenomena. Nevertheless, Weber's voluminous writings on religion represent a deeply theoretical effort to ascribe the content of different worldviews, in part, to the content of different religious belief systems. Protestantism, Catholicism, Confucianism, and Hinduism, he argues, have different ways of relating to economic structures because those different religious traditions represent very different ways of defining the ultimate reality underlying human life and human meaning.

For his part, the anthropologist Clifford Geertz explicitly ties religion to the notion of world views (two words for Geertz), or what he also calls "way[s] of seeing."[35] Geertz defines religion as "a system of symbols which acts to establish powerful, persuasive, and long-lasting moods and motivations in men by formulating conceptions of a general order of existence and clothing these conceptions with such an aura of factuality that the moods and motivations seem uniquely realistic."[36] The key to this definition is the characterization of religion as a "system of symbols" that serves to "synthesize a people's . . . world view – the picture they have of the way things in sheer actuality are, their most comprehensive ideas of order."[37] These religious world views rest on conceptions of what is

---

[33] Bendix 1977: 141.   [34] Bendix 1977: 197.   [35] Geertz 1993: 111.
[36] Geertz 1993: 90   [37] Geertz 1993: 89.

"really real," a commitment to the proper ordering of supernatural and natural experience that the "symbolic activities of religion ... are devoted to producing, intensifying, and rendering inviolable."[38]

The potential political significance of a "system of symbols" that undergirds "comprehensive ideas of order" should be obvious. Geertz argues that religion, understood in this way, "objectivizes moral and ethical preferences by depicting them as imposed conditions of life, implicit in a world with a particular structure."[39] To cite the metaphor we are using here, this conception of religion imagines a "garden" constructed in intricate detail. The garden's form, structure and layout are all understood by those who live within its borders as absolute givens of the natural order and profoundly symbolic of the cosmic reality that gives meaning to earthly design. For their religious advocates, then, opposition to homosexuality, say, or insistence on faithful stewardship of creation are not merely "positions" to be argued, equal in epistemological validity to their opposites. They are, instead, "mere common sense given the unalterable shape of reality." "Religious symbols formulate a basic congruence," in other words, "between a particular style of life and a specific metaphysic, and in so doing sustain each other with the borrowed authority of the other."[40] Political interests grounded in metaphysical worldviews claiming congruence with *The Truth* are not likely to be particularly open to negotiation, compromise, or (sometimes) even rational justification.

These symbolic systems also produce widely accepted understandings of important aspects of human experience. Questions about the very existence of life itself, the perennial problem of human suffering, and the presence of evil in the world can all be answered through religious conceptions of general order. And, of course, conflict can be (and often is) based in contact between and among peoples whose "experiential evidence for their truth"[41] lead them to differing "conception[s] of the established world of bare fact."[42]

9.5   The Sacred and the Profane

Geertz links religious systems of symbols and everyday life through the ultimate meaning that those symbols grant to "common sense" and "order." Many other theorists, however, have drawn a clearer distinction between two realms of human experience, identifying them most often as the "sacred" and the "profane." In a seminal work titled *The Sacred and*

---

[38] Geertz 1993: 112.   [39] Geertz 1993: 90   [40] Geertz 1993:90.   [41] Geertz 1993: 90
[42] Geertz 1993: 119.

the Profane: The Nature of Religion, Romanian historian Mircea Eliade identifies the two realms of his title as two very different "modalities of being," or "ways of being in the world."[43] "*Homo religius,*" he argues, "always believes that there is an absolute reality, *the sacred,* that transcends this world but manifests itself in this world, thereby sanctifying it and making it real."[44] These manifestations of absolute reality, or "hierophanies,"[45] drive the ritual orientation and construction of sacred space, space which for adherents to the resulting religious tradition is experienced as "the only real and real-ly existing space" amid "the formless expanse [that] surround[s] it."[46]

It is important to note here that Eliade is talking about actual physical space, the sacred designation of which powerfully influences the worldviews of those who acknowledge the sacrality of "our world" and its centrality in the cosmos. According to this conception, religious believers are quite literally "viewing the world" either from the confines of a sacred space itself, or at the very least from a frame of mind and spirit that is defined in terms of a very particular sacred space. "Our world," as understood by adherents, is situated at the center of the universe – indeed, *is* the center of the universe – given that it is the place where the hierophany took place or where it is ritually recognized and re-enacted. Eliade offers the examples of "an entire country (e.g. Palestine), a city (Jerusalem), [and] a sanctuary (the Temple in Jerusalem)"[47] as examples of the kinds of sacred space he has in mind.

Indeed, for many Jews, the Land of Israel is idealized as the "geographical center of the universe and the point of contact between the spiritual and material spheres."[48] Zionism is one central manifestation of this understanding of sacred space, and the status and destiny of the modern legal state of Israel has resided near the center of contemporary debates concerning Jewish identity, as well as of contemporary constructions of how many Jews understand their place in an often hostile world. There is no Jewish creed, no Jewish Church. There is, instead, a Jewish *people,* albeit a diverse and complex one. And as a people, Jewish interests tend to revolve around the survival, sustainability, and flourishing of the collective. This is not merely a theoretical or mystical notion, of course, but rather a practical responsibility and duty, carried out through a history of unimaginable suffering, struggle, and forbearance. As Michael Barnett shows in Chapter 5, membership in that people, participation in that enduring history of struggle and survival, is what binds Jews together

[43] Eliade 1959: 14.   [44] Eliade 1959: 202.   [45] Eliade 1959: 11   [46] Eliade 1959: 20
[47] Eliade 1959: 42.   [48] Schweid 1987: 538.

across vast geographic distances and amid significant diversity in terms of belief and practice.

The Christian religion, obviously, is more creedal in nature. Despite the great diversity of Christianity in institutional, social, and pastoral terms, the vast Christian Church is united in the belief that Jesus of Nazareth represents the unique, direct intervention of the divine into human history. Jesus is, in a sense, the ultimate hierophany, whose own manhood redefined human experience itself as sacred space, and whose own sacrificial death and redeeming resurrection redefined humanity's relationships with death, eternity, and the divine.

For their part, Muslims valorize Medina and Mecca as paradigmatic sacred spaces out of which grew a people (umma) who should ideally be governed by rulers and legal systems attuned to God's authoritative message, as contained in the Qur'án. Moreover, the call to pray (toward Mecca) five times a day, as well as the requirement (if possible) to visit Mecca at least once, have the effect of placing "our world" at the center of the universe, a center around which the proper ordering of human affairs ought to be oriented.

Eliade also argues in a vein directly relevant to our purposes here that this spatial cosmology serves to breed communal interests that tend to be exclusionary, geographically based, and absolutist. The idea that "our" communal space, in both physical and symbolic senses, is uniquely sacred and uniquely central to the meaning of human experience is not something that can be easily extended to outsiders or compromised with competing claims. Indeed, worldviews based in conceptions of sacred space often include within them definitions of outsiders as particularly odious and illegitimate: "As 'our world' was founded by imitating the paradigmatic work of the gods ... so the enemies who attack it are assimilated to the enemies of the gods, the demons, and especially to the archdemon ... conquered by the gods at the beginning of time."[49] When identity and conflict are defined in this way, it is no wonder that so many theorists and practitioners of IR have tried since at least 1648 to marginalize the role of religion in global affairs. It really can be that disruptive, dangerous, and noncompromising of a force.

No theorist of religion, of course, is more closely associated with the sacred/profane dichotomy than Emile Durkheim. For Durkheim, religion is defined as "a unified system of beliefs and practices relative to sacred things, that is to say, things set apart and surrounded by prohibitions – beliefs and practices that unite its adherents in a single moral community called a church."[50] The whole key to this understanding of religion is its

---

[49] Eliade 1959: 47–48.   [50] Durkheim 1995: 44

emphasis on *function*, on the mutually constitutive role of religion and society. Based in an examination of Totenism, and then applied to other religions, Durkheim argues that sacred objects represent both the divine *and* the group through the group's shared understanding of the divine. A central function of religious belief and practice, in other words, is actually to form and define the group engaged in the belief and practice itself, and to construct "solidarity" among adherents. As Kunin puts it: "ritual practice serves the social function of validating and strengthening group cohesion."[51] The whole enterprise, for Durkheim, is definitively collective.

Sacred objects and rituals give meaning to life, but in an even more fundamental way they also function to create the social realities from which a collective can actually have a shared worldview. At its most basic core, this type of religious worldview is defined by the conviction that *we* are sacred while *they* are profane; *our* system of identity and solidarity is based in ultimate reality while *theirs*, to put it mildly, is not. At the same time, as Durkheim stated in his original definition, this conception of religion's functional role in constituting society also involves the recognition of "prohibitions" that serve to construct moral ethos and to "devalue the importance of the individual as a mediator for social facts."[52] Religion forms identity, defines it in collective terms, and works to focus the collective's worldview on that which renders its social structures sacred.

History shows us, of course, that these sacred systems of solidarity can, and often have been, closely linked to national identity and state sovereignty. In cases as diverse as Poland, Iran, Israel, India, and Tibet, religious worldviews can define a people's understanding of their place in the global order and define the interests that the society's leadership is expected to advance. But in our modern era, it is just as common for religious solidarity to cut across national identities and state borders. Numerous sacred social structures are defined in "transnational" terms as systems of solidarity and belonging that are constructed through shared belief and, perhaps even more profoundly, shared ritual.

I have spent many years, for example, studying the political role of transnational Catholicism in a variety of settings.[53] Along the way, I have never failed to be impressed by the consistency of ritual that I have encountered in Catholic communities all across the globe. The order of service, the role of music, and, most importantly, the centrality of the Eucharist in Catholic worship clearly function as experiences of effervescence that construct the Catholic Church, *as such*, and form bonds of

---

[51] Kunin 2003: 21.   [52] Kunin 2003: 23   [53] Byrnes 2001; Byrnes 2011.

solidarity among more than a billion Catholic adherents worldwide. In a similar way, the transnational Islamic umma is not just knit closer together by the Five Pillars of Islam. It is, in Durkheimean terms, actually constructed by that set of divinely mandated ritual practices that function to engender solidarity and define identity. And of course, in the words of Huston Smith, "Judaism is a faith of a people."[54] There is great significance placed within Judaism on the preservation and cohesion of that people, and on the functional construction of that people into a nation. From Abraham's acceptance of the covenant with God, through the exodus from Egypt to the Promised Land, to the eventual dispersal in a global diaspora, the national identity of the Jewish people – separate and apart from any other definitions and articulations of sovereignty – has been a basic element of how many Jews have viewed their place in the world.

In this way of viewing religion, then, a "Catholic worldview," or an "Islamic worldview," or a "Jewish worldview," or any other religious worldview is more than a way of seeing the world based on theological tenets. Such religiously defined worldviews are, at a deeper level, ways of *being* in the world; they are ways of constructing the most meaningful and most basic social structures, and ways of delineating who qualifies for being recognized as part of the sacred order.

The implications of including these religious worldviews in our approaches to global politics can be immediate and profound. Much of modern International Relations theory, for example, identifies survival – in both individual and collective terms – as *the* overriding "interest" that needs to be protected and advanced in virtually all political interactions. Religious worldviews that do not acknowledge death as final, however, or that do not even conceive of death in particularly negative terms – some even prominently value and reward martyrdom – will be at odds with, and potentially problematic for, systems of global order that assume survival as an overriding value. Common military considerations such as deterrence and the avoidance of collateral damage may look very different if one is viewing this world as a prelude to the next, if one sees earthly death as a moment of clarifying transition to a faithfully anticipated eternal unification with a Divine Being and coreligionists who have previously gone on to their "heavenly reward."

9.6   Conclusion

Describing what he called "Islamic exceptionalism," Shadi Hamid wrote that "the tendency to see religion through the prism of politics or

---

[54] H. Smith 1991: 31.

economics (rather than the other way around) isn't necessarily incorrect, but it can sometimes obscure the independent power of ideas that seem, to much of the Western world, quaint and archaic."[55] Applying Hamid's point more generally, I argue here that religious "ideas" – or, more broadly conceived, religious beliefs and practices – have played and continue to play central roles in the construction of politically relevant worldviews in a wide variety of contexts. In fact, rather than claiming that the relationship between religion and politics should be viewed as the former constructing the latter (rather than the other way around), I argue that these two foundational aspects of human life and community relate to each other as mutually constitutive elements in "systems of order," "ways of viewing the world," and, most essentially, ways of "being." According to this way of viewing religion's place in modern life, beliefs, practices, and meaning that we generally classify as religious in nature are not epiphenomenal or incidental to some other dynamic that is "really going on." They are not atavistic holdovers that we can either wish away or presume will go away soon. They are, instead, in many places and for many people, the defining features of contemporary life.

To be sure, secularism does seem to be on the rise in some societies and polities,[56] and it is certainly plausible to imagine that those secularizing dynamics might spread geographically and demographically in the coming years, decades . . . centuries? But even modern political orders that are based in liberal individualism and that place humanity at the center of individual and collective meaning still have to contend today – and will continue to have to contend in the future – with nonsecular and anti-secular elements of their populations that view the world from very particular perspectives. What I have chosen to call religious worldviews – while acknowledging their great diversity – are manifestly still animating the way that many people understand their identity, their interests, and their conception of how the political order should be structured. That being the case, we who purport to illuminate the workings of global politics – or, if you like, International Relations – should take these religious worldviews as seriously as do those who embody them.

Bibliography

Bendix, Reinhard. 1977. *Max Weber: An Intellectual Portrait*. Berkeley: University of California Press.
Berger, Peter L. 1996/97. "Secularism in Retreat," *National Interest* 46, Winter: 3–12.

---

[55] Hamid 2016: 10.   [56] Norris and Inglehart 2004.

Burnidge, Cara Lee. 2016. *A Peaceful Conquest: Woodrow Wilson, Religion, and the New World Order*. Chicago, IL: University of Chicago Press.

Byrnes, Timothy A. 2001. *Transnational Catholicism in Postcommunist Europe*. Latham, NY: Roman & Littlefield.

Byrnes, Timothy A. 2011. *Reverse Mission: Transnational Religious Communities and the Making of US Foreign Policy*. Washington, DC: Georgetown University Press.

Carlson, John D. and Erik O. Owens, eds. 2003. *The Sacred and the Sovereign: Religion and International Politics*. Washington, DC: Georgetown University Press.

Casanova, José 1994. *Public Religions in the Modern World*. Chicago, IL: Chicago University Press.

Durkheim, Emile. 1995. *The Elementary Forms of Religious Life*. New York: The Free Press.

Eliade, Mercia. 1959. *The Sacred and the Profane: The Nature of Religion*. San Diego, CA: Harcourt Brace Jovanovich.

Geertz, Clifford. 1993. *The Interpretation of Cultures: Selected Essays*. London: Fontana Press.

Goldberg, Michelle 2006. *Kingdom Coming: The Rise of Christian Nationalism*. New York: W.W. Norton & Co.

Hamid, Shadi 2016. *Islamic Exceptionalism: How the Struggle Over Islam is Reshaping the World*. New York: St. Martin's Press.

Kidd, Sue Monk. 2020. *The Book of Longings*. New York: Random House Large Print.

Kunin, Seth D. 2003. *Religion: The Modern Theories*. Baltimore, MD: The Johns Hopkins University Press.

Mandaville, Peter. 2020. *Islam and Politics*. 3rd ed. New York: Routledge.

Mehrotra, Rajiv, ed. 2005. *The Essential Dalai Lama: His Important Teachings*. New York: Penguin.

Niebuhr, Reinhold. 1953. *Christian Realism and Political Problems: Essays on Political, Social, Theological, and Ethical Themes*. New York: Scribner

Norris, Pippa and Ronald Inglehart. 2004. *Sacred and Secular: Religion and Politics Worldwide*. Cambridge: Cambridge University Press.

Petito, Fabio and Pavlos Hatzopoulos. 2003. *Religion in International Relations: The Return from Exile*. New York: Palgrave Macmillan.

Philpott, Daniel. 2002. "The Challenge of September 11 to Secularism in International Relations," *World Politics* 55: 6–95.

Savakar, Vinayak Damodar. 1923. *Hindutva: Who is a Hindu*. Bombay: S.S. Savarkar.

Schweid, Eliezer. 1987. "Land of Israel," in Arthur A. Cohen and Paul Mendes-Flohr, eds., *Contemporary Jewish Religious Thought: Original Essays on Critical Concepts, Movements, and Beliefs*. New York: The Free Press, pp. 55–60.

Smart, Ninian. 1973. *The Science of Religion and the Sociology of Knowledge: Some Methodological Questions*. Princeton, NJ: Princeton University Press.

Smart, Ninian. 1996. *Dimensions of the Sacred: An Anatomy of the World's Beliefs*. Berkeley: University of California Press.

Smith, Christian. 2017. *Religion: What it is, How it Works, and Why it Matters.* Princeton, NJ: Princeton University Press.

Smith, Huston. 1991. *The World's Religions* (rev. ed.). San Francisco: Harper San Francisco.

Smith, William Cantwell. 1962. *The Meaning and End of Religion: A New Approach to the Religious Traditions of Mankind.* New York: The Macmillan Company.

Thomas, Scott M. 2005. *The Global Resurgence of Religion and the Transformation of International Relations: The Struggle for the Soul of the Twenty-First Century.* New York: Palgrave Macmillan.

Wald, Kenneth D. and Clyde Wilcox. 2006. "Getting Religion: Has Political Science Rediscovered the Faith Factor?" *American Political Science Review* 100, 4: 523–29.

Weber, Max. 1976. *The Protestant Ethic and the Spirit of Capitalism.* London: Unwin Paperbacks.

Part IV

Conclusion

10   Of Gardens, Forests, and Parks

Peter J. Katzenstein

> The task becomes not one of looking for some single thing, but managing . . . multiple shifting perspectives, and negotiating . . . between irreducibly different contexts. If one wants to call this a "world view" then I have no objection to that.
>
> Raymond Geuss (2020)[1]

Why are scholars of world politics unable to recognize the importance of uncertainty in world politics? I argued in Chapter 1 that humanist Newtonian and hyper-humanist Post-Newtonian worldviews shape analytical perspectives on risk and uncertainty. Humanist Newtonianism is central to conventional analyses of world politics. With most students of world politics following, economics took the lead by viewing reality as timeless; it deployed the lens of probability and paid little attention to uncertainty.[2] Since much of twentieth-century economics has resembled, roughly speaking, the physics of the 1870s and 1880s, this is not surprising.[3] Post-Newtonianism takes uncertainty for granted and is conceptually better equipped to explore terrains of world politics marked by uncertainty. The worldview of the analyst makes a difference: worldviews inform basic understandings of world politics.

Accepting the predictable/controlled and the unpredictable/uncontrollable as linked aspects of human experience, garden, park, and forest (or jungle) metaphors offer a convenient way to organize my discussion in this concluding chapter. Is the world neat or unkempt? We can make things look similar by failing to examine them closely. There exists a difference in intellectual styles between the mind of the French and the mind of the English. In understanding the laws of the natural (and we might add, the social) world, did God think like a French mathematician

---

I thank Matthew Evangelista for his careful reading and invaluable comments on an earlier draft of this chapter; Richard Price for making me consider some of the normative implications of my argument; and Begüm Adalet, Peter Gourevitch, and Stephen Krasner for their general reactions.
[1] Geuss 2020: 163.   [2] Smolin 2013: 258–63.   [3] Mirowski 1989.

or did she have the untidy mind of the English?[4] My answer is a resounding "both." Leaving gods aside, Newtonian humanists imagine the world as a garden to be observed and controlled. Often, the garden fights back, revealing itself to be a jungle that is not tamed and might not be tamable. Hyper-humanist Post-Newtonians seek to understand the jungle as it is, well aware that this task is impossible due to the problem of radical uncertainty: not knowing what one does not know, one hence does not know what to include in a predictive model. My interest in uncertainty inclines to Post-Newtonianism, yet I remain tethered to visions of the garden in which I was raised. I thus find refuge in parks, which offer vistas to both garden and jungle.

Section 10.1 explores gardens and forests; it summarizes the core arguments of Henry Nau and Prasenjit Duara (presented in Chapters 6 and 7); and investigates the garden of experiments and the forest of experimentation as different ways of operating under conditions of putatively controllable risk and acknowledged uncertainty. Section 10.2 considers parks as zones of contact between gardens and forests; inquires into the complementarities between worldviews; surveys Newtonian and Post-Newtonian workarounds; and addresses the role of values. The final section (10.3) discusses the arguments of Bentley Allan and Timothy Byrnes (in Chapters 8 and 9) and science and religion more broadly as the two reigning worldviews that help us navigate a world filled with uncertainties.

10.1   Garden and Forests, Experiments and Experimentation

Drawing on a broad variety of literary and cultural sources, Robert Harrison meditates on humanity, nature, and society as he explores gardens and forests.[5] Harrison's gardens embody care and cultivation as quintessentially human traits. Life without them is soulless and humanity loses its defining purpose. Harrison shows gardens of many different types and in many different places: real, mythical, historical, literary, monastic, republican, princely, and imperial. All of them are central to the care of mortal life and defend against the ever-threatening reign of inhumane, passive, stillborn sterility. Lack of care drove Eve, the first human planter (of the seeds of the forbidden pomegranate), and Adam

---

[4] Cartwright 1999: 19.

[5] I thank my colleagues and friends in Cornell's Circle seminar, as well as Caryl Clark, Patchen Markell, and Divya Subramanian for directing me to some of the sources used in this section. I also would like to thank Roderick Floud for reading this section and offering helpful criticisms and suggestions. Unlike Munroe (2008: 7–14) and others, I am not interested here in theorizing spatial and social relations. Harrison 1992; 2008.

out of God's garden. Care, "in its self-transcending character, is an expansive projection of the intrinsic ecstasy of life."[6] For gardeners, as for teachers, cultivation is not the same as creation. Planting seeds and nourishing life is what gardeners do and teachers aspire to do in the garden of young minds.

For Harrison, as in Rome, forests are birth sites of city and civilization; of profane pagan worship resisting Christianity; of spiritual solitude and savagery; of chivalrous knights gone mad; of royal prerogatives for hunting; of outlaws pursuing justice; of lyric nostalgia and error-filled tradition; and of presumed national essences. What is true of forest ecosystems holds also for the entire biosphere of the earth: a complex and integrated system of relations. Humanity is part of a diverse web of jungle- or forest-like, planetary sprawling relations. The Greek word *logos* originally "means 'relation.' *Logos* is that which binds, gathers or relates. It binds humans to nature in the mode of openness and difference."[7] It is true that past civilizations have typically encroached on the wilderness of forests in the interest of economic efficiency.[8] Yet, it is also true that in most classical Indian texts *jangal* refers to dry lands that turned out to be suitable for agriculture.[9] Forests are about ever-changing relations.

Metaphors that capture the awe-inspiring wilderness of forests and the tamed harmony of gardens express different worldviews.[10] Are gardeners and forest-dwellers occupying altogether different spaces? Are they experiencing a similar world differently? Or are they sharing some similar experiences in the world? These are old questions. Materialist and mechanistic Newtonian beliefs express a view of nature as lifeless matter, in motion and subject to universal laws. Vitalists and organicists saw instead an active nature filled with living entities and swarming matter much closer to the Post-Newtonian worldview of quantum mechanics and scientific cosmology. Mechanically interacting lifeless matter is more legible than a world teeming with always changing possibilities. Calvin, gardener extraordinaire, could not stand that "filthy dog" Lucretius and other vitalists who concealed the craftsmanship of an omniscient God that diligent astronomers, to Calvin's great satisfaction, highlighted so well.[11]

---

[6] Harrison 2008: 33.   [7] Harrison 2008: 200.

[8] Skaria 1999: vi–vii. Modest elevations protected peasants in Southeast Asia and Europe alike from the powers of taxation and conscription by the urban centers of civilizations.

[9] Skaria 1999: viii; Barton 2000: 557, 572–73. To complicate matters further, in contemporary Pakistan *jangal* refers to forest or jungle even though its etymological antecedent, the Sanskrit term *jangala*, referred to a man-made savanna. See Dove 1992: 231.

[10] Cooper 2006.   [11] Allan, Chapter 8.

Garden and forest metaphors capture experiences in and views of the world that reach deep and resonate profoundly. Forests often depict sites of solitude and resistance. In the Middle Ages, European peasants saw in forests a wilderness that differed starkly from their plowed fields. "Wood" and "*wald*" derive etymologically from "wild": inhospitable domains of lawless unpredictability.[12] Forests were sites of contestations over power, authority, and identity in places as far apart as historical Germany and contemporary Southeast Asia. The introduction of modern forestry methods in eighteenth- and nineteenth-century Prussia and Saxony exemplified the power of the modern state. Carefully planned seeding, planting, and cutting aimed at transforming wild forests into predictable and profitable enterprises – a metaphor for the modern state's effort of making civil society fully legible.[13] It was precisely that legibility that made Ernst Jünger's fictitious forester a militant loner and solitary elitist willing to fight the authoritarian and dictatorial tendencies of modern social and economic systems.[14] Between the 1950s and 1970s, insurgency and counterinsurgency warfare in Southeast Asia occurred in forested territories invariably referred to as jungles. Discursively, institutionally, and practically, these spaces became objects for military conquest and political incorporation into national societies.[15] By the beginning of the twenty-first century, the jungle had become a rainforest – a fragile ecosystem deserving of humankind's collective, defensive mobilization.[16] In America the sequence was reversed. In the first half of the nineteenth century, Thoreau's *Walden* became an introspective call for a return to simple authenticity and a declaration of independence from society.[17] By the first half of the twentieth century, Americans had come to think of jungles as grim landscapes, the realm of dangerous apes and violent peoples. In memories and imaginations, the characteristics of forests are not firmly fixed.

England offers many examples of this fluidity. Shakespeare's "sea-walled garden" was Edenic and set on the road to discovery and, eventually, world domination. Garden design changed dramatically from intimate medieval to expansive estate gardens, marked first by manicured, formal areas and later by more natural, though carefully planned, parks.[18] Kitchen gardens were common among all social strata; formal gardens with trimmed hedges and geometric arbors were only for elite households. Despite many attempts at imitation, eighteenth-century England had no Versailles, where "aesthetic displays of control over natural forces yielded stunning

---

[12] Jackson 1984: 45.   [13] Harrison 1992: 108, 115–23; Scott 1998: 11–22.
[14] Jünger 2013.   [15] Peluso and Vandergeest 2011: 589.   [16] Enright 2008: 556.
[17] Cronon 1983.   [18] Tigner 2012: 1–2, 5; Hunt and Willis 1975: 1–46.

visual effects ... In the microcosm of the garden, the tools of French land-based politics were revealed in all their glory."[19] In contrast, London's Vauxhall was an innovation. It evolved from a formal garden catering to an aristocratic clientele to a kaleidoscopic pleasure garden and vivacious capitalist enterprise offering a public space wherein people who otherwise would never encounter each other could mingle.[20] Reflecting the growing complexity of social identities, nineteenth-century England proliferated a variety of gardens: wild, cottage, formal, and various syntheses.[21] And with the spreading of the British empire in the eighteenth and nineteenth centuries, landscaping practices linked imperial centers and colonial outposts.[22] Botanical gardens became one of the domestic symbols of empire.[23] It was only fitting when a young Princess Elizabeth compared the British empire in 1946 to an "English garden"– not formal and forced, but natural and organic.[24]

Garden and jungle or forest metaphors come up frequently in the sciences, the humanities, and the arts. Oxford mathematician Marcus Du Sautoy, for example, writes that "for any scientist the real challenge is not to stay within the secure garden of the known but venture out into wilds of the unknown."[25] For Fields Medal winner Maryam Mirzakhami, "doing research ... is like being lost in a jungle and trying to use all the knowledge that you can gather to come up with some new tricks, and with some luck you might find a way out."[26] Neuroscientists conceptualize the development of the synapses between brain neurons in garden termin-ology, as a process in which synapses are first exuberantly overproduced and subsequently "pruned."[27] And in his discussion of different kinds of scientific fraud, Charles Babbage writes about the trimming of experi-mental data, "clipping off little bits here and there from those observa-tions which differ most in excess from the mean."[28]

The Garden of Eden and other paradisal depictions of the Golden Age are the religious and classical mothers of European garden metaphors. Bereft of nature's seasonal cycle – birth, life, and death – God's garden lacked a defining sign of humanity. Did Eve perhaps take a bite from the forbidden fruit to find in nature's cycle the humanity that remained inaccessible to her in the celestial realm? Exiled to the real world, she did not lose touch with the divine – for on earth, a gardener's bottom is often pointing to heaven. In contrast to theological tracts, Hobbes's state of nature did not allow for any Edenic discourse.[29] Eventually, however,

---

[19] Mukerji 1997: 2.   [20] Dubois 2015; Coke and Borg 2011.   [21] Helmreich 2008: 274.
[22] Casid 2005; Herbert 2011; Barton 2000; Drayton 2000.   [23] Tigner 2012: 159–94.
[24] www.bbc.co.uk/archive/princesselizabeth/6602.shtml.   [25] Du Sautoy 2016: 8.
[26] Carey 2014.   [27] Neniskyte and Gross 2017.   [28] Chevassus-au-Louis 2019: 2.
[29] Moloney 1997.

the Hobbesian jungle, governed by Leviathan, was challenged by Proudhon's anarchist utopia.[30] More than a century later, while advocating social coordination without the state, public choice theorists searched for their utopian "equilibrium in the jungle."[31]

In eighteenth-century music, the free fantasia occupied a jungle-like space combining composition with improvisation – "fragmentary, subjective, open-ended, it simultaneously resists interpretation and offers itself promiscuously to multiple readings."[32] More generally, discourses of nature have been a major preoccupation for classical composers. Nature, natural settings, and outdoor spaces are recurrent opera themes. Many Baroque and later operas feature enchanting, bewitching, or seductive garden scenes.[33] Music composed by Mahler, Sibelius, Grieg, Bartok, and Copeland incorporate folklore traditions that have close connections to nature.[34] And in the twentieth century, Duke Ellington developed jungle jazz. Initially it was an exotic form of entertainment for white audiences frequenting Harlem's Cotton Club in the 1920s and 1930s. In the 1960s and 1970s, late in Ellington's career, jungle became a self-conscious reclaiming of a diasporic history for African and African-American audiences. A generation later, as part of the rave scene, jungle became a genre of electronic music.

In philosophy, theater, movies, and literature, gardens and forests are also persistent metaphors. Acknowledging its intrinsic value, philosopher Michael Smith advocates "letting the jungle in," arguing that ethical concerns about the jungle and the environment more generally should not focus on the relative distance between moral objects and ourselves, but on a community of relationships that commands respect and care.[35] The French poet and playwright Antonin Artaud sought a radical break from the carefully scripted, grammatically correct language and its predictable order that modern audiences had rejected for their pretentious and unrealistic claim of France, and the French, as a well-tended garden.[36] He pleaded instead for the primacy of the body as a jungle where anarchic impulses could be acted out. The 1955 movie *Blackboard Jungle* stirred debate about its treatment of teenage violence in America's inner-city schools.[37] For Werner Herzog, writer and director of the epic 1982 film *Fitzcarraldo*, the jungle was the attractive and yet repulsive epitome of excess. Rudyard Kipling's *The Jungle Book* offered a series of

---

[30] Coyne 2003: 557–58.   [31] Piccione and Rubinstein 2007.   [32] Richards 2001: 15.

[33] Hunter 1993. Haydn's oratorios, Act IV of Mozart's *The Marriage of Figaro*, the middle acts of Wagner's *Tristan*, and Klingsor's magic garden in *Parsifal* all draw on garden and jungle or forest metaphors.

[34] Peattie 2015: 8; Grimley 2006.   [35] Smith 1991: 152.   [36] Artaud 1958: 74–83.

[37] Stoever-Ackermann 2011.

animal fables set in the Indian jungle, where fantastically unpredictable events were set in motion.[38] And Upton Sinclair's *The Jungle* became a classic depiction of the raw capitalism of America's meat-packing industry at the outset of the twentieth century.[39]

The American West is also filled with jungle or forest and garden imagery. Nineteenth-century American landscape painting shaped popular imaginations by depicting the frontier west of the Mississippi as an idyllic, unspoiled land inhabited by "noble savages."[40] The frontier's most famous and persistent proponent, Jackson Turner, disagreed. The West was a meeting point of forest and garden, savagery and civilization. American democracy emerged from the forest as it regenerated from America's forever moving frontier.[41] In the twentieth century, America's pastoral dreams and imagination were transformed by the assault of an industrial machine that wreaked havoc inside the garden without destroying its mythical powers. Nick Carraway, the narrator in F. Scott Fitzgerald's *The Great Gatsby*, struggles emotionally with the "garden" and "wilderness" images of the New World. Gatsby impersonates the American Adam, and America exemplifies a "complex pastoralism" forged in history and through politics.[42] A century later, the experience with garden cities and the environmental necessity of lowering the carbon imprint of urban life points to a possible narrowing of the difference between machine and garden.[43] Some have gone so far as calling postwar Oakland an "industrial garden."[44]

The garden metaphor aptly captures Nau's analysis in Chapter 6, just as the forest metaphor shines through much of Duara's Chapter 7. Nau expresses a profound worry that high modernity may rob humanity of the ability to make individuals accountable for their choices. We risk, he argues, losing sight of the importance of the self-extending gardener's care for and cultivation of the welfare of life nourished in humanity's garden. Expressing a worldview that goes beyond humanist Newtonianism, Duara looks for civil society actors whose holistic cosmologies and religious resources may equip them to address the counterfinalities that are threatening the planet's very existence in high modernity.

---

[38] Kipling 1894.   [39] Sinclair 1906.   [40] Goetzmann and Goetzmann 1986.
[41] Smith 1950: 251, 253.   [42] Lewis 1955: 197; Marx 1964: 356–57, 363.
[43] Hurley and Reynolds 2014: 77.
[44] Self 2003: 23. The "jungle" of Japan's chaotic cities conveys a dynamism lacking from planned cities in other parts of the world. Half a century later, a proposed design for Berlin's new Humboldt Forum museum would conceal the façade of the restored historical Hohenzollern palace with lianas and plant a jungle on its roof. http://hybridspa celab.net/project/humboldt-jungle/. Accessed 03/12/20.

Nau pushes back against what he regards as relationalism's attack on the Enlightenment values of rationality and individuality.[45] Following Max Weber, he contends that individual human beings, with their capacity for self-consciousness and reason, give meaning to the social and natural world. While reason is only one among several human faculties, it is the one that creates space for choice and hence accountability in human affairs. Relationalism, by contrast, accords greater influence to nonrational faculties – emotion, religion, intuition, habit – and diffuses the agency for change throughout a holistic universe that leaves little room for individual responsibility.

In line with Dilthey and Weber, Nau argues that it is a mistake to model social science after natural science. The Newtonian worldview was never simply atomistic and disenchanted. It was inspired by a Christian (Protestant) worldview valuing individual human beings and a predictable cosmos. Weber secularized that view: human beings, not the divine, give meaning to life. For Nau, relationalists hold that the quantum world implies a universe of entanglement and nonlocality that dispenses with reasoning individuals and insists on the observed world as the only one we can know. For Nau, the individual and an objective universe do not disappear in quantum science or scientific cosmology. The investigator becomes more important than ever, but as an "outside" actor who asks the questions. And for Nau the objective world exists and remains the only basis for supporting or disproving quantum propositions.

Because the world is holistic and is open to interpretations offered by all worldviews, Nau argues, relationalism has nothing to say about individual or collective ethical and moral responsibilities. It simply denies the human freedom to choose and be held responsible. What's left are sciences that blend diverse values with localized (not universal) experimentation (trial and error) and are compatible but not commensurable, harmonious but not integral, and equivalent but not competitive. Multiple beliefs and realities cut or "smear" into one another like quantum waves. They blend and harmonize. But what if multiple worldviews do not harmonize? What if some worldviews condone slavery, genocide, discrimination against women (Islam in Saudi Arabia) or minorities (Uighurs in China), holy war against the infidel, and so on? Do we welcome those worldviews too, or consider them wrong only in their specific time but not in general (respecting quantum locality)? The Weberian worldview – the human capacity for individual agency, free

---

[45] Chapter 6.

thinking, and choice – for Nau is an indispensable defense against those sorts of evil.

In Chapter 7, Duara's hyper-humanist concern with the Anthropocene and planetary politics offers a striking contrast to Nau's humanist engagement with international politics as it is conventionally understood. Duara works within a conceptual approach that relies on individual and distributed agency, relational and processual thinking, layered and interactive temporalities, and a willingness to explore worldviews other than Newtonian humanism. He focuses on China's rise, as well as on an issue that receives no specific mention in Nau's chapter: the ocean as a concrete illustration of the metaphorical jungle. Duara responds to a profound crisis of high modernity that China's rise accentuates as the world is struggling to find a sustainable future.[46] Since the ocean (or jungle) threatens to submerge the planet, Duara is profoundly skeptical of Nau's claim of the overwhelmingly beneficial control of humanist Newtonianism over nature.

Duara locates his argument at the point where humanism meets hyper-humanism and Newtonian science meets Post-Newtonian science. He builds on both the substantialism of Newtonianism and the relational and processual ontology of the world of quantum physics and scientific cosmology, embodied in and by the ocean. For Duara, efficiency-driven, resource-exploiting, nature-controlling, and competing nation-states are the epistemic engine driving the conventional realist or liberal worldview that frames current world orders and world politics. Central to that worldview is nationalism as a secular religion that has transfigured salvation into progress – testimony to the dynamic achievements of the Enlightenment projects and modern science and technology.

In China's past, the issue of otherness differs from the sharp distinction between national self and other in the Westphalian system. Indifference, conversion, negotiation, and occasionally conquest were played out in a world conceptualized as concentric discs that went out of focus the further removed they were from the Heavenly City. Insiders were civilized people who belonged. Outsiders were beasts who did not. And an intermediary disc consisted of various kinds of semi-barbarians who might become civilized and absorbed through continuous interaction with insiders.[47] Expressed in open-ended, flexible tribute practices and language games, the traditional Chinese world order and worldview, Duara argues, differed greatly from the codes and rules of the Westphalian system. The Chinese order was hierarchical and paternalistic rather than constituted by states equal in legal status. Unlike European states,

[46] Duara 2015.   [47] Katzenstein 2012: 3, 6.

the rulers of imperial China were for the most part uninterested in controlling space lying beyond imperial frontiers. Military operations, mostly limited, were designed to stabilize the tributary system at the frontier rather than seeking to control the foreign territories beyond it. What mattered was the symbolic subordination of neighboring states, communities, and groups that were otherwise peripheral to China.

The contrast among different kinds of cosmopolitanism and nationalism is unmistakable, as Michael Barnett shows in Chapter 5. Barnett distinguishes between a revisionist Zionism that builds on a mixture of territorial and particularistic components and a rooted cosmopolitanism indebted to deterritorialized and universal building blocks. These conceptions fit into the Westphalian system more readily than traditional Chinese notions of hierarchically negotiated harmony. Duara argues that, at least to some extent, that system lingers on in contemporary China's worldview, expressed in the ideals of harmony, authority, and nonintervention. This vision appears to be at odds with Westphalia, even though the Belt and Road initiative has unfolded along Westphalian lines of capitalism, nationalism, and statism. Duara is uncertain what differences may emerge as China becomes a superpower. China has become a driving force of the contemporary epistemic engine shaping global developments. It entered the garden of modernity on a path different from the one charted by the Enlightenment projects; but we know it arrived because its worldview's reliance on Newtonian humanism can be seen everywhere. Within this framework, China has invested greatly in clean energy and poor countries, while at the same time outsourcing its requirements for natural resources and intensifying its authoritarian techniques of surveillance and suppression. In the foreseeable future, Duara argues, China is unlikely to offer a new vision of a global order.

Coupled tightly with China's ascendancy, the rising ocean is destroying life as we know it. High modernity contains unknowable futures toward which nations are racing, perhaps unstoppably. Such counterfinalities point beyond the walls of the Newtonian-humanist garden, toward dimly perceived alternatives with different cosmologies, moralities, and possibilities. Even though there exist no ready-made alternatives, the bulk of the world's population may not fully believe in the disenchanted cosmology of modernity. The *Panchashila* "principle-based development" movement of decolonizing nations, Iranian theocracy, and Saudi Arabia's neofeudalism are not viable alternatives to the "hegemonic doxa" of Newtonian humanism and the Westphalian state system that currently organize world politics. In the future, pandemics and other natural disasters may become more effective brakes than the competition between states. For Duara, the ocean is the real and metaphorical incarnation of planetary processes that create unpredictable effects that Newtonian humanism struggles to explain and cope with. Duara ends with the thought that protection of human rights and the defense of a world endangered by the intellectual forces that made those rights more or less secure offer a dual moral mandate for an era that both builds on and transcends conventional Newtonian-humanist premises, exhortations, and critiques.

Experiments. Before presenting my overall argument that parks comprise bridges between garden and jungle, let us first stroll through the garden of experiments and trek in the forest of experimentation. [48] Since the world is conceptualized in Newtonian terms as a decomposable system, theories are tested via application on its constituent parts.[49] Specifically, the testing of large theories is helped by scrutinizing subsidiary propositions or exploring causal mechanisms in controlled environments. Furthermore, experiments are conducted under the presumption that the world is marked by discrete causes and effects that can be captured by probabilistic or deterministic laws.[50] The attempt to control for all but one or, at most, a small number of variables, is central to experimental studies that cannot rely on randomization in a laboratory setting.[51] Experimental work sometimes reports statistical significance tests even when those effects are small, of short duration, and highly unstable over time. Most of the time, however, we are interested in the size of a statistical effect rather than its existence.[52] And the assessment of size requires substantive argumentation and agreement among communities of experts and, perhaps, as in physics, a priori theoretically informed specification. There is no substitute for scientific, policy, or personal judgments. Physicists do not rely much on standard tests of statistical significance and are wary of replacing judgments with tables of conventionally defined goodness-of-fit measures.[53]

---

[48] I am grateful to David Bateman, Alexandra Blackman, Alexandra Cirone, Ilene Grabel, Sabrina Karim, Sarah Kreps, Douglas Kriner, Adam Levine, Bryn Rosenfeld, Geoffrey Wallace, Jeremey Wallace, and Christopher Way for their critical comments and suggestions on earlier drafts of this section.

[49] Green and Gerber 2002: 822–23, 828.

[50] Druckman, Green, Kuklinski, and Lupia 2011; Teele 2014; Gerber and Green 2012; Chilton and Tingley 2013; Hyde 2015.

[51] Conjoint experiments seek to identify the causal impact of a potentially larger number of factors on some quantity or outcome of interest. See Hainmueller, Hopkins, and Yamamoto 2014.

[52] Gaines, Kulinski, and Quirk 2006; McCloskey and Ziliak 2008a; Gerber and Green 2012: 65–66. The field of American politics, and public policy more generally, typically focuses on the magnitude of effects, for example of different modes of increasing voting. Green and Gerber's (2015) focus on behavioral outcomes makes it more intuitive and easier to calculate effects than the attitudinal outcomes typically measured in the survey experiments reported by students of international relations.

[53] McCloskey and Ziliak 2008b: 42–44, 51–52.

In contrast to students of American politics, comparative politics, and public policy, students of international relations rely heavily on survey experiments. Most often, they simply are in no position to conduct field experiments on substantively important questions. Unfortunately, the external validity of survey experiments is highly suspect; for example, asking respondents about their policy choices in an imagined nuclear crisis simply cannot duplicate decision-making dynamics in a real nuclear crisis. Furthermore, in the analysis of international politics, experiments are typically considered a neutral mirror of reality, leaving little or no trace in the world. This presumed distancing between observer and objects in the world is a marker of the Newtonian worldview that often does not bear out when applied in the social sciences. With quantum mechanics very much on his mind as early as 1946, Morgenthau warned against the use of experiments, for both theoretical and practical reasons.[54] In taking measurements of the social world, the social scientist cannot help but change that world. She "does not remain an indifferent observer but intervenes actively as both product and creator of social conditions."[55] Measurement alters the characteristics of the object that is being measured.[56] It is thus very difficult, if not impossible, to create proper experimental setups. In the field of economic development, for example, foreign agencies and their local agents have heavy boots and deep pockets. In the administration of treatments in the field, a lot goes on other than the treatment.[57] Since phenomena are difficult to replicate reliably, especially outside of a laboratory, "experimental regularities should perhaps be interpreted in terms of human skill rather than [of] stable, underlying entities and the functioning of the laws of nature."[58]

Understandably, proponents of experiments disagree. They believe that tight controls over all plausibly relevant conditions except the treatment establish a firm ground for causal inference. A philosopher of physics, Nancy Cartwright, and a heterodox economist, George DeMartino, disagree. Cartwright argues that as we shift from controlled micro- to uncontrolled macro-environments, we run into the fact that all "generalizations" in the natural and, by extension, social world are ceteris paribus laws.[59] They are not general; they obtain only under specifically defined circumstances. This limits greatly their contribution to the search for generalizability and simplification. Furthermore, DeMartino argues, all causal arguments about the past, present, and future depend on counterfactual reasoning.[60] It is not only our knowledge of the future

---

[54] Morgenthau 1946: 125–44.   [55] Morgenthau 1946: 143.
[56] Morgenthau 1946: 141, 143–44.   [57] Deaton and Cartwright 2018: 11.
[58] Porter 1995: 13.   [59] Cartwright 1999: 25–29.   [60] DeMartino 2018.

that is fictitious and uncertain, as critics of rational expectation theories have argued. It is also our knowledge of the past, for we do not and cannot distinguish between contending counterfactuals concerning past events. This is true of all randomized control trials in field and survey experiments.[61] Whether World War I would have happened in the absence of the assassination of the Archduke is based unavoidably on a constructed narrative about the past. In sharp contrast to Newtonianism, all causal claims in a quantum worldview are based on counterfactuals about different, possible worlds. Theories are based not on what is seen but on what can't ever be seen. Epistemically insecure, theories "hold to distinct fantasies, generated by their distinct theoretical frameworks, which cannot ever be subjected to knock-out empirical or theoretical tests for assessing who, if anyone, has the uniquely correct counterfactual."[62] We solve this thorny problem by adhering to the convention that only one framework is feasible or legitimate. For the proponents of experiments, that one convention is a Newtonianism that denies a constitutive role of uncertainty. Put differently, we accept without further thought what we purport to test empirically.

In survey and field experiments, randomized controlled trials (RCTs) are the gold standard. In one over-the-top endorsement, the *British Medical Journal* wrote that "Britain has given the world Shakespeare, Newtonian physics, the theory of evolution, parliamentary democracy – and the randomized trial."[63] Nancy Cartwright is more laconic when she writes that randomized control trials are not the gold standard, for the simple reason that there are no gold-standard experiments beyond those held under extremely narrow scope conditions and thus resistant to generalizations.[64] The average of a treatment effect, though useful, does not tell us what percentage of the population is affected positively, or negatively, or not at all.[65] We need to understand not only the experiment but also its context and operative mechanisms before we can evaluate its relevance to our understanding of the world we are part of. In a world marked by heterogeneity and large numbers of covariates, the knowledge gained from randomized control trials is often oversold.[66] Experiments are good for isolating specific treatment effects. They are narrow by design. Local average treatment effects apply only to the specific treatment applied to a specific sample. External validity remains a huge challenge when it comes to generalizing the results of one or a few experiments. When all is said and done, experiments are precise and narrow.

---

[61] DeMartino 2018: 10.   [62] DeMartino 2018: 13.   [63] Deaton 2010: 438.
[64] Quoted in Deaton 2010: 426.   [65] Deaton 2010: 449.
[66] Deaton and Cartwright 2018: 3, 10.

To understand "what works," we need a theory of why things work rather than just experiments that test whether things work.[67] Simple extrapolation and generalization from repeated successful replication is not a theory in and of itself. Many practitioners of experiments agree that well-established results do not necessarily export to other settings. It takes good reasons to justify even making the attempt. And such reasons often do not exist.[68] Local results must be linked to more general mechanisms. The chicken infers from repeated evidence that when the farmer comes in the morning, it will be fed. A good inference, until Christmas morning when the farmer comes, wrings the chicken's neck, and feeds it to his family. Both randomized control trials and field and survey experiments run this chicken risk. To be sure, proper specification of scope conditions, heterogeneous treatment effects, and how to address problems of replication offer avenues for protecting experimental research against the charge of claiming more than it can prove. However, the deeper problem is not with the method itself but with a possible lack of understanding of the social conditions that give rise to the causal relationship the chicken, or experimenter, observes.[69]

At best, randomized control trials can establish "circumstantial" causality that points to observable effects under specific historical circumstances, rather than generalized causality. All too often experiments are based on the assumption that "the universe proceeds by causality and so the future that lies ahead of us is as determined as our history."[70] But, as Blaug mischievously suggests, history repeats itself because "historians repeat each other."[71] Since for many historians (and some physicists) the past is as open and indeterminate as the future, this is at best an argument for a world of weak causal effects, with the concept of cause encompassing Aristotle's four different kinds of causes rather than being restricted only to Hume's notion of efficient cause. Furthermore, long chains of causation cannot be foreseen with "any degree of certainty."[72] No easy shortcuts get us around the problems raised by differences in contexts, mechanisms, ceteris paribus conditions, and counterfactuals – other than the confidence instilled by a Newtonian worldview of politics.

Experimentation.[73] Experimentation that reflects a Post-Newtonian worldview proceeds along a different line of reasoning. It assumes that appropriate scientific practice is rooted not in a better philosophy of epistemological and ontological claims or a better set of methods, but in

---

[67] Deaton 2010: 442.   [68] Deaton and Cartwright 2018: 10–12.
[69] Deaton and Cartwright 2018: 11–14.   [70] Basu 2014: 459.   [71] Blaug 1963: 152.
[72] Morgenthau 1946: 127.
[73] I would like to thank Ilene Grabel for commenting critically on an earlier version of this section.

a better understanding of the scientific enterprise. Rather than imagining that a well-designed experiment can yield insights on widely generalized phenomena, it starts with the proposition that one well-designed and focused experiment can yield insights that, at best, another such experiment can build on.[74] Experiments are events; experimentation is a process. In practice, both the natural and the social sciences are based on trial and error. They are "multifaceted, epistemologically opportunistic" and not dogmatically associated with a particular philosophy.[75] But, in contrast with the practice of experiments, experimentation "disavows the notion ... that causality and its measurement can be fixed across time and place and that any occurrence can be isolated from its context."[76] This is no small matter. In the analysis of world politics, Henry Kissinger, a realist here turned Post-Newtonian, holds that context is everything.[77] Stressing a profound similarity between the natural and the social sciences, experimentation is informed by a Post-Newtonian worldview.

Albert Hirschman was a man of forests. He developed his very own Post-Newtonian social scientific approach. It was well attuned to making things work without searching for law-like generalizations, relying on any one "ism," or touting any one "killer method."[78] He was a heterodox economist with wide-ranging interests who disliked blueprint economics and its cookie-cutter application to any issue, including development economics. Opposed to any and all orthodoxies, he valued experimentation with new forms of practice and institutional arrangements. His belief in small-scale experimentation resonates with those who advocate experiments more generally. However, he rigorously opposed the temptation to argue that any lesson learned from small-scale experiments could be scaled up to larger settings marked by unknown yet surely different conditions. Learning by doing, listening rather than preaching, humility, and the capacity to adjust and adapt to changing circumstances were the hallmarks of his approach. He favored incoherence over coherence and pragmatism over plans.

Simple approaches to complex problems were anathema to him, and so were overblown grand claims in the name of Science (with a capitalized S), often enunciated as part of a Newtonian worldview. Urbinati writes that "in a time in which ... nothing seemed to work without the predefined guidance of a weltanschauung, Albert persisted in living outside of and without any weltanschauung."[79] Not quite. His disposition was

---

[74] In this it resembles Weber's suggestion of the usefulness of ideal types drawn from empirical research as abstract stepping stones for the next empirical inquiry.
[75] Wight 2013: 340.   [76] Adams 2020: 360.   [77] Mead 2018.
[78] Grabel 2017: 29–54; Meldolesi 1995.
[79] Urbinati 2015. See also the epigraph to Chapter 1.

Post-Newtonian. In a complex world filled with unknowable uncertainties, he opposed reductionist models, epistemic certainty, and the pretense of scientifically based authority over policy. Hirschman's writings from the late 1950s did much to end the "big push, high development" theory of the 1940s and 1950s.[80] After half a century of obscurity, development economics has recently been swept up by the excitement of RCTs, which was both widely noted and criticized when it was recognized with the 2019 Nobel Prize for Economics.[81] Taken together with the macro approach of large-N statistical studies, this micro approach may undergird a new and better development economics.[82] But Hirschman would have presented both epistemic and ethical grounds for skepticism of the positivist RCT approach in general, and especially its dubious claim that microscopic experiments can lead to actionable knowledge about how to achieve large-scale growth and development. He would likely have been repulsed by the power disparities between economic experts and vulnerable populations exposed to ethically dubious experiments. More likely, he would have welcomed the pragmatic learning-by-doing approach to development through an inclusive growth strategy, as illustrated by China since 1979.[83]

Intellectual opportunism is central to experimentation. Searching out uniqueness and novelty requires taking advantage of spaces for innovation rather than relying on preconceived notions and plans. Deep knowledge of local contexts, awareness of sequential and cumulative changes that are not legible from quick visits of research sites made accessible by local gatekeepers, and suspicion of efforts to transplant observed local average treatment effects to unrelated and distant sites are hallmarks of an experimentation approach. Most importantly, it is the faith in and embrace of what is possible.[84]

Experimentation is based on a worldview that acknowledges the existence of uncertainty, and incomplete, dispersed, partial, tacit, and limited knowledge. It is also marked by humility. Knowledge of the future is irreducibly uncertain and typically cannot be accessed by probabilistic thinking. For Hirschman, the need for predictability and the embrace of epistemic certainty and parsimony supporting general paradigms and laws was a serious neurosis that afflicted economics and other social sciences that were also grounded in Newtonianism.[85] His commitment to complexity was as unshakable as his commitment to intervention. Practical intervention always has unknowable effects that are set in motion by contending forces and a totality of circumstances that is

[80] Hirschman 1958.   [81] Reddy 2013; Dehejia 2016.   [82] Grabel 2017: 32–33.
[83] Ang 2016.   [84] Grabel 2017: 33.   [85] Grabel 2017: 37.

unknown to the researcher or practitioner at the time the intervention is made.

For Hirschman, the world is an open and complex system that is contingent, adaptive, and unknowable in many of its features. Shorn of the epistemic error of viewing the world as a simple, linear, decomposable, and analytically tractable system, Hirschman's approach expressed the hope of exploiting unforeseen possibilities for improving it.[86] Hirschman's "possibilism," Ilene Grabel writes, "is grounded in faith in the demonstrated capacities of individuals, institutions, and societies to develop diverse, creative solutions to unforeseen challenges and development problems. Possibilism encapsulates the enduring bias for hope."[87] Hirschman regarded a nonprojected, open future as a truly inalienable right for every person or nation.[88] As did Russian Nobel Prize–winning physicist and human rights activist Andrei Sakharov, who wrote in a letter from his exile in Gorky: "fortunately, the future is unpredictable and also – because of quantum effects – uncertain."[89] As for the social sciences, in Hirschman's view they often "consider it beneath their scientific dignity to deal with possibility until *after* it has become actual and can then at least be redefined as a probability."[90] Convinced of the importance of uncertainty, he resolutely refused to cede possibilistic ground to probabilistic thinking.

Playing off Adam Smith's "invisible hand," Hirschman's "hiding hand" principle captures many of these observations.[91] The hiding hand recognizes ignorance as a precondition for rather than an obstacle to progress. In most domains, actors unavoidably are ignorant and make mistakes as they operate under conditions of uncertainty. This ignorance can be highly productive. Embarking on a project that seems manageable at the outset and then turns out to be fiendishly difficult, ignorance cultivates unknown capacities for innovation and adaptation. Hirschman's hiding hand beneficially conceals those difficulties and thus frees previously untapped powers of creativity. Without our ignorance, we would not start projects and thus forego the possibility of learning and the creation of possibly long-term beneficial outcomes or effects. We stumble into progress rather than plan for it. Predictions based on laws of change are misleading, and predictive failures breed success. We can literally "fall from error into truth."[92] Hirschman did not

---

[86] Hirschman 1971.   [87] Grabel 2017: 46.   [88] Hirschman 1971: 30.
[89] http://people.bu.edu/gorelik/AIP_Sakharov_Photo_Chrono/AIP_Sakharov_Photo_Chr onology.html. Accessed 09/30/20.
[90] Hirschman 1980: xii.
[91] Hirschman 1967; Gladwell 2013; Meldolesi 1995: 38, 118–20.
[92] Hirschman 1967: 13, 20.

believe that context-independent and timeless factors, such as economic fundamentals, determine the success or failure of our projects in the world. Instead, he acknowledged the importance of a norm-based, practical wisdom that embraces "possibilism" and humility as two of its guiding principles.

How can experimentation be made workable in the analysis of world politics that relies heavily on survey experiments? In a paper indebted to quantum theorizing, Leonardo Orlando points to "elicitation" interviews as a research method that may bolster an experimentation approach.[93] It offers a way of probing consciousness and experience through "introspection" as an alternative to treating humans as responding to set questions in survey experiments. The elicitation method seeks to get around a well-established finding in psychology that shows reliable self-reporting to be impossible because mental processes cannot be accessed introspectively.[94] However, being unaware of a mental act does not mean we cannot access it with an interview method that differs from the conventional approach. Retroactive awareness can activate passive memory and the constant, involuntary memorization of lived experience that escapes our notice.[95] To access that awareness requires bypassing explanations as to *why* a subject did or did not do X and guiding the subject to her cognitive processes through the "elicitation interview method," which leads the subject to share increasingly detailed elements of how past choice processes unfolded. Elicitation interviews rely on rigorous protocols that direct attention to the description of fine-grained elements of the evoked choice process while deflecting the subject's attention from explanations and abstractions.[96] This method seeks to remedy our normal blindness to lived experience and avoids diving ever deeper into the trap of providing post-hoc reasons for past choices.[97] Decision points are productively conceptualized as choice processes that are inherently indeterminate. This method self-consciously foregoes the search for universal laws or generalizations.

Beyond issues of methodology, how we think about the world has causal effects and will affect how we might want to change it. Hirschman's possibilism sidesteps both the overconfidence that we can fix everything and the fatalism that nothing can be changed. Instead of

---

[93] Orlando 2020: 468–471. I thank Dr. Orlando for reviewing the accuracy of this paragraph for me.

[94] Orlando 2020: 469–70.   [95] Orlando 2020: 470.   [96] Orlando 2020: 470–71.

[97] Orlando 2020: 472–74 disarms the criticisms of interpretive, retrospective, and unverifiable representational biases by quantizing introspection – that is, by linking minimally interpreted descriptions of decision processes to transversal structures operating like Schrödinger's equations without depending on individual subjects or specific contexts.

epistemic certainty, he believed in the importance of path-dependent change, small steps, local contexts, unintended consequences, and adaptive learning. Above all, he prized experimentalism and improvisation as practices, along with slow reform-mongering that creates the possibility for substantial change.

Conclusion. Informed by different worldviews, as we make our way in the world we typically are unaware of uncertainty or unwilling to acknowledge its existence. Experiments help us understand the risk-based world we seek to control on the basis of results gleaned either after manipulating conditions in a laboratory or performing smartly designed field or survey experiments. Experiments share in the hope of studying the effects of treatment assignments and then, perhaps, scaling up local results to offer general solutions to real-world problems. Experimentation has less lofty aspirations. It is based on the notion of learning by doing under always shifting conditions in a dynamically evolving world filled with uncertainties that resist law-like generalizations. Like risk and uncertainty, experiments and experimentation are two halves of one walnut.

Bentley Allan concludes his chapter with an ecumenical argument for a processual social science that strives to generate general or middle-ground theories. The aim is not to create a catalogue of laws or mechanisms, supported by experiments. Rather, processual social science should offer an "agile base for an experimental approach to politics."[98] This stance might help in orienting us to the uncertainties of the world, juggling several causal factors, observing trade-offs, and locating potential points of engagement: "By mapping the complexity of social worlds within legible frameworks, we can provide a flexible starting point for understanding and action without the dream of control."[99]

A similar sense of intellectual openness in an indeterminate world is also central to Milja Kurki's capacious treatment of how to think about causation and Peter Galison's detailed studies of the material culture of microphysics. Kurki seeks to free the concept of cause from the deterministic and mechanistic connotations that it has for many students of world politics and social theorists.[100] She probes a multiplicity of meanings that the concept of cause can have, so that we can appreciate the many

---

[98] Chapter 8.

[99] Chapter 8. A similar sense of intellectual openness in an indeterminate world is also central to Milja Kurki's capacious treatment of how to think about causation and Peter Galison's detailed studies of the material culture of microphysics. Kurki seeks to free the concept of cause from the deterministic and mechanistic connotations that it has for many students of world politics and social theorists.

[100] Kurki 2008: 11–12. Clarke and Primo (2012) remind us repeatedly and helpfully that different models serve different purposes. In testing models "final cause" may therefore be as important, or more important, than "efficient cause." Most scholars of world

nondeterministic senses in which causes can work. In doing so she embeds the Humean notion of efficient cause (observed regularity relations of patterned events) within Aristotle's broader conceptual apparatus, which acknowledges three additional notions of cause: material (the passive potentiality of matter), formal (defining shapes or relations), and final (purposes that guide both rest and change). Kurki thus provides a rich and flexible understanding of causation that locates efficient causes in their relation to final causes and within the constitutive or causally enabling or constraining context understood in terms of material and formal causes. The task of analysis is not to isolate one kind of cause, but to focus on the complex concatenation of different types of causes, thus resisting the reductionist impetus to focus only on risk and thereby neglect uncertainty as a constitutive part of world politics.

Focusing on what he calls zones of exchange, Galison warns against the barrenness of all dichotomies.[101] Here: positivism and science as a series of prescribed and rigorous rules for discovery, replication, verification, and confirmation, and theory-independent data offering an empirical form of knowledge drawn from raw experience. There: creative muddling through and adaptive learning catching emergent processes. What holds physics together, Galison argues, is not a single scientific apparatus or a veneer of rationality concealing the exertion of raw interests, but a patchwork of many things and practices. Instrument makers, theorists, and experimenters generate and operate in distinct cultures connected by trading zones and border regions that reveal how the whole of physics fits together. Communication is made possible by different pidgin and creole languages that pre-Einsteinians, Einsteinians, and post-Einsteinians fashion as they seek contingent, local forms of coordination among dynamically evolving material and epistemic traditions marked by different interpretive practices. This is where and how the whole of physics is worked out. It should be no surprise, then, that in the polycultural history of physics – and perhaps the social sciences and the analysis of world politics – the meanings of "experiments" and "experimentation" have

politics are unaware of conceptions of cause that differ from and go beyond the concept of efficient cause.

[101] She probes a multiplicity of meanings that the concept of cause can have, so that we can appreciate the many nondeterministic senses in which causes can work. In doing so she embeds the Humean notion of efficient cause (observed regularity relations of patterned events) within Aristotle's broader conceptual apparatus, which acknowledges three additional notions of cause: material (the passive potentiality of matter), formal (defining shapes or relations), and final (purposes that guide both rest and change). Kurki thus provides a rich and flexible understanding of causation that locates efficient causes in their relation to final causes and within the constitutive or causally enabling or constraining context understood in terms of material and formal causes. The task of analysis is not

been unstable and contested for the last 350 years. This would not be a surprise for Harry Lipkin, a theoretical particle physicist. He writes that "the best physics I have known was done by experimenters who ignored theorists completely and used their own intuitions to explore new domains where no one had looked before."[102]

Expressed as the practice of experiments and experimentation in the history of physics, Newtonian and Post-Newtonian worldviews resonate with a long arc of intellectual history. Toulmin argues that for about 300 years, from the middle of the seventeenth century to the middle of the twentieth, philosophy focused on the general, the timeless, and the theoretical. Before and after, in its medieval and post-Wittgensteinian forms, it focused instead on the local, the timely, and the practical.[103] Montaingne and Descartes exemplify this difference, as reflected in "the practical modesty and the intellectual freedom of Renaissance humanism, and the theoretical ambitions and intellectual constraints of 17th-century rationalism."[104] For Toulmin, "cosmopolis" offers a comprehensive account of the world that binds things together in politico-theological as much as in scientific-explanatory terms. In the early eighteenth century, the cosmopolitical function of the Newtonian worldview counted for more than its explanatory function.[105] Today, Newtonianism's cosmopolitical function has fallen silent. And it is largely forgotten that Newton was an accomplished experimentalist. Unaware, we now focus only on the explanatory presuppositions of Newtonianism's worldview. Hirschman's plea for experimentation reminds us of the existence of a different, Post-Newtonian alternative that acknowledges uncertainty as an irreducible aspect of world politics.

10.2   Inhabiting the Same Park? Complementarities, Workarounds, and Values

Parks mix elements of forest and garden, sometimes in unexpected ways. Parks are designed to suppress the appearance of a garden's artificiality, its rigid imposition of discipline and fixed borders.[106] Seventeenth-century English gardens were highly artificial, walled environments. But as wilderness began its slow retreat from the English countryside, aesthetic preferences for fertile and cultivated scenery faded. Eighteenth-century sensibilities and fashions ran toward irregular, asymmetrical, and "natural" forms of gardening.[107] In the second half of that century,

---

[102] Quoted in Clarke and Primo 2012: 104.
[103] Toulmin 1990: 36; Toulmin 1982: 12, 231.   [104] Toulmin 1990: 42.
[105] Toulmin 1990: 128, 132.   [106] Zetzel 1989: 331.   [107] Williamson 1995: 1–4.

picturesque perspectives on nature invited visitors to participate in park landscapes guided by their own imaginations and interpretative freedoms. Nature was not seen as an immutable thing that reflects either garden or forest. Parks emerged as a hybrid of both.

In the words of Walpole, "the contiguous ground of the park without . . . was to be harmonized with the lawn within; and the garden in its turn was to be set free from its prim regularity, that it might assort with the wilder country without."[108] Parks were tended by livestock, not gardeners. Visually, gardens and parks began to resemble one another. Recessed methods of landscape design, such as the ha-ha, created a vertical barrier that cattle could not cross to enter the garden while preserving an uninterrupted view of the wider park landscape. Classical buildings, lakes, blocks of woodlands, or clumps of trees became widely accepted design elements of parks. And after parks were no longer treated as a habitat for deer, they became unfenced landscapes. Curvilinear and serpentine forms replaced linear plantings and geometric vistas. Appearing close to untreated nature, the visual simplicity of parks concealed a complex landscape design. Parks blurred the boundary between aesthetic and functional landscape, and between leisure and production.[109] English parks became models for Germany. One of the largest public parks in Europe, Munich's English Garden, dates back to the late eighteenth century. Many other German public gardens followed. Combining park and garden elements, Hamburg's *Stadtpark* was created in the early twentieth century.[110]

In an increasingly urban America, parks also offered a compromise between fast-paced city life and the more sedate countryside: "Machine and garden exist in a state of continual tension . . . [the park] was, in short, a pastoral 'middle' landscape in every sense of the term."[111] One of America's foremost landscape architects, Frederick Olmsted, argued that "the pastoral middle landscape was an appropriate compromise" between city and wilderness.[112] City parks were a place to reconstruct a way of life that had been lost.[113] Weaving together images of domesticated and wild nature, *Garden and Forest* was a weekly magazine in late nineteenth-century America that offered an integrative vision of city and nature.[114]

America's national parks offer a sharp contrast to such a peaceful vision. At the very moment that the frontier was vanishing, Americans sought to protect and celebrate the wilderness of the West as a symbol of its manifest destiny. But American ideas about wilderness changed over

---

[108] Quoted in Williamson 1995: 2.   [109] Williamson 1995: 75–78, 122–23.
[110] Richards 2001: 10, 28–30.   [111] Zetzel 1989: 291, 295.   [112] Cranz 1982: 24.
[113] Miller 1976: 181, 184.   [114] Hou 2012.

time. The country's first national park, Yellowstone, opened in 1872 to a delighted public who admired it mostly from afar. But by the end of the century, the wilderness of the national parks was linked indelibly to the Indian reservation policy, restricting Indians to isolated patches of land or assimilating native peoples into American society. In fact, it took decades to remove Indian populations from three of America's iconic parks: Yosemite, Yellowstone, and Glacier. Yosemite, for example, was a large-scale experiment of keeping "the animals in and the humans out."[115] Wilderness preservation and native dispossession were two aspects of one complex process that stretched over more than half a century. Wilderness was not natural and empty but populated and shaped by native populations who thought of the wilderness as tame.[116] Depopulation became the precondition for creating a man-made, artificial wilderness. Massive acts of human violence and cruelty were thus indelibly stamped as constitutive elements of America's national identity.

Not so in Olmsted's most important creation, New York's Central Park. Designed together with Calvert Vaux, it was modelled on Birkenhead, one of England's first public parks. Olmsted's approach to landscaping self-consciously and deliberately differed in both style and scale from gardening. It reflected design principles that diverged greatly from those of the gardeners of his day. He avoided flower-bedding and specimen-planting of hybrids as they violated the character of a park's natural surroundings. Letting things alone was central to Olmsted's art – an almost impossible dictum for any gardener.[117] He infused a combination of the pastoral and the picturesque with his philosophy of unconscious recreation and the importance of contemplation. A deliberate, eye-level interplay of light and shadow was intended to convey a heightened sense of mystery. The thick planting style in some parts of Olmsted's parks was borrowed from his encounter with the tropical jungles and forests he had wandered through while travelling in Central America in 1863.[118] "The result was a series of designs that combined richness and wildness of planting with unified composition."[119] Olmsted's reliance on picturesque landscapes broke with the geometrical and symmetrical designs of European gardens and parks that were laid out in a gardenesque style. Knowing that pure wilderness could not be recreated in urban settings, Olmsted opted instead for a compromise between pastoral transcendentalism and rural landscapes.[120]

---

[115] Schama 1995: 7.   [116] Spence 1999: 4–5.   [117] Howett 1998: 83.
[118] Beveridge 1977: 39–41.   [119] Beveridge 1977: 43.   [120] Taylor 1999: 436–38.

Olmsted's efforts to build pastoral scenery into parks were belittled by John Muir and other wilderness enthusiasts who found his scenery too tame. Philosophically, Olmsted was antagonistic to the idea of wilderness, and specifically to the semi-Hobbesian state of nature reigning at the American frontier. He regarded that state as antithetical to "civilization" as he defined it, with reference to principles of cosmopolitan community, common culture, and genteel order. He saw beautiful landscapes created in public parks both as powerful instruments for a vibrant democracy and profound symbols of a civilized society.[121] Central Park followed an explicitly political logic and a design inspired by a dual vision of democracy and landscaped art tailored to plutocratic and polyglot New York.[122] It was a space understood in terms not only of ownership and management, but also of public use and inclusiveness – a kind of modern village commons set up, in Thomas Bender's words, by a combination of Olmsted's "sincere feeling for the less fortunate with a somewhat manipulative concern."[123] Grounded in a stubborn democratic faith, Olmsted's approach also reflected the logic of social control and a "profoundly conservative concept of reform."[124]

Complementarities of Newtonian and Post-Newtonian Worldviews. Faith in order helped define Olmsted's vision of parks as a zone connecting gardens and forests. Similarly, Stuart Kauffman holds that nature's evolution is partly governed by the laws of nature, yet moves partly outside and beyond them.[125]

Haas and Nau appear to suggest that Newtonianism and Post-Newtonianism must be rivals.[126] The rhetorical strategy of their chapter conceals to the casual reader a possibility that they themselves suggest: Newtonianism and Post-Newtonianism may coexist in a complementary relationship with one another. "Lets assume," Haas and Nau write,

that the specific questions we are asking as investigators trigger the relationalist quantum world to yield the Weberian world ... That assumption is not inconsistent with the new relationalism and allows this Weberian analysis to proceed. After all, if Newtonian science is good enough for understanding tennis balls, but not quanta and galaxies (black holes), it may be good enough for the study of politics since the latter operates on the level of tennis balls not quanta or galaxies.[127]

---

[121] Lewis 1977: 388–89, 392–403.   [122] Blackmar and Rosenzweig 1994: 113–14.
[123] Quoted in Cranz 1982: 286.
[124] Blodgett 1976: 870. For example, the Olmstedt-designed Morningside Park in Northern Manhattan eventually became an effective barrier separating the predominantly minority, poor neighborhood of West Harlem from the predominantly white, middle-class neighborhood of Morningside Heights. See Solecki and Welch (1995: 95) and Schaffer and Smith (1986: 358).
[125] Kauffman 2008: 231–33, 287–88.   [126] Chapter 2, this volume.   [127] Chapter 2.

This is true. In comparison to Planck's constant h (which establishes the small but nontrivial difference between classical and quantum measurements), quantum effects are dependent on the size of an object multiplied by its typical momentum. When predicting the path of a flying tennis ball, uncertainties due to quantum theory are infinitesimal (about ten million billion billion billionths). When trying to describe the path of electrons moving in an atom, quantum uncertainties dominate.[128] Haas and Nau do not address, let alone resolve, the inherent contradiction between the inert materialism of their Newtonianism and the importance of human experience in their Weberianism. And they do not spell out the implication of their important point. Shaped by the laws of gravity, does world politics operate at the level of tennis balls, as they suggest? The world's leading physicist of tennis, Howard Brody, would probably have disagreed, acknowledging that individual ball control, motivation, mutual weakness recognition, and interaction with the spectators produce enough uncertainty to make the score of any match unpredictable.[129] Excitement-generating uncertainty completes its task before Newtonian physicists begin theirs.

Furthermore, in a worldview that includes Groves' notion of space-time, "there are relations at every scale crossing into every other scale. Which relations are most important, most operative, and most determinative ... depends upon the region investigated."[130] If the scale of a tennis match were like that of world politics, then both of them constitute regions that are a far cry from the Newtonian world of mechanistic laws yielding accurate predictions. Indeterminacy, unpredictability, and quantum weirdness thus can enter the orderly, classical model and become the stage for a Weberian analysis of world politics. Despite all their differences, there is a connection between Nau and Kurki: in different formulations, they both suggest that Newtonian and Post-Newtonian worldviews are complementary. For Kurki

[r]elational traditions pry open seemingly well-sealed liberal individuals or national communities, and reveal the "other aspects of ourselves," the porosity and comaking, the overlaps, the complex constitution of individuals and communities and species ... what is needed is fewer new total single global visions – a worldview; rather, what is needed is "multiplying viewpoints so as to complicate all 'provincial' or 'closed' views with new variants."[131]

Grove and Allan suggest such multiplying viewpoints by embedding a Weberian Newtonianism in more encompassing, complementary perspectives. Grove's analysis is deeply relational. He points to Weber's

---

[128] Pagels 1982: 90.   [129] The Economist 2015.   [130] Chapter 4, this volume,
[131] Chapter 3, this volume.

individualism as profoundly relational, constituted by four different modes of action: instrumental rationality, value rationality, emotions, and habits. The individual, in his reading of Weber, is not a unified actor (as Nau argues in his critique of relationalism in Chapter 6), but is constituted by a deep relationality between these four distinctive Weberian categories marked by "a plastic and oscillating intensity of relations" that constitute human consciousness and senses.[132] Grove's analysis of the Cuban missile crisis puts into a different scale the conventional depiction of the American President as the heroic leader holding in her hands "the football" that contains the codes for starting nuclear war. It was not the President that replaced a collectivity, Congress, in October 1962. Instead, it was one collectivity, the "nuclear-sovereign-assemblage," that replaced another, Congress.[133] Executive power rests on complex and evolving networks of a myriad of systems. In this relational account, individual accountability is submerged in a variety of assemblages and relationships. Grove argues that a perspective that only focuses on the accountability of a sovereign individual or groups of individuals, as do Haas and Nau in Chapter 2 and Nau in Chapter 6, downplays that the individual is embedded in relays, connections, resonances, and actants that are presupposed in each subsequent iteration of sovereign decisions layered into multiple streams of time: "The decision and the decider only appear singular when we truncate time and space to the moment the president 'pushes the button.'"[134] Put differently, individualism primes us to discern only an already constituted, single decider situated in time and space. This individualist orientation may undermine the capacity of members of a polity to resist or steer nuclear politics. Grove does not seek to replace sovereign decisions with assemblages. He insists instead that those decisions are embedded in fields of relations and resonances from which decisions emerge. In October of 1962, he argues, President Kennedy was "the titular focal point of an assemblage, a mascot not a quarterback."[135]

Similarly, conventional Weberian analysis, Allan argues in Chapter 8, is beholden to too narrow a worldview. Weber analyzes the rationalization of life embodied in scientific ideas that undermine traditional worldviews as constraints on action. Rationalization thus furthers disenchantment. Weber's failing was to not place himself reflexively within that history. Pushing historical analysis further and deeper, as Allan does, generates a vision of a relational self. It is constituted by cosmological elements that, propelled by individual choices and actions, generate changing worldviews. Two mainstays of

---

[132] Chapter 4.   [133] Chapter 4.   [134] Chapter 4.   [135] Chapter 4.

Newtonianism – materialism and object-orientation – are cosmological elements that have been incorporated into European and American political discourses and traditions. This makes Weberian value-orientations possible and natural, including the valorization of reason: "Reason could now be conceptualized and defined in means–ends terms as knowledge of the outside for the manipulation of the outside in the service of internal ends. Rationality itself is a value-orientation."[136] Put differently, rationalism is a product of history. It is not a natural object. And this crucial point, Allan argues, is missed by defenders of rational worldviews, like Haas and Nau in Chapter 2. Their "defense of individualism … is unpersuasive because it ignores the history of the concepts they themselves deploy."[137] Affirming agency, Haas and Nau make us see it as operating at the surface. For Allan, this is less than fully convincing. It simply does not go deep enough. Their Weberian map misses the territory, the cosmological background that constrains actors by placing them into a specific political landscape. The agency Haas and Nau highlight is relationally constituted. It is made possible by specific configurations of historical legacies and interactions with other actors. If a materialist and mechanical ontology had not prevailed over vitalist and organicist views in the nineteenth century, then the relational scientific worldview of emergence that informs Kurki's chapter would perhaps not be "new," as Kauffman calls it. And a much messier and less predictable world would perhaps be taken for granted, rather than the rationally legible world of mechanically interacting matter.[138] Allan's historicized relationalism situates Weberian analysis in a deeper history and thus opens up multiple viewpoints of the kind that Kurki's chapter advocates and evokes.

Finally, writing on religion in Chapter 9, Byrnes adopts an argument that resonates with the possibility of complementarities between Newtonian and Post-Newtonian thought. Religious worldviews are in some contexts meticulously maintained Newtonian gardens. In other contexts they are deeply relational Post-Newtonian forests, grounded in the intricate and evolving connections between the human and the divine, and within humanity, as cocreative forces of "a world that is always in the process of becoming."[139] This formulation is remarkably close to Kauffman's reinvention of the sacred as a new scientific worldview in which God as the generator of life is akin to the reverence-instilling creativity of the natural and social universe itself.[140]

---

[136] Chapter 8, this volume.   [137] Chapter 8.   [138] Kauffman 2008.
[139] Chapter 9, this volume.   [140] Kauffman 2008: xi, 283.

Despite their profound differences, Newtonian and Post-Newtonian worldviews thus can exist in complementary relations.[141] After all, initial doubts about the classical model at the outset of the twentieth century and, eventually, its replacement by quantum physics arose within Newtonianism and a shared view of ignorance. Newtonianism and Post-Newtonianism both think of epistemic uncertainty as a function of the present state of ignorance. In the form of better models and improved theories, additional knowledge will reduce ignorance and, with it, uncertainty. Predictive accuracy is highly prized in the practical work of classical and quantum physics. Confirming a theoretical claim made almost half a century earlier by a group of physicists, the discovery of the Higgs Boson in 2012 was a widely celebrated achievement. And so was a 2017 experiment of nonlocality that provided extremely strong support for entanglement, Einstein's "spooky action at a distance," on a cosmic scale. Theoretical claims and experimental data lined up according to the classical view of how science should operate. Quantum mechanics embeds discrete cause-and-effect sequences in an encompassing relationalism.[142] It thus is able to identify specific domains of efficient cause-and-effect relations within a broader set of entanglements subject also to material, formal, and purposive causation in the natural and social world.[143] Time and again, quantum mechanics has generated hypotheses with a fabulously high predictive accuracy about the natural world, accounting for observations covering a range of 25 orders of magnitude, from the smallest particles of matter to the cosmos.[144] The theory works with spectacular success at scales many millions of times smaller than those for which it was originally developed.[145] It works while economics, the "queen" of the social sciences most eager to imitate physics, does not, as physicist David Mermin observed caustically.[146]

At least in principle, classical and quantum physicists believe ignorance will increasingly be overcome as science advances. For physicist and public intellectual Marcelo Gleiser, this assumption is questionable. He argues that "as the Island of Knowledge grows, so do the shores of our ignorance – the boundary between the known and the unknown."[147] But the growing reach of instruments and practices do more than extend the vast horizon of our ignorance. They also extend the limits of our thinking, as we probe our ignorance and seek to comprehend our own mortality in a world of

---

[141] Sil and Katzenstein (2010a, b) have made the same basic point in writing about analytic eclecticism of different paradigms and research traditions in international relations.
[142] Wendt 2022b.   [143] Kurki 2008.
[144] Barad 2007: 110 fn21, 415–16 fn55, 423 fn21, 419 fn28.
[145] Mermin 2016: 58, 62–63.   [146] Mermin 2016: 132.
[147] Quoted in Ahmari 2020: 25.

incomprehensible complexity and infinitude. The only thing we do seem to know is that science, philosophy, and religion will continue in the future as they have in the past: seeking meaning as they engage with the unfathomable.

Illustrated by the neglect of uncertainty, in the words of international relations scholar Robert Jervis, "many of the social-science attempts to understand behavior in classical terms are at best incomplete."[148] For him, quantum physics

provides better analogies for reality than does classical mechanics, with its faith in invariant relationships and its radical separation between the observed and the observer. In the social world, and even more in international politics, uncertainties (of both scholars and actors) reflect not only lack of knowledge that in principle could be gained, but multiple possibilities that have yet to be realized.[149]

Jervis appeals metaphorically to postclassical theory as a way of helping the classical model overcome specific forms of ignorance about the social and political world. Left unaddressed in his acknowledgment of the complementary relations between these two worldviews are the specific terms of their coexistence.[150] Below I argue that two workarounds exemplify different kinds of coexistence. In the first, complexity and subjective probability leave some room for elements of Post-Newtonianism in a Newtonian worldview. In the second, subjective beliefs and human experience in quantum physics offer an innovative theoretical intervention into a debate about the meaning of Post-Newtonianism and Newtonianism.

Newtonian Terms of Coexistence: Complexity and Subjective Probability. Unable or unwilling to break with the conventional Newtonian worldview, scholars have relied on different argumentative moves to address the issue of uncertainty. Here, I briefly consider two. A Newtonian worldview does not preclude conceptualizing world politics as a complex, open system that evolves within a complicated yet closed Newtonian system.[151] Furthermore, scholars can sidestep the issue of uncertainty by insisting that the main thing that matters is what unites conditions of uncertainty and probability: they are both experienced subjectively.

[148] Jervis 2017: 171.   [149] Jervis 2017: 186.

[150] The term 'complementary' is used in this section in its conventional rather than quantum sense. Warm thanks to Begüm Adalet, Jill Frank, Patchen Markell, and Alexander Wendt for giving detailed comments on this and the following section, to my colleagues at the Wissenschaftszentrum Berlin for reacting to these sections in two seminars convened on January 6 and 7, 2021, and to Patchen Markell for suggesting how to bring the two sections together.

[151] The intermediate case of a loosely coupled mechanical system that is partly decomposable is discussed by Simon 1962.

The determinist or probability-inflected Newtonian world can be thought of as a special case that reveals itself when the quantum world of infinite possibilities and radical uncertainty collapses. Following the insights of relational cosmology and quantum mechanics, the world can thus be conceived of as indeterminate and open, nested in a closed Newtonian universe. We are not observing that universe, be it natural or political, at a distance; we are part of it. Something resembling Quantum weirdness thus can enter the orderly classical, Newtonian model of world politics once we substitute the assumption of an open system for that of a closed one. Complexity theory applied to world politics thus accommodates some nonclassical possibilities and potentialities within a Newtonian worldview while excluding others, such as nonlocality.[152] It is the closed system assumption that makes the classical model of world politics gloss over uncertainty. Complexity theory thus affirms what Newtonianism denies: the existence of uncertainty that also marks the broader Quantum context in which the Newtonian world exists.

All too often we are stunned by events in world politics and ask ourselves "how was that possible?"[153] Complexity theory answers that question by focusing on the adaptive characteristics of open systems, their emergent properties, and their uncertainties. It distinguishes between *complicated* systems, which can be predictable and are made out of tightly or loosely coupled modules, and *complex* systems, which are not predictable and cannot be readily decomposed. The management of complexity demands persistent experimentation, incessant improvisation, successive approximation, continuous innovation by recombination, local knowledge, and accumulated experience. It acknowledges the inescapability of uncertainty. Even when uncertainty yields to local predictability, at a system level "a high degree of complexity and unpredictability" coexist.[154] All too often the confluence and interaction of many factors form wholes that are not readily captured by simple models of how small things follow from large ones. Indeed, large things may follow from small ones in complex systems. This is a world of clouds, not clocks.[155] Large-scale weather patterns can be predicted with growing accuracy, but the movement, size, and shape of individual clouds remain mysteries. There is no bell-shaped curve, yet, charting the future of a world of individual clouds.

---

[152] Kellert 1993; Axelrod and Cohen 1999; Jervis 1997; Byrne and Callaghan 2013; Kiel and Elliott 1996; Harrison 2006.
[153] This discussion of complexity theory builds on Seybert and Katzenstein 2018: 16–21.
[154] Jervis 1997: 16.
[155] Almond and Genco 1977; McClosky 1991; Tetlock and Gardner 2015: 8–10.

In complex systems, many group and individual behaviors and events are inherently unpredictable and seemingly erratic. Historical probabilities offer no reliable guide to a future that remains radically open. Complexity thus brings risk and uncertainty into one view. It opens a perspective on a world of emergent properties and regularities with a short half-life that leaves space for human inventiveness and low probability or totally unpredictable conjunctions. Pervasive chaos and disequilibria mark processes in the natural worlds of biology, geological patterning, climate, and other open systems. Creative evolution is its hallmark, not predetermined laws. System evolution can be tracked ex post; it is not predictable ex ante.

In open systems with emergent properties, predictive capacity is limited by the time it takes a system to run through sufficient repetitions to record how things eventually map out. Human interactions make uncertainty an integral part of world politics for four separate reasons.[156] First, slowdowns on interstate highways without accidents and stampeding crowds with no apparent trigger point to unexpected results that are not related to human intentions; human interactions can produce "emergent" phenomena. Second, in the social world of incessant human interaction, probabilities are forever changing; social processes are often nonrepeating or "non-ergodic." Third, human interactions are so complex that they elude attempts to anticipate correctly; the world is filled with "computational irreducibility." Finally, the belief that we live only in a world of knowable, manageable risk is sheer fantasy; instead, often we live in a world marked by "radical uncertainty," and the probability of some kinds of outcomes is simply unknowable. Complexity thus forces us to adopt an inherently humble approach to our understanding and conduct of world politics.[157]

A second workaround that avoids breaking with a Newtonian worldview takes on the problem of uncertainty more directly, by circumventing the distinction between risk's known probability distributions and uncertainty, where distributions are unknown.[158] What really matters is that all conditions of risk and uncertainty can be known only subjectively. A subjective probability is defined for situations in which one cannot know the correct probability which one should assign to the state of the

---

[156] Bookstaber 2017; Kay and King 2020.
[157] Bousquet and Geyer 2011: 1; Kauffman 2008: 258.
[158] Friedman 2019. I am very grateful for an extended email exchange with Jeffrey Friedman that helped clarify my thinking. Here, I am bypassing risk-based models that seek to integrate strategic uncertainty by including the possibility of ignorance about player preferences and beliefs. Such ignorance can yield suboptimal strategies. Uncertainty is thus reduced to a lack of information, in this case about the payoff matrix and attributes of one of the players. Common knowledge and common prior beliefs about the rules of the game are still assumed to exist. See Weinhardt 2017, 2020.

world based on the information that is available. The quantification of subjective probabilities pushes back against the idea of a 'correct' or 'objective' probability assessment about the state of the world – say, a crisis in national security decision-making.[159] Only subjective assessments are possible. In this view, assessments of uncertainty are only considered to be "correct" in as far as they coherently reflect an actor's personal beliefs given specific circumstances. Since ultimately everything rests on personal conviction, objective assessments of or correct answers about probability and uncertainty are unobtainable. But the ability to give well-structured and coherent assessments of judgments is not.[160] Although we cannot assess uncertainty in any objective fashion, we should exploit fully and consistently the subjective insights we do have. This requires distinguishing clearly between "assessments of probability (which reflect the chances that a statement is true) with assessments of confidence (which reflect the extent to which analysts believe they have a sound basis for drawing conclusions)."[161] Confidence depends on the reliability of available evidence, the range of reasonable opinion surrounding a judgment, and the susceptibility of a judgment to new information that might be forthcoming.[162] Put simply, confidence is analytic.[163]

This is where Keynes makes his central contribution. After he had abandoned the effort of making a compelling case for objective probability that did not ultimately rest on personal convictions, and after years of speculating in financial markets, Keynes developed a broader conception of confidence.[164] Practical men and women, he reasoned, had no choice but to rely on "conventions, stories, rules of thumb, habits, and traditions in formulating our expectations and deciding how to act."[165] All of these instill confidence as an essential ingredient of decision-making under uncertainty. Confidence is "a state of mind, a belief or feeling about the adequacy or otherwise of the knowledge base from which the forecasts of an inescapably uncertain future are derived."[166] In financial markets,

---

[159] Friedman 2019: 51–52; Gillies 2000: 55–58.

[160] Bayesian statistics offers a more formal approach to subjective probabilities. Compared to a more flexible and integrative approach, in the area of national security studies its usefulness is currently restricted by very large calculative tasks that may exceed human intellectual capacities. But the humanism that inheres in the Newtonian worldview which supports subjective probability approaches is an unnecessary restriction. A Hyper-Humanist Post-Newtonian worldview could readily accommodate approaches in the field of Artificial Intelligence that manages very large calculative tasks with greater ease.

[161] Friedman 2019: 23; see also 51, 57, 62, 63 fn37.   [162] Friedman 2019: 61–63.

[163] Friedman 2019: 14, 58–63; Friedman and Zeckhauser 2018.

[164] Friedman 2019: 59; Gillies 2000: 25–52; Keynes 1937.

[165] Skidelsky 2009: 87. See also Lawson 1986, 916.   [166] Gerrard 1994: 332.

Keynes did not see "analytic confidence" at work but rather "animal spirits ... of daring and ambitious entrepreneurs taking risks and placing bets in an environment characterized by uncertainty: that is by crucial unknowns and unknowables."[167]

Most scholarship on subjective probability assumes implicitly that accuracy is the only concern that influences a decision-maker's choice. Yet in American foreign policy it is implausible to think that presidents care simply about predictive accuracy when they confront risk and uncertainty in international affairs. The widespread resistance of decision-makers to rely only on probabilistic reasoning that Friedman reports in his book suggests as much.[168] Logic, cognition, and rigor are surely relevant.[169] But typically they work along with other factors, including individual or group emotions, religious and other beliefs, and social conventions.[170] Besides accuracy, all of these factors also are relevant for instilling the confidence that decision-makers have in their subjective beliefs.[171]

In sum, as these workarounds illustrate, a Newtonian worldview can accommodate elements of a Post-Newtonian one. Scholars committed to a Newtonian worldview can introduce uncertainty into the analysis of world politics by drawing on complexity theory. And they can erase the distinction between uncertainty and risk by relying on a subjective probability approach. Both moves are workable. For reasons that remain opaque, however, both resist letting go of the conventional Newtonian worldview and making space for a broader range of insights into world

---

[167] Kirshner 2009: 532. Friedman (2019: 59) calls Keynes's argument "logically coherent" but with consequences that are "untenable for anyone who seeks to contribute to foreign policy debates." Perhaps. Elsewhere (Friedman 2019: 193) he acknowledges the relevance of factors such as emotions, values, and organizational and other cultures that also shape the confidence of decision-makers. Until those factors are fully integrated into a comprehensive explication of decision-making under conditions of uncertainty, for the practice of foreign policy the pessimistic skepticism of the many decision-makers that he is reporting in his book appears to me to be as tenable as Friedman's optimistic rationalism.

[168] Friedman 2019: 12, 96–98.   [169] Friedman 2019: 12, 34, 49.

[170] This argument assumes that various criticisms of subjective probability can overlap. And it accords greater importance to factors such as values and emotions that Friedman's analysis of analytic confidence excludes, at least for now. See Friedman 2019: 6–10, 192–95.

[171] Friedman 2019: 12, 14–15. He concedes (pp. 67, 88) that the distinction between "mathematicians" and "poets" may make sense from organizational and cultural perspectives. This concession acknowledges the limits of the scope of analytic confidence that concerns Friedman's analysis. More generally, Bayesian decision theory is not the only rational way to make decisions in all situations. Savage (1954: 16) restricted the application of his theory to "small worlds" that sidesteps the enormous cognitive challenge of evaluating all possible action paths in a "large world." It is descriptive rather than prescriptive. See Binmore 2017: 260, 263–64.

politics. Such broadening would have the advantage of taking more fully into account developments that have transformed the natural sciences during the last century and avoid extending the record of frequent and shocking failures of predictive accuracy in the Newtonian study of world politics. Stuart Kauffman writes that "scientists tend to live with philosophies of science that are decades out of date."[172] In the case of the study of world politics, it has been more than a century. Early formal modelers in political science were drawn to nineteenth-century views of scientific theories: "The Received View, with its origins in classical mechanics, seemed a natural fit for scholars looking to put their young discipline on an equal footing with the 'hard' sciences … Soon after, philosophers abandoned the Received View as a description of scientific theories."[173] Most students of world politics, however, have stuck with the received view and have thus failed to incorporate uncertainty as a constitutive part of world politics.[174]

Post-Newtonian Terms of Coexistence: Individual Beliefs and Subjective Experience. Quantum mechanics works. [175] Compared to all other theories in physics, it has had the most spectacular success. Its understanding of the structure of matter is so powerful and precise that most contemporary technology rests on it. Physicists learn how to use quantum mechanics. But there exists no consensus about what they are talking about. As David Mermin argues, "there is an unprecedented gap between the abstract terms in which the theory is couched and the phenomena the theory enables us so well to account for. We do not understand the *meaning* of this strange conceptual apparatus that each of us uses so effectively to deal with our world."[176] In contrast to the theoretical workarounds of Newtonianism, Post-Newtonianism's is philosophical. In the form of Quantum Bayesianism (or QBism), it restates the insights of quantum mechanics in a language congruent with subjective probability theory and consonant with Dilthey's writings on worldviews.[177] QBism is a way of thinking about uncertainty, quantum mechanics, and

---

[172] Kauffman 2008: 293.   [173] Clarke and Primo 2012: 65–66.

[174] Wendt (2015: 154–73) discusses quantum decision theory as a serious alternative to a humanist substantialist analytical perspective grounded in the humanist Newtonian worldview that characterizes decision theories based on subjective probabilities.

[175] I am grateful for the detailed comments that David Mermin made on this section. For an informative critical engagement of Qbism, see Mohrhoff 2014a, 2014b and 2019a, 2019b.

[176] Mermin 2019: 1.

[177] Confounded by the weirdness of the quantum world that they can measure and manipulate without grasping its meanings, realist interpretations of quantum mechanics view quantum states as objective properties of the quantum system and thus disagree with QBism. For two sharply differing views, see Becker 2018: 89–162, 289–94 and Baeyer 2016: 235–39. Mermin (2019: 2, 13–15) argues that the insights of QBism are relevant

the sciences generally.[178] For Mermin, "QBism is as big a break with 20th-century ways of thinking about science as cubism was with 19th-century ways of thinking about art."[179] QBism grapples with the "weird-ness" of central aspects of quantum physics. David Mermin has attempted to reduce the puzzles of quantum mechanics to just one: interpreting quantum probabilities.[180]

Q stands for quantum and B for Bayesian. QBism offers a radically subjective interpretation of probability, stipulating that each actor makes bets and updates odds.[181] The question of probability goes to the heart of physics, "where everything had seemed to be regulated by firm laws that were universal and irrevocable."[182] In QBist interpretations, all probabilities in quantum states are interpreted as the private beliefs of individuals. Based on past experience and following the rules of Bayesian probabilities, agents calculate the probability of what might happen next. Based on evolving experience that creates new information, agents update their prior beliefs to improve their predictions of future events. This process involves only the agent's evolving experiences and beliefs through continuously updated information. Einstein refused to believe that God played dice: "If he had wanted to do this, then he would have done it quite thoroughly and not stopped with a plan for his gambling. In for a penny, in for a pound [*Wenn schon, denn schon*]. Then we wouldn't have to search for laws at all." Rüdiger Schack answers Einstein: "God *has* done it quite thoroughly. That's the message of QBism. It is not a plan for *his* gambling, but for *ours*."[183]

In QBism, wave functions are the products of an individual's experiences. Like other interpretations of quantum mechanics, QBism thinks of the wave function not as an objective entity but as a mathematical abstraction. Wave functions do not exist 'out there in the real world.'[184]

---

also for puzzling, though less vexing, aspects of the classical world such as the problem of 'Now'; for those instances he suggests the label CBism.

[178] Mermin 2016: 232–48; Fuchs, Mermin and Schack 2014; Healey 2016.

[179] Mermin 2016: 233.   [180] Mermin 1998; McCall 2001; Fuchs and Schack 2009: 48.

[181] Caves, Fuchs, and Schack 2002a, 2002b; Fuchs 2017; Mermin 2016: 232–48. There is a vast technical literature on these matters in physics that is inaccessible to me. Baeyer 2016, Timpson 2008, Bächtold 2008, Bacciagaluppi 2014, and Healey 2016, 2017 provide expositions and critical reviews; Bächtold and Healey develop the link to American pragmatism.

[182] Rovelli 2016: 18.   [183] Fuchs 2017: 20.

[184] As Baeyer (2016: 131–43) argues, QBism is anti-realist. Because of "quantum weirdness" it wholeheartedly agrees with Carlo Rovelli (2017), no QBist by any means, that *Reality is not what It Seems*. And it disagrees with the thrust of Adam Becker's (2018) *What Is Real?* And because QBism zeroes in on the personal experience of individual agents, it also differs from most Copenhagen interpretations: Objective for those interpreting Bohr as focusing only on the material aspects of measurement apparatuses, intersubjective for those interpreting Bohr as focusing also on the verbal or written

Experience is an agent's inner manifestation of what other interpretations take to be on the outside and call the collapse of the wave function. Experience "confers meaning by anticipating future information in relation to an organism's evolving purposes through time. The effect of this appropriation of the future is to transform objective information into subjective meaning – and it is on the basis of the latter that people act."[185] QBism focuses on beliefs and information and captures the idea that individual experience is intrinsically private and inaccessible to other observers.

In QBism, nature's deterministic laws do not exist. QBism postulates that "nature and its parts do what they want, and we as free-willed agents do what we can get away with. Quantum theory, on this account, is our best means yet for hitching a ride with the universe's pervasive creativity and doing what we can to contribute to it."[186] As is true also for Lee Smolin's version of scientific cosmology, humans are part of a participatory rather than an inert universe.[187] In this view, the big bang at the origin of the universe is a continuing occurrence rather than an event that happened about 13.8 billion years ago. Billions and billions of elementary observer-participatory acts help constitute the shape of the universe but without determining it.[188] Acts of observation and participation cannot be separated. Quantum mechanics is not a description of the world, but a technique for navigating and operating in it.

Laws and mechanisms are invented by observing scientists who are part of the natural and social world. They are developed as hypotheses, tested, and, over time, if confirmed by the private experiences of large numbers of individuals, they are crystallized into conventional wisdoms.[189] The source of the laws of nature "must be the books of human authors and not the original Book of Nature. What we end up with through this process is bound to be a thoroughly human and social construction, not a replica of the very laws that God wrote."[190] The laws of nature are an accretion of dispersed, variegated human experiences. Ours is a *Dappled World*, as Nancy Cartwright argues.[191] For Leonard Savage it is "small."[192] Classical physics works well in some domains; quantum physics in others. It is a patchwork of practices, each more or less successful in its more or less well-bounded domains. It is not experience that

communications of measurement practices. See Mermin (2016: 241–44) and Barad (2007) for different interpretations of Bohr's positions.
[185] Wendt 2015: 141. See also Fierke 2017: 145, 147; Baeyer 2016: 187–95; Timpson 2008: 18.
[186] Fuchs 2017: 20.   [187] Baeyer 2016: 202–10.   [188] Fuchs 2017: 5–6.
[189] Baeyer 2016: 196–201.   [190] Cartwright 1999: 46.
[191] Cartwright 1999: 2; Daston 2019: 24–25.
[192] Savage 1954: 16; Binmore 2017: 260, 263–64.

yields to the world, as the classical model holds. It is the world that yields to experience – until the accumulation of experience changes. Laws of nature are never absolute, and always provisional. Shaped by the beliefs of scientists, we do not need to search for nature's laws and mechanisms any further than the beliefs and experiences expressed in scientific theories and experimental practices. In brief, scientific practices in the classical model represent the natural and social world; in the quantum model, they coproduce that world.[193]

QBism holds that self's understanding of the world rests entirely on the experience gained over a lifetime. "When I sleep or die," writes Oswald Spengler, "my world ends with me, but the world of the others remains. With every newborn child awakens also its world."[194] It is self's uncommunicable experience that matters – the individual "I" not the intersubjective "we." It is "each of us" as a singular entity and not a collective "us."[195] This is *not* to argue that the world exists only in the head of self.[196] The material from which self constructs a picture of its external world includes the effects that the world has on self's experience in response to her measurement and argumentative practices. For self's practices normally do not control how the world acts back. Self's experience of other leads self to reason that other is very much like self, with its own private experiences. This is as firm a belief as any that self has. Self could not function in the world without it. Asked to assign a probability to this statement, self would choose p=1.[197]

QBism's subjectivity does not mean that the world exists only in the mind of the individual agent. Although self does not have any access to the private experience of other, a very important part of self's private experience is the impact on self by other's effort to communicate in speech or writing other's personal experience. Through language and other forms of communication, different agents affect private perceptions and create a state of deep entanglement.[198] Communication makes it possible for agents to plausibly conclude that each of them has private experiences that are quite alike, though perhaps not identical to, their own. Bridging

---

[193] Jasanoff 2004; Camic, Gross, and Lamont 2011.
[194] Spengler 1965: 54. My translation.
[195] Mermin 2016: 233 fn1, 238; Mermin 2019: 5–6.
[196] Becker 2018: 25–27, 29–30, 48, 168, 234.
[197] "Probablity-1 measures the intensity of a belief: supreme confidence: It does not imply the existence of a deterministic mechanism ... That probability-1 assignments are personal judgements, like any other probability assignments, is essential to the coherence of QBism" (Mermin 2016: 244, 245, and 219–26). Alien to the conventional view of frequentist probability, Mermin insists that this interpretation is perfectly congruent with Hume's views on induction: Mermin 2019: 4–5, 7.
[198] Fierke 2017: 151; Wendt 2015: 207–21; Mermin 2019: 2–4, 6.

the privacy of subjective individual experiences, they thus can arrive at common or intersubjective understandings of the outside world. Hence, QBism does not give any space to the reification of a common external world. Language enables self and other to share a portion of what each has experienced. And the effects of their measurement and argumentative practices constitute the world, external to each actor's subjective beliefs. QBism is not a solipsistic theory that holds that each of us is free to make up our own private world.

There exists, then, a world external to each agent.[199] This proposition is more useful and strongly confirmed by experience than any other empirical hypothesis. That, however, does not mean that the concepts of quantum mechanics correspond directly to features in the world. When we think that physicists "measure" the world we imply, conventionally, that as measuring agents they themselves are described by their theory of the external world rather than taking the measuring agent as a given (or primitive). The orthodox view makes the agent inert and passive when, arguably, she is active and engaged. QBism holds to a strongly subjective and active view of agency. Agents act on their personal experiences and beliefs and, based on their measurement practices of the world, they acquire wholly personal experiences. This does not mean that the theory is only about self and not about other. Anyone can use the theory and, in using it, each assures herself that beliefs about the consequences of their encounters with the world are consistent. Every action by self can be met by uncontrollable and unforeseen consequences from the world; "The objective world asserts itself unmistakably, unpredictably and uncontrollably in its immediate response to any of our interventions."[200] When actors prod the external world, the world can and often does generate something new that no agent could have predicted. The core, then, is about the relationship between something that is both profoundly personal and profoundly relational.

It is surprising how much of the discussion of knowledge and experience in quantum physics resonates with Dilthey's writings.[201] Individual experience and belief are central for both. Dilthey's insistence on the creative power of life as an engine of all human experience offers a humanist's worldview not unlike QBism's scientific one. If we view Dilthey as a QBist before QBism, the metaphorical description of Dilthey as the Newton of the humanities needs to be corrected.[202] For Dilthey,

[199] Fuchs and Schack 2009: 48–55.   [200] Mermin 2019: 8.
[201] Mermin 2016: 165–66, 232–48; Wendt 2015: 29–32, 141–43.
[202] Rickman 1979: 1.

I and world are given components in lived experience before questions of object-ivity and representations are raised. . . . to live is to be situated in a world prior to the split between theory and practice. The theoretical world of the natural sciences arises as an abstraction from this lived, practical context, and it is given mediately as a representational construct.[203]

The conventional view of quantum mechanics may miss much of what QBism and Dilthey have to offer.[204]

Dilthey's theory of life is consonant with QBism. Both offer their theories "for the use of agents immersed in and interacting with the world."[205] This is not to deny some important differences between the two. Dilthey rejects the empiricism that QBism embraces. And compared to QBism, he distinguishes less self-consciously between individual experiences and collective beliefs.[206] Equating science with Newtonian physics, Dilthey laid the groundwork for the venerable two-cultures view of science and humanities, or "hard" or "soft" versions of Kuhn's para-digms. QBism and Smolin's scientific cosmology suggest otherwise. Versions of the two-cultures paradigm are part of the human effort of meaning-making, with the world acting back on human intervention in more or less unpredictable ways. The abstract concepts of quantum physics, such as waves and particles, are human creations to make sense of specific personal experiences. They are not real. "For practical pur-poses," as Mermin said,

it does not matter if, like most physicists, I confer objective reality on the theoret-ical abstractions that enable me to calculate the likelihood of my subsequent experience. But for resolving certain conceptual puzzles . . . it is essential not to reify what are fundamentally intellectual tools, and not to treat what is fundamen-tally subjective and personal as if it were objective and universal . . . It can be hard to acknowledge that it is humanity all the way down, in all fields – even physical science.[207]

Different points of departure for the humanities and the natural sciences thus meet at the same intersection as the human sciences overlap with the natural sciences.[208] For both Dilthey and QBism, knowing is not a spectator sport played at a distance by impartial and objective observers. Knowing is part of life. The knowing subject is not a self-aware, self-contained, independently rational agent that comes to knowledge fully

---

[203] Owensby 1994: 32–33.   [204] Fuchs and Schack 2009: 47.
[205] Fuchs and Schack 2009: 48.
[206] Dilthey thus runs afoul of the "shifty split" between quantum and classical that Bell identified and that Mermin (2016: 219–26, 239–40) discusses.
[207] Mermin 2019: 15. Clarke's and Primo's (2012) view of models as objects expressing human purpose aims in the same direction.
[208] Hodges 1944: 34–35.

formed. Instead, knowledge is a distributed practice that includes material and argumentative arrangements. Humans are part of the larger configuration of the world and its open-ended articulation.[209] For both QBism and Dilthey, knowing is not the playing of ideas in the mind of a Cartesian subject that stands outside and apart from the world the subject seeks to know. It is, rather, a practice of engagement with a world that is made explicable in terms of scientific theories, philosophical inquiries, artistic creations, and religious practices.

QBism has restored the important role of senses in understanding nature.[210] Intellect seeks to understand the world as it really is, trying to discover its true essence. It focuses on the object of inquiry. Senses insist that they are indispensable for learning what nature tries to teach us. Humans are equipped with senses that convey the surfaces of things. "It is," as Lorraine Daston writes,

appearances all the way down ... The surfaces that nature presents so abundantly and incessantly to view are also ordered, in ways more obvious, more reliable, and more permanent than most artifacts. It is the natural appearances of day-in, day-out experience, not the natural depths revealed by electron microscopes and cyclotrons, which still shape some of our most sturdy intuitions about what an order can be.[211]

Senses remind us of the role subjectivity plays in science generally. Specifically, they help account for Newtonianism's enduring appeal. Modern physics had done away with senses and the subject – until the weirdness of quantum states prompted the articulation of QBism. Einstein established in 1905 that the observer's frame of reference was indispensable for making sense of mechanics, thus eliminating the unvarnished objectivity of Newton's absolute notions of time and space. The wave/particle duality in quantum mechanics staged another assault on objectivity. An electron is not a wave or a particle, but a hybrid revealing different properties, depending on the questions agents ask and the measurement and argumentative practices they engage in. Extending well beyond dispassionate reason, the questions scientists pose and the answers they offer are shaped by what William James called temperament. This includes the senses. Will, taste, emotions, and passion are all implicated in and contribute to scientific practice, just as they are present in all other human affairs. Temperament conditions our receptivity for heuristic and obfuscating concepts, confirmatory and disconfirming evidence, and illuminating and distracting methods of inquiry.[212]

---

[209] Barad 2007: 341–42, 379.   [210] Baeyer 2016: 144–55.   [211] Daston 2019: 65–67.
[212] Fuchs 2017: 5–6.

Numbers play a central part in science and in the study of world politics. They are stories self and other can share, rooted in their private experiences. They are fictions, like poems and paintings, and they become instruments of taking imaginative leaps with which we try, Deborah Stone argues, to make others leap with us. Numbers are accumulated experiences and judgments. They have souls that become social conventions when shared.[213] Because counting forces things into categories that ignore differences, numbers have power. As is true of the collapsing wave function that creates one real world from an infinity of possible worlds, we construct numbers by making our own decisions about how to separate things into groups. In the split second before we decide, things could go either way: "It could be *this* or it could be *that*. Numbers are a magic wand that resolves ambiguity into one-ness."[214] We fool ourselves into believing that they are objective or inhere in the world outside. As in QBism, numbers are our creation, our way of making sense of the world. And, just like language, they can never pin things down definitively.[215]

Like Smolin's scientific cosmology, QBism demands thinking of science in "radically unfamiliar ways."[216] It asks us to trade in deeply held Newtonian convictions about the existence of an objective, external world for a view of the world based on individual beliefs rooted in personal experience. Its radical subjectivism is grounded in the firmest of beliefs that in their own private experiences self and other are very much alike. And this belief makes it possible for self to function in the world. QBism thus contains a close link to the idea of intersubjectively shared beliefs. The objective world is affirmed by the fact that other acts back on self.

Conclusion. Workarounds such as subjective belief and human experience offer, as is true of complexity and subjective probability, specific terms of coexistence between Post-Newtonianism and Newtonianism. Confronted by uncertainty, QBism insists that the world is constituted by subjective beliefs and human experience all the way down. In contrast, Newtonian workarounds do not let go of the notion of risk in a closed classical world governed by objective laws and mechanisms. With QBism, Post-Newtonian workarounds offer a radical subjectivist argument that does away with the notion of a law- or mechanism-governed external world, while at the same time excelling in the conduct of controlled

---

[213] Stone 2020: xiv–xvi, 12, 61, 115, 218, 241–42.   [214] Stone 2020: 4.

[215] Stone 2020: 217. In her review, Cheng (2020: 37) insists on the importance of rigor, logic, consistency, and controlled experiments that Stone does not question. But she also extends Stone's argument: "Higher-level math involves exactly the complexities she [Stone] is asking us to be aware of elsewhere."

[216] Mermin 2019: 2.

experiments in a world radically open to human intervention and interpretation.

The conventional understanding of uncertainty is Newtonian, as it applies to statistical distributions that defy the assignment of probabilities. Newtonianism even accommodates subjective probability theory, which elides a clear distinction between risk and uncertainty and links up with the more radical subjectivism of QBism. Both subjective probability theory and QBism distinguish clearly between subjective probabilities and objective conditions.[217] A subjective probability expresses a degree of belief about the truth of some proposition. In the form of subjective probability theory and QBism, Bayesian theory thus distinguishes clearly between subjective and objective parts of its arguments. The subjective part relates to the initial judgment of an agent that leads to the assignment of the probability of prior beliefs. The objective part is the application of the rules of probability to such priors. Even probabilities produced by physical laws have subjective roots: "Probabilities are degrees of belief, not facts. Probabilities cannot be derived from facts alone. Two agents who agree on the facts can legitimately assign different prior probabilities."[218] The epistemic state of an actor is part of the reason for her prediction about the world, not part of some process that occurs in the world. Subjective probability theory lives in a halfway house. It wagers that information updating and careful calibration of different streams of information will reconcile subjective perceptions with an objective external world governed by determinist laws, probabilistic tendencies, and causal mechanisms. The classical model operates quite well for many practical purposes since statistical quantum effects wash out at the macro level. For many, the decohered world that the classical model describes is thus thought to be an adequate approximation of the macro social and political world.[219] But the classical model has no room for nonlocality (Einstein's "spooky action at a distance"), where cause-and-effect relations operate without mechanisms, and it fails to acknowledge uncertainty as a constitutive part of the world, be it natural or political.

Taking a subjective view of probability leads unavoidably to a QBist interpretation.[220] Quantum probabilities offer a complete description of the quantum system, an infinity of potential realities. Quantum mechanics describes the probabilities of finding some specific properties when they are being measured rather than the properties of material objects and forces in the classical world. Like subjective probability theory, QBism narrows the concept of probability to apply only to single agents. But, in

[217] Caves, Fuchs, and Schack 2007: 1–2. [218] Caves, Fuchs, and Schack 2007: 6.
[219] Waldner 2017; Nau, Chapter 6, this volume. [220] Mermin 2019: 7, 10.

contrast to subjective probability theory, it broadens the concept of probability by including all personal experiences, subject only to the constraints of being free from mathematical contradictions. This broadening captures a web of shared individual probability assignments that makes science a powerful endeavor for collective human inquisitiveness and ingenuity. It has generated a large common core of experiences that organize our scientific and common sense of how the world works.

Quantum mechanics and the classical model are not antithetical. The former covers the latter as it recovers classical theory at the limit. The infinity of possible quantum worlds collapses, with measurement, into the classical world in which we live. That transition, or "decoherence," remains one of the great mysteries in quantum mechanics. Evidence in several fields, including quantum decision theory, points to quantum effects in the classical world that Post-Newtonianism may explain better than Newtonianism.[221] Unsurprisingly, in navigating the practicalities of life, common sense often makes us rely on the "both/and" logic of quantum probability that is multivalent and nonlocal, rather than the "either/or" Boolean logic that is binary and local.

QBism's radical subjectivist stance does not sit well with the many quantum physicists who hold to a realist interpretation of science.[222] Most quantum physicists step back when they confront the weirdness of the natural world. For all intents and purposes, they have stopped probing the meaning of doing physics, throwing up their hands before the unfathomable strangeness they navigate so expertly. In Nobel Prize-winner Richard Feynman's possibly apocryphal but often quoted words, "No one understands quantum mechanics. Do not keep saying to yourself, if you can possibly avoid it, 'But how can it be like that?' because you will go 'down the drain' into a blind alley from which nobody has yet escaped. Nobody knows how it can be like that."[223] Feynman's advice is readily understandable. Why heed the implication of the radically subjectivist call of QBism, if the experimental practice of quantum mechanics has worked so well in helping physicists to navigate the world even without understanding it? Furthermore, the success of that practice provides a strong and durable link to the Newtonian worldview of scientific practice.

This pragmatic move breaks the symmetry in the partial accommodation of Post-Newtonian elements in Newtonianism and of Newtonian elements in Post-Newtonianism.[224] For Post-Newtonian science to create circumscribed cause-and-effect chains to conduct experiments with great accuracy,

---

[221] Wendt 2022a, 2022b. Wendt 2015: 91–108. [222] Becker 2018.
[223] Quoted in Pagels 1982: 135.
[224] Patchen Markell pushed this point so compellingly that I have used some of his language in the rest of this paragraph. Thank you.

based on situationally specific human purpose, for Post-Newtonianism to treat Newtonianism seriously as a special case when the wave function collapses, and for Post-Newtonianism to define substantively its terms of coexistence with Newtonianism would require sustained inquiry into the meaning of Post-Newtonianism and the reasons why Newtonianism is valid in delimited ways but not in general. The practical success of quantum physics has been so great, however, that it has sidelined inquiry into the meaning of twentieth-century particle physics. To the extent that physicists working with a Post-Newtonian worldview unquestioningly take for granted the goal of predictive accuracy as a matter of undisguised practicality, they share a view of science that is familiar to those holding a Newtonian world-view. As committed a QBist as David Mermin suggests that, "if and when quantum mechanics is successfully modified, the motivation will come from unambiguous deviations of actual data from its predictions, and not from discomfort with any interpretations of its formalism."[225]

Newtonianism expresses a combination of common and tacit know-ledge, as in commonsensical Newtonianism and tacit, experimentally triumphant Post-Newtonianism.[226] This combination is arguably the main reason why Newtonianism retains such a powerful grip on our understanding of the world and our inability to recognize uncertainty as a constituent part of world politics.

Common knowledge focuses on what actors consciously think about and which information they rely on to make their choices and coordinate their behavior. Tacit knowledge highlights what agents think *from* and take for granted: their unspoken worldviews. In the analysis of world politics, most scholars share in the common knowledge that the world is fundamentally orderly and predictable and that it is their task to discover the laws and mechanisms revealing the enabling conditions of order and predictability. They hold this commonsensical Newtonian view, fortified by the tacit knowledge of the experimental success of Post-Newtonianism. Together, Newtonian commonsense and Post-Newtonian experimental success offer a compelling combination of common and tacit knowledge.[227] The inter-pretation of reality as consisting only of risk is not readily open to rational reconstruction or refutation.[228] Most students of world politics thus hold that their subject is defined by risk. Uncertainty as a constitutive principle is ignored.

Scholars and commentators alike lavish attention on risk, expressing a profound belief in an orderly universe. In doing so their contingent,

---

[225] Mermin 2019: 2.
[226] For a longer discussion of common and tacit language, see Katzenstein 2018: 383–88; Adler 2019: 18–20, 301; Collins 2010.
[227] Collins 2010: 119–38.   [228] Jackson 2002: 70–71.

mid-level, probabilistic propositions have not come close to the explanatory rigor, predictive accuracy, and prescriptive practicality of Newton's theory of gravity. In focusing on risk to the exclusion of uncertainty, they subscribe, often unwittingly, to a whole slew of other contested and inherently contestable foundational ideas marking Newtonian and Post-Newtonian thought. Efficient causation, neutralist epistemologies, individualist ontologies, linear temporality, and asocial space are taken for granted; constitutive causality, entangled epistemologies, relational ontologies, nonlinear temporality, and social space are ignored.

Greater awareness of these foundational differences has implications for the analysis of world politics. The complementarities between Newtonianism and Post-Newtonianism provide ample intellectual justification for engaging in self-reflection and increasing toleration of intellectual pluralism in the analysis of world politics.[229] This could make some of us less hesitant to acknowledge personal experience and emotions as relevant factors in research. It could make the study of methods less interesting, and the study of epistemology more so. It could lead to trading in the aspiration for unobtainable predictive accuracy in favor of greater explanatory depth. It could encourage searching out approaches, theories, and models that are open to or informed by both Newtonian and Post-Newtonian worldviews. And it could lead us to reject Dilthey's widely accepted argument that there exists an irreconcilable difference between the natural sciences and the humanities. Post-Newtonianism offers perspectives on the natural sciences that make us question the conventional equation of Newtonianism with science: "Just as it would be mistaken to rule out explanation from the interpretive human sciences, so quantum theory and the cosmology of dark matter have raised unresolved questions about the universe and its origin that make it unreasonable to exclude interpretation from the natural sciences."[230]

The analysis of world politics thus confronts a deep predicament. Both the commonsensical appeal of Newtonianism and the practical successes of quantum mechanics are deeply appealing. In contrast, the practical accomplishments of scholars of world politics are small. Compared to quantum mechanics, their record of predictive accuracy is embarrassingly poor and shows little prospect of improving. Refusing to inquire into the meaning of this failure amounts to an act of willful ignorance. The analysis of world politics in current research practice remains so strongly tethered to Newtonianism that it confronts enormous difficulties in entertaining alternative worldviews. And, in so doing, it continues to deny the constitutive role uncertainty plays in world politics.

[229] Kauffman 2008: 258.   [230] Makkreel 2020: 323.

Values. Because measurement and observation have a great deal to do with the world we make and experience, Newtonian and Post-Newtonian workarounds underline the importance of ethics and accountability.[231] In this view, science is constituted by collections of ethical communities.[232] This evokes theorist Satkunanandan's calculable and extraordinary responsibilities.[233] We ordinarily focus on our countable and discharge-able responsibilities. But this calculative move does not free us from confronting our ontological condition of uncountable responsibility constitutive of being human. Calculative responsibility is attractive because it gives a sense of control over our lives. It coexists with the incalculable dimension of the world and the enormity of freedom. Although the first often effaces or conceals the second, both responsibilities are important for an inquiry into moral values.

In the social sciences and the study of world politics, this is especially clear when numbers are used to characterize the world. Deborah Stone reminds us of the dual meaning of the verb "count": to add things up reciting numerals in ascending order, and to matter in the sense of being included and having importance. The two meanings are always inter-twined, and always implicate values and power in, for example, the national accounts of GDP, in the assessment of teacher performance, in the evaluation of a slave in the Constitution as a three-fifths person, and in the many other examples she thoughtfully analyzes.[234] Despite their sharp disagreements on many issues, Nau's humanist Newtonian advocacy of individual accountability in Chapter 6 and Kurki's hyper-humanist Post-Newtonian plea for a morally infused practice of all sentient beings in Chapter 3 are less divided than one might think. Worldviews compel us to take a stand as they incorporate world-inquiring and action-coordinating policies and practices.[235] Whether and to what extent ethics or power shape argumentative outcomes and different normative standards is a proper subject of empirical and the-oretical inquiry.[236] Worldviews tolerate dilemmas, tensions, and contradictions that philosophy, science, and religion seek to resolve once and for all. This is their weakness – and their strength.

Values are inextricable components of all worldviews that offer an ethical universe linking the here-and-now to the supernatural, and the practical to the metaphysical.[237] To the world's jungle, worldviews offer

[231] I thank Richard Price for helping me think through this point.
[232] Kurki, Chapter 3, this volume.   [233] Satkunanandan 2015: 6–7.   [234] Stone 2020.
[235] Brown and Eckersley 2018: 7–8; Reus-Smit 2008: 67–70, 76–77.
[236] Price 2008: 11–12, 43–46; Martineau and Squires 2012: 530–34; Checkel 2013: 228–30, 235–36; Erman and Möller 2013.
[237] Reus-Smit 2008: 54–57; 2013, 601–03.

a transcendental canopy.[238] Henry Nau argues as he does in Chapters 2 and 6 because of his deep commitment to individual choice and accountability; Milja Kurki in Chapter 3 because of her equally deep sense of care about the environment and ecological collapse. The intensity of the debates and disagreements during our meetings and in the different chapters was perhaps not as great as the two-generation split between climate change denier Donald Trump and climate change advocate Greta Thunberg. But it was qualitatively different from normal academic disagreements. Everybody felt and understood that the stakes under discussions were very high. For different worldviews lead to different expectations of what world orders are or might be feasible and what ethical considerations could or should come into play.

Because humans are self-reflective, their practices are inextricably linked to their worldviews. And because values are baked very deeply into our scientific theories and religious beliefs, we may not be able to recognize them easily in our daily discourses and practices. But they exist nonetheless.[239] What is true of all metatheoretical discussions of ontology, epistemology, and methodology holds also for a praxis-shaping morality: it is always provisional and contestable. Political engagement of citizen practices and government policies matter no less than philosophical arguments, scientific discoveries, or religious beliefs. As part of worldviews, moral values and social purposes gain strength and salience, for "individuals cannot escape the moral language embedded in the social conventions which have previously constituted them as moral subjects."[240]

This is true also for an empirical theory of world politics that leans heavily on Newton and is indebted to Weber. While struggling with the difference between fact and value, Weber insisted on the mutual relevance of science, normative discourse, and human choice. Weber's arguments sharpen our thinking rather than bridge the gaps between is and ought, means and ends. We can choose to accept basic values. Seeking to justify them, however, is a hopeless endeavor. There exists no ultimate rational foundation for our most basic values. One of the classical functions of theory is its practical efficacy, its formation of an orientation toward practical action. In the conduct of social science and international

---

[238] Barnett, Chapter 5, this volume.

[239] Monteiro and Ruby 2009; Bernstein 1976: 61–62, 104, 110–11, 113–14; Adler 2019: 2, 265–94. Operating at different levels of abstraction, Levine and Barder (2014) and Paipais (2017) make the same point in their critiques of how prominent realist and liberal international relations scholars and different philosophical schools of thought deal with issues of pluralism and difference.

[240] Linklater 1998: 64.

relations, this is often constrained by various barriers – theoretical, methodological, and otherwise – that create an intellectual and practical vacuum between theory and practice. Marked by their action-inducing features, worldviews do not give rise to such restrictions. They fill the void left by theory and methods.

Take, for example, pressing environmental issues. Although many scholars of world politics worry about the environment, that concern is not yet reflected in their publications. Between 2011 and 2015, three leading IR journals published virtually no articles on conventionally understood, noncatastrophic environmental issues.[241] It is a safe assumption that catastrophic scenarios are a negligible proportion of these very small numbers.[242] Attended by scholars from all over the world, the 2015 annual meeting of the International Studies Association featured 1,250 panels; only one paper title referred explicitly to the Anthropocene.[243] And even though they ranked climate change as the most important issue facing the world, only 2.4 percent of about 4,000 international relations scholars listed the environment as their main area of research.[244] To the extent that the environment matters, however, debate expresses two different worldviews travelling under cornucopian-exemptionalist and catastrophic-ecological labels. A "cornucopian" position centers on core values such as economic growth and humankind's justified mastery of nature. A "catastrophic" worldview questions the rightfulness of a man-over-nature stance and foresees doom unless changes in individual and socially transformative values move us away from a materialist status-quo. Relatedly, an "exemptionalist" worldview insists that unique achievements in science and technology free humankind from ecological limitations that constrain other species. An "ecological" worldview holds instead that the human species is embedded in rather than emancipated from ecological constraints.[245] In Chapters 3 and 6, Kurki and Nau articulate these differences. Both positions ground themselves in the achievement of or aspiration for Enlightenment values understood in the singular, such as freedom, human rights, and economic prosperity.[246] Nau champions an abstract ethics to justify action on

---

[241] 0% in *International Organization*, 0.3% in *International Studies Quarterly*, and 1.6% in the *European Journal of International Relations*. It is a safe assumption that the catastrophic possibilities that Pelopidas (2020) focuses on are a tiny proportion of these very small numbers. Underdal 2017: 170.

[242] Pelopidas 2020.

[243] I thank Colin Chia for his assistance in generating these figures. See also Kelly 2019

[244] Harrington 2016: 486–87.   [245] Dake 1991: 64.

[246] Nau (Chapter 6) and Duara (Chapter 7) differ in their recognition of Enlightenment thought. Nau talks about the Enlightenment in the singular; Duara calls attention to its different strands. It is very rare that the work of African philosophers Yacob and Amo is

universal grounds; Kurki advocates an intense practicality without offering answers to questions of public policy. Kurki challenges Nau's claim that self-reflective experience makes humans stand apart from and above the environment and that humans operate in a Newtonian world of things against a background of empty space and linear time. It is that difference which animates the clash of two scientific worldviews and their different value commitments.

Hirschman's possibilism provides an opening for future explorations.[247] Possibilism does not reject the individual accountability standards that concern Haas and Nau in Chapter 2 and Nau in Chapter 6. And it embraces the social normativity of engaging the other in open dialogue that Kurki espouses in Chapter 3. Grove and Barnett (Chapters 4 and 5) develop variations of these normative stances. Exposure to different values and ways of being and viewing the world can contribute to an ecumenical outlook and the practical and ethical injunction for toleration that is at the heart of different Enlightenment traditions. As Duara shows in Chapter 7, with the world at the brink of planetary catastrophe, even in the absence of a clearly and rationally articulated path, it may be necessary to explore further the morality of possibilism. In Chapter 8 Bentley Allan historicizes nineteenth- and twentieth-century values such as "civilization" and "economic growth" as constituted by cosmological elements. Finally, without denying that faith can lead to value absolutism, Timothy Byrnes stresses in Chapter 9 that humble recognition of the uncertainty that accompanies faith can also engender an ecumenism grounded in empathy with and respect for other religious traditions.

Considerations of values are the subject of metatheoretical debates in the analysis of world politics.[248] Such debates make the stability of any foundational commitments inescapably provisional and inherently contestable.[249] Chris Reus-Smit, for example, does not believe that "fundamental questions of epistemology and ontology – the stuff of metatheory – are resolvable in any final or absolute sense."[250] This is not to deny that even though "debate with a view to resolution" is an unobtainable objective, "reflection with an eye to consequences" is not.[251] The Newtonian worldview that permeates

---

ever acknowledged, even though they preceded and anticipated many of the European Enlightenment's core tenets. Not grounded in notions of salvation (through science or religion) such non-European worldviews highlight alternatives, such as tearing and repairing, yielding different ethical and political arguments. Robbie Shilliam's interventions in our discussions made this point several times. See also Herbjørnsrud 2017; Rutazibwa and Shilliam 2020; Trownsell et al. 2020.

[247] I thank Richard Price for this line of thought.   [248] Wendt 1991: 383.

[249] Gunitsky 2019; Monteiro and Ruby 2009: 17, 25–26.

[250] Reus-Smit 2013: 590, 594–95; Hamilton 2017; Levine and Barder 2014: 868–72.

[251] Reus-Smit 2013: 605.

the major paradigms of international relations has led to this bet: the best scientific knowledge can be gained by presupposing that the world is governed only by risk.[252] In contrast, Post-Newtonianism is more ready to acknowledge the constitutive role of uncertainty in world politics. This leads to inescapable conflicts that are both important and unresolvable.

Newtonian and Post-Newtonian worldviews offer complementary ways for engaging with and navigating the world in never-ending, partly self-correcting processes of trial-and-error. Newtonianism has sidelined uncertainty as a constitutive feature of world politics. Too often, therefore, students of world politics are left speechless by stunning surprises. Creating a park out of garden and forest, and adopting Post-Newtonianism, not to the exclusion of Newtonianism, would help to account better for uncertainty as a central feature of world politics.

10.3   Science and Religion

Parks exemplify the possibility of a meaningful coexistence of garden and forest, here science and religion – the most deeply anchored worldviews. On this point, Acquinas and Newton appear to have agreed.[253] People are drawn to science or religion, and sometimes to both at the same time, as they seek to navigate the uncertainties of their lives. But today, Mark Lilla argues, humankind is not well equipped to deal with uncertainty. We are an impatient lot, and we demand that god, science, or both satisfy our craving for knowledge about the future. We are not content when told that some kinds of knowledge are unobtainable and are drawn to those who, in the end, promise more than they can deliver. Priestesses then and pundits now eagerly offer to provide an unlimited supply of unobtainable knowledge. We have a hard time acknowledging uncertainty because it makes us come to terms with our vulnerability. We want to be on a power walk into the future "when in fact we are always just tapping our canes on the pavement in the fog."[254] This is not surprising. Most occurrences in the world, philosopher Nancy Cartwright argues, are "subject to no law at all ... the claims to knowledge we can defend by our impressive scientific successes do not argue for a unified world of universal order, but rather for a dappled world of mottled objects." The search for universal laws governing nature and society is a fool's errand. Yet, the belief in the existence of universal laws embodied in a single scientific system of inquiry exists across all sciences: "The yearning for 'the system' is a powerful one; the faith that our world must be rational

---

[252] Jackson and Nexon 2013: 549; Wæver 1997.   [253] Konyndyk 1995.
[254] Lilla 2020.

and well-ordered through and through plays a role where only evidence should matter."[255] And, in the field of international relations, that evidence points powerfully to the importance of uncertainty as an important aspect of global politics.

As we slowly stumble through the fog, Michael Barnett writes in Chapter 5, we "blend the worldly and the heavenly." Along the way we rely on worldviews to steady us as we seek to secure our anxious sense as fleeting beings in this world. The search for ontological security, like the politics of fear, seeks to eradicate uncertainty through fight-or-flight responses and their conservative or reactionary political consequences. But as Catarina Kinnvall and Jennifer Mitzen argue, it can also steady us as we try to cope with a more diffuse anxiety.[256] Such a disposition permits a broader range of political responses than the emotion of focused fear, including resistance, exploration, anticipation, and even excitement. Even though fear and anxiety may be difficult to sort out empirically, ontological insecurity avoidance differs from ontological security seeking. In either case, the experience of the fundamental contingency of being is mitigated by scientific and religious worldviews.

Moving in a fear- and anxiety-inducing fog, science and numbers can acquire a semi-magical power. Even though we are their creators, we put an extraordinary faith in them as modern oracles of truth: "Numbers acquire their power the same way the gods acquire theirs – humans invest them with virtues they want their rulers to have . . . Our numbers, like our gods, promise to govern us well . . . We count to learn what's happening in our world and to gain control over our lives."[257] Confronted with uncertainty and chaos,

science is a quintessentially human method of trying to control that chaos . . . Adrift in the world, uncertain of the future, hostage to fate, but possessed of increasingly powerful tools for carving up pieces of the world and putting them under the microscope, is it any wonder that we increasingly turn to science when looking for deliverance from our human predicaments? . . . We want the comfort of certainty.[258]

Or we crave the comfort of religion. As conventionally used today, the concept of religion is barely 200 years old. Most communities had to invent new categories – such as *shukyo* in Japanese and *zongjiao* in Chinese – to describe a novel foreign phenomenon. They simply lacked indigenous categories that corresponded to the contemporary under-standing of religion. Even ancient Greece lacked a single word that corresponded to the Latin *religio*.[259] Over time, religions have changed

---

[255] Cartwright 1999: 16–17.   [256] Kinnvall and Mitzen 2020.
[257] Stone 2020: 100–1, 178.   [258] Klay 2020: 10.
[259] Casanova 2012: 193; Byrnes, Chapter 9.

from compact to complex symbolic systems and practices that tie humankind to the ultimate conditions of its existence. Established binaries such as sacred–profane, transcendent–mundane, and religious–secular do not really capture the multiplicities that this change has wrought.[260] Religious worldviews reflect, inform, and simplify more or less explicit understandings that individuals or groups share as they search for the meaning of being a very small part of a very large whole.[261]

"The world's great religions provide world views; but so does the scientific rationality that is emblematic of modernity."[262] Religious and scientific worldviews can shift, sometimes gradually, sometimes quickly. The rise of Axial Age religions and the rise of modern science are two of the most notable shifts that humanity has experienced. The Axial Age witnessed powerful and independent cultural developments in China, India, Iran, Palestine, and Greece. This gave rise to the world's great religions. At that pivotal moment, humankind moved from a less reflective to a self-reflexive striving for human agency, transcendence, criticism, self-determination, and, eventually, future-oriented progress. Around the year 1,000 the first wave of globalization was powered by a desire to spread religious beliefs and by religious conversions. The vast majority of today's believers subscribe to one of the major religions that spread across the globe at that time.[263] In the sixteenth and seventeenth centuries, scientific advances discovered new ideas about motion and matter in a universe governed by the laws of nature. In the eighteenth and nineteenth centuries, geological and biological scientists transformed the understanding of time, development, and progress. In the twentieth century, quantum mechanics probed the infinite possibilities and uncertainties of the subatomic world while scientific cosmology developed new ways of thinking about the universe. Religion and science have evolved along plural and often contradictory lines. Today, the two provide foundations for worldviews that give meaning to the experience of being in a world marked by inescapable uncertainties.

Religion. Though often unacknowledged, theology has retained an important influence in modernity. Gillespie argues that the hidden origins of modernity precede the Age of Enlightenment and are to be found in "the great metaphysical and theological struggle that marked the end of the medieval world": the struggle between nominalism. with its insistence on nonteleological singularities accessed by biblical revelation or mystical experience, and scholasticism, with its belief in divinely created and revealed

---

[260] Casanova 2012: 193, 200, 202.
[261] Ossio 1997: 549; Hamilton 2018b: 377–78; Hamilton 2018a.
[262] Goldstein and Keohane 1993: 8.   [263] Hansen 2020.

universals.[264] At stake in this struggle were questions about the nature of God and the nature of being rather than, as emerged subsequently, the process of human self-assertion and control. Modern science neither opposed nor displaced religion. Unwittingly, it became an extension of earlier theological debates. And this, Gillespie argues, has created a concealed theology of philosophical disagreements that has stretched throughout modernity down to the present. God does not disappear. His attributes and capacities are transferred to nature and man. In the shift from divine to natural law, disenchantment thus merges with re-enchantment.[265]

Religious worldviews also remain deeply embedded in contemporary world politics in other ways, as Byrnes shows in Chapter 9. For example, they provide a hidden script about order in anarchy that lies at the center of realist theories of international relations.[266] As the founder of modern political science, Hobbes offers a "worldly application of a theological pattern."[267] Existing in the state of nature, man is a believer in God and acknowledges his obligations under God's law. These are real obligations rooted in real law, made and enforced by men on the basis of and legitimized by their worldviews. Just as God created the universe, so man can create the commonwealth and an international order, even if their sovereign is only imagined. In Bain's reading, Hobbes is thus a theorist of interstate society rather than of international anarchy.[268] Contemporary realist theories of order are not strictly modern or secular; traces of medieval theological discourses can be discerned by those who choose to look. In our accounts of world politics, religion remains constitutive of how we think about the world. Nominalist theology remains embedded in modernist conceptions of sovereignty as immanent and necessary or imposed and contingent order.[269] In this view, religion lives on in the era of secular science and the study of world politics. "The core constituents of the Judeo-Christian world-view have traveled in a multiplicity of forms to make up the dominant 'secular' cosmology characteristic of much of 'western thinking' and 'science' today ... the theological origin of the search for order, in our everyday discourse and indeed in science, is important to recognize" as a way to reason from natural phenomena or God as the first cause of the universe.[270] Today, the connections between religious, social, and political cosmologies typically are implicit, often contradictory, and always consequential.[271]

---

[264] Gillespie 2008: 12, 14.   [265] McClure 2010.   [266] Bain 2020.
[267] Mitchell 1993: 78, quoted in Bain 2020: 129; Bain 2015.   [268] Bain 2020: 130–31.
[269] Bain 2020: 9–10; Gillespie 2008.   [270] Kurki 2020: 26–27.
[271] Kurki 2020: 39–40, 67–68, 79–80; Kragh 2004: 12, 51.

It follows, as Byrnes argues in Chapter 9, that religion and politics are not separate "variables" as Haas and Nau hold in Chapter 2, but coconstitutive ways of "being in" the world. Haas and Nau, Byrnes writes,

> want to insist that relational worldviews imply their own kinds of … "Gods" that pose a threat to human freedom because we don't really possess the capacity to truly know or resist their effects. But if a relational cosmology is grounded in faith or in the pursuit of what is "really real," then the unknown itself is the basis of Truth and the human propensity to resistance is ultimately futile. We are, some religious worldviews might suggest, in the act of "becoming" through our relationships not only with each other, but also with that which we cannot measure, define or know through Newtonian scientific methods.

In contrast to nondogmatic religions such as Buddhism and Hinduism, which tolerate the uncertainties of forests and the foibles of divine personages, fundamentalist political projects of doctrinal religions wish to create orderly and predictable gardens. Cosmological uncertainty unleashes a yearning for clarity and the comforts of the promise of eternal life. But even dogmatic Catholicism, Byrnes argues, invites believers to more than conformity and oppression resting on unshakable ontological certainty. Communion with God requires acts of courageous faith. And "faith," as Block says in Bergman's *Seventh Seal,* "is a torment. It is like loving someone who is out there in the darkness but never appears, no matter how loudly you call."[272] "Confronted with the inexplicable problem of suffering and in a state of profound unknowing," Byrnes suggests, believers turn to Jesus "in a search for meaning within uncertainty and suffering. In this context then faith is the acceptance of uncertainty, not a search for comforting explanations that will dispel it."[273] In the end, all religions require "the life-defining act of leaping, faithfully, into the unknown."[274] Reflecting on Wittgenstein's philosophical astonishment about the existence of the world, author John Kaag articulates a similar idea: "Philosophy is the activity of climbing a ladder, and once you reach the top, the ladder disappears."[275]

In its current global resurgence, religion is not an idiom of the discontented or the displaced. It is a set of ideas, values, practices, and traditions that shape many communities and their political struggles in all parts of the world. Often it is not religion per se but its various manifestations that matter politically, "as cognitive statements of truth, identificatory symbols, comprehensive ways of life, modes of voluntary association, moral and ethical obligations, vulnerable collective identities, and so forth." What matters politically is not religion as such but "the multiple values

---

[272] The Economist 2020: 68.   [273] Byrnes, email sent to the author 04/12/2020.
[274] Byrnes, Chapter 9.   [275] Kaag 2020.

that particular dimensions of religion realize."[276] Religious resurgence is not a "fundamentalist" or "anti-modernist" reaction to science and modernity. It is part of modernity and often a normative critique of developments that have failed to deliver on the promises of the Enlightenment project.

Enlightenment expectations of the inevitable march of secularization and rationalization turn out to have been mistaken. As a legacy from the past and an adaptation to the present, religion continues to shape contemporary worldviews and world politics. In America's social and political life, the "fourth great awakening" has made religion once again a vital force. The enlargement of the European Union toward the South and East has broadened the scope for human population flows, yet a growing stream of illegal migrants and refugees have made religion a vital concern in secular Europe.[277] Catholicism thrives in Africa, Protestantism in Latin America. Folk religions flower in East Asia, specifically China and Japan. And Islam is going through a global resurgence. Indeed, religious traditions all over the world are showing a great capacity to reinvent and reinvigorate themselves.

Science. Allan argues in Chapter 8 that worldviews are local, temporary, and political stabilizations of cosmological elements. In contrast to ascetic Protestantism, "the world remained a great enchanted garden" for Asia's popular religions, in the words of Weber. Concretizing further Weber's historical account, Allan highlights the constitutive effects that two cosmological elements – materialism and object orientations – have had for modernist values of rationality and control and thus for the very basis of the contemporary science of world politics. In other works, Allan shows how economy and climate became in the twentieth century objects of governance that lent themselves to the exercise of control in a putatively law-governed yet highly unpredictable universe.[278] He also shows how the separation of object and subject creates in history the very basis for the concept of rationalization that Weber deploys. Referring to Shilliam's discussion of the importance of Vodou (*lwa*) in the Haitian revolution, Allan concurs with Byrnes: the historical evolution of the conceptual apparatus of the modern natural and social sciences has created enormous barriers to reckon with the importance of religious worldviews. Furthermore, that apparatus simply cannot acknowledge that the *lwa* might have real agency in the world, and thereby misunderstands the way that cosmology forges action in ways that differ from Western concepts of modernity.[279]

---

[276] Laborde 2017: 2.   [277] Katzenstein 2006.   [278] Allan 2017.
[279] Allan, Chapter 8; Shilliam 2017; Byrnes, Chapter 9.

Although the scientific method buttresses a worldview that has acquired global significance in the last 400 years, different sciences can embody different worldviews.[280] A radical break in scientific worldviews occurred in the sixteenth and seventeenth centuries. Leading scientists put on a different "thinking-cap" that permitted them to leave behind an Aristotelian worldview that had been unassailable for centuries.[281] The ascendant scientific worldview replaced that of a well-ordered, hierarchical cosmos with visions of an "indefinite and even infinite universe."[282] Over time, this scientific worldview increasingly supplanted the views embodied in the world's major religions. For modern orders science became a secular equivalent to religion.

Kuhn's celebrated theory of scientific revolutions offers a good illustration. Central in the evolution of his thinking about science was the "Aristotle Experience" Kuhn had in the summer of 1947 in Harvard's Kirkland Hall. Kuhn discovered for himself the fundamental difference between the Aristotelian and Newtonian views of the world. At one moment Aristotle seemed to be just a bad and ignorant physicist.[283] And then, suddenly, "the fragments in my head sorted themselves out in a new way, and fell into place together. My jaw dropped, for all at once Aristotle seemed a very good physicist indeed, but of a sort I'd never dreamed possible."[284] Aristotle's physics suddenly seemed plausible and it was no longer puzzling why his view of the world had been so widely shared for so many centuries. Throughout his life Kuhn reflected often on this revelatory experience. He writes that scientific "paradigms are constitutive not only of science but of nature ... in a scientific revolution, what we take to be nature must itself, in a sense, change."[285] And he described scientific revolutions as "conversions" prompted more by transformative personal experiences or leaps of faith than reason, observation, and careful experimentation.[286] For those following Kuhn, different paradigms have "incommensurable ways of seeing the world and practicing science in it."[287] Scientific revolutions can change the meaning of conventionally accepted concepts and thus reconfigure "the conceptual network through which scientists view the world."[288]

---

[280] Becker 2018: 284.   [281] Butterfield 1957: 1–2.   [282] Koyré 1957: 2.

[283] Weinberg 2015 writes that Aristotle was the first scientist to insist on the need for observation to check speculative theories. But he had no sense that mathematics could be an important part of the study of nature and did not recognize the importance of experiments. Over the centuries and millennia science has progressed.

[284] Kuhn 2000: 16.   [285] Bernstein 1976: 87.

[286] My discussion follows Reisch 2019: xxxii–xiii, 61–62, 65–68, 79; Bernstein 1976: 87, 92; and Weinberg 1998: 8–9, 12–13.

[287] Kuhn 2012: 4.   [288] Kuhn 2012: 102.

Classical and quantum physics are both part of modern science and thus are not separated by as dramatic a shift in scientific worldviews as were Aristotle's and Newton's. But as specimens of modern science, their view of nature is arguably very different. One holds that nature is passive and subject to control; the other that nature is active and always threatening to escape control. One neglects uncertainty; the other builds on its constitutive effects. One holds a determinist or probabilistic view of the world that excludes uncertainty; the other incorporates uncertainty. These are foundational differences in outlook on the natural and, by implication, also on the political world.

Science and Religion. Religious worldviews share some features with Post-Newtonian scientific worldviews. Building on Schütz and in agreement with Post-Newtonianism, Bellah argues that we live in multiple worlds.[289] Much of the time, we live in the world of ordinary daily life, organized by the coordinates of standard time and standard place. Pragmatic and practical interests and means-and-ends calculations rule that life. But we do not spend all of our time in the ordinary reality of daily life. Sleeping and dreaming, for example, do not operate in standard time and standard space. They contradict the logic of daily life. So do other activities: watching a sports event, movie, or play; gazing at a piece of art; reading; listening to stories or music; playing games. All of these divert us from daily life and suspend or alter its rules. Both science and religion are part of those other worlds.

Newton personifies the intimate relations of religion and science. While he drafted the *Principia Mathmatica,* covertly and intensely during a quarter of a century, "Copernicus and Faustus in one," he also wrote extensively about alchemy and magic.[290] Einstein believed that objective reality could be understood; he called this belief a "religion."[291] Both science and religion are variegated practices of different ways of knowing. Neither one takes the appearance of daily life for granted. Neither suspends, as we do in daily life, a disbelief in the world as it appears. Both inquire into the possibility that the world might be different than it appears. Both are instances of us living in multiple realities and thus are examples of the profound human capacity of meaning-making. Physicists who believe in God are "unusual" but "not rare." Religious and scientific practices are rooted in the world of play. The practice of seeking an understanding of the universe is a good in and of itself, with consequences that can reflect back on and shape our daily life.[292]

---

[289] Bellah 2011: 1–3.   [290] Keynes 1951: 323.   [291] Henderson 2020: 39.
[292] Bellah 2011: 112–14.

In scientific as in religious odysseys, the journey matters more than the destination. Both trips are open ended. Another bend in the road always awaits and always promises a new vista. It could be an old idea thought anew, or a new idea no one has thought before. The culture wars between science and religion – and between competing scientific explanations of nature and society and humanistic interpretations of meanings – are worldviews expressed by and within science and religion. Michael Barnett ends Chapter 5 by recounting Marin Buber's personal odyssey. In the final stage, Buber adopted a relationalism steeped deeply in both the immanent and the transcendental, the particular and the universal. This relationalism provides the foundation for his magisterial *I and Thou* and the fluidity between being and becoming that he pleads for. Barnett concludes that Buber might well have been critical of the metaphysics and the ethics of both humanist substantialism and hyper-humanist relationalism; both threaten to destroy the human. Perhaps. But this book points to possible variants and combinations of substantialism and relationalism, and science and religion. They constitute part of the fleeting and contested multiple realities that enrich our daily life.

Newton knew this only too well. On account of religion, he refused to speculate about the causes of gravity. He considered himself to be God's right hand and not his opponent. For him and other modern scientists, like Descartes, the link between science and religion was explicit. Both theologians and scientists conducted astro-theological inquiries into the order of the world and God's role in upholding it. Now the link is implicit. Many today believe that Science (with a capital S) is looking for a theory that can explain the world. Eternal and universal Laws of Nature are not in this world but stand behind it;[293] "This implies at least the possibility, if not the existence, of a god."[294] Unger and Smolin label this a "transcendental folly."[295] Like God, such a scientific theory would embody absolute and eternal principles that account for the order of the world; it would work toward unveiling a transcendental reality that somehow lies "behind" the world we experience. In a public address given in November 1951, Pope Pius XII went so far as to assert that the big bang theory confirmed the story of Genesis. He soon realized that much of his flock was not prepared to consider such an explicit and direct link between religion and science.[296]

Many physicists working with the standard model are extremely reticent to probe the conditions that made the big bang possible.[297] Scientific

---

[293] Smolin 1997: 193–94, 198–99.   [294] Smolin 1997: 200.
[295] Unger and Smolin 2015: 366.   [296] Rovelli 2017: 204–05. Healey 2016: 2–6.
[297] Kurki 2020: 48–49.

cosmology is neutral science as it is conventionally understood, but it also has speculative aspects not normally associated with modern science. The Standard Model is mute on what existed before the big bang moment of singularity. How could that moment have emerged? Why are the laws of physics what they are today? Why are conditions in the universe so constant? These questions push scientific cosmology to its very boundaries, and perhaps beyond. Roger Penrose, winner of the 2020 Nobel Prize in physics, suggests – without, yet, any strong evidence – that universes existed before the big bang and others might well follow the end of this one.[298] The current inability to conceptualize convincingly what came before the big bang puts scientific cosmology in touch with religious worldviews: "The question of what happened during, and perhaps even before, the Big Bang is slowly coming into focus in the last years of this century in the same way that the question of what happened before the origin of our species came into focus during the last."[299] In seeking to answer that question, why should the sciences assume that the laws of nature are eternal rather than the creation of time-bound natural processes?[300]

Today, ordinary language presents religion as about beliefs while science is about facts. But for others, including some of the twentieth-century's leading physicists, the border between quantum mechanics and religion is porous and, in the case of Schrödinger, best captured by the concept of worldview.[301] Werner Heisenberg is less than definitive about the separation between religion and science: "In science a decision can always be reached as to what is right and wrong. It is not a question of belief, or *Weltanschauung* [worldview], or hypothesis; but a certain statement could be simply right and another statement wrong ... It is decided by nature, or if you prefer by God, in any case not by man."[302] But what happens if we replace the singular Science with plural sciences and their different worldviews? Do the encounter with the code of the cosmos and the surrender of notions of absolute space and time really render scientific worldviews implacably opposed to religion and philosophy? Or are both more or less successful attempts to stabilize and imbue with meaning a world filled with gut-wrenching uncertainties? Niels Bohr appears not to have cared. According to a possibly apocryphal story told by Elaine Pagels, a colleague visiting him in Denmark was taken aback by a horseshoe nailed over Bohr's barn door. He asked assertively that surely Bohr did not believe such stuff. Bohr's answer was telling: "Of course not! But it works whether you believe in it or not."[303]

---

[298] Healey 2016: 8–9.   [299] Smolin 1997: 17.   [300] Smolin 1997: 18.
[301] Schrödinger 1985; Burgess 2018; Wilber 1984; Smetham 2010.
[302] Quoted in Pagels 1982: 74.   [303] Pagels 2019: 13.

The legacies and interrelations of Axial Age religions and science affect our worldviews to this day. Each of them has evolved along plural and often contradictory lines. Together, they constitute much of the discursive forms informing world politics today. Charles Taylor sees secularization as furthering both science and faith.[304] A meaningful life can be had by all. Religion is a matter of choice. Believers and nonbelievers alike must lead a morally demanding life. Instead of fitting into a slotted place in the cosmos, everyone is called to construct a good life through personal development and choice. Believers believe while doubting. And nonbelievers are not indifferent to the transcendental. The outcome is not a clash between atheism and religious devotion. Instead, science and religion accommodate each other and, together, feed a spiritual pluralism.

In Taylor's terms, we should avoid conceiving of religion and science in the singular, each as an overarching, coherent worldview. Instead, their various elements are loosely coupled and circulate in scientific, religious, philosophical, social, and political discourses. They provide the raw material for actors who try to construct more or less compelling and more or less contested religious and scientific narratives that place humanity in the world. We can engage these narratives as we cling to the categorical assertion of a universally valid truth, or we can seize the opportunity, subject ourselves to the requirements of "warranted assertability" by relevant communities of practice, and learn something new as we enter "a different world of definitions and procedures" – all at the risk of disrupting earlier certainty.[305] Religion and science and their various traditions inhabit the park which contains most of the worldviews that individuals hold and argue about today.

Stuart Kauffman agrees, in his reverential awe of the ceaseless creativity of the web of life and human history, which tumbles forward and breaks no laws of physics, while always remaining partially lawless. This is one way of naming God. It is "our chosen name for the ceaseless creativity in the natural universe, biosphere, and human cultures . . . we typically do not and cannot know what will happen. We live our lives forward, as Kierkegaard said. We live as if we knew, as Nietzsche said. We live our lives forward into mystery, and do so with faith and courage."[306] This worldview has a place for both the promise and the inadequacy of reason. Uncertainty is not a problem to be solved but a condition to be experienced.

This broad understanding of the relation between science and religion offers a productive way of thinking about the relationship between Newtonian and Post-Newtonian science and between humanism and hyper-humanism. Steven Weinberg, for one, suggests that, in the end,

---

[304] Taylor 2007; Brooks 2013.   [305] Jackson 2015: 16–17.   [306] Kauffman 2008: xi.

the coming together of cosmology and particle physics in two widely accepted "standard models" will produce one story.[307] Dark matter and dark energy are central in a 13.8 billion-year-old "transparent" universe that is accessible to science. (The "nontransparent" universe that preceded the big bang remains accessible only to faith). Weinberg concedes that a "crude anthropic explanation" may be the best we can do since the particular "bubble" in the multiverse or assemblies of an unknown and perhaps unknowable number of universes that we inhabit may constrain our ability to construct a "rational explanation" for all multiverses. The values for the matter and energy that we do know might be no more than an accident of the particular part of this particular multiverse we inhabit. "Any beings like ourselves that are capable of studying the universe must be in a part of the universe in which the constants of nature allow the evolution of life and intelligence. Man may indeed be the measure of all things, although not quite in the sense intended by Protagoras."[308]

Eager to disobey his orders at the Battle of Copenhagen, Admiral Nelson reportedly inverted his looking glass, put it on his blind eye and shouted – "Mate! I cannot read the signal!" And so it is with worldviews when they encounter "a relatively sudden and unstructured event" that reorders our perceptions of the world.[309] The pandemic of 2020 may be one such event that creates a moment of profound epistemic uncertainty about the future of world politics. As the crystallizations of comforting worldviews confront the contingencies of a world in unfathomable flux, perhaps the time has come to fully acknowledge this uncertainty and to start waking up from our "deep Newtonian slumber."[310] This suggestion is in tune with Tom Stoppard's *Arcadia* and its many allusions to gardens and forests. The play's mathematical biologist, Valentine, ruminates that "the unpredictable and the predetermined unfold together to make everything the way it is. It's how nature creates itself, on every scale, the snowflake and the snowstorm. It makes me so happy. To be at the beginning again, knowing almost nothing."[311] Does not the study of world politics share this with the study of nature? And if it does, why wouldn't we want to acknowledge the obvious – the existence of uncertainty as a constitutive part of world politics?

Bibliography

Adams, Thomas Jessen. 2020. "A Lesson in Eventful Temporality: Pedagogies of Donald Trump from Abroad," *PS: Political Science & Politics* (April): 360–61.

---

[307] Weinberg 2013.   [308] Weinberg 2013: 8; Kauffman 2008: 27–30.
[309] Jackson and Nexon 2009: 909.   [310] Kavalski 2012.   [311] Stoppard 1993: 47.

Adler, Emmanuel. 2019. *World Ordering: A Social Theory of Cognitive Evolution.* Cambridge: Cambridge University Press.

Ahmari, Sohrab. 2020. "They Blinded Us with Science: The History of a Delusion," *Commentary* (May): 23–29.

Allan, Bentley B. 2017. "Producing the Climate: States, Scientists, and the Constitution of Global Governance Objects," *International Organization* 71, 1: 131–62.

Allan, Bentley B. 2018. *Scientific Cosmology and International Orders.* New York: Cambridge University Press.

Allan, Bentley B. 2019. "Paradigm and Nexus: Neoclassical Economics and the Growth Imperative in the World Bank, 1948," *Review of International Political Economy* 26: 183–206.

Almond, Gabriel A. and Stephen J. Genco. 1977. "Clouds, Clocks, and the Study of Politics," *World Politics* 29, 4: 489–522.

Ang, Yuen Yuen. 2016. *How China Escaped the Poverty Trap.* Ithaca, NY: Cornell University Press.

Artaud, Antonin. 1958. *The Theatre and Its Double.* Translated by Mary Caroline Richards. New York: Gove Press.

Asad, Talal. 2003. *Formations of the Secular: Christianity, Islam, Modernity.* Stanford, CA: Stanford University Press.

Axelrod, Robert and Michael D. Cohen. 1999. *Harnessing Complexity: Organizational Implications of a Scientific Frontier.* New York: Free Press.

Bacciagaluppi, Guido. 2014. "A Critic Looks at QBism," in M.C. Galavotti, S. Hartmann, M. Weber, W. Gonzalez, D. Dieks, and T. Uebel, eds., *New Directions in the Philosophy of Science.* Switzerland: Springer International, pp. 403–15.

Bächtold, Manuel. 2008. "Interpreting Quantum Mechanics According to a Pragmatist Approach," *Foundations of Physics* 38, 9: 843–68.

Baeyer, Hans Christian von. 2016. *QBism: The Future of Quantum Physics.* Cambridge, MA: Harvard University Press.

Bain, William. 2015. "Thomas Hobbes as a Theorist of Anarchy: A Theological Interpretation," *History of European Ideas* 40, 1: 13–28.

Bain, William. 2020. *Political Theology of International Order.* New York: Oxford University Press.

Barad, Karen. 2007. *Meeting the Universe Halfway: Quantum Physics and the Entanglement of Matter and Meaning.* Durham, NC: Duke University Press.

Barton, Gregory. 2000. "Keepers of the Jungle: Environmental Management in British India, 1855–1900," *The Historian* 62, 3: 557–74.

Basu, Kaushik. 2014. "Randomisation, Causality and the Role of Reasoned Intuition," *Oxford Development Studies* 42, 4: 455–72.

Becker, Adam. 2018. *What Is Real? The Unfinished Quest for the Meaning of Quantum Physics.* New York: Basic Books.

Bellah, Robert N. 2011. *Religion in Human Evolution: From the Paleolithic to the Axial Age.* Cambridge, MA: The Belknap Press of Harvard University Press.

Bernstein, Richard J. 1976. *The Restructuring of Social and Political Theory.* New York: Harcourt Brace Jovanovich.

Beveridge, Charles E. 1977. "Frederick Law Olmsted's Theory of Landscape Design," *Nineteenth Century* 3 (Summer): 38–43.

Binmore, Ken. 2017. "On the Foundations of Decision Theory," *Homo Oeconomicus* 34: 259–73.

Blackmar, Elizabeth and Roy Rosenzweig. 1994. "The Park and the People: Central Park and Its Publics: 1850–1910," in Thomas Bender and Carl E. Schorske, eds., *Budapest and New York: Studies in Metropolitan Transformation: 1870–1930*. New York: Russell Sage, pp. 108–34.

Blaug, Mark. 1963. "The Myth of the Old Poor Law and the Making of the New," *The Journal of Economic History* 23, 2: 151–84.

Blodgett, Geoffrey. 1976. "Frederick Law Olmsted: Landscape Architecture as Conservative Reform," *Journal of American History* 62 (March): 869–89.

Bookstaber, Richard. 2017. *The End of Theory: Financial Crises, the Failure of Economics and the Sweep of Human Interaction*. Princeton, NJ: Princeton University Press.

Bousquet, Antoine and Robert Geyer. 2011. "Introduction: Complexity and the International Arena," *Cambridge Review of International Affairs* 24, 1: 1–3.

Brooks, David. 2013. "The Secular Society," *New York Times* (July 8). www.nytimes.com/2013/07/09/opinion/brooks-the-secular-society.html. Accessed 08/29/20.

Brown, Chris and Robyn Eckersley. 2018. "International Political Theory and the Real World," in Chris Brown and Robyn Eckersley, eds., *The Oxford Handbook of International Political Theory*. New York: Oxford University Press, pp. 3–18.

Burgess, J. Peter. 2018. "Science Blurring Its Edges into Spirit: The Quantum Path to Ātma," *Millennium* 47, 1: 128–41.

Butterfield, Herbert. 1957. *The Origins of Modern Science 1300–1800*. London: G. Bell and Sons.

Byrne, David and Gill Callaghan. 2013. *Complexity Theory and the Social Sciences: The State of the Art*. New York: Routledge.

Camic, Charles, Neil Gross, and Michèle Lamont, eds. 2011. *Social Knowledge in the Making*. Chicago, IL: The University of Chicago Press.

Carey, Bjorn. 2014. "Stanford's Maryam Mirzakhani wins Fields Medal," *Stanford News* (August 12).

Cartwright, Nancy. 1999. *The Dappled World: A Study of the Boundaries of Science*. New York: Cambridge University Press.

Casanova, José. 2012. "Religion, the Axial Age, and Secular Modernity in Bellah's Theory of Religious Evolution," in Robert N. Bellah and Hans Joas, eds., *The Axial Age and Its Consequences*. Cambridge MA: The Belknap Press of Harvard University Press, pp. 191–221.

Casid, Jill. H. 2005. *Sowing Empire: Landscape and Colonization*. Minneapolis: University of Minnesota Press.

Caves, Carlton M., Christopher A. Fuchs, and Rüdiger Schack. 2002a. "Quantum Probabilities as Baysian Probabilities," *Physical Review A* 65, 022305: 1–6.

Caves, Carlton M., Christopher A. Fuchs, and Rüdiger Schack. 2002b. "Unknown Quantum States: The Quantum de Finetti Representation," *Journal of Mathematical Physics* 43, 9: 4537–59.

Caves, Carlton M., Christopher A. Fuchs, and Rüdiger Schack. 2007. "Subjective Probability and Quantum Certainty," *Studies in History and Philosophy of Modern Physics* 38, 2: 255–74.

Checkel, Jeffrey. 2013. "Theoretical Pluralism in IR: Possibilities and Limits," in Walter Carlsnaes, Thomas Risse and Beth Simmons, eds., *Sage Handbook of International Relations*, 2nd ed. Newbury Park, CA: Sage Publications, pp. 220–42.

Cheng, Eugenia. 2020. "Two plus Two: An Argument for not Putting too Much Stock in Numbers," *The New York Times Book Review* (November 8): 37.

Chevassus-au-Louis, Nicolas. 2019. *Fraud in the Lab: The High Stakes of Scientific Research*. Translation Nicholas Elliott. Cambridge, MA: Harvard University Press.

Chilton, Adam and Dustin Tingly. 2013. "Why the Study of International Law Needs Experiments," *Columbia Journal of Transnational Law* 52, 1: 173–239.

Clarke, Kevin A. and David M. Primo. 2012. *A Model Discipline: Political Science and the Logic of Representation*. New York: Oxford University Press.

Coke, David and Alan Borg. 2011. *Vauxhall Gardens: A History*. New Haven, CT: Yale University.

Collins, Harry M. 2010. *Tacit and Explicit Knowledge*. Chicago, IL: The University of Chicago Press.

Cooper, David E. 2006. *A Philosophy of Gardens*. Oxford: Clarendon Press.

Coyne, Christopher J. 2003. "Order in the Jungle: Social Interaction Without the State," *The Independent Review* 7, 4: 557–66.

Cranz, Galen. 1982. *The Politics of Park Design: A History of Urban Parks in America*. Cambridge, MA: The MIT Press.

Cronon, William. 1983. *Changes in the Land: Indians, Colonists, and the Ecology of New England*. New York: Hill and Wang.

Dake, Karl. 1991. "Orienting Dispositions in the Perception of Risk: An Analysis of Contemporary Worldviews and Cultural Biases," *Journal of Cross-Cultural Psychology* 22, 1: 61–82.

Daston, Lorraine. 2019. *Against Nature*. Cambridge, MA: The MIT Press.

Deaton, Angus. 2010. "Instruments, Randomization, and Learning about Development," *Journal of Economic Literature* 48 (June): 424–55.

Deaton, Angus and Nancy Cartwright. 2018. "Understanding and Misunderstanding Randomized Controlled Trials," *Social Science & Medicine* 210: 2–21.

Dehejia, Vivek. 2016. "The Experimental Turn in Economics," *Livemint*. www.livemint.com/Sundayapp/IM5bHpfFjniYIONzr1qJWJ/The-experimental-turn-in-economics.html. Accessed 03/19/20.

DeMartino, George. 2018. "The Specter of Irreparable Ignorance: The Confounding Problem of the Counterfactual in Economic Explanation." Presidential Address, Association of Social Economics, Atlanta, GA (January 5).

Dove, Michael R. 1992. "The Dialectical History of 'Jungle' in Pakistan: An Examination of the Relationship between Nature and Culture," *Journal of Anthropological Research* 48, 3: 231–53.

Drayton, Richard. 2000. *Nature's Government: Science, Imperial Britain, and the 'Improvement' of the World*. New Haven, CT: Yale University Press.

Druckman, James N., Donald P. Green, James H. Kuklinski, Arthur Lupia, eds. 2011. *Cambridge Handbook of Experimental Political Science*. New York: Cambridge University Press.

Du Sautoy, Marcus. 2016. *The Great Unknown: Seven Journeys to the Frontiers of Science*. New York: Viking.

Duara, Prasenjit. 2015. *The Crisis of Global Modernity: Asian Traditions and a Sustainable Future*. New York: Cambridge University Press.

Dubois, Pierre. 2015. "Porous Places: Music in the (Late) Pleasure Gardens and Social Ambiguity," *XVII-XVIII* 72: 115–28.

The Economist. 2020. "Pandemic Cinema: Will and Grace," (August 1): 68.

Enright, Kelly. 2008. "On the Jungle," *Environmental History* 13, 3: 556–61.

Erman, Eva and Niklas Möller. 2013. "Political Legitimacy in the Real Normative World: The Priority of Morality and the Autonomy of the Political," *British Journal of Political Science* 45: 215–33.

Fierke, Karin M. 2017. "Consciousness at the Interface: Wendt, Eastern Wisdom and the Ethics of Intra-Action," *Critical Review* 29, 2: 141–69.

Friedman, Jeffrey A. 2019. *War and Chance: Assessing Uncertainty in Politics*. New York: Oxford University Press.

Friedman, Jeffrey A. and Richard Zeckhauser. 2018. "Analytic Confidence and Political Decision-Making: Theoretical Principles and Experimental Evidence from National Security Professionals," *Political Psychology* 39, 5: 1069–87.

Fuchs, Christopher A. 2017. "Notwithstanding Bohr, the Reasons for QBism," *Mind and Matter* 15, 2: 245–300.

Fuchs, Christopher A., N. David Mermin, and Rüdiger Schack. 2014. "An Introduction to QBism with an Application to the Locality of Quantum Mechanics," *American Journal of Physics* 82: 749–54.

Fuchs, Christopher and Rüdiger Schack. 2009. "Quantum-Bayesian Coherence," arXiv:0906.2187v1 [quant-ph] (June 11).

Gaines, Brian J., James H. Kuklinski, and Paul J. Quirk. 2006. "The Logic of the Survey Experiment Reexamined," *Political Analysis* 15, 1: 1–20.

Galison, Peter. 1997. *Image and Logic: A Material Culture of Microphysics*. Chicago, IL: The University of Chicago Press.

Gerber, Alan S. and Donald P. Green. 2012. *Field Experiments: Design, Analysis, and Interpretation*. New York: W.W. Norton.

Gerrard, Bill. 1994. "Beyond Rational Expectations: A Constructive Interpretation of Keynes's Analysis of Behavior under Uncertainty," *The Economic Journal* 104, 423: 327–37.

Geuss, Raymond. 2020. *Who Needs a World View?* Cambridge, MA: Harvard University Press.

Gillespie, Michael Allen. 2008. *The Theological Origins of Modernity*. Chicago, IL: The University of Chicago Press.

Gillies, Donald. 2000. *Philosophical Theories of Probability*. New York: Routledge.

Gladwell, Malcolm. 2013. "The Gift of Doubt: Albert O. Hirschman and the Power of Failure," *The New Yorker* (June 24). www.newyorker.com/magazine/2013/06/24/the-gift-of-doubt. Accessed 03/15/20.

Goetzmann, William H. and William N. Goetzmann. 1986. *The West of the Imagination*. New York: W.W. Norton.

Goldstein, Judith and Robert O. Keohane. 1993. "Ideas and Foreign Policy: An Analytical Framework," in Judith Goldstein and Robert O. Keohane, eds., *Ideas and Foreign Policy: Beliefs, Institutions, and Political Change*. Ithaca, NY: Cornell University Press, pp. 3–30.

Grabel, Ilene. 2017. *When Things Don't Fall Apart: Global Financial Governance and Developmental Finance in an Age of Productive Incoherence*. Cambridge, MA: MIT Press.

Green, Donald P. and Alan S. Gerber. 2002. "Reclaiming the Experimental Tradition in Political Science," in Ira Katznelson and Helen V. Milner, eds., *Political Science: The State of the Discipline*. New York: Norton, pp. 805–32.

Green, Donald P. and Alan S. Gerber. 2015. *Get Out the Vote: How to Increase Voter Turnout*, 3rd ed. Washington, DC: The Brookings Institution.

Grimley, Daniel M. 2006. *Grieg: Music, Landscape and Norwegian Identity*. Rochester, NY: Boydell Press.

Gunitsky, Seva. 2019. "Rival Visions of Parsimony," *International Studies Quarterly* 63, 3: 707–16.

Hainmueller, Jens, Daniel J. Hopkins, and Teppei Yamamoto. 2014. "Causal Inference in Conjoint Analysis: Understanding Multidimensional Choices via Stated Preference Experiments," *Political Analysis* 22, 1: 1–30. https://doi.org/10.1093/pan/mpt024.

Hamilton, Scott. 2017. "A Genealogy of Metatheory in IR: How 'Ontology' Emerged from the Inter-Paradigm Debate," *International Theory* 9, 1: 136–70.

Hamilton, Scott. 2018a. "The Measure of all Things? The Anthropocene as a Global Biopolitics of Carbon," *European Journal of International Relations* 24, 1: 33–57.

Hamilton, Scott. 2018b. "Foucault's End of History: The Temporality of Governmentality and Its End in the Anthropocene," *Millennium* 46, 3: 371–95.

Hansen, Valerie. 2020. *The Year 1000: When Explorers Connected the World – and Globalization Began*. New York: Scribner.

Harrington, Cameron. 2016. "The Ends of the World: International Relations and the Anthropocene," *Millennium* 44, 3: 478–98.

Harrison, Neil E. ed. 2006. *Complexity in World Politics: Concepts and Methods of a New Paradigm*. Albany: State University of New York Press.

Harrison, Robert Pogue. 1992. *Forests: The Shadow of Civilization*. Chicago, IL: The University of Chicago Press.

Harrison, Robert Pogue. 2008. *Gardens: An Essay on the Human Condition*. Chicago, IL: The University of Chicago Press.

Healey, Richard. 2016. "Quantum-Bayesian and Pragmatist Views of Quantum Theory," *The Stanford Encyclopedia of Philosophy* (Spring 2017 Edition), Edward N. Zalta (ed.). https://plato.stanford.edu/archives/spr2017/entries/quantum-bayesian/. Accessed 10/10/2017.

Healey, Richard. 2017. *The Quantum Revolution in Philosophy*. New York: Oxford University Press.

Helmreich, Anne. 2008. "Body and Soul: The Conundrum of the Aesthetic Garden," *Garden History* 36, 2: 273–88.

Henderson, Bob. 2020. "The Quantum Mechanic," *The New York Times Magazine* (June 28): 36–39, 54–55.

Herbert, Eugenia W. 2011. *Flora's Empire: British Gardens in India*. Philadelphia: University of Pennsylvania Press.

Herbjørnsrud, Dag. 2017. "The African Enlightenment," Aeon (December 13). https://aeon.co/essays/yacob-and-amo-africas-precursors-to-locke-hume-and-kant. Accessed 2/2/2021.

Hirschman, Albert O. 1958. *The Strategy of Economic Development*. New Haven, CT: Yale University Press.

Hirschman, Albert O. 1967. "The Principle of the Hiding Hand," *The Public Interest* 6 (Winter): 10–23.

Hirschman, Albert O. 1971. *A Bias for Hope: Essays on Development and Latin America*. New Haven, CT: Yale University Press.

Hirschman, Albert O. 1980 [1945]. "Preface to the Expanded Paperback Edition," in *National Power and the Structure of Foreign Trade*. Berkeley: University of California Press, pp. v–xii.

Hodges, H.A. 1944. *Wilhelm Dilthey: An Introduction*. New York: Oxford University Press.

Hou, Shen. 2012. "Garden and Forest: A Forgotten Magazine and the Urban Roots of American Environmentalism," *Environmental History* 17, 4: 813–42

Howett, Catherine. 1998. "Ecological Values in Twentieth-Century Landscape Design: A History and Hermeneutics," *Landscape Journal* 17: 80–98.

Hunt, John Dixon and Peter Willis, eds. 1975. *The Genius of the Place: The English Landscape Garden 1620–1820*. London: Paul Elek.

Hunter, Mary. 1993. "Landscapes, Gardens, and Gothic Settings in the Opera Buffe of Mozart and his Italian Contemporaries," *Current Musicology* 51: 94–104.

Hurley, Amanda Kolson and Timothy J. Reynolds. 2014. "The Machine is a Garden," *Foreign Policy* 208 (2014): 72–77.

Hyde, Susan D. 2015. "Experiments in International Relations: Lab, Survey and Field," *Annual Review of Political Science* 18: 403–24.

Jackson, John Brinckerhoff. 1984. *Discovering the Vernacular Landscape*. New Haven, CT: Yale University Press.

Jackson, Patrick T. 2002. *International Relations and Scientific Progress: Structural Realism Reconsidered*. Columbus: Ohio State University Press.

Jackson, Patrick T. 2015. "Fear of Relativism," *International Studies Perspectives* 16: 13–22.

Jackson, Patrick T. and Daniel H. Nexon. 2009. "Paradigmatic Faults in International Relations Theory," *International Studies Quarterly* 53: 907–30.

Jackson, Patrick T. and Daniel H. Nexon. 2013. "International Theory in a Post-Paradigmatic Era: From Substantive Wagers to Scientific Ontologies," *European Journal of International Relations* 19, 3: 543–65.

Jasanoff, Sheila. 2004. "The Idiom of Co-Production," in Sheila Jasanoff, ed., *States of Knowledge: The Co-Production of Science and Social Order*. New York: Routledge, pp. 13–45.

Jervis, Robert. 1997. *System Effects: Complexity in Political and Social Life*. Princeton, NJ: Princeton University Press.

Jervis, Robert. 2017. "One World or Many?" *Critical Review* 29, 2: 170–88.

Jünger, Ernst. 2013. *The Forest Passage*. Candor, NY: Telos Press.

Kaag, John. 2020. "Being and Time: How Wittgenstein, Benjamin, Cassirer and Heidegger Altered the Way We see Reality," The New York Times Book Review (September 27): 13.

Kalberg, Stephen. 2016. "Protestant Ethic," in George Ritzer, ed., *The Blackwell Encyclopedia of Sociology*. New York: Wiley. https://doi.org/10.1002/97814051 65518.wbeos0826.

Katzenstein, Peter J. 2006. "Multiple Modernities as Limits to Secular Europeanization," in Timothy A. Byrnes and Peter J. Katzenstein, eds., *Religion in an Expanding Europe*. New York: Cambridge University Press, pp. 1–33.

Katzenstein, Peter J. 2012. "China's Rise: Rupture, Return, or Recombination?" in Peter J. Katzenstein, ed., *Sinicization and the Rise of China: Civilizational Processes Beyond East and West*. New York: Routledge, pp. 1–38.

Katzenstein, Peter J. 2018. "The Second Coming? Reflections on a Global Theory of International Relations," *The Chinese Journal of International Politics* 11, 4: 373–90.

Kauffman, Stuart. A. 2008. *Reinventing the Sacred: A New View of Science, Reason, and Religion*. New York: Basic Books.

Kavalski, Emilian. 2012. "Waking IR Up from its 'Deep *Newtonian Slumber*'," *Millennium* 41, 1: 137–50.

Kay John and Mervyn King. 2000. *Radical Uncertainty: Decision-Making Beyond the Numbers*. New York: Norton.

Kellert, Stephen H. 1993. *In the Wake of Chaos: Unpredictable Order in Dynamic Systems*. Chicago, IL: The University of Chicago Press.

Kelly, Duncan. 2019. *Politics and the Anthropocene*. Cambridge: Polity.

Keynes, John Maynard. 1937. "The General Theory of Employment," *Quarterly Journal of Economics* 51, 2: 209–23.

Keynes, John Maynard. 1951. "Newton the Man," in Geoffrey Keynes, ed., *Essays in Biography*. London: R. Hart-Davis, pp. 310–23.

Kiel, L. Douglas and Euel Elliott. 1996. *Chaos Theory in the Social Sciences: Foundations and Applications*. Ann Arbor, MI: The University of Michigan Press.

Kim, Sabrina. 2017. "Using Experimental Methods in Post-Conflict Countries to Understand the Effects of Gender Reforms in the Liberian National Police," in Andreas Kruck and Andrea Schneiker, eds., *Researching Non-state Sectors in International Security: Theory and Practice*. London: Routledge, pp. 187–203.

Kinnvall, Catarina and Jennifer Mitzen. 2020. "Anxiety, Fear and Ontological Security in World Politics: Thinking with and beyond Giddens," *International Theory* 12, 2: 240–56.

Kipling, Rudyard. 1894. *The Jungle Book*. New York: Doubleday.

Kirshner, Jonathan. 2009. "Keynes, Legacies, and Inquiry," *Theory and Society* 38, 5: 527–41.

Kirshner, Jonathan. 2021. "Keynes and the Elusive Middle Way," in Jonathan Kirshner and Peter J. Katzenstein, eds., *The Downfall of the American Order: Liberalism's End?* (in production).

Klay, Phil. 2020. "Human Experience Can't be Quantified," The New York Times (November 8): 10. www.nytimes.com/2020/11/07/opinion/sunday/dat a-science-limits.html. Accessed 12/12/20.

Konyndyk, Kenneth J. 1995. "Aquinas on Faith and Science," *Faith and Philosophy: Journal of the Society of Christian Philosophers* 12, 1: 3–21.

Koyré, Alexandre. 1957. *From the Closed World to the Infinite Universe.* Baltimore, MD: The Johns Hopkins University Press.

Kragh, Helge. 2004. *Matter and Spirit in the Universe: Scientific and Religious Preludes to Modern Cosmology.* London: Imperial College.

Kuhn, Thomas S. 2000. *The Road Since Structure,* ed. James Conant and John Haugland. Chicago, IL: Chicago University Press.

Kuhn, Thomas S. 2012. *The Structure of Scientific Revolutions.* 4th ed. Chicago, IL: The University of Chicago Press.

Kurki, Milja. 2008. *Causation in International Relations: Reclaiming Causal Analysis.* New York: Cambridge University Press.

Kurki, Milja. 2020. *International Relations in a Relational Universe.* Oxford: Oxford University Press.

Laborde, Cécile. 2017. *Liberalism's Religion.* Cambridge, MA: Harvard University Press.

Lawson, Tony. 1986. "Uncertainty and Economic Analysis," *Economic Journal* 95 (December): 909–27.

Levine, Daniel J. and Alexander D. Barder. 2014. "The Closing of the American Mind: 'American School' International Relations and the State of Grand Theory," *European Journal of International Relations* 20, 4: 863–88.

Lewis, Robert. 1977. "Frontier and Civilization in the Thought of Frederick Law Olmsted," *American Quarterly* 29, 4: 385–403.

Lewis, R.W.B. 1955. *The American Adam: Innocence, Tragedy and Tradition in the Nineteenth Century.* Chicago, IL: Chicago University Press.

Lilla, Mark. 2020. "No One Knows What's Going to Happen," *The New* York Times (May 24). www.nytimes.com/2020/05/22/opinion/sunday/coronavirus-prediction-future.html. Accessed 2/2/2021.

Linklater, Andrew. 1998. *The Transformation of Political Community: Ethical Foundations of the Post-Westphalian Era.* Columbia: The University of South Carolina Press.

Makkreel, Rudolf A. 2020. "Metaphysics and the Hermeneutical Relevance of Worldviews," *The Review of Metaphysics* 74: 321–44.

Martineau, Wendy and Judith Squires. 2012. "Addressing the 'Dismal Disconnection': Normative Theory, Empirical Inquiry and Dialogic Research," *Political Studies* 60: 523–38.

Marx, Leo. 1964. *The Machine in the Garden: Technology and the Pastoral Ideal in America.* New York: Oxford University Press.

McCall, Storrs. 2001. "The Ithaca Interpretation of Quantum Mechanics and Objective Probabilities," *Foundations of Physics Letters* 14, 1: 95–101.

McCloskey, Donald N. 1991. "History, Differential Equations, and the Problem of Narration," *History and Theory* 30: 21–36.

McCloskey, Deirdre N. and Stephen T. Ziliak. 2008a. *The Cult of Statistical Significance: How the Standard Error Costs Us Jobs, Justice and Lives.* Ann Arbor, MI: University of Michigan Press.

McCloskey, Deirdre N. and Stephen T. Ziliak. 2008b. "Signifying Nothing: Reply to Hoover and Siegler," *Journal of Economic Methodology* 15, 1: 39–55.

McClure, Kirstie M. 2010. "Reflections on Michael Gillespie's Theological Origins of Modernity," *The Review of Politics* 72, 4: 697–704.

Mead, Walter Russell. 2018. "A Word from Henry Kissinger," *The Wall Street Journal* (February 6): A17.

Meldolesi, Luca. 1995. *Discovering the Possible: The Surprising World of Albert O. Hirschman.* Notre Dame, IN: University of Notre Dame Press.

Mermin, N. David. 1998. "The Ithaca Interpretation of Quantum Mechanics," *Pramana* 51: 549–65.

Mermin, N. David. 2016. *Why Quark Rhymes with Pork: And Other Scientific Diversions.* New York: Cambridge University Press.

Mermin, N. David. 2019. "Making Better Sense of Quantum Mechanics," *Reports of Progress in Physics* 82: 1–16.

Miller, Ross L. 1976. "The Landscaper's Utopia versus the City: A Mismatch," *The New England Quarterly* 49, 2: 179–93.

Mirowski, Philip. 1989. *More Heat than Light: Economics as Social Physics – Physics as Nature's Economics.* New York: Cambridge University Press.

Mitchell, Joshua. 1993. "Hobbes and the Equality of All under the One," *Political Theory* 21, 1: 78–100.

Mohrhoff, Ulrich J. 2014a. "QBism: A Critical Appraisal." arXiv preprint: arXiv:1409.3312.

Mohrhoff, Ulrich J. 2014b. "First-Person Plural Quantum Mechanics." http://p hilsci-archive.pitt.edu/11130/1/FPPQM.pdf

Mohrhoff, Ulrich J. 2019a. "Bohr, QBism, and Beyond."arXiv preprint: arXiv:1907.11405.

Mohrhoff, Ulrich J. 2019b. "'B' is for Bohr." arXiv preprint: arXiv:1905.07118.

Moloney, Pat. 1997. "Leaving the Garden of Eden: Linguistic and Political Authority in Thomas Hobbes," *History of Political Thought* 18, 2: 242–66.

Monteiro, Nuno P. and Kevin G. Ruby. 2009. "IR and the False Promise of Philosophical Foundations," *International Theory* 1, 1: 15–48.

Morgenthau, Hans J. 1946. *Scientific Man vs. Power Politics.* Chicago, IL: The University of Chicago Press.

Mukerji, Chandra. 1997. *Territorial Ambitions and the Gardens of Versailles.* New York: Cambridge University Press.

Munroe, Jennifer. 2008. *Gender and the Garden in Early Modern English Literature.* Burlington, VT: Ashgate.

Neniskyte, Urte and Cornelius T. Gross. 2017. "Errant Gardeners: Glia-Cell-Dependent Synaptic Pruning and Neurodevelopment Disorders," *Nature Reviews Neuroscience* 18 (November): 658–70.

Orlando, Leonardo. 2020. "The Fabric of Agency: Navigating Human Potentialities through Introspection," *Security Dialogue* 50, 5: 467–81.

Ossio, Juan M. 1997. "Cosmologies," *International Social Science Journal* 49, 154: 549–62.

Owensby, Jacob. 1994. *Dilthey and the Narrative of History*. Ithaca, NY: Cornell University Press.

Pagels, Elaine. 2019. "Faith and Reason," *The New York Times Book Review* (December 1): 1, 12–13.

Pagels, Heinz R. 1982. *The Cosmic Code: Quantum Physics as the Language of Nature*. New York: Simon and Schuster.

Paipais, Vassilios. 2017. *Political Ontology and International Political Thought*. London: Palgrave MacMillan.

Peattie, Thomas. 2015. *Gustav Mahler's Symphonic Landscapes*. New York: Cambridge University Press.

Pelopidas, Benoît. 2020. "Power, Luck, and Scholarly Responsibility at the End of the World," *International Theory* 12, 3: 459–70.

Peluso, Nancy Lee and Peter Vandergeest. 2011. "Political Ecologies of War and Forests: Counterinsurgencies and the Making of National Natures," *Annals of the Association of American Geographers* 101, 3: 587–608.

Piccione, Michele and Ariel Rubinstein. 2007. "Equilibrium in the Jungle," *The Economic Journal* 117, 522 (July): 883–96.

Porter, Theodore M. 1995. *Trust in Numbers: The Pursuit of Objectivity in Science and Public Life*. Princeton, NJ: Princeton University Press.

Price, Richard M. 2008. "Moral Limit and Possibility in World Politics," in Richard M. Price, ed., *Moral Limit and Possibility in World Politics*. New York: Cambridge University Press, pp. 1–52.

Reddy, Sanjay G. 2013. "Randomise This! On Poor Economics," *Review of Agrarian Studies* 2, 2: 60–73. www.ras.org.in/randomise_this_on_poor_eco nomics. Accessed 03/19/20.

Reisch, George A. 2019. *The Politics of Paradigms: Thomas S. Kuhn, James B. Conant and the Cold War "Struggle for Men's Minds."* Albany, NY: SUNY Press.

Reus-Smit, Christian. 2008. "Constructivism and the Structure of Ethical Reasoning," in Richard M. Price, ed., *Moral Limit and Possibility in World Politics*. New York: Cambridge University Press, pp. 53–82.

Reus-Smit, Christian. 2013. "Beyond Metatheory?" *European Journal of International Relations* 19, 3: 589–608.

Richards, Annette. 2001. *The Free Fantasia and the Musical Picturesque*. New York: Cambridge University Press.

Rickman, H.P. 1979. *Wilhelm Dilthey: Pioneer of the Human Studies*. Berkeley: University of California Press.

Rovelli, Carlo. 2016. *Seven Brief Lessons on Physics*. New York: Riverhead Books.

Rovelli, Carlo. 2017. *Reality is Not What It Seems: The Journey to Quantum Gravity*. New York: Riverhead Books.

Rutazibwa, Olivia U. and Robbie Shilliam, eds. 2020. *Routledge Handbook of Postcolonial Politics*. New York: Routledge.

Satkunanandan, Shalini. 2015. *Extraordinary Responsibility: Politics Beyond the Moral Calculus*. New York: Cambridge University Press.

Savage, Leonard J. 1954. *The Foundations of Statistics*. New York: Wiley.

Schaffer, Richard and Neil Smith. 1986. "The Gentrification of Harlem?" *Annals of the Association of American Geographers* 76, 3: 347–65. www.jstor.org/stable/ 2562585. Accessed 12/12/20.

Schama, Simon. 1995. *Landscape and Memory*. New York: Knopf.

Schrödinger, Erwin. 1985. *Mein Leben, Meine Weltansicht*. Wien: Paul Zsolnay.

Scott, James C. 1998. *Seeing Like a State: How Certain Schemes to Improve the Human Condition Have Failed*. New Haven, CT: Yale University Press.

Self, Robert O. 2003. *American Babylon: Race and the Struggle for Postwar Oakland*. Princeton, NJ: Princeton University Press.

Seybert, Lucia A. and Peter J. Katzenstein. 2018. "Protean Power and Control Power: Conceptual Analysis," in Peter J. Katzenstein and Lucia A. Seybert, eds., *Protean Power: Exploring the Uncertain and Unexpected in World Politics*. New York: Cambridge University Press, pp. 3–26.

Shilliam, Robbie. 2017. "Race and Revolution at Bwa Kayiman," *Millennium* 45, 3: 269–92.

Sil, Rudra and Peter J. Katzenstein. 2010a. *Beyond Paradigms: Analytic Eclecticism in the Study of World Politics*. New York: Routledge.

Sil, Rudra and Peter J. Katzenstein. 2010b. "Analytic Eclecticism in the Study of World Politics: Reconfiguring Problems and Mechanisms across Research Traditions," *Perspectives on Politics* 8, 2: 411–31.

Simon, Herbert A. 1962. "The Architecture of Complexity," *Proceedings of the American Philosophical Society* 106, 6: 467–82.

Sinclair, Upton. 1906. *The Jungle*. New York: Doubleday.

Skaria, Ajay. 1999. *Hybrid Histories: Forests, Frontiers and Wildness in Western India*. New York: Oxford University Press.

Skidelsky, Robert. 2009. *Keynes: The Return of the Master*. New York: Public Affairs.

Smetham, Graham. 2010. *Quantum Buddhism: Dancing in Emptiness – Reality Revealed at the Interface of Quantum Physics & Buddhist Philosophy*. Brighton: Shunyata Press.

Smith, Henry Nash. 1950. *Virgin Land: The American West as Symbol and Myth*. Cambridge, MA: Harvard University Press.

Smith, Michael F. 1991. "Letting in the Jungle," *Journal of Applied Philosophy* 8, 2: 145–54.

Smolin, Lee. 1997. *The Life of the Cosmos*. New York: Oxford University Press.

Smolin, Lee. 2013. *Time Reborn: From the Crisis in Physics to the Future of the Universe*. Boston, MA: Houghton Mifflin Harcourt.

Solecki, William and Joan Welch. 1995. "Urban Parks: Green Spaces or Green Walls?" *Landscape and Urban Planning* 32: 93–106. https://doi-org.proxy.library .cornell.edu/10.1016/0169-2046(94)00193-7. Accessed 12/12/20.

Spence, Mark David. 1999. *Dispossessing the Wilderness: Indian Removal and the Making of the National Parks*. New York: Oxford University Press.

Spengler, Oswald. 1965. *Urfragen: Fragmente aus dem Nachlass*. Ed. Anton Mirko Kotanek. Munich: C.H. Beck.

Stoever-Ackerman, Jennifer. 2011. "Reproducing US Citizenship in 'Blackboard Jungle': Race, Cold War Liberalism, and the Tape Recorder,"*American Quarterly* 63, 3: 781–806.

Stone, Deborah. 2020. *Counting: How We Use Numbers to Decide What Matters*. New York: Norton.

Stoppard, Tom. 1993. *Arcadia*. New York: Farrar, Straus and Giroux.

Taylor, Charles. 2007. *A Secular Age*. Cambridge, MA: Harvard University Press.

Taylor, Dorceta E. 1999. "Central Park as a Model for Social Control: Urban Parks, Social Class and Leisure Behavior in Nineteenth-Century America," *Journal of Leisure Research* 31, 4: 420–77.

Teele, Dawn Langan, ed. 2014. *Field Experiments and Their Critics: Essays on the Uses and Abuses of Experimentation in the Social Sciences*. New Haven, CT: Yale University Press.

Tetlock, Philip and Dan Gardner. 2015. *Superforecasting: The Art and Science of Prediction*. New York: Random House.

Tigner, Amy L. 2012. *Literature and the Renaissance Garden from Elizabeth I to Charles II: England's Paradise*. Burlington, VT: Ashgate.

Timpson, Christopher G. 2008. "Quantum Bayesianism:A Study," *Studies in History and Philosophy of Modern Physics* 39, 9: 579–609. arXiv:0804.2047v1 [quant-ph].

Toulmin, Stephen. 1982. *The Return to Cosmology: Postmodern Science and the Theology of Nature*. Berkeley: University of California Press.

Toulmin, Stephen. 1990. *Cosmopolis: The Hidden Agenda of Modernity*. New York: The Free Press.

Trownsell, Tamara A. , Arlene B. Tickner, Amaya Querejazu, et al. 2020. "Differing about Difference: Relational IR from around the World," *International Studies Perspectives* 22, 1: 25–64.

Underdal, Arild. 2017. "Climate Change and International Relations (After Kyoto)," *Annual Review of Political Science* 20: 169–88.

Unger, Roberto Mangabeira and Lee Smolin. 2015. *The Singular Universe and the Reality of Time*. Cambridge: Cambridge University Press.

Urbinati, Nadia. 2015. "'Proving Hamlet Wrong': The Creative Role of Doubt in Albert Hirschman's Social Thought," *Humanity* 6, 2: 267–71. http://humanity journal.org. Accessed 03/19/20.

Wæver, Ole. 1997. "Figures of International Thought: Introducing Persons instead of Paradigms," in Iver B. Neumann and Ole Wæver, eds., *The Future of International Relations: Masters in the Making*. New York: Routledge, pp. 1–37.

Waldner, David. 2017. "Schroedinger's Cat and the Dog that Didn't Bark: Why Quantum Mechanics is (Probably) Irrelevant to the Social Sciences," *Critical Review* 29, 2: 190–233.

Weber, Max. 1946. "Religious Rejections of the World," in H.H. Gerth and C. Wright Mills, eds., *From Max Weber: Essays in Sociology*. New York: Oxford University Press, pp. 323–59.

Weinberg, Steven. 1998. "The Revolution That Didn't Happen," *The New York Review of Books* (October 8). www.nybooks.com/articles/1998/the-revolution-that-didnt-happen. Accessed 9/10/2019.

Weinberg, Steven. 2013. "Physics: What We Do and Don't Know," *The New York Review of Books* (November 7). www.nybooks.com/articles/2013/11/07/physics-what-we-do-and-dont-know/. Accessed 03/20/20.

Weinberg, Steven. 2015. "Eye on the Present – The Whig History of Science," *The New York Review of* Books (December 17). www.hrstud.unizg.hr/_news/3

4443/Pages%20from%20New%20York%20Review%20of%20Books%20-%
2017%20December%202015-2.pdf. Accessed 03/20/20.

Weinhardt, Clara. 2017. "Playing Different Games: Uncertain Rules in EU–West
Africa Trade Negotiations," *International Studies Quarterly* 61: 284–96.

Weinhardt, Clara. 2020. *Negotiating Trade in Uncertain Worlds: Misperception and
Contestation in EU–West Africa Relations*. New York: Routledge.

Wendt, Alexander. 1991. "Bridging the Theory/Meta-theory Gap in
International Relations," *Review of International Studies* 17: 383–92.

Wendt, Alexander. 2015. *Quantum Mind and Social Science: Unifying Physical and
Social Ontology*. New York: Cambridge University Press.

Wendt, Alexander. 2022a. "Why IR Scholars Should Care about Quantum
Theory: Part I. Burdens of Proof and Uncomfortable Facts," *International
Theory* 14:1: 119–129.

Wendt, Alexander. 2022b. "Why IR Scholars Should Care about Quantum
Theory: Part II. Critics in the PITs," *International Theory* 14:1: 193–209.

Wight, Colin. 2013. "The Dualistic Grounding of Monism: Science, Pluralism
and Typological Truncation," *Millennium* 41, 2: 326–45.

Wilber, Ken, ed. 1984. *Quantum Questions: Mystical Writings of the World's
Greatest Physicists*. Boston, MA: New Science Library.

Williamson, Tom. 1995. *Polite Landscapes: Gardens and Society in Eighteenth-
Century England*. Baltimore, MD: The Johns Hopkins University Press.

Zetzel, Susanna S. 1989. "The Garden in the Machine: The Construction of
Nature in Olmsted's Central Park," *Prospects: An Annual of American Cultural
Studies* 14: 291–339.

Index

Cambridge Studies in International Relations

9 781009 068970